Confronting Racism

Confronting Racism

Arthur Garfield Hays and the
Fight for Equality,
1925–1954

RICHARD F. HAMM

Published by State University of New York Press, Albany

EU GPSR Authorised Representative:
Logos Europe, 9 rue Nicolas Poussin, 17000, La Rochelle, France
contact@logoseurope.eu

For information, contact State University of New York Press, Albany, NY
www.sunypress.edu

Library of Congress Cataloging-in-Publication Data

Name: Hamm, Richard F., author.
Title: Confronting racism : Arthur Garfield Hays and the fight for equality, 1925–1954 / Richard F. Hamm.
Description: Albany, NY : State University of New York Press, [2025]. | Includes bibliographical references and index.
Identifiers: LCCN 2025016913 | ISBN 9798855804751 (hardcover : alk. paper) | ISBN 9798855804775 (ebook) | ISBN 9798855804768 (pbk. : alk. paper)
Subjects: LCSH: Hays, Arthur Garfield, 1881–1954. | Civil rights lawyers—New York (State)—New York—Biography. | Race discrimination—Law and legislation— United States—History—20th century. | Racism—United States—History—20th century. | Race relations—United States—History—20th century. | LCGFT: Biographies.
Classification: LCC KF373.H39 H36 2025 | DDC 340.092 [B]—dc23/eng/20250703
LC record available at https://lccn.loc.gov/2025016913

For Ben

Contents

Preface

Arthur Garfield Hays was, in his lifetime, a famous and consequential lawyer. He was best known as an advocate of civil liberties. Yet he also became what today we might call an anti-racist. This book is an exploration of how an elite member of the legal profession confronted and fought against the ingrained racism of his society. A hundred years ago, Hays began his race work, battling against policies and practices that limited the lives of African Americans. The issues he confronted continue today: police mistreatment of African Americans, housing discrimination, limits on African Americans in the professions, racial discrimination in the military, and how to build government structures to limit discrimination. Thus, this book speaks to our time as well as Hays's time.

I have lived with Hays for too long. Many, many years ago, my then doctoral student Laura Wittern-Keller, who was working on the fall of film censorship in the United States, asked me a question about the role of Hays in a case. I told her to consult the standard biography on Hays. When she reported there was no biography at all, my interest in him awakened. I had long considered writing a biography of a lawyer, and preliminary investigation revealed Hays's interesting career and that he had left a collection of records behind. I obtained funding to conduct research in his papers but discovered that there was not quite enough there to undertake a full biography. Nevertheless, I persisted in working on him and wrote a series of articles from the digging I had done. As I sketched out more to write from that research, the linkage of fighting racism came into focus, and I began to think about writing a book about Hays's work against the color line. But I had many other interests, duties, and obligations that kept me from beginning such a book. I shelved it. Then the convergence of a sabbatical leave and the Covid pandemic gave me the opportunity to begin writing this work. Along the way I have been supported and aided by many people and institutions that must be acknowledged.

Financial support was provided by a National Endowment for the Humanities Summer Stipend, two Individual Development Awards from the State of New York and United University Professions, a Faculty Research Award Program Grant from the University at Albany, and a Sabbatical Leave from the University at Albany. Beyond that, I must acknowledge the generous research, writing, and publishing funds made possible by Deans of the College of Arts and Sciences Edelgard Wulfert and Jeanette Altarriba, Provost Carol Kim, and Chair of the History Department Patrick Nold.

The professionalism and aid of the staffs of the Seeley G. Mudd Library, Princeton University), University at Albany library, and Schomburg Center for Research in Black Culture, New York Public Library made the months of research that stretched into years both enlightening and efficient.

The responses of those who heard me when I presented parts of this work at conferences or events helped me steer the book in the right direction: the Tri University Conference, University of Guelph; Jews Along the Hudson, the Center for Jewish Studies, University at Albany and New York Civil Liberties Union; Public Policy History Conference; the Conference on the Legacy of Charles W. McCurdy, Miller Center and Law School, University of Virginia; and New York University Law School Faculty Workshop.

The editors and readers for the *American Journal of Legal History* provided good insights when I published an earlier version of chapter 4. I thank Oxford Journals for permission to publish a revised version of that material.

Colleagues, past and current, from the History Department at the University at Albany Laura Wittern-Keller, Allen Ballard, Gerry Zahavi, Laurie Kozakiewicz, Rick Fogarty, Sheila Curran Bernard, Kendra Smith-Howard, Dave Hochfelder, Carl Bon Tempo, Barry Trachtenberg, Kori Graves, Ryan Irwin, Mitch Aso, Chris Pastore, and Maeve Kane all have been generous in sharing their insights and reactions to my work on Hays. I have learned much from each of them. Patrick Nold, in particular, stands out for keeping me moving forward when I hit the obstacles all too common for authors.

The first writings that became this book benefited from insightful comments from Anette Lippold. After it became a full manuscript, the comments of several people reshaped it. Molly Guptill Manning took time to read the first draft and provided critical impetus for me to refine it. Richard Carlin of SUNY Press, the anonymous readers for SUNY Press, Paul Grondahl of New York State Writers Institute, Mary Ann Short, and Laura Tendler helped to tighten and streamline the work.

Even though I stood at my writing desk in my basement to write and revise this work, I did not work alone. It takes a family to write a book. Robin D. Campbell brought a different perspective and proved a fount of good sense and suggestions. She sustained me at the end of this journey. And if my son, Benjamin F. Hamm, had not urged me to think big, I would not have undertaken this task. Thus, this work is dedicated to him.

Richard F. Hamm
Delmar, New York

Introduction

In 1955, when the American Civil Liberties Union (ACLU) was planning a memorial service for Arthur Garfield Hays organized around the work he did for causes, it asked Roy Wilkins of the National Association for the Advancement of Colored People (NAACP) to participate. Wilkins responded, "I am honored to be asked to say a few words about Arthur's great—even vital—work in legal cases along the color line." In 1903 W. E. B. Du Bois famously asserted that "the problem of the Twentieth Century is the problem of the color line." The color line encompassed the many social, economic, and political barriers that separated people of color from white people, especially the formal legal barriers that blocked people of color from accessing the same rights and opportunities as white people. In the United States, the color line (directed mostly, but not exclusively, against African Americans) was manifested in many forms, including formal segregation by race declared in law, discrimination by government agents, bigoted administration of the criminal law, and discrimination by private bodies and individuals. African Americans sought to dismantle the color line, undertaking a host of efforts that later scholars have characterized as "the long civil rights movement." They were joined in many of their campaigns by white allies. This book is an examination of the work of one of those white allies. Hays was a prominent civil libertarian, and his work against the color line reveals the motivations for racial activism among some whites and delineates the range and limits of interracial cooperation in the period.[1]

Today the scope and nature of Hays's civil rights activism is mostly unknown; it is overshadowed by his civil liberties activism. Hays is familiar to legal scholars as a corporate lawyer who became a leading civil liberties lawyer. He was from a well-to-do family, and his early years showed few signs that he would be any sort of activist. After establishing himself as a lawyer, events during and after World War I pushed him to become an indefatigable supporter of civil liberties. Hays became a key lawyer for the young ACLU and its co-general counsel from 1929. A self-labeled "nut" on the Bill of Rights, Hays was one of the first free speech absolutists in the organization. He represented ACLU in many cases and was also an important figure in the organization's policymaking. To promote civil liberties awareness, he participated in public debates, staged media events, delivered lectures, and wrote four books. Moved by his conception of a good society, one that valued democracy and individualism, Hays fought for civil liberties. Those same impulses carried him into struggles against the color line.

From the 1920s into the 1950s Hays was a public figure who presented a steady, if complex, persona. Hays identified as a Jew, but did not practice Judaism. He was not a tall man, at five feet seven inches, and tended toward stockiness. He was "fair-complexioned," according to one interviewer, and his 1928 passport labeled his eyes blue and his hair brown. He had a pronounced limp caused by an injury to his hip and often used a cane. This bad hip did not keep him from physical activity; he played tennis and was "a sailing enthusiast." His other recreation was playing chess. He was a heavy smoker, using both pipe and cigarettes. For an important, wealthy member of the establishment, he was remarkably informal outside the courtroom. How that informality was perceived depended on the observer's stance toward his causes. Thus, during the Scopes trial, his critics in the press described him as being "a thickset stocky individual, democratic-looking, with a rough shirt open at the throat." Yet others would see him as "a genal personality, simple, unassuming and possessed of a rare fund of humor." All would agree he possessed one of the characteristic traits of a New Yorker: He was fast-talking. He estimated in the 1940s that "ordinarily I speak about 150 words a minute." Hays could both name-drop and give others credit. He wrote the line "I was playing squash one day at the London Automobile Club with William J. Donovan," famous now as the first director of what would grow into the Central Intelligence Agency. But such lines were balanced with others: "I owe the title of my first full-length book to . . . my friend Fulton Oursler." He was hungry one night and while "we raided the icebox" he suggested the title. Hays symbolized for many intellectual and social ferment. A reviewer of Hays's first book, *Let Freedom Ring*, put it this way: "Once I lingered on a tropical island for days watching incoming ships and wishing that Mr. Hays would get off one. There was a judge in the old brick tower on the island who said that he would 'become actionable' the moment he stepped ashore, and it would have been great fun to see him do it in such a drowsy place."[2]

Hays's entry into work against racism came in 1925 when the NAACP brought Clarence Darrow and Hays into the Sweet trials. Two participants, Walter White of the NAACP and Hays himself, published accounts of the meeting on October 8, 1925, when a delegation from the NAACP met with Clarence Darrow in Hays's Greenwich Village home. Arthur Spingarn, Charles Studin, James Weldon Johnson, and Walter White wanted to retain Darrow to represent the Ossian Sweet and ten others who had been charged with murder after they fired into a mob of white people intent on driving the family of the African American physician from the home he had just purchased in Detroit. Spingarn and Studin were white lawyers, and White and Johnson (according to Hays) were "leaders of the colored race and officers of the Association." As a representative of the legal committee, Spingarn summarized the case to Darrow. Spingarn was, according to Hays, "a man with black hair and swarthy complexion," White wrote, whose "naturally dark skin had been deeply tanned during his service in the Army and weekends at his country place in Dutchess County." According to White, "Darrow listened with deep sympathy" and upon Spingarn finishing said, "I understand I know the suffering your people have endured." Hays recounted that Spingarn replied that "he was not a negro, whereupon Darrow turned to Charles Studin and said, 'Well, you understand what I mean.'" White wrote that "Charles laughed and told him that he also was white. In desperation Mr. Darrow turned to me. 'Well, with your blue eyes and blond hair I could never make the mistake of thinking you colored.'" I smiled and told him I *was* colored." White in his retelling probably added words to his account, as Hays's version has Darrow say simply, "I would not make that mistake with you." But Hays's account of White's reply is even more fanciful: "White raised his blonde head, spoke through his blue eyes and proudly said he was a negro." No matter whose account you follow, the point is clear: Race was not easily determined, and the implication was that to limit people by their race was impractical as well as a fundamental denial of equal citizenship rights.[3]

Hays recounted that conversation flowed into a discussion about race. There was "some discussion as to why people with more white blood in their veins than negro (and this applies to large part of the race in this country) should "identify their lives with the more unfortunate class and thus subject themselves to prejudice?" Hays declared, "We learned then a fact which was emphasized in our later associations in this case: that to negroes there is no problem so vital as that of color; that race consciousness and race pride have solidified our colored citizens." It should be noted that Hays has in this account flipped the racist narrative that presumed black inferiority. What African American citizens were proud of was their color. Race consciousness and pride were things that united them. Moreover, the subsequent discussion showed that Hays thought that African Americans were an "unfortunate class" not because of inherent inferiority but because of discriminatory treatment. According to Hays, the conversation segued to the legal means and violence directed at African Americans to enforce segregation of the races, exposing the manifest interlocking problems of the color line.[4]

Up to this point in his life, Hays had not involved himself in any fights against the discriminations and injustices that people of color faced in the United States. He was, by this time, a successful corporate lawyer, a liberal voice, and a leading figure in civil liberties activism. But from this point on, Hays would sporadically, until the end of his life in 1954, fight segregation and other racial discriminations. What follows is an examination of Hays's roles in confronting the racial order in America during his career. It details the work of one well-known activist, shedding light on the ways in which white liberals could challenge segregation and work in close collaboration with African American activists and those less engaged without ever actually breaking through the color line in their personal lives.

As a white man with a good income, and as a Jew who confronted the rising anti-Semitism of the era, Hays was not a typical activist. He was a man of good will, but not a racial revolutionary. Hays's efforts against the color line were an outcrop of his overall stance, rather than the product of a specific understanding of or support for African Americans. The program behind Hays's racial activism was a vision of American society that required every member of society to have access to the full measure of civil liberties. As in his larger civil liberties career, Hays showed a disposition to work with a wide range of people. In his race work, he collaborated with African Americans whose affiliations spanned the political spectrum from Republicans through Socialists, and he worked with both members of the NAACP and former Marcus Garvey supporters.

While Hays saw more clearly than most others of his class and ethnicity the injustice of segregation, there is no evidence that he had any friends or lasting social associations across the color line. African Americans deserved the same civil liberties as any other group in American society. Approaching the color line from that perspective, Hays fought for African Americans' legal rights under the Constitution. He thought if the legal barriers were removed, African Americans would come to enjoy full membership in American society. Perhaps because he was an affluent corporate lawyer, he did not question deeply the economic implications of the racial order. And his commitment to individualism and his tempered fear of a large and strong state that intervened in economic matters and life carried over into how he thought the government should approach racial policies.

Hays did not particularly broadcast his commitment to ending legal racial discrimination, and some unaware of the extent of his contributions have denigrated them. Hays's own accounts downplayed his role in the first Sweet trial, and two of the later actions challenging the segregated draft and desegregating the American Bar Association came after he had written his final book. Jack Greenberg, in talking of his own entry into civil rights work, recounted that in 1945 he had "developed an amorphous notion that I'd like to be someone like Arthur Garfield Hays, whom I'd never met and about whom I knew next to nothing except that his name appeared in the paper frequently, that he represented the American Civil Liberties Union, and that he had something to do with the NAACP" not as a staffer but he "apparently made enough of a living in his private practice that he could afford to take civil liberties cases." Greenberg did become a paid employee of the NAACP but became disillusioned with Hays. "Years later when Hays and I were in a case together . . . I was appalled by his poor performance, he was unprepared and disorganized, couldn't answer questions and rambled on. He became a role model of a reverse sort—I vowed I never would make a presentation like that." In addition, Greenberg's disenchantment with Hays might have prompted him in his account of the ending of the color bar in the American Bar Association to omit Hays's key role in the process. A more measured account from the historian Kevin Boyle notes in passing that Hays after the Sweet trials "continued his peripatetic campaign to secure justice for those the nation made marginal." He lists Hays's involvement in the appeals for Sacco and Vanzetti, the fight for free speech in Jersey City, and his protest against the violent repression of Puerto Rician nationalists, and he mentions one race matter: his work in Harlem, "demanding justice when police brutality reached such obscene levels it triggered nights of rioting."

Boyle gives the right weight to Hays's range of work; race activism was not central to Hays's career, it was part of it. Also, it reflected an America that Hays believed in, where the minorities made up the majority, and if all minorities worked to protect not their own rights but other minorities' rights, then everyone's rights would be secure.[5]

Hays's race work almost spanned his whole career as a civil liberties lawyer, peaking in the period from the late 1930s through the early 1940s in conjunction with the rise of Hitler's racialist state and the struggle to advance racial egalitarianism during World War II. He was motivated in these efforts by his civil liberties values that he had formed in the 1920s. Through five major episodes, the book illustrates that it was his vision of society (in which all Americans were guaranteed their civil liberties) that inspired Hays to work on race relations in the United States and informed his activism. The opening chapter details Hays's life and career before he began civil rights work. After the Sweet case he worked to challenge racism's effects in American life. His awakening to racial issues almost brought him into the Scottsboro case and did prompt him to write about both the Sweet and Scottsboro cases in his first two books. The second chapter examines Hays's approach to the issue of police brutality in African American neighborhoods through his service on the Mayor's Commission investigating the Harlem disturbance of 1935. In this instance, he led the hearings to expose discriminatory policing, believing that bringing the problems to light would prompt reform. The third chapter covers a 1937 Westchester County, New York, case challenging restrictive covenants. Hays used this case to undermine the common definitions of race: the very basis for the legal color line. The book then turns to how Hays leveraged the ideology of the war against Hitlerism to advance race relations in the United States. The fourth chapter shows how Hays attacked racism in his own profession when he resigned in protest from the American Bar Association over its racist exclusion policy. As early as 1938, he considered taking this step but delayed it until 1943 when the anti-racist rhetoric of the war better ensured success. The fifth chapter turns to Hays's role in challenging the practice of segregation in the military draft, bringing the only case questioning segregation in the military during World War II to the United States Supreme Court. The final chapter looks at how—driven by his wariness toward the administrative state and his view of how Jews should combat anti-Semitism—Hays came to oppose the creation of strong fair employment opportunity laws in the 1940s. His stance was revealing of the limits of Hays's work against the color line.

1

Arthur Garfield Hays

Roots and Branches

Little in his early life—from childhood and up until his civil liberties
work—indicated that Arthur Garfield Hays would become an active opponent of segregation. But there were actions, inclinations, and occurrences
that would lead him to oppose the color line and use tools that he had
mastered in his civil liberties work against it. The turning point would
come with his entry into the Sweet trial of 1925. From then on, racial
discrimination would be among the causes he would take on, even as his
fame increased and his determination to spread his ideas prompted him
to write two books exploring limits on freedom of speech and action
as well as miscarriages of justice caused by social prejudice. He became
recognized as someone engaged with the issues raised by race.

Arthur Garfield Hays was born in Rochester, New York, in 1881. His
grandparents' generation were Jews who immigrated to the United States
from central Germany. Both sides of his family were owners of clothing
factories or wholesalers. The families were part of a thriving community.
While most were pillars of the local temple, there was some religious
experimentation in the family. One grandfather became an agnostic and
the other a spiritualist. Attendance at seances as a child started Arthur
Hays on the path to skepticism. Hays later asserted, "There was little
racial consciousness in our household," giving as evidence that as a boy
he called another boy "you little Jew," which earned him punishment. He
admitted the phrase meant little to him, and he could have used "any other
designation," such as "mick" or "wop." While German was spoken among

the family, English was the predominant language. The family name had long been Anglicized from Haas to Hays. His father's prosperity meant they lived in an affluent suburban neighborhood. The children attended public school and also went to an expensive experiment in summer camp. Hays was inseparable from his brother Harold, who was one year older than he; doted on his sister, Alma, who was three years younger; and was a bit more distant with Robert, nine years younger.[1]

In 1893, when Arthur was twelve, the family moved to New York City, first taking up residence in a brownstone on West 80th Street but moving several times over the years. He again attended public schools. The family planned that Harold would become a doctor and Arthur a lawyer. So it was not surprising that Arthur became a member of the school debating club. The move to New York City loosened the family's attachment to religion, as they stopped going to synagogue. Arthur's was a sheltered life within a bustling city. He was trusted to go out and play and be in charge of his younger brother, but limited in his activities when he did so: no playing baseball in Central Park when Bob tagged along. He did not remember experiencing any anti-Semitism, though he remembered that "my people, German Jews, were passionately prejudiced against Polish and Russian Jews." He claimed to learn of prejudice against Catholics only in college. While Harold went to a private school to prepare him for Columbia University, Arthur started at City College, first as one of the "subfreshmen," and after three years transferred to Columbia as a sophomore. Hays may have attended City College to save on costs, as his father's business was suffering one of its periodic downturns. He remarked years later, "As I remember my early life, the only difference in the standard of living of our family when my father's business was bad and when it was good was that in the former event my parents didn't go to opera or theatre or take a carriage, or indulge in any luxuries whatever. We always had the same number of servants and lived in pretty much the same style." Both Harold and Arthur worked as tutors during the summers throughout their college years.[2]

Hays's experiences at Columbia University and later Columbia Law School shaped the rest of his life, but not because of what he learned in class. He majored in philosophy and studied modern and ancient languages as well as mathematics. But he ended his formal education without "the slightest grounding in the sciences, music, the arts, or any other cultural study"; they "were just names to me after the sessions had run their course." In law school he worked hard, though the "tasks often seemed dull and unrelated to practical daily affairs." He was appointed to law review and both enjoyed that work and relished his only academic distinction. However, it was the collegiate spirit, the bonding with his classmates, that was pivotal for his future. He was "an enthusiastic collegian" engaging in college pranks and was a regular attendee at the football games, especially the Columbia-Yale matches. Hays was active in debate, musical, and athletic pursuits. He played lacrosse—often coming home battered and bloodied from the contests to the consternation of his father, who wanted him to "quit the game." Hays understood his father's attitude, as "he lived in an entirely different world," but he persuaded him of the importance of lacrosse "by explaining that shooting a goal meant outstripping competitors and selling a bill of goods."[3]

Hays formed lifelong friendships and associations at Columbia, most notably with McAlister Coleman, a scion of a wealthy family with some skill as a writer. He coached others in debate who would go on to careers in journalism and law, including Walter Lippmann and Osmond Frankel. Friends from his years at Columbia were among his first partners and clients when he later launched his own law firm. More than thirty years after he graduated the college he still referred fondly to the connections he formed there, telling a classmate: "Often I have thought of the early days at the Columbia and regretted that our lines don't cross more often. You have no idea of the respect and affection that a fellow holds in his heart always for those he admired in his college days." He had more distant associations with his classmates Felix Frankfurter (from City College) and William Donovan, but even those marked him for what he would become, a member of the American establishment.[4]

Hays passed the bar exam for New York in June 1905 and after a speedy European grand tour embarked on his legal career. Through the intercession of friends from college he gained a position as a clerk in the firm of Bowers and Sands, which practiced mostly securities and real estate law. He got the interview at the firm because they believed he was the son of a different, more prominent Hays, but did well enough at the interview to land the position. It was quickly noted he knew all the clients: "I explained that among the old Jewish settlers each family was acquainted with the other and since most of our clients were Jews in real estate business I was apt to know them." He worked to impress the partners, but more importantly studied how the elite law firms worked and learned important lessons. He quickly calculated that he could earn more money in his own firm than by continuing to work as a clerk. In

1907, Hays formed a partnership with three other classmates, S. Walter Kaufmann, Norvin R. Lindheim, and T. Raymond St. John, opening an office at 60 Wall Street. The firm was unusual in that the partners were not exclusively of one religion or ethnicity, with Hays, Lindheim, and Kaufmann being Jews of German descent but St. John a Baptist, the son of a minister. Moreover, they tolerated each others' different opinions; for instance, Lindheim was a noted Zionist, while Hays opposed Zionism. And while not particularly profitable, the firm put out an air of success. The Kaufmann family was established in the book publishing industry, and Walter was well connected to bring in clients. Lindheim's family's business was supplying raw materials for the garment industry and introduced the firm to clients in the fur and leather business, many of which entailed overseas connections, especially in Germany and Russia. St. John did not land clients but rather did the "laborious spadework." They were open-minded; for instance, they recruited William Abramson as office factotum but, recognizing his talents, encouraged his training; he would later become a partner in the firm. They also recruited John Schulman from another firm. Their firm was successful enough that it moved to a larger location at 43 Exchange Place. Because of the publishing clients brought in by Kaufmann, Hays learned copyright law, the first of his many acquired legal specialties.[5]

Hays settled into the life of a successful lawyer. A sign of his affluence was that he took up horseback riding—an expensive proposition in New York City, which required belonging to a club and using commercial facilities. And once he had made enough money to make a living for himself, what he considered "biological urges and normal emotions soon led to . . . making a life which includes someone else." He overcame his trepidations of the responsibility of marriage, and he and Blanche Marks married in 1908. Rabbi Stephen Wise (a leader of the Reform Judaism movement) presided over the ceremony. Wise's participation points to the couple's religious orientation and prominence within the community, though it did not show the reality that Blanche was more devoted in her religion than Arthur. After the marriage they moved to New Rochelle "and settled down to an active suburban existence." Their daughter Lora was born in 1910. They soon obtained the material possessions of the well-to-do: a fine house, a car, and servants. Hays was a progressive Republican and active in local politics; in 1912 he bolted to Theodore Roosevelt's Bull Moose Party, becoming the leader of the local organization.[6]

For the early part of World War I, Hays was in England practicing international law, an area of practice that he learned as he went along. The economic warfare between Great Britain and the Central Powers threatened the interests of many shippers and importers. Hays interceded with government officials and also appeared in the Prize courts, often asserting a particular seized cargo shipped from the United States was not in violation of English restrictions on trade with Germany and thus should be released. He also represented German and Austrian shippers who had non-war material goods they wished to ship to the neutral United States. Several things stand out about Hays's stint in international law. He mastered the topic, and this mastery did not just show up in his filings and pleadings, but in the public arena. Hays engaged in print debate about the nuances on the law of trade during wartime in the press. His life there was congenial: Blanche and Lora had gone to England with him, and his relations with the English legal establishment were exceptionally convivial and close, as shown by "The Very Blue Book." This was a comic set of letter templates that Hays put together and presented to opposing counsel, puncturing the posturing that marked the prize court practice concerning the disputes over shipping during the war. And Hays also boldly would reach out to the media to tout his accomplishments. Thus, while he received permission from the British government to allow the importation of a wide range goods ordered but not paid for before the restrictions (including laces, woolens, cotton goods, and paper), what he highlighted were high-end toys produced in Germany. Hays later delighted in the stories reporting that he was a lawyerly Santa Claus for getting the goods released.[7]

Considering that Hays's partner Lindheim was decidedly pro-German before the war, that Hays was often accusing the British of abusing the American neutral shipping, and that he thought nothing of attending functions at the German embassy, he gained a reputation of being pro-German. He worked to have non-contraband goods be allowed to go to Germany. With American entry into the war, that was of course a financially precarious position to hold for a lawyer. The bar was "blatantly patriotic," and its members often worked as informants for the government. Hays however did support the war. His friends often vouched for his pro-war stance and that he was "OK" when government agents raised questions about his loyalty. Hays could also point to his older brother, Harold, who signed up on the day the United States declared war and served in France. And after his return to the United States, Hays undertook work for the Red Cross, helping to raise money for war relief. In early January 1918 he wrote a lawyer friend in England: "Most lawyers here are busily engaged in war work of one kind or another," especially staffing draft boards. "So far I have not participated because I have found it extremely difficult to attend to my own work and to this other work at the same time. I prefer to draw the line perpendicularly rather than horizontally—that is, to stick to business for a few months and then to volunteer for a definite period." Much of his private work in this time grew out of representation of enemy aliens whose property was seized. From this work Hays produced a legal treatise: *Enemy Property in America*. In the summer of 1918, he volunteered for Red Cross supervisory work. He also sought admission into the military. He first tried through the special officer training camp developed by Grenville Clark in Plattsburgh, New York. However, a long-standing injury to his left hip from a horse-riding accident had left him with serious limp. Most of the rest of his life he walked with the assistance of a cane. His weak hip kept him from being accepted at the Plattsburg officer's training camp. However, in June 1918 he used his connections with "a friendly draft board" to waive his age and marital status exemptions and subjected himself to conscription. He passed the physical by disguising the weakness of his leg: When his group of draftees were asked to hop across the room on their left leg, he hopped on his right. His call to service came on armistice day and was quickly canceled.[8]

If Hays's German connections did him no harm, his partners could not say the same. Hays's firm had represented the German Embassy before the war. The partners were divided over which side they favored when the United States was neutral but their German connections brought them much business. The firm was involved in a number of transactions where Germans bought or invested in certain corporations. The extent of the firm's handling of business was revealed by the theft (by American intelligence agents) of the briefcase of the German Embassy's commercial attaché. Among the documents were some relating to the newspaper *The Evening Mail*. It had been a strong advocate of American neutrality before the United States entered the war. A subsidy of the paper was eventually revealed to have come secretly from the German government. Eventually Kaufmann and Lindheim were prosecuted along with the owner of *The Mail* for filing a false declaration to the alien property custodian. Hays escaped prosecution, as he was not directly involved in filing the document as he was away on Red Cross work. Kaufmann and Lindheim were tried and convicted of the charge and sentenced to a year and day in prison. They were also disbarred.[9]

Hays always believed that Kaufmann and Lindheim were victims of prejudice and war hysteria. At the time of the investigation and the trial, Hays was part of the team that represented them. He later denounced the questioning of Kaufmann during the investigation that took no notice of his near blindness and the implication that the vagueness of his descriptions of places revealed that he was lying. Soon after the conviction he publicly called them "victims of war hysteria." He detailed what he considered underhanded methods by the prosecutor in having the defendants stipulate to a fact that the prosecutor knew was not true to block the calling of an exculpatory witness. Hays later argued that Lindheim was added to the case so the government could "parade before the jury" the matters he had handled for the German government and thus prejudice it. He successfully worked with the City Bar Association of New York for their commutation (they served a month before President Calvin Coolidge commuted their sentences) and the restoration of their law licenses (Lindheim's came posthumously) and eventual pardons. More than twenty years after their convictions, Hays saw them as "victims of the spirit of the times, of forces beyond their control, casualties of the war." The destruction of his original partnership was not the only blow that Hays endured in 1918. His youngest brother died of influenza in November of that year.[10]

The anti-German feeling, fear of the Russian Revolution, and the government's encouragement of the "snooping, spying, tattletale fraternity" awakened Hays's interest in civil liberties. In a December 1918 draft article titled "American Liberalism, Hays recounted the story of a dinner guest who wondered if they were getting all the news from Russia, what "the other side of the story" was, and whether the United States should not have intervened. This guest also argued that Socialists were not all Bolshevists, and not all "Bolshevists are Anarchists." The guest worried about rumors of punitive indemnities on Germany, wanted the Espionage Act to be repealed, and spoke in favor of the British Labour Party. After the guest left early, he was called a Socialist and an Anarchist, and a third person declared, "I am sure you will all agree that he's a pacifist and pro-German. And they all did." This little snippet was designed to show the suppression of individual thought prevalent right after the end of the war and was Hays's plea for Americans to reassert their rights to think what they wanted and not be afraid to say what they thought.[11]

His political and personal life also carried him toward civil liberties work. Hays continued to be active in politics; in 1919 he joined a group called the Committee of 48, which aimed to form a new progressive political party—eventually it became the Farmer Labor party. The activity of the Committee of 48 was widely denounced as "radical and red" by "patriotic organizations." Hays was thus directly aware of the many attempts to suppress "radical" organizations in this period. He rejoined his family (they had returned to the United States before him) in their suburban existence as another member of "the family circle." In particular, Blanche Hays deepened his interest in civil liberties and brought him into his first free speech case. She was the more radical of the couple; she was acquainted with various members of the Socialist parties in nearby towns. When the mayor of Mount Vernon, New York, denied the Socialist Party a permit for a public rally in the town (where for years they had held such meetings), she joined with two of its leaders on the night of October 2, 1920, in attempting to speak and was arrested for violating an ordinance requiring a permit. On petitions filed by Arthur Hays, they were all released on writs of habeas corpus on October 6. Blanche Hays supported her habeas corpus petition by stating that she was not a Socialist but she believed in free speech and said that she had told the gathered crowd, "I have come here to Mount Vernon to find out if Mount Vernon is a free city." Arthur Hays represented all the arrested, and after a victory in the New York Supreme (trial) Court, wrote briefs and argued the case in the Appellate Division and Court of Appeals, where they lost. His long, involved, well-researched briefs argued that the mayor abused his legal powers by denying the Socialist Party a permit, as he wished only to suppress their views. The state reply rejected that free speech had anything to do with the denial of the permit, but rather that this was a question of regulation of the streets for public safety reasons alone. The higher state courts settled the issue on that ground; Hays's appeal to the United States Supreme Court was denied on the grounds that the case was settled at the state level on a non-federal question.[12]

The case is revealing of Hays's early conception of freedom of speech, one that he would adhere to with little change for the rest of his life. The ending of his brief for the Court of Appeals is a full-bodied statement of the principles of political free speech grounded in the realities of 1920s America. Hays asserted that such suppression of speech was commonly happening across the country, "in some cases in order to stop religious meetings, in others to prevent meeting of Negroes, in others to prevent meetings of the American Federation of Labor; in other parts to prevent meeting of those who are said to hold Socialist or radical views." He portrayed this as a "new method of combating so called un-Americanism. Instead of the method of free men meeting error with truth, with the confidence that in the competition of ideas truth will prevail, the new method is that of prevention and repression." While earlier in the brief he carefully asserted that he was not attacking the permit system, by the end he presented a parade of horribles where future laws requiring permits for halls would lead to Democrats preventing the meeting of Republicans. He closed with fundamentals and a call to judicial action to protect political speech: "Our institutions are founded on the theory that the people are to be trusted; that they will not be deluded by false theories; that free speech provides a safety valve and assures that a spirit of discontent where it exists, will find means of expression other than through force and violence." The mayor's action was "the mob spirit exercised officially" crushing "the rights of the citizen." The courts stood "as a bulwark of personal liberty." The officials' discriminatory action gave "the courts the opportunity to determine what is the true meaning of an ordinance." Here the law was not about public safety but suppressing unpopular speech, as the local government knew the Socialists neither could afford a hall nor would likely be able to find one to rent in Mount Vernon for their meeting. "Free speech and the right of assemblage have never been limited to those who can afford to pay for a hall. The passion for liberty does not permit of equivocation."[13]

Also, in 1920 the Hays family moved to 47 West 12th Street in the Greenwich Village neighborhood in Manhattan. Blanche Hays was involved in the theater and became associated with the famous Provincetown Players. In the city, she and Hays were members of an artistic set with social and political radical inclinations. Louise Bryant and John Reed were both friends, as were Socialists and peace advocates like Crystal Eastman and her husband, Walter Fuller. Their daughter Lora was in the first class of the Walden School, the famous progressive private school. Thus began the bifurcated life, personal and professional, where Hays associated with Wall Street financiers and mine owners during the day and with social and political radicals at night. His law work was similarly divided. As he wrote in 1926, "I conduct a general law practice" with partners, and "our clients are chiefly conservatives, commercial and banking houses," but he also represented those who had suffered restrictions on their freedoms. He never hid his radical associations or his actions from his partners; in fact, he memorialized them by putting photographs of the events on his office walls. This was a practice that he continued until the end of his career.[14]

In the first six years of the 1920s, Hays's private practice diversified. Beyond "lines of brokerage, estate, commercial, and constitutional law," he continued his work in international law. This area of his practice encompassed trade across international boundaries but also dealt with two new topics: the complications of restriction placed on immigration and movement in the period and migratory divorce, overcoming the restrictive divorce laws of one nation by procuring divorce in another. He also assisted clients with theatrical law, musical rights, and libel matters. Of course, the bread and butter of his firm, corporate law, dominated his practice and chiefly concerned corporate governance, securities issuance, and contracts. His office on Exchange Place was described as "large" and "simply furnished," sending the signal that it was a space for work. His labors made him a wealthy man with high status in the profession. He was a member of the American and the New York State Bar Associations. And he was also a member in the County and City Bar Associations of New York City. The latter organization marked him as one of the elite lawyers in the nation. He was also a member of two country clubs. But wealth and influence were not everything to Hays; he also involved himself in causes, which often circled back into work for the firm.[15]

The divorce work of the firm stemmed from Hays's friendship with Dudley Field Malone and points to how the personal, business, and civil liberties work all tended to merge. Malone and Hays knew each other through their efforts on behalf of women's suffrage. Malone fell in love with Doris Stevens, a leader of the suffrage movement. He got a divorce in Paris from his first wife to marry Stevens. Then Hays and Malone went into loose partnership to carry on such work for others. By 1922, Arthur and Blanche's marriage began to break up because he had fallen in love with Aline Davis. They separated and then too sought a French divorce. As he put it, "After a time we were divorced, and I married Aline. It was just as clear and simple as that." Hays became a vocal advocate of both easier divorce and companionate marriage. He was most familiar with the law of divorce in his own state, which was one of the most restrictive in the nation, and saw migratory divorce as a workaround at best. He wanted the law to reflect social reality: that marriage was for love and companionship, and when they faded from a relationship, divorce should be an option—even if it would end the divorce business of his firm. He appeared on radio debates advocating divorce reform. His advocacy of easy divorce was part of Hays's worldview, which embraced modernism. And his embrace of modernism had much to do with how he came to see the American Civil Liberties Union (ACLU).[16]

Hays drifted into the orbit of the ACLU, which was founded in 1920. It grew out of an earlier organization, the National Civil Liberties Bureau, established by radicals and pacifists to meet the challenges of conscription and repression of dissent provoked by World War I and the Red Scare. Roger Nash Baldwin dominated the ACLU, which was a strange mixture of labor leaders, pacifists, and economic radicals of different stripes. Hays and Baldwin became friends. As Baldwin later told an interviewer: "Of all my associates Arthur Hays was the closest over the longest period of time"—despite Baldwin saying the same about Scott Nearing, Norman Thomas, and John Holmes. But Baldwin said Hays "was also my own lawyer and my friend—in fact, I lived almost a year with him and his family in his home at 20 East 10th Street." The connection was close despite the difference in demeanor and political views, Baldwin was remarkably austere and forbidding while Hays was gregarious and generous. Baldwin asserted that for Hays, "the left never tempted him. He didn't get involved in the various United Fronts that I and some of the others in the ACLU got into, so he balanced some of the rest of us and gave the Union a more solid reputation as a defender of the Bill of Rights." Their connection was over ideas of civil liberties. Baldwin remarked: "I think he was the most extreme civil libertarian among us. He didn't believe in banning anything. . . . He looked with intense suspicion on any restraint on thought or expression." Under Baldwin, publicity campaigns, lobbying, direct action, and lawsuits were all tactics embraced by the early ACLU, and each vied for primacy in its early years. In the 1920s it focused primarily on labor issues and protection of political speech. It frequently represented Communist groups and individuals when they ran afoul of state anti-syndicalism laws. Hays was not directly involved in any of the ACLU's major Communist cases. The ACLU did little about prohibition, censorship, and minority rights—even though a member of the National Association for the Advancement of Colored People (NAACP) always had a seat on its governing board. Hays's role in the organization grew throughout the decade, culminating in his being named co-counsel with Morris Ernst in 1929. In fact, Hays had convinced Baldwin to bring Ernst into the organization. The naming of the two co-counsels was "a decisive shift in ACLU priorities: from that point on lawyers were a major force."[17]

Hays was involved in the ACLU's attempts at direct action to test the restrictions put on, especially, labor unions to mobilize. The organization sent observers and investigators into coal regions where miners' attempts at organization and strikes had led to violent reaction, and where even speech about the issue of unionizing was forbidden. Sometimes the suppression of speech came under the umbrella of a court injunction but more often just through threats or use of disorderly conduct laws invoked selectively against the speakers. The ACLU followed its earlier actions by sending in teams of activists and lawyers to support unions in their attempts to have meetings and sometimes even calling a meeting to demonstrate the right of freedom of speech. Members of the press always joined the attempts. Hays participated in such challenges in 1922 and 1923 in Pennsylvania and West Virginia. Hays reported that when he returned home, "my conservative partners—we had and still have an office on Wall Street—were stunned and shocked." He saw in person the intimidation tactics of the privatized police and regular police. He was manhandled and threatened more than once. He and others used the law to back up their direct actions, ironically seeking injunctions against those who would suppress their speech and prosecuting those who had arrested them for false imprisonment. Like their fleeting meetings, often these legal maneuverers were mere sound and fury. Because swaying minds was central to the ACLU's goals, publicity—even if the legal or practical victory was elusive—was welcome. But to succeed, the organization needed members, and Hays was one of their members who recruited others into the organization.[18]

Hays was charismatic and drew people into causes, as was shown by the career of Charles Abrams, who idolized Hays and cast his life in Hays's mold. A Polish-born immigrant Jew raised in the slums of Brooklyn, Abrams worked as a child and climbed out of poverty through education. Directly from high school he entered night law school and started working as clerk in various law firms. Eventually, in the 1920s, he ended up in Hays's firm for a three-year stint. He modeled himself on Hays: "for a while he even walked with a limp because Hays had a game leg, and he also took to smoking a pipe in what he hoped was a convincing imitation of Hays' profound, brooding manner." At Hays's firm, "Abrams began to form some idea of what he wanted to make of his life." Like Hays, he wanted to make money but also to fight for "unpopular social causes." Abrams recalled "the atmosphere in Hays' office when civil-liberties cases were being worked on as a rousing one of derring-do in the quest for social justice." Recognizing his talent, Hays gave Abrams important criminal law and civil liberties cases to work on and loaned Abrams six hundred dollars to start his own firm, which quickly prospered. Abrams patterned his work on Hays, mixing private practice and public service. Abrams went on to make a fortune as a real estate speculator, then turned to housing reform in the 1930s, leading the way in experiments in public housing. He later turned to fighting racial discrimination in housing. In the 1950s, he became the chairman of the State Commission Against Discrimination, revitalizing that body. Abrams's causes may have been different from Hays's, but his style—the mix of amassing private wealth while crusading for social causes, the use of press publicity, the writing on a range of topics, and the employment of catchy quips to deflect criticism or draw attention—all echoed Hays.[19]

By 1922, Hays's civil liberties foundations were formed. He revealed them in an interview to the *New York World*. Described as a successful lawyer but "not a radical" and associated with the ACLU, Hays was hopeful that "the spirit of Liberty is reviving in these United States." But there were forces to be battled: "Prohibition, the Ku Klux Klan and movie and other censorship." He traced the attack on liberty to the war, where the nation developed "a mania of intolerance." Hays thought this was part of war in general, "but, for some reason or other, Americans suffered from it much more than most of the nations of Europe." The Post Office suppressed unpopular opinions, and the Department of Justice "gave itself over to heresy hunting." As a member of the ACLU, he said he would defend the Ku Klux Klan and others he hated and explained that the ACLU rushed to labor's aid because "they are being picked upon." Hays mentioned that his wife was arrested for speaking at a Socialist meeting in Mount Vernon, even though she was not a Socialist, but believed "in right to speak, even without a permit." The goal of his activism was to awaken the public to the threat to liberty. "Public opinion is the highest tribunal in America. Unless the public wants liberty . . . this will not be a free country. "[20]

National publicity and fame came to the ACLU (and Hays) through the 1925 Scopes trial in Tennessee, and Hays was pivotal in how that event developed. It was through his intervention with reluctant ACLU leaders that Clarence Darrow was kept in the case. Darrow's role, coming on the heels of his dramatic work in the notorious Leopold and Loeb case, guaranteed that the trial would become a media spectacle. The ACLU had prepared for a constitutional case and developed a deep cadre of scientific and biblical experts to challenge the Tennessee law criminalizing the teaching of evolution. Hays was responsible for developing that aspect of the case, but the judge excluded that evidence. That decision led the defense to call opposition counsel and proponent of anti-evolution laws William Jennings Bryan to the witness stand as an expert on the Bible. Darrow's examination of Bryan became the stuff of legend and sealed the popular image of the case of being a struggle of science and modernism against ignorance and tradition. Scopes lost his case, technicalities denied the ACLU an appeal on the constitutional issue, and anti-evolution laws continued to be passed in states. But press writers, especially H. L. Mencken, proclaimed that modern society was prevailing over the hide-bound past and mercilessly flayed Fundamentalists, legislators, jurists, as well as most of the people of the South as backward. Hays certainly perpetuated that view. As an interviewer paraphrased him: The "trial according to Mr. Hays was the logical result of the medieval background still existing in some districts of this country." He always portrayed the trial as one where "unreasoning, blind, religious bigotry was fighting modern science."[21]

Some of the Scopes trial lawyers, including Hays, became celebrities, and some of the participants became friends. Both developments would reshape Hays's life. Hays made enduring personal ties with both Mencken and Darrow. The connection with Darrow was far more significant. It intensified Hays's practice of expressing his views in in public forums. Hays determined to make himself, as Darrow had, into a public intellectual. Where previously Hays had pursued politics and civil liberties activities as an outlet, he now instead engaged in many more public debates, delivered more speeches, and began writing for popular audiences. This development was taken furthest in his undertaking to write books, with the ghostwriting help of his friend McAlister Coleman. The friendship also gave Hays a hero in Darrow. Years after Darrow's death, Hays declared that Darrow "was to me, the greatest man I ever met." And "the better I knew Darrow, the more I admired him. He was so essentially and ruggedly honest. He never fooled even himself." Extending this view, Hays wrote in a letter: "Ordinarily, when you get to know well a person of high reputation, the bubble of greatness is punctured. In the last fifteen years of his life, I knew Darrow intimately, and the better I knew him the more I loved and respected him." For Hays, Darrow was the epitome of a certain kind of liberal that Darrow had called "our kind." In his 1942 book *City Lawyer: the Autobiography of a Law Practice*, Hays wrote, "Darrow's notes of introduction to me always read the same way: 'Dear Art, Here's one of our kind." Hays defined "our kind" as men of goodwill, who follow chance, who welcome different viewpoints, and who are not conventional in any sense. This openness (as Hays defined liberal) was "an attitude of mind by which one considers any proposition on its merits, without reference to dogma and tradition." Darrow's materialism and determinism began to infuse Hays's worldview. For instance, when asked why he engaged in "hopeless causes," Hays answered (sounding very much like Darrow), "I go into these things because I get a pleasant emotional reaction out of activities along this line. Naturally, if I feel indignant, I am uncomfortable if I do nothing." But he also would marry these ideas with the conventional understanding that people should struggle to change people's attitudes to bring about change: "I think that fights along these lines are sometimes won and never lost. The important thing is education and the publicity given these cases bring home to people what is going on." He took on Darrow's causes, becoming a governing board member of the League to Abolish Capital Punishment and joining the legal advisory committee of the NAACP. The latter connection shows that one of the issues that Hays came to espouse because of his connection with Darrow was civil rights for African Americans, but it was only one of his many causes.[22]

Hays took the tactics used in the labor disputes and Scopes trial and carried them into a different cause, censorship. Hays was involved in a number of legal and public relations actions against censorship of print media starting in 1922. His first foray into censorship battles was outside the ACLU and came from his connections in the publishing industry. He represented Horace Liveright, a new publisher willing to challenge the censorship efforts of government and private bodies. Then in the wake of Scopes, which had shown the power of publicity, Hays jumped on the chance to use the same combination of publicity and legal action against a censor. When his new friend H. L. Mencken's magazine was banned by the Boston Watch and Ward Society for a story about prostitution, Hays and Mencken launched a multifront attack on censorship. They arranged to have Mencken personally sell a copy to the head of the Watch and Ward society under the eyes of a crowd that had been alerted to the stunt and a large contingent of reporters. The ensuing legal actions and publicity damaged the reputation of the society and prompted a nation-wide engagement with censorship. Its importance was not lost on Hays, who hung a commemorative photo of the event signed by Mencken on his office wall and wryly noted that "Massachusetts became the Tennessee of the North."[23]

In the 1920s and early 1930s, Aline became a shaper of the direction of Hays's work. Aline Davis was from a well-to-do Jewish family. She attended art school but did not finish after she married and began having children. She designed and made the clothing for her daughters, and her work caught the eye of a bespoke dress shop who hired her to design. Her work then carried over to "designing stage costumes and directing lighting and scenic effects." It was probably through the theater that she and Arthur met. At the time of her marriage with Hays in 1924 she was the mother of two children with her first husband. Together she and Hays had one daughter, Jane. Aline Hays worked during their marriage and had a notable career as a stylist and textile designer—in 1927 and 1928 she was a stylist with R.H. Macy & Company (later Macy's), and she left that position to become a textile designer with Ameritex. There, her innovations with cotton weave gained her some renown. Some of her cloth was made into items shown at a Paris fashion show. In her professional role she preferred to be called Miss Hays, apparently a practice common among stylists in this period. Aline and Arthur (and his ghostwriter, McAlister Coleman) occasionally worked together on writing projects. Aline Hays was also more radical in her political and economic beliefs than her law-yer husband, and she shared his inclination to be a joiner and for direct action. In 1935 she founded the "League of Women Shoppers," which sought to raise working standards in the garment industry by organized boycotts of shops by well-to-do and well-dressed women. They put into practice the idea that "a mink coat counts more on the picket line than a pair of overalls." Aline was arrested in early 1936 for picketing a Brooklyn department store. Hays had a picture of her arrest on his office wall. She often joined Hays when he delivered speeches or participated in debates and even trials.[24]

Unlike others in his circle, Hays never exhibited great attraction to communism. Probably at both Aline Hays's and Roger Baldwin's urging he visited Russia for six weeks in 1926. Arthur and Aline's trip to Rus-sia started with a crossing on an ocean liner in first class and included stops in Paris and Berlin beforehand with stays in luxury hotels. The children—Aline's two children and their daughter, Jane—were with them on the first part of the trip but not on the tour of Russia. They returned by way of Constantinople and Budapest on the Orient Express. Hays's commitment to civil liberties and free enterprise made him aware of the limitations of the Communist utopia. In 1926, while praising the Soviet Union's extension of medical care to workers, he criticized it for developing a class society: Communists got privileges and the rest of the population did not. He particularly attacked the lack of political liberty and free speech as well as the remorseless indoctrination of the population. In a 1931 debate at the Labor Temple in New York City over whether "the United States would remain a democracy or adopt the dictatorship of the proletariat," Hays based his defense of democracy on the freedom of speech and action "even if it sometimes curbed," which he compared to the lack of liberty in the Soviet Union. The economics worried him too. In February 1927, he declared that "all initiative of the individual to make money was prevented by the Communist policy." In 1928 and 1929, Hays was even stronger in his rejection of Marxism, not limiting it just to Communism. He told a reporter that "most Socialists and radicals have a scheme for transforming the universe and they espouse this with a religious conviction that the economic system is bound to work out according to their philosophy. As a matter of fact, economics have a way of their own." In a later debate with a Communist, Hays asserted that "the most important characteristic of democracy is liberty" and that it was lacking under the Soviet system. "Democracy protected the weak against the strong . . . and the people themselves are responsible for what they have in democracy." On the other hand, that liberty included the right for Communists to proclaim their ideas in the United States.[25]

Hays's thinking about the issues of freedom was caught up in his view of law in a democratic society. In a speech to the Freethinkers' Society in February 1928, Hays emphasized popular sovereignty—through nullification. "Any community which observed laws of which it did not approve only because some Legislature had passed them . . . would be living in slavery." He called such law "blue laws" but defined them in his own way. "A law against reading the Bible in the schools in not a blue law . . . as it has the sanction of most of the community." On the other hand, "Anti-evolution laws are blues because they are not enforceable. It is impossible to teach scientific facts . . . without teaching evolution." This was a general proposition, true to "any law that attempts to curb active thought." Thus, in Hays's estimate, divorce laws and prohibition laws were blue laws." New York's divorce laws were unenforceable, as someone wanting a divorce could get one by "going to another jurisdiction." He saw couples living together as natural and not commanded by marriage, "and they will separate if they want to in spite of laws." People "behave as they please, and laws should be an expression of their views, not prohibitions of their conduct." His view was modernist and clearly shaped by his experiences in his private practice (managing migratory divorces), his personal life (his separation from Blanche and joining with Aline as well as the influence of Darrow's idea of humans being driven by innate urges), and his work for the ACLU (the references were to both Bible reading and the evolution case). His views at that point tended toward tempered absolutism and clearly did not deal with the problem of the tyranny of the majority. Over time, his ideas would develop and adjust, becoming more friendly to the protection of minority rights.[26]

The event that moved Hays to undertake work against the color line pervasive in American society was the trial of Ossian Sweet and his co-defendants. Hays was part of that larger story: He was involved in only one of the two Sweet trials, and his participation was overshadowed by that of his friend Clarence Darrow. In 1925, Dr. Ossian Sweet bought a house in a white neighborhood of Detroit. During the great migration and the auto industry's growth, Detroit's African American population mushroomed, and decent housing for upper income African Americans was scarce. Prior to Sweet buying the home there had been incidents, including mob intimidations, of other African Americans who had purchased property in predominantly white areas. Sweet assembled a team of family and friends to help with the move and to guard him, his wife, and baby against a potential violent reaction from people in the neighborhood. The white people of the neighborhood formed an association that had as a goal keeping African Americans out of the district. Crowds gathered outside the Sweet house over the course of two nights and a day. The second night the crowd turned into a mob and despite police presence assaulted the house by throwing stones at it. In response to the mob attack, the Sweets and their associates opened fire. Their one volley killed Leon Breiner, who was more a bystander than an active participant. The police response was to arrest every adult in the house.[27]

Detroit was rife with both racial and ethnic tensions, as tremendous growth had outstripped services and the disorder created by the flouting of prohibition laws had upset many. The Ku Klux Klan was quite active in the city, and the pitting of new immigrants (especially Catholics and Jews) and African Americans against Protestants resulted in fierce rhetoric and near violence. The city newspapers fueled racial antagonism, and thus the police department denied key aspects of the story: that there had been a crowd, that they had turned into a mob, and that they had stoned the house. The prosecutor's office, which could have gone beyond these transparent lies and refused to bring charges, instead accepted and augmented them. Eventually they would charge all eleven adults in the house with conspiracy to commit murder. The local NAACP at first thought this case could be handled like previous incidents and worked with the leading African American lawyers of the city to represent them and also secured a white lawyer of some repute, aiming for a dismissal. Meanwhile, the national NAACP, led by Walter White and James Weldon Johnson, saw the Sweet case as a chance to dramatize to the nation the problem of housing segregation and moved to take over the case. As they saw the forces lining up against them in Detroit and also the prospects for national attention, the leaders of the NAACP sought to bring in the most famous courtroom lawyer of the age, Clarence Darrow. Darrow happened to be visiting New York and staying with his friend Hays. Their appeal to Darrow also captured Hays. Darrow agreed to go to Detroit to consider representing the Sweets and their associates with the assumption that Hays would join him as co-counsel.[28]

Darrow's entrance into the case made it front page news across the nation. Darrow met with the defendants, and with the help of the NAACP formed a defense team of the original three African American lawyers who had been representing the Sweets: Cecil Rowlette, Julian Perry, and Charles Mahoney, as well as a white Detroit lawyer, Walter Nelson; and Herbert J. Freidman from Chicago along with Hays from New York. As in the Scopes trial, there was an element of socializing and learning outside the courtroom that pervaded the trial. Darrow gave speeches at various locales on all of his standard topics, and members of the greater defense team attended. Aline accompanied Arthur to Detroit. She was among the group that went to nightclubs in the African American district with Darrow, Hays, and Johnson. The NAACP officers and the lawyers stayed up well into the night talking and drinking. From all indications, Hays found both Johnson and White to be good company. Hays also spent time with Ossian Sweet, though not in relaxed circumstances as Hays prepared Sweet for trial in the jail.[29]

Darrow during the Sweet trial, "invariably deferred to Hays" when it came to legal questions. In the courtroom, Hays yielded to Darrow the jury selection and all cross-examination. Hays help set out trial strategy and prepared legal points for Darrow to raise. The defense decided there should be one trial, not separate trials, and offered up a self-defense argument. Working with Nelson, Hays fashioned the key point: that a person under Michigan law had the right to use deadly force if threatened by a mob, even if that person's perceptions of the mob's intentions were erroneous. Hays did not just stay on the law, he also asked the NAACP to provide their fact-rich, vigorously checked accounts of white mob actions against African Americans, including some from the riot-torn summer of 1919; the Elaine, Arkansas, massacre that had prompted the Supreme Court to overturn trumped-up jury verdicts against African Americans; and the terror of the 1921 Tulsa, Oklahoma, riot. These horrors become central to the case and were brought into focus in the trial by Hays. But before that defense could be mounted, the prosecution put on its case.[30]

Even in that phase, Hays's mastery of legal technicalities shaped the trial. Hays asked that the prosecution be required to file a bill of particulars as to what it would prove to establish conspiracy—that the defendants had decided in advance to arm themselves and to shoot to kill and they had done so. Hays also displayed significant courtroom tactical expertise. As the prosecutor was presenting, Hays repeatedly objected. As Boyle writes, "time and again" Hays "used his intimate knowledge of precedent and finely honed debater's skills" to knock the prosecutor off stride and weaken the impact of the evidence. His objections were often learned and lengthy. Otis Sweet (Ossian's brother) long after assessed him as bold. "He never asked the court. He demanded the court and brought up law to prove that he had a right to demand it." He may have come off as "a little too smart for the court," but he won a surprising number of objections and weakened the prosecution's case.[31]

After the prosecution finished its case, the defense asked for a dismissal, as the prosecution had not proved conspiracy. Hays invoked the technicality that circumstantial evidence if it had lawful purpose could not prove a conspiracy charge. Darrow insinuated that the witnesses for the state were lying and that the prosecution was animated by racial prejudice. And Hays was not above courtroom trickery. He had the Sweets' baby brought into the court on the day the defense would argue for the dismissal of charges. And with a wink he related years later that the baby cried out during his argument for motion to dismiss: "What inspired the child to break out at that special moment I don't know . . . I am certain that my instructions were merely to bring the child" to court. When the judge asked why a baby's cry was interrupting the court, Hays admitted he had the child brought in. "I wished to point out with illustrative emphasis that there is no more reason on the evidence here for holding any particular defendant than there would be for holding that baby who was in the house at the time of the shooting." Even though the prosecution was weak in rebutting it, the judge refused to grant the dismissal.[32]

Self-defense tied to the psychology of race would be the crux of the. Hays's opening statement stressed the equality of citizenship as applied to race: "We are not ashamed of our clients and we shall not apologize for them. We are American citizens; you men of the jury are American citizens; they are American citizens." American citizens had a legal right to self-defense. That right "in Anglo-Saxon history is centuries old and is well expressed in the old phraseology of Lord Chatham: 'The poorest man may in his cottage bid defiance to all the forces of the Crown; it may be frail, its roof may shake, the wind may blow through it, the storm may enter, the rain may enter; but the King of England cannot enter.' " By reaching back in history Hays may have risked losing the jury, but he did not linger there long; he declared that self-defense was "the dearest right of a free man" and necessary to civilized society, especially for the "humble citizen and particularly to one who is subject to prejudice because he differs in race, creed or color from the ruling class in any community." Hays said the defense would take the jury inside the minds of the defendants so they could see the events "as they appeared to eleven people of the black race who had behind them a history, who were affected by knowledge of the appalling and almost uncivilized treatment of their race by those who should be their brothers." They would show the reasonable ground for fear of mob violence in the mind of a "colored man" who had "knowledge that people" had threatened to bomb the house, drive them out, and kill the occupants; and had formed an organization to keep the neighborhood white and, most importantly, had "knowledge of what mobs do and have done to colored people."[33]

The burden of showing the mental state of the defendants was placed on Ossian Sweet. Hays guided that key witness for the defense in his testimony. Hays told him to "stand up so the jury can look you over" as he recounted his biography: the grandson of a slave, the son of a farmer and minister, who along with his brothers, a dentist and college student, had risen in American society. "Dr. Sweet gives one pride in America, just as the story of this case makes one ashamed for America." For Hays, Sweet was an appealing figure, one who was "born on a farm of humble people, gradually rising through life to become after years of work, study and earnest application, a member of an honored profession." Yet he was one who was always stalked by the reasonable fear of mob violence against his race, one who knew that police had recently and repeatedly failed to protect African Americans from mobs. There were ten other defendants, but the doctor, the homeowner, was the focus of Hays's opening statement. It set the stage for Ossian Sweet's testimony.[34]

The essence of Ossian Sweet's testimony explained to the jury the state of mind of the African Americans who fired into the mob on that September night in 1925. He told his life story, mixing in accounts of, in the words of historian Kevin Boyle, "the racial incidents that scarred him most." Over the prosecution's objections, the evidence was admitted to show the state of mind of the defendants. His recounting of the events leading up the shooting ended with Hays asking, "What was your state of mind at the time of the shooting? Sweet's answer was masterful, "When I opened the door and saw the mob, I realized I was facing the same mob that had hounded my people throughout its entire history. . . . I was filled with a peculiar fear, the fear of one who knows the history of my race. I knew what mobs had done to my people before." In Hays's later condensed version, "Dr. Sweet told something of negroes' tragic story, the lynchings . . . in various parts of the country . . . of negroes taken from policemen said to be guarding them and killed." These were not just stories; Sweet connected them to his own history and status. For instance, he was in the Washington riot against African Americans in 1919 and in Elaine, Arkansas, professional men like himself were slaughtered. In the closing statements of the trial, Darrow handled this theme masterfully in Hays's estimation: "The ordinary lawyer collates facts, analyzes evidence and makes his appeal. There are few who use history, psychology and philosophy in order to show the real underlying facts. He showed how race prejudice animated the mob and fear led the Sweets and their friends to defend themselves against it.[35]

This trial of the Sweets and associates ended in a hung jury. While the defendants were released on bail, the defense changed its strategy and sought separate trials for all. The prosecution countered with trying Ossian's brother, Henry Sweet, who had confessed to shooting out of the home. The defense team was reshaped and a noted criminal lawyer from Detroit, Thomas Chawke, was added. Darrow participated as he had before, but Hays did not take part. He had involved himself in a different cause, one that would also allow him to continue to work in New York City. The Countess Cathcart had been refused entry into the United States because of her known adultery in the past. This challenge to both modernism and freedom was a cause Hays embraced easily. But even though Hays did not come back for the second trial (and his later accounts ascribed too much credit to Darrow alone for the not-guilty), the Sweet trial added racial discrimination to the menu of wrongs he would attempt to right. The Sweet trial was where Hays came face-to-face with African Americans, worked with them, came to admire some of them, socialized with some, and learned to embrace the cause of equal rights for them. The lessons from the Sweet experience stayed with Hays and shaped how he approached race relations in later years.[36]

If Hays had any doubts about how civil rights were tied to civil liberties, his and James Weldon Johnson's treatment by the New York City school board would have settled them. Hays and Johnson had been invited to speak at a Peace Week celebration held by the League of Neighbors and the Union of East and West in May 1926. Both Hays and Johnson were denied the use of the school by the director of extension activities. The ACLU protested, and an extended controversy as to whether there was a blacklist and the reasons for Hays's and Johnson's exclusions were aired. The superintendent of schools said the schools needed to protect young minds against subversive ideas. "We will not permit speakers in the school to undo our work with the children. We are teaching patriotism and the love of American institutions. We cannot admit people who are subversive, who preach doctrines calculated to overthrow the Government by unlawful means." Much of the discussion focused on whether the ACLU and the NAACP, with Hays and Johnson as their representatives, were blacklisted groups, as well as Hays's role in the evolution case. The meeting was shifted to another, non-school locale and recast as "Old Fashioned Free Speech." There Hays and Johnson addressed the controversy. Hays denounced the school officials as "prudes and pigmies, ignorant alike of the principles under the American Government and of the Constitution." He railed against the kind of teaching about American government that their stand implied, stating that it would not teach the importance of dissent and important ideas like the right of revolution and the right to question religion. Johnson said he presumed he was regarded as dangerous because he belonged to the NAACP, an organization that condemned lynching, adding, "If this is radicalism, I must plead guilty." The ACLU's allies and opponents joined the debate either denouncing or defending the school officials. The ACLU tested the superintendent's policy by applying to use a school building for another free speech event. It was denied. The school board justified its decision by quoting testimony by ACLU members to a congressional committee where they had supported the right of aliens to advocate communism, and the school board said that New York Legislature's Lusk Committee (which had investigated radical groups) had declared the ACLU an organization that advocated dangerous views. Eventually the matter was carried to State Commissioner of Education Frank P. Graves, who upheld the school's position. An appeal to the courts resulted in an order requiring the board to give the ACLU a hearing. After that hearing, the board allowed the ACLU to sponsor a meeting at a school building on an innocuous topic: the growth of New York.[37]

A press release concerning this flap, which Hays drafted, provided a snapshot of his thinking about freedom of speech. "The Board of Education does not seem quite clear as to why I am on the Blacklist." Maybe because "I was unfriendly to the Government." Or maybe because "I bested the Department of Immigration in the Cathcart case and the Post Office Department in the Mencken case." Or maybe it was because "I am anti-religious because of the defense of Scopes. Apparently, then, those who oppose anti-evolution laws seem anti-religious to our educators, for of course, no distinction can be drawn between those who merely oppose such a law and those who try to do something about it." Or, worst of all, Hays feared his skepticism and open mind threatened those "in control who use the schools to teach that this the best of all possible worlds, that this the best of all possible countries, that this is the best of all possible cities, and that a complacent satisfaction and an ignorance of true conditions must be the background of American education." Later he recast the piece as an attack on the Board of Education and broadened it beyond himself to include Johnson. "So why was the League of Neighbors and Union of East and West, during the Peace Week not permitted to use a high school? Because James Weldon Johnson, one of the foremost colored poets and literary men in the United States and secretary of the National Association for the Advancement of Colored People and were on the Board of Education blacklist." Hays added that what stood out was that he and Johnson were members of the ACLU. To Hays's thinking, the Board was "afraid of a breath of freedom coming through the windows into the stuffy atmosphere of conventional school. They have not the faith in Democracy which should lead them to favor the expression of all opinion."[38]

In the wake of the Scopes and Sweet trials, Hays used his fame to push for individualism and overcoming social boundaries and correcting the direction of American politics. He advised a college audience, in *The Frater*, to avoid becoming Babbitts and not to continue to allow the decline of democracy shown by American intervention in the Caribbean. He urged them not to be conformist "bond salesmen, business-men, lawyers, doctors, engineers, and others "but to become non-conformists, dissenters." He challenged them to make the Bill of Rights have a real effect in American society. He urged men (and his gender limits were clear) to break with the "training toward economic success, with acquiescence in our institutions" as they currently were. He instead called on them to challenge the status quo. He held up dissenters like Roger Baldwin and John Thomas Scopes. "[Scopes] has received a scholarship at Chicago University where he is now studying, and is the envy of other school teachers in Tennessee, who thought it would pay to 'conform.'" He wanted them to deal with was the lack of democracy in American overseas ventures in Haiti, Santo Domingo, and the Virgin Islands.[39]

As part of his resistance to the trends in American society, Hays began giving speeches on public topics as well as engaging in debates. In July 1927, Hays sought to reclaim the label of patriotic from the groups he thought were restricting liberty. In a radio address, he labeled the various conservative groups as "unpatriotic." He called the Woman's Christian Temperance Union and the Ku Klux Klan censorship organizations. He linked them together, saying they were by degrees reducing "the fundamental rights of free speech, free press, and assemblage." In phrases that would be repeated in his 1928 book *Let Freedom Ring*, he said, "you can speak on any subject but unionism in a time of strikes in West Virginia and New Jersey, in Tennessee on any topic save religion." And African American rights were among the rights that were endangered, as he retold the struggles of Ossian Sweet in Detroit. Hays condemned the restrictive immigration laws. He denied the ACLU was radical and insisted it was "quite old fashioned" and had on its board of directors Republicans and Communists. He attacked the American Legion for its "intolerance and oppression." This was not just talk: Hays had previously sought to use the law of libel to curb the activities of those who were red baiting. Along with others, including his friend McAlister Coleman, he filed a libel suit against the publishers of a pamphlet that named him as member of an organization allied with the Communist movement during the 1924 presidential campaign when Hays backed the Progressive Party's Robert La Follette.[40]

Hays's fame prompted him to explain his dual lawyerly roles—those of private lawyer and civil liberties advocate. In a draft article, "My office is on Wall Street," he explained, "my work has largely to do with corporate matters, brokerage and general commercial cases. My clients are mostly conservatives who do not approve of my view or work for the American Civil Liberties Union." He explained, "I suppose I am chiefly interested in this work because I resent the hypocrisy of people who pretend to be Americans who always talk about the Constitution, but do not believe in its principles." He made a point of saying that he used libel law only "for good causes," and that because his only "criminal cases having been those where some matter of principle was involved . . . these I have usually taken without pay." (The emphasis should be on "usually" as Hays took a fee of three thousand dollars plus expenses from the NAACP for the Sweet trial.) And his range of projects for the ACLU had been extensive, including his work on the coal town free speech drives; Scopes; representing the *American Mercury* against the censors; championing Countess of Cathcart's plea for entry into the United States; his work on the appeals and request for commutation for Sacco and Vanzetti; working with Darrow on the murder trials of two anti-fascists, Calogero Greco and Donato Carrillo; and the trials of labor organizers, some of them Communists, who were tried for murder after a violent strike in Gastonia, North Carolina. He admitted he "gained national prominence" through the ACLU actions, and he thought this work advanced the cause of freedom.[41]

Another way Hays made his case for freedom, including freedom from racial discrimination in housing, was through writing. His fullest treatment came in *Let Freedom Ring*, which included a chapter on the first Sweet trial. The account rightly featured Darrow, almost to the exclusion of all other actors, including himself. For instance, he reproduced the opening statement for the defense in the book, but he did not say he gave it. Nor did he write that he also led Ossian Sweet through his testimony. His account strongly makes the case that Sweet was a worthy individual whose freedom was threatened.[42]

Even though battling for equal rights, Hays did not escape racialist thinking, but the racialist categories were used to attack any supposed superiority of the white race. In his account of the white witnesses in the Sweet trial, he wrote: "Lies, evasion, prejudice and stupidity characterized their expression. Physically they were low-browed, mean and unintelligent looking, ugly." He contrasted them to "the colored witnesses" with their "clear features, good looks and unusual intelligence" who "were people of a distinctly higher type than the whites who testified for the prosecution. "At no point did the Nordics show to advantage." Indeed, concluded Hays: "Surely, Sweet was moving to a neighborhood of his inferiors." This twist had been put into the case by Darrow in his closing argument in the case in even stronger terms. But it had also been done with more sub-tlety by having Walter White testify about mob violence (to support the psychological defense) to explain why Sweet feared for his life. "The last question asked of [White] was, 'are you a negro?'" and the answer 'Yes' brought home to the jury that one might be a negro and still be white." Thus, while racialist thinking was there, the use of it undercut common racial assumptions of white superiority. In the trial Hays had used such thinking and in later accounts had shared the lesson he learned that day when the NAACP came calling for Darrow. He would invoke it in other circumstances later in his career.[43]

There are also off notes in his account that undercut its focus on equal rights. For instance, in his 1928 account, Hays did not supply the first name of all the African American lawyers who first represented the clients in the case. Instead, they were "Three local colored lawyers, Messrs. Perry, Rowlette and Mahoney." On the other hand, the two other white members of the team, "Mr. Walter Nelson and Herbert J. Freidman," were identified by their full names. This was legal snobbery and latent racism and clearly indicated the limits of Hays's racial liberalism. He apparently did not think of these men as professional equals. He may not have been impressed with Rowlette's work, which, while it was the basis for the defense, buried the key precedent. These lawyers stood in contrast to Dr. Sweet, whom Hays clearly portrayed as a superior individual. But still, Hays could see that freedom should apply to all in America's democratic society. The defense had also called other African Americans who were passing through the neighborhood in their cars that night and were threatened with lynching. The prosecution attempted to discredit their testimony in cross-examination by highlighting small inconsistencies. Hays recounted that one witness "seemed to resent the cross-examination as a species of impertinence. He was asked where he had had dinner, how long he had been driving, whom he had seen. Finally in a burst of impatience the old colored gentleman exclaimed, 'I eats where I please, goes where I please and I pays my bills.'" The story is inserted to lighten a serious topic, but it is not just a laugh at the man's phrasing. The unnamed witness in colloquial language was asserting the point Hays always returned to in explaining the Sweet case. It was a case of freedom—in this case, that of residence, to live where one pleased. That was part of being an equal member of society. To deny it was to erode freedom. He ended his chapter by invoking Lord Chatham, whom he had quoted in his opening at the trial about the legal sanctity of the home. In 1928, he wrote that the Sweets had not secured that right. The house stood empty. There were many reasons why the Sweets may not have wanted to live there, as their child had died or they may have feared for their safety. Racism was still alive, and "residence in Detroit is not free so long as that house stands idle."[44]

Publishing the book, which contained many of Hays's more notable cases, kept his fame alive. *Let Freedom Ring* was widely reviewed in newspapers across the nation. Predictably it gained favorable coverage in Northeastern city papers and criticism in both the South and West. One reviewer wrote that books like this "should be issued every six months to keep the flame of liberalism alive," while another dismissed it and him: "Hays is a New York lawyer. . . . His militant study leaves the impression that freedom will succeed in wringing our necks if we don't watch out." Hays courted fame; as he would do with all his works, he purchased copies and sent them to influential people. Hays was particularly impressed with Oliver Wendell Holmes's handwritten letter in thanks (he had it typed for his files and inserted it into his final book). Holmes thought him a "little overwrought" on issues of civil liberties and cautioned him against getting carried away with his own conclusions and bending evidence to support it. And Holmes was optimistic, writing, "I rather more than hope that there is more intelligent and high-minded thinking on public matters than ever before." The reminder to be skeptical appealed to Hays, but ran in opposition to his desire to sway people and to be famous. Hays would bend the rules to try to bring it about; thus, in a move that was doubly self-serving, Hays agreed to be interviewed by his ghostwriter (but not identified as such) in a radio broadcast over the Socialist radio station WEVD soon after the book was released.[45]

The synergy of Hays's fame, willingness to write about civil liberties, and role in the ACLU came together when the ACLU promoted Hays's *Let Freedom Ring* through a mass mailing. Typical of the early ACLU, it claimed repression was new in American life, having "grown up since the war." It aimed to "build up over the country a counter-sentiment against the prevailing intolerance and indifference." It asked people to take on the issues on their own. When it suggested investigations by the interested, it mentioned a wide range of police actions and school board actions but nothing about segregation. Racial discrimination, while always an ACLU target, was never a central target, and Hays's activism shared that trait.[46]

In Hays's career after the Scopes and Sweet trials, family, fame, friends, business associates, and fellow civil libertarians all came together to reinforce his work. For instance, his divorce from Blanche never fully severed their relationship. They coparented successfully, and he continued carrying on business with clients that had come his way through Blanche. Thus, he represented the Provincetown Playhouse for years, a connection that came to him through her. Indeed, there was always a smell of greasepaint and limelight in the family. Alan S. Hays, a cousin of Arthur who worked in his law firm, was the son of Walter Hays who had been "a pioneer in the motion picture industry." Alan met his future wife probably through Arthur and Blanche's daughter Lora, as the she attended the same drama school as his future wife. Horace Liveright, the publisher, was a friend, and through their friendship Hays was drawn into the fight against the New York censor over the staging of the lesbian play *The Captive*. Friendship also led to business connections. Hays continued to do legal work for friends and even family of friends. Thus, in 1930 he represented Paul Darrow, son of Clarence Darrow, in a suit over fraud in the purchase of bonds.[47]

Beyond his inner circle, there was an established world of civil liberties camaraderie that sustained Hays. In the 1920s Roger Baldwin stayed for at least one extended period of almost a year in Hays's home. Throughout the 1930s, Hays and Baldwin and others in the ACLU mixed during summers on Martha's Vineyard. Even during the most intense periods of activism, the social connections were part of the ACLU. For example, during the height of the attempts to stop Jersey City Mayor Frank Hague's suppression of speech he did not like, a Hays radio broadcast over WEVD was interrupted by a woman throwing pepper at his eyes. Later, the radio station reenacted the scene with Connie Ernst, daughter of Morris Ernst, playing the role of Aline Hays, who had been in the audience at the original broadcast. This casting shows a closer connection than one could project from the strong debates Hays and Ernest engaged in when it came to ACLU positions on various issues.[48]

Hays was linked with Darrow in the public mind, and this lifted his salience. A reporter portrayed him as a "Modern crusader" in the "vast arena of conflicting ideas and ideals" who was "Clarence Darrow's right hand man." Darrow promoted him. He told a reporter that "I have known a great many men, good, bad and indifferent, but I have never known one who was superior to Arthur Garfield Hays in ability, idealism, courage and devotion." Darrow noted "his willingness to serve any righteous cause that needs a champion." Even after Darrow's death, his name was linked with Hays's. For instance, a short biography of Hays read: "ARTHUR GARFIELD HAYS ranks with the late Clarence Darrow as one of the outstanding liberal lawyers of this generation. He was a close personal friend and associate of Darrow, who called him 'the warrior of the courtroom.'" His image morphed over time, as his corporate practice was glossed over. His *Current Biography* entry for 1933 presented Hays as a civil libertarian. "As counsel of the Civil Liberties Union since the early '20s he has participated in the defense of Sacco and Vanzetti, Tom Mooney, the Gastonia Communists, the Scottsboro Negroes, John Strachey, Harry Bridges and others." The entry continued, "He has fought for the right of free speech for German-American Bundists, Henry Ford and William Randolph Hearst, as well as for Communists and labor organizations." Hays confessed he was "a 'nut' on the Bill of rights." But that was because he thought that no one "can live a satisfactory experience without the full right to express himself." He was no Adam Smith liberal, though, or even New York Governor Al Smith. Because while Hays wanted the government to leave individuals alone, he also wanted every citizen to be guaranteed "at least a minimum standard of living."[49]

Hays's political orientation moved from progressive Republicanism, to Bull Moose, through the Committee of 48 and its progressive politics, to the Progressive Party, and ended at New Deal Democrat. He seemed to struggle to find a home for his liberalism. At times his identification with the Progressive Party idea vied with his image as a high-powered lawyer or ACLU activist in the press. Hays identified himself as a liberal while participating in a symposium on radicalism in the United States held by the League for Industrial Democracy. Other speakers represented more radical viewpoints (communism and socialism) while yet others espoused the Catholic views on labor. Unlike the other speakers, he claimed to have "no beliefs," and he said he welcomed the accomplishment of liberal aims by others who weren't identified as liberals, like Governor Al Smith. To Hays, the key to liberalism was flexibility in trying to advance humanity. Hays warned radicals "against becoming rigid and doctrinaire." Paraphrasing and extending Oliver Wendell Holmes's formulation from the *Abrahams* case, he said, "Liberty consists in the competition not the repetition of ideas." In a 1932 radio address he argued for submitting the prohibition amendment to the vote of the American people through a referendum. He was sure it would be voted down, as it could not be enforced. "It was wrong in theory, wrong in practice, goes against American liberty." By the election of 1932, Hays was supporting Franklin Delano Roosevelt and argued others should too because "it would throw out Hoover," lead to "the elimination of the stupid, vicious and indefensible prohibition laws," would bring a more "liberal program" to the nation, and "bring a more humanitarian point of view to Washington on all social problems." He added, "I like the idea of balancing the budget with beer. . . . I'd rather drink with Roosevelt than protest with [the Socialist Norman] Thomas."[50]

Even though Jews as a group were becoming part of the Democratic coalition, Hays's embrace of the party did not stem from his Judaism. Hays was a Jew when anti-Semitism was on the rise. In 1928 the *Jewish Tribune* described him as "a Jew—but a Jew with a universal perspective, and as he himself said, he was 'not a self-conscious Jew.'" As was common, this piece defined Judaism not as just as a religion but as a race and asserted that Hays "always has affirmed his racial identity." Others attacked him because of his religion. Opponents to his position in the Scopes trial used stereotypical anti-Semantic tropes to describe him. It was part of the age. Henry Ford's anti-Semantic propaganda was ramping up. Immigrant restriction, aimed in part at Eastern European Jews, was instituted in the 1920s. The elite universities stepped up their efforts to limit the number of Jews admitted. The legal profession waged a multifront campaign to limit the number of Jews who entered it. Before the rise of Hitler in Germany, in the face of the stirring of anti-Semitism, Hays fought back behind the scenes, especially through his work for "the non-sectarian but filled with Jews fraternity," Pi Lambda Phi (PLP). The American college fraternity system was segregated, with many societies restricting membership to whites and Christians. And in many places there was resistance to allowing Jewish or nonsectarian fraternities on campus. Hays was involved in efforts to open chapters or resolve issues that had arisen from chapters' behavior. In the late 1920s he was drawn into disputes at Brown University, the University of Wisconsin, and Amherst College. Unlike most of his other work, these efforts were conducted with no attempts at publicity. The Supreme Rex (president) of PLP, in thanking Hays for his work, praised his ability "to avoid provocation." Hays was named Supreme Rex in 1933. Still, Hays wore his Judaism lightly. When asking the famous reform journalist Heywood Broun to come to a PLP event, Hays wrote, "Do you want to do me a favor? Pi Lambda Phi, a Jewish fraternity, of which I am Supreme Rex or Kleagle or big Elephant or something of the kind, is having a dinner on Tuesday night, the 21st. I think they are going to give me my regalia. At any rate, won't you come to that dinner? The boys are all anxious to hear you."[51]

In this period, Hays's relationships with African Americans were professional but, considering how his world of work carried over into the social, also a bit social. Yet there were limits. There is no indication that he had close social associations across the color line. Hays socialized with some African Americans, but, significantly, they courted him. For instance, in between the first and second Sweet trials, Walter White went out of his way to "nurture" their relationship. As Keven Boyle points out, in December 1925 "there was a tasteful get-together one night at White's apartment on Edgecombe Place, another evening at the theater to see Hamlet performed in modern dress, and a somewhat more raucous night touring Harlem's hotspots." But, as always with Hays, the social was also mixed with work. Thus, James Weldon Johnson's invitations and arrangements showed a familiarity between the men. In arranging a joint talk before the [NAACP] Newark branch, he wrote Hays, "You can see now what you have let yourself in for. I hope, however, that you can go. If you can arrange to do so, why, we will motor over. In that way we will make the trip as pleasant as possible." After that engagement Hays committed to talk in April before the Philadelphia branch to help with its membership drive. Yet there was a limit to Hays's melding his race work with his civil liberties portfolio; thus, when accepting an invitation to speak at the faculty club at Princeton University, he did not suggest his work in the Sweet case as a suitable topic: "I don't know what to suggest as a subject. It might be 'American Freedom,' or 'Decay of the Constitution,' or 'American Hypocrisy.'" He also listed the Scopes case, the Cathcart controversy, and Mencken's censorship battle in Boston.[52]

Two years after the Sweet trial, Hays was willing to travel to talk about the trial and considering writing about social relations between African Americans and whites. Significantly, he sketched out his ideas to Darrow and asked for his help. He wrote to him that he was "thinking of writing an article for 'Harlem,' a new Negro paper, on the subject of the self-consciousness that usually exists in social relations between colored people and whites." His starting point would be that "The colored people are of course tremendously race-conscious. The white man is in the position of not wanting to appear too friendly for fear it might be thought patronizing, and on the other hand, does not like to appear cool." He thought Darrow had "lots of thoughts on this subject" that he could share in writing or in person. "You are sure to have anecdotes or items from your own experience." Darrow replied that it was a good idea and thought they should talk about it in person as he soon would be in New York, though it's unclear whether the article ever got written. Hays's calling on Darrow for anecdotes and ideas implies that his interactions with African Americans were rather limited.[53]

The limited interactions with African Americans was a constraint to Hays in shaping his activism, as experience mattered as much as ideology for him. After he published *Let Freedom Ring*, Hays in an interview revealed the influence the Scopes trial preparation had on him. He found exchanges among the scientists at the hotel about the development of science to be fascinating. And that knowledge seeped into his assessment of the anti-evolution laws. He portrayed them as doomed to failure because the church had already accepted more fundamental changes. "It is strange that a world which accepts the heliocentric theory should be troubled about the theory of evolution. If the earth is not the center of the universe . . . it is hard to conceive man as the center of God's attention." He thus not only repeated the idea that the trial was about a struggle between modern science and old religion, but also emphasized that religion had already lost the contest. This view also informed his modernism. Thus, he would telegraph Margaret Sanger about her struggle for legalizing birth control, telling her that "our Moral system has developed from Tradition and Theology. Were Rational consideration given weight, your battle would be won." This notion of progress that would shift boundaries of knowledge would reemerge in Hays's later race work.[54]

Established during the Scopes trial, Hays's and Darrow's friendship deepened after the Sweet cases and survived the ups and downs of economic fortune. This relationship increased Hays's involvement in the cause of African American rights. After the Sweet trial, "much of Darrow's time" was "spent furthering the cause of Negro rights from the lecture platform." And Darrow tied Hays to the NAACP. Both Darrow and Hays suffered serious financial losses from the stock market crash of 1929, and while Hays recouped his fortune, Darrow did not. Hays mused philosophically about the changing economic fortunes, exaggerating how luck had shaped his income: "from commercial cases, trials, estates, corporation work and various other sources I make a substantial living. Unless several cases came in each year that paid big fees, I would be broke. At the beginning of the year I never know where they will come from. It's the breaks!" Darrow was far more desperate. Hays himself admitted that he kept Darrow's legal career going, writing that "in the last ten years of his life there were few cases that he tried without my having been his associate." Some think that Darrow would never have tried another case if Hays had not pulled him into various cases. "Hays was active in cases of the type that interested Darrow and furthermore could be relied upon to do the spadework that Darrow himself was not prepared to do." But Hays thought he got the better part of the deal. "Nothing has been more inspiring or humanly helpful than [Darrow's] company, his example and his friendship."[55]

Thus, from their friendship Hays was drawn into the plight of the nine young African American men convicted of the rape of two white women in Scottsboro, Alabama, which became the cause célèbre of the

1930s. The NAACP had been slow to involve itself in the case even as an investigation by its ally, the ACLU, showed that the two women were probably lying about the crime. The NAACP had difficulties finding local lawyers to take the case; eventually two sets of local counsel were involved, one working with the NAACP and another with the International Labor Defense (ILD) of the Communist Party. Following the lead of the party, which was trying to court African Americans, the ILD went into the case with great fervor. The men and boys agreed to representation by the ILD, which prompted the leaders of the NAACP to overcome their doubts about the cost of Darrow's fee and his atheism and ask him, and Hays, to take on the appeal and presumably new trials if the appeal was successful. Darrow and Hays asked to join the case, but the ILD said they could only if they repudiated the NAACP's involvement and agreed that the ILD would determine tactics and strategy. In reply, Darrow and Hays proposed that the ILD lawyers team up with them, jettisoning all organizations to "work together as attorneys to try to save these boys, and our responsibility is to them and to them only." The ILD lawyers refused, and Darrow and Hays withdrew. The Scottsboro appeal continued, with Hays keeping a close watch on it while engaged in other matters.[56]

When he published his book *Trial by Prejudice* in 1933, Hays was less the cultural warrior he had been in *Let Freedom Ring* and more an advocate for righting legal wrongs. That focus took him into many areas: persecution of a radical at the time of a strike, "a banker when his bank fails, a pacifist in wartime," and an African American in the South. The longest section of *Trial by Prejudice* was the chapter on Scottsboro. He discussed his writing of this section in a later work, showing how he had tried to move beyond his immediate reactions on learning that the Scottsboro boys were victims of vicious and cruel "men who framed and persecuted their fellows." He had realized that people influenced by "emotion, predisposition, and prejudice" sorted through the evidence and followed only the lines that reinforced their beliefs. He showed the draft to Aline, who told him that he had "shown your own prejudices very clearly" and that this version "reads like a frame-up" of the defendants. His revision stressed every bit of evidence that favored the prosecution's case and caused her to inquire, "Do you still believe those negroes are innocent?" This dialectic gave him the means to pull the book together to treat the "human factors" that went into miscarriages of justice despite "constitutional safeguards." Yet that racial injustice had become fully a part of Hays's panoply of prejudices to be combated is made clear by the frontispiece of his book, an illustration by Carl Rose and first published in *The Nation*. It shows a black man, standing with head bowed, facing a jury. The jury is all white and male. But looming in the back corner of the box is a larger-than-all hooded figure. That juror represented what Hays called "the ominous presence of the thirteenth juror—prejudice."[57]

Hays's account of the Scottsboro trials gave the Communists their due by praising their hiring of Walter Pollak and Samuel Leibowitz for handling first the appeal and then the retrials. While he decried "their blustering threats" toward Southern officials, he thought their tactics "stirred up tremendous excitement all over the world." But he had his doubts about the wisdom of this course. He reported that he said to Joseph Brodsky of the ILD (with whom he had good relations), "Joe if you were an illiterate Negro and on trial for your life . . . would you not feel that charge [of rape] alone was a sufficient burden, without having your counsel hang about your neck the added weight of social equality for the Negro, self-determination of the Black Belt, Northern prejudice, Jew Money, revolution, and Communism?" His account also ably captured what was so effective about Leibowitz's courtroom tactics in exposing the lies that constituted the evidence against the defendants and the almost insurmountable prejudices that worked against him. Hays faulted the leaders of the Southern Bar for not taking on the case and detailed how the Communists made Leibowitz's job harder. Nevertheless, Hays always proclaimed that the ILD saved the Scottsboro boys' lives. His book was written soon after the end of the Decatur trial, where the judge had set aside the jury's guilty verdicts as being contrary to the evidence. Hays was guardedly optimistic, quoting a Tennessee newspaper that "we cannot conceive of a civilized community taking human lives on the strength of the miserable affair." And though eventually the state did give up trying to condemn the men to death, the long retrials and the state's intractability made a case for Alabama not being a civilized community.[58]

That idea of advancing civilization—which had manifested itself in his understanding of the Scopes trial—was in tension with Hays's near faith in common-law criminal protections. Part of Hays's worldview was the common view among American lawyers that the American system of jurisprudence was the best because of the protections it afforded criminal defendants. Hays's embrace of this was particularly old-fashioned in that he described the system as Anglo-Saxon: "Anglo-Saxons are proud of their criminal legal system," he declared in the opening lines of *Trial by Prejudice*. Remarkably, he racialized the system as Anglo-American in an argument for equitably applying the system to all races. This high regard for the American system was established by the time Hays was in law school, where he no doubt acquired it, and he never abandoned it. When talking of criminal law processes in the United States, Hays admitted that the protections of procedure and due process were not implemented, and he detailed how practice did not comport with theory: Forced confessions, evidence seized illegally, and lack of adequate counsel were common and undermined the fairness of the process. Even if the "safeguards are often denied," an ordinary defendant in an "ordinary case" who was an innocent man was "in little danger of conviction." But if the case "arouses the emotions, if it involves question of race, color, religion, politics, or opinions," it was no longer ordinary. "An unpopular minority, a despised class or an heretical group" facing trial by human beings—whether judges or jurors—found their cases decided based on prejudice. Thus, he wrote a book to "present the facts in cases where prejudice has caused injustice," with the aim of arousing "the righteous indignation of decent men" to seek justice where juries had erred and not just complacently accept the jury verdicts. He hoped to bring about changes in the law to allow for easier changes of venue at trial, fuller scope to appellate courts in being able to set aside verdicts, and governors to issue pardons.[59]

In a 1934 draft article about Scottsboro, an expansion on his ideas in *Trial by Prejudice*, Hays again proclaimed how good the "Anglo-Saxon" criminal legal system was. But he admitted the theory was undercut by aroused emotions in a case "if it involves questions of race, color, religion, politics or opinions." When those factors were involved, it was no longer an ordinary case and prejudices came into play. Hays asserted there was not "a conscious intention or desire to kill innocent men." Just as the people of Alabama were led by the media to believe the defendants guilty, the defendants' supporters (Communists, the NAACP, and liberals) jumped too soon to the conclusion they were innocent. After the first trials, the idea that it was a "frame up" was embedded in Communists' minds. Prejudice derailed justice. Though always interested in grabbing a headline, Hays also usually carefully prepared any public speaking event (and often sought transcripts of his comments, if available) and issued corrections when he thought he had been misquoted. For example, in 1932, after the Supreme Court in *Powell v. Alabama* had mandated new trials for the Scottsboro defendants, a *New York Times* article said he attributed success in the court to the Communists' tactics of "mass pressure and mass protest." He wrote to the editor that he had not said that, and what he did tell the *Times* "was dictated by me over the telephone after I had carefully written out the statement." His view was that the Communists stirred up interest in the case, and that got their case to the Supreme Court. He gave them credit "for pushing the case to the limit." But he decried that "the fight against injustice is too often left to those who do not believe in our institutions" like the Communists. He closed with an echo of his modernist, civil libertarian 1920s worldview: "Certainly this case shows up the respectables."[60]

As the *Times* approaching him for a comment showed, by the end of the 1920s and the beginning of the 1930s, Hays was regarded as having expertise in African American legal issues. For example, the *Harvard Law Review* requested that he write a review on a recent book on lynching, and the *Yale Law Journal* wanted him to write an article on proposed federal anti-lynching legislation. Hays did neither, because "when one is in practice his time is not his own and these legal articles require a great deal of thought and work." He did write a piece (which the editor considered "a magnificent little article") for *The Survey* on African American agitator Angelo Herndon's prosecution in Georgia for sedition. That case, since it involved both freedom of association and questions of race, was more familiar ground for Hays.[61]

The ACLU's support of the NAACP anti-lynching legislation drive drew Hays into public discourse on that topic. In his 1934 review of James Chadbourn's *Lynching and the Law*, Hays showed familiarity with both the federal legislative proposal and the pushback against it. He praised Chadbourn's book for is presentation of the facts, noting that it was the work of a Southerner that undercut the "usual claims of lynchers." He emphasized how the book showed the racial nature of the practice, with whites lynching blacks. Hays knew of the "wholesale opposition of Southern Lawyers and judges" to federal anti-lynching legislation. Also, in an August 1934 address in Washington DC, Hays for the ACLU argued for the passage of a federal anti-lynching bill that would punish state officers who failed to protect prisoners and punish counties where lynching occurred. But anti-lynching legislation was only a small part of the ACLU agenda. It also sought restrictions on the power of the Post Office to ban items from the mail and overturning of the court cases that denied aliens citizenship if they were pacifists. It advocated for freeing political prisoners, including Angelo Herndon, and defended parts of the New Deal.[62]

But it was not just in the legal realm that others assumed Hays had familiarity with African Americans, and these more general topics were revealing of Hays's views on race. For instance, the publisher Harper & Brothers asked him to read the manuscript "Home to Harlem" by Claude McKay and "blurb" it. This would be McKay's hit novel after publishing his famous poem "If we must die." Hays's write-up said it was a direct and earthy story of "a simple, decent negro in modern negro civilization. The characters and situations appeal probably because they are a white man's ideas of negroes." He added: "The actions are human, animal and natural. . . . No white man could have written the book." In particular, he praised its rich vocabulary, some new to him, such as "sweet man" and "buffet-flats," which "without the context one would often wonder at meanings." He said the "language is crisp, the action staccato, the reactions honest. Hays asserted that McKay's work showed a full range of characterization of African Americans and that some of the negative views held by white men "of some negroes isn't so far wrong." He stressed that it was not race that defined them: "These are like whites of the same class and McKay doesn't pretend that they are different." Hays noted that for McKay, "colored people are not just negroes or blacks. They ranged from "high yellows" to "laquer [sic] black." He listed seventeen different phrases used to describe people. This obsession with color range contradicted the stark racist notions so prevalent in America and Europe.[63]

The rise of Hitler in Germany brought these racist notions, especially anti-Semitism, to the forefront of Hays's mind. He kept up with the ominous developments in Germany. He talked with German visitors and refugees. After attending as an observer the Nazi-organized trial of the men accused the burning down the Reichstag, he publicly and repeatedly attacked the Hitler regime on multiple levels, but especially for its treatment of Jews. He contrasted Germany with the United States. "Americans cannot comprehend how the Germans can submit to control by morons and gangsters," how the people were made into "slaves," and how fear pervaded the country, with everyone "apprehensive and worried." Hays asserted he valued his "country where he is protected against the tyranny of government, where he has a right to a writ of habeas corpus and to a fair trial, where he can think and say what he pleases, where different points of view are expressed." To those praising the German economic recovery from the depression and asserting that fascism was a way to fix the American economy, Hays rebutted them: "Fascism is just plain old-fashioned tyranny. King Canute could not stop the waves; Hitler cannot stop the forward progress of the race" (apparently referring to the human race). In his speech at the Madison Square Garden anti-Nazi event of 1934, Hays said that the "Hitler regime has many defenders but no defense." If Germany wanted equal rights on the world stage, it must give equal rights to its citizens. He bashed the "pathological exaggeration and tyranny of the state which leaves no one safe and under which the government is in no way restrained from seizing individuals and placing them in concentration camps." Nazis had stolen the "elemental rights for which individuals have fought and died for hundreds of years." To Hays, "democracy and liberty never seem a more valuable heritage than when one contemplates the tyranny and oppression which has terrorized the German people."[64]

Hays folded the anti-Semitism of the Nazis into their general oppression of all minorities. "The Jews are only one of the minorities which were suppressed. Their treatment is peculiarly shocking because they suffer the cruelest of punishment for the least of crimes—that of Judaism—a crime shared by some of the greatest figures in world history and of which no one is penitent." Even when it sounded like he was going to talk about anti-Semitism alone, Hays did not. In June 1934, he placed a long article in *Liberty*, a magazine edited by his friend C. Fulton Oursler, titled "What the Jews Want from Hitler." Hays's own witnessing of Nazi Germany's anti-Semitism, his rejection of fascism, and his rejection of racialism were on display, but his solution (which was totally unrealistic) emphasized what he valued. He proposed that Germany pursue the ideal of equal protection of the law for everyone, including Jews, as the path to improving its position in the "eyes of the world."[65]

Hays did take action against anti-Semitism. For the first time in its history, instigated by Hays, the PLP fraternity gave an award. It bestowed a medal on James G. MacDonald, High Commissioner for Refugees from Germany. In announcing the award, Hays warned of intolerance on American campuses and in the world. Still, he often preferred to not call an anti-Semite an anti-Semite. Thus, when a New Jersey newspaper attacked him with veiled anti-Semitic terms over his debate in a New Jersey school advocating prohibition repeal, he responded, but not by calling them out for it. The paper described him as "a sarcastic, ungentlemanly, conceited, cheap speaker." He was "unworthy of the names of the three presidents of this country and should reassume the name of the family to which he was born." Hays's printed response in the paper stated: "I was born in Rochester New York December 12, 1881 and am the son of Isaac M. Hays who lived in that community for a great many years. I resent the slur. I neither have changed my name nor have I never had any occasion to: in fact I am rather proud of it." (As he had told a reporter for the *American Hebrew* several years before who had asked about the shift, "it had been changed three generations back from Haas to Hays.) He framed the attack as one on his character, hinting that the New Jersey paper implied he had changed his name because he had done something disreputable. Coming from Hays, who had an active libel practice, this statement was quite barbed. But in taking this tack he slid over the implication that he was trying make his name sound less "Jewish." His response also underscored his religious heritage by pointing out his father's first name, as Old Testament names had fallen out of favor with Christians in the United States.[66]

By the 1930s fascism had come to America. Though the ACLU, encouraged by Hays, was adamant in protecting the free speech rights of the right as well as the left, Hays was also interested in making sure that fascists engaged in criminal actions would have the law enforced against them. In 1933, he took on a criminal case defending leftists who had been in an altercation with American fascists. It was a complicated story with obvious elements of Hays's worries about prejudice's power over courts. A fascist group from Philadelphia visited a brother organization in Queens, and sporadic violence resulted. In the aftermath of a rally, a fight broke out on the street between leftists and rightists. Two fascists died and two anarchists were prosecuted, one for murder. But the fascists had framed the anarchists. Hays, bringing in a very frail Darrow for marquee value, dominated a defense composed of different leftist groups, including the ILD. The defense won an acquittal, and then some of its members sought to have the district attorney and perjury-peddling witness legally punished. The working relationship between Hays and the ILD almost broke down, as he preferred invoking the press against the district attorney. Hays worked hard to put this story in the public eye, writing an article on it that he tried (and failed) to place in a number of publications, including *The New Republic*. It was an example of how he raised awareness of the causes he believed in and warned of dangerous trends in the hope that enlightened public opinion would result in improvement in society.[67]

Hays's friendship with Darrow pulled him into the Sweet case, and his work in that case propelled him into fighting against discrimination against African Americans as a new cause among the many he espoused. It mixed easily with his civil liberties work and was no more at odds with his private practice than his espousal of free speech rights for Communists. Advocating for the end to the color bar also fit well with Hays's conception of himself as a Jew in American society and how he thought Jews (and all minority groups who were persecuted) should go about protecting their rights. It also fit his personality. He wanted to battle for the underdog. But there is another aspect to it: Race was part of the fabric of every aspect of the United States. To be involved in the public arena would necessarily involve questions of race. In the 1930s, Hays's race work led him to join Darrow in trying to represent the Scottsboro boys. But race problems also manifested themselves much closer to home for Hays. And in 1935 Hays would be at the center of the attempt to confront the prejudices that fueled police brutality in Harlem.

2

"The stupidity of the city police"

The Harlem Riot Commission

According to a member, "the hearings before the Mayor's Commission" on the Harlem disorder of 1935 "were as exciting and dramatic as anything ever put upon the stage." Arthur Garfield Hays, "as Chairman of the subcommittee on the riots, allowed the fullest latitude to witnesses, to lawyers, to the representatives of the Communists, and even to the spectators." The hearings he conducted exposed "the intense bitterness and antagonism to the police" by the people of Harlem, which proved "a shock and revelation to all who heard." The Harlem disturbance of 1935 was the first major incident where, inside a racially segregated district, some of the African American inhabitants attacked property, engaged in violence, and looted stores. Hays spearheaded the commission's investigation of the policing abuses that sparked both the disturbance and blighted life in the neighborhood. He came to the job with orientations that set his course: As a liberal, especially after the start of the Great Depression, Hays embraced the use of government to both regulate the economy and redress the suffering brought on by economic calamity. However, his liberal strain was built on a civil libertarian foundation. Hays's civil liberties ideology celebrated the individual and turned a skeptical eye toward government action against people. Thus, there was always a tension between his liberal and liberties stances. He also came primed to deal with the issue of abusive policing from his work in the American Civil Liberties Union (ACLU); indeed, Hays approached this problem of racial discrimination as a civil libertarian, and much of what he was told in the hearings reinforced that approach. After the hearings, he helped to shape series of reforms aimed at limiting police abuse and repeatedly pushed for their adoption.[1]

Harlem, stretching from 110th to 155th streets between Third and Amsterdam Avenues, by 1930 was the largest African American neighborhood in the nation. The African American population there rose most dramatically in a short time from 1925 to 1930. In central Harlem, the African American population increased from 32.4 percent in 1920 to 70.2 percent in 1930 and rose again to 89.3 percent in 1940. The Harlem Renaissance gave rise to an outpouring of cultural creativity that defined the 1920s and the early 1930s. James Weldon Johnson in his 1930 book *Black Manhattan* portrayed the African American experience in Harlem as "a large-scale laboratory experiment" in which "the Negro" was "helping to form American civilization" and showcasing new, positive conceptions of the race. Johnson concluded, "Possessing the basic rights, the Negro in New York ought to be able to work through the discriminations and disadvantages."[2]

There were discriminations and disadvantages aplenty; they grew worse as the Great Depression pushed New Yorkers into smaller and shoddier living spaces and jobs disappeared. African Americans in Harlem experienced a more severe depression than whites across the city. The housing crisis affected them severely, as Harlem's rents already were disproportionally high and stayed so. African Americans suffered levels of unemployment at least twice the rates for whites, and the jobs open to them were usually low paying. In New York City, "entire industries were kept lily-white even for menial employment." In Harlem, the chain and department stores long refused to hire African American clerks. In September 1935, 43 percent of the African American families in Harlem qualified for food relief. The chief judge of the domestic relation courts commissioned a report in 1934 showing that African American childhood crime had risen more than 240 percent since 1921, and African American families constituted 25 percent of all parental nonsupport cases in the city even though their proportion of the population was less than 6 percent. Added to these woes was discrimination by those who were supposed to help people through the depression. The city's Home Relief Bureau, the State Employment Service, and other "programs designed to help the poor openly discriminated against" African Americans. Not surprisingly, prostitution became a job of last resort for many, and many more placed their hopes in winning illegal street lotteries.[3]

Long before 1935, "the legitimate grievances of Harlem's population were being articulated by its leaders, albeit ignored by the city's political

actors." Activist-led marches and boycotts drew large numbers of participants. Their goals were clear: fair hiring by relief agencies, more and better
relief, ending employment discrimination in the private sphere—including
the hiring of African American workers by the stores in the area. In the
summer of 1934, the target of such demands was Harlem's largest department store. For five months, hundreds of protestors at a time picketed the
store. But the boycott was broken by a court ruling at the end of 1934 and
progress erased as the African American clerks hired in the response to
the protests were fired. Picketing of stores continued but in the hands of
radical groups and under the watchful eyes of New York City police, who
were more than willing to use force to enforce both the law of picketing
and their own sense of what should be, prompting complaints of police
brutality.[4]

In New York City, charges of police brutality were centered around
the liberal use of police clubs, especially in suppressing strike demonstra-
tions, street political events, and in questioning suspects. For most of its
history, police brutality was linked to corruption. Thus, often the claims of
excessive force would be tied to misconduct and abuse of authority through
illegal searches and false arrest. In the early twentieth century, added to
brutality of street clubbings—either random or along racial, ethnic, or
political lines—came the practice of official torture. The so-called "third
degree" was the means (ranging from psychological pressure to beatings)
used by the police to secure confessions. It became more common when
the police role expanded into solving crime and was sanctioned within
the police department. The perceived rise in crime due to Prohibition led
the New York City police to use dragnets and strong-arm squads, further
institutionalizing brutality. Mayor Fiorello La Guardia's obsession with
rooting out illegal gambling and organized crime drove this endorsement
of brutality. The practice was entrenched under Commissioner Grover
Whalen and later was sanctioned by La Guardia's Police Commissioner
Lewis Valentine. After seeing press photos of an arrested gangster in stylish
clothing, Valentine said the police should "muss 'em up." He did not want
them to look like "fashion plates." The statement was widely reported and
denounced. Thus, Valentine, an officer who had made his reputation by
pursuing corrupt cops, secured the support of his officers by supporting
their existing violent practices.[5]

The New York City police's determination to use force to control
the streets meant that it was at the forefront of curtailing labor and leftist
activism. Also, Commissioner Whalen used the police to wage political

war against the Communist Party. The Communists, in turn, found police brutality an effective tool for recruitment. Mayor La Guardia, with his labor background and the rising awareness that suppressing labor made the city administration look like the fascist governments of Europe, announced a noninterference policy for street gatherings and meetings. He even banned the police from carrying their clubs when patrolling picket lines. Early in his tenure he met with representatives of the ACLU; its recommendations for handling outdoor meetings and parades, after the appointment of Commissioner Valentine, silently became the department's policy. Whatever credit the mayor and commissioner gained from the liberals and leftists as a result of their stand was balanced by criticism from conservatives.[6]

Policing in Harlem was marked by pervasive abuse—intrusive street searches, brutality, and warrantless searches of homes—and fruitless complaints by the residents and their organizations about this abuse. To the police, Harlem was an unrespectable and dangerous place; the prevalence of prostitution, illegal drinking (especially during Prohibition), and illegal gambling defined the area. The mobster-controlled enterprise of policy gambling, or betting daily on certain numbers showing up in certain innocuous public publications, generated thousands of arrests annually and many, many more encounters as police searched for policy slips. Between 1931 and 1935, half of all arrests in Harlem were for possessing policy slips. And in the same period, three-quarters of all women arrested were charged with vagrancy or prostitution. It was widely believed that Valentine assigned officers to Harlem as punishment for infractions elsewhere in the city. Officers, white and African American, gained the reputation of being brutal, corrupt, and rude.[7]

The community tried and failed to get the authorities to stop the police abuse. In the 1920s and 1930s, the African American newspapers ran story after story about police abuse. They attacked the third degree, searches of homes, verbal abuse, and clubbing. Some Harlemites blamed police violence on the "lawlessness in the community" and advocated the idea that just a few bad actors on the force caused the abuse. But the long-lasting, pervasive, and never-rebuked nature of police violence toward civilians undercut these assertions. The press action was matched by violence; in 1928, a vicious clubbing during an arrest provoked a riot in which more than a thousand people threw objects at the police. But nothing prompted either the police hierarchy or the District Attorney's Office to prosecute brutal officers.[8]

The issue of police brutality raised the Communists' "profile and credibility in Harlem." There emerged a rough alliance of the left and African Americans against police brutality. Crowds booed and hissed at the police who showed up to curtail Communist events in the area. Not surprisingly, police officers in Harlem did not welcome this development and found ways to harry the Communists. As the white Communists routinely mingled more with African Americans, they caught the attention of the police. From 1933 on, party members complained of police harassment of interracial couples. By March 1934, the emerging dynamic of street violence in response to police violence was clear and known to Commissioner Valentine and Mayor La Guardia. A police attack on an International Labor Defense (ILD) demonstration on behalf of the Scottsboro boys prompted an hour-long riot in Harlem. Soon after, the Communists held an interracial meeting against police brutality on the site of the previous demonstration. And this time the police, by the mayor's order, were restrained and the event passed without violence. More importantly, the mayor empowered then Chief Inspector Valentine to investigate. He allowed full press coverage of the hearing and invited lawyers from the ACLU to the ILD to cross-examine witnesses. After the hearing, Valentine concluded that the police were mostly responsible and recommended discipline of a number of police officers, though apparently it was not carried out.[9]

The ACLU and Hays were primed to confront issues of police brutality. From its founding, the ACLU protested against police abuse, and in Hays's visits to coal towns he had been manhandled by private police empowered by law. In 1929, Hays, on behalf of the organization, wrote a letter decrying Whalen's policy of violent roundups and raids against organized crime. When city police violently broke up a Communist rally in 1930, beating and arresting many, the ACLU held a meeting of lawyers to plan prosecuting individual officers for assault. A critic of these plans wrote to Hays to justify the use of violence against the Communists because it had "outgrown the soapbox stage of oratory and has become a mass movement against the very institutions which you . . . seek to defend." Hays responded that the violent repression probably helped the Communists in that their right to free speech was being suppressed, making their message about the plight of workers in the Depression more attractive. Hays asserted that democracy rested on the theory of "counting heads rather than cracking them." He did more than broadcast his ideas.

In 1930, Hays used his position as a member of the Citizenship Committee of New York County Lawyer's Association to attempt to discipline the police officers who severely beat a Communist after he was thrown out of City Hall during a protest. The police stonewalled this white-shoe organization's investigation. In another instance, Hays, of behalf of a citizens committee, represented a fare jumper severely beaten by two subway policemen. Neither effort was successful; thus, Hays was well aware of the problems of investigating police misconduct.[10]

In the heart of Harlem on March 19, 1935, sometime after 2:00 p.m., store workers in the Kress five and dime store at 256-258 West 125th Street caught Lino Rivera, a sixteen-year-old Puerto Rican boy, stealing a pocket knife. The employees, as they usually did for shoplifting by youths, summoned the crime prevention officer attached to the youth court. Meantime, Rivera resisted, biting his captors. Seeing the struggle, nearby police intervened. The boy was taken to the back of the store, out of sight of customers. To avoid the crowd at the front of the store, a police officer released Rivera on the 124th Street side of the store on the basement level. The policeman also left. The crowd of customers and concerned people continued to grow in the store, which drew another police officer. A woman shopper cried out that "they" had taken "the boy to the basement to beat him up." When an ambulance arrived to treat a store clerk who had fainted, the woman's charge gained credibility among the crowd. When the ambulance left empty, it "gave color to another rumor that the boy was dead. A hearse parked nearby added credibility to the rumor. The "death of the boy" became "an established fact," linked to "deep-seated sense of wrongs. . . . One woman was heard to cry out that the treatment was 'just like down South where they lynch us.'" At least a dozen police officers were now at the store, and they responded to almost all requests from the crowd for information about the boy with replies that it was "none of their business" and attempted to shove the crowd out of the store. By 5:30 the store was closed, but the disturbance had spread to the street.[11]

A Communist-affiliated interracial group attempted to give speeches about the event at a traditional "free speech corner," and after being moved by the police ended up in front the Kress store. Before the speaker could truly begin, the police broke up the group, and "someone threw a missile through the window of the Kress store." Another speaker, Harry Gordon, tried to address the crowd and was arrested and beaten by police. The crowd grew and spread to Seventh and Lenox Avenues. They threw things at the police and broke store windows. By 7:30, placards and leaflets from a local, Communist-affiliated group, the Young Liberators, appeared. The Young Liberators leaflet blared "Child Brutally Beaten!" It called it a lynch attack and advocated picketing the store. Leaflets from the Young Communist League (which appeared later) said the store's "special guard" had brutally beaten "Riviera [sic]" and demanded the guard and store manager be prosecuted and the arrested protestors released. Without leaders or coordination, the rumor spread. People reacted by gathering in crowds and throwing things through the windows of stores, and looting began. Violence broke out, with African Americans attacking the few whites who ventured into the area, and attacks by and against the police escalated. Police cordoned off the neighborhood, but the violence lasted all night. Groups "dispersed by the police, . . . often re-formed." Police were showered with projectiles thrown from apartment buildings as they broke up the groups. Eventually, the police brought forth Rivera and posed him with the African American police lieutenant Samuel Battle to show that the rumors were false. About 1,000 people participated in these actions. About 250 shop windows were broken, more than 128 people arrested, and five were dead—including two African Americans killed by the police. The next day the police lined the streets of Harlem but carefully avoided the use of force.[12]

Reaction was immediate. The mayor asked District Attorney Copeland Dodge to summon a special grand jury. Dodge, perhaps hoping to embarrass the La Guardia administration as well as weaken the Communist Party, began his investigation. Dodge, described by one scholar as "a hack who would not blow his nose without Tammany's blessing," saw the Communists' "inflammatory leaflets on the streets" as the cause of the riot. His crusade against the Reds was urged on by the Hearst newspaper chain and even supported by a leader of the New York branch of the Urban League. The investigation was short-lived, however; Dodge suspended the grand jury by March 26, 1935, after indicting only three Communists who attempted to speak during the riot, before the first window was broken. But the cries of Communist influence, according to Hays, pushed La Guardia into saying that the Communists were "at the bottom" of the disorder. Less concerned with causes, the Uptown Chamber of Commerce (an association of large commercial establishments—most white-owned—that served Harlem) called for mobilization of the state guard to protect property. The Communists denounced the police and mobilized labor unions in which they had influence to send telegrams to the mayor, denouncing the "brutal tactics of police against Negro workers" and demanding the mayor arrest those responsible "for beating and shooting innocent workers in Harlem." On the same day the Communists denounced the police, Walter White of the National Association for the Advancement of Colored People (NAACP) sent the mayor a telegram suggesting that he appoint a biracial commission to investigate the root causes of the unrest, which he identified as "economic distress of the Negroes," and reminding the mayor that after the race riots of 1919 across the United States, many communities had appointed commissions to find ways to avoid future violence.[13]

Mayor La Guardia responded in an open letter to the "people of New York City." He assured them that "the overwhelming majority of the negro population of West Harlem are splendid, decent, law-abiding American citizens." He blamed "the unfortunate occurrence" on "a few irresponsible individuals." The "malice and viciousness of the instigators are betrayed by the false statement contained in mimeographed handbills and placards." He appealed "to the law-abiding element of Harlem to carefully scrutinize any charge, rumor or gossip of racial discrimination being made at this time." He promised that every agency in the city would be investigating charges of discrimination and reporting to him and that he would release those reports. He also declared that he was appointing "a committee of representative citizens to check all official reports and to make a thorough investigation of the causes of the disorder and a study of necessary plans to prevent a repetition of the spreading of malicious rumors, racial animosities and the inciting of disorder." The mayor's letter, while taking the NAACP's advice to create an investigatory body, ignored its statement of the underlying roots and seemingly embraced the idea that Communists were behind the riots. Yet he deliberately chose commissioners who would return to the idea of systemic causes to the riot.[14]

La Guardia's creation of the commission allowed him to take the lead in finding a liberal solution to the issues of race. White had written the mayor a five-page, single-spaced letter to propose an ambitious program of sociological analysis along the lines of the famous Chicago Commission on Race Relations, formed in response to the Chicago race riot of 1919. He pointed out that the Commission would likely entail high costs and also recommended E. Franklin Frazier as a lead investigator. In response, La Guardia cut costs by making commissioners volunteers. He took a bold step in whom he named as commission members. The mayor's secretary described the commissioners as "predominantly negro, and the white members are intelligent, liberal, and sympathetic." The African American members were all prominent figures in Harlem society, including Dr. Charles H. Roberts, a dentist and important figure in the city's Republican party who was the first African American member of the Board of Aldermen; Eunice H. Carter, a rising star in Republican politics in the city; and A. Phillip Randolph, a Socialist and head of the International Brotherhood of Sleeping Car Porters, the most powerful African American union in the nation and a vocal opponent of the Communist Party. The white members were chosen for their previous interests in similar concerns. For instance, Hays and Morris Ernst were co-counsels of the ACLU, and in 1934 Ernst had served the mayor as an arbitrator between striking taxi drivers and their employers. Oswald Garrison Villard was a reform journalist and publisher of both the *New York Post* and *The Nation* (and a founder of the NAACP and long a proponent of investigatory commission into the plight of African Americans). Colonel William J. Schieffelin was a trustee of the Tuskegee Institute as well as member of the NAACP. After protests from African American church leaders and anti-Communists, two more members were added: the prominent African American minister John W. Robinson and the Catholic priest W. R. McCann. Before holding a single hearing, the Commission issued a statement declaring that "the disturbances" were "merely symbols and symptoms" and blamed "economic and social conditions which the depression has intensified."[15]

Formed just days after the disturbance, the Commission organized and then reorganized itself and began work; it operated for more than a year. After some jostling, it, selected Roberts as chair and Villard as vice chair. The job of secretary was settled on the only woman, Carter. The Commission identified areas of focus—work, housing, education and recreation, relief, and crime and police—each with a subcommittee that would hear evidence. Hays was named chair of the subcommittee on crime and police, whose purview included finding what had sparked the disturbance. The other members were Carter, Robinson, Toney, and Villard. Frazier was hired on April 24 but did not start work until May 1. By the time he began his investigations, the first hearing on crime and police had already been held. The hearings were all scheduled in Harlem and usually held on Saturdays at the courthouse on 151st Street. In the course of its investigations, the commission held twenty-five hearings, listening to more than 160 witnesses. Lacking subpoena powers, the commission sought information from various sources: Carter solicited information from African American women and Hays from the Communists. It issued an open call to the community to share what they knew. And many did.[16]

For Hays and the crime subcommittee, the call for information opened the door to people willing to participate, which snowballed into further contacts. Hays's connections in the Harlem community were not deep, but through his civil rights and other work, he had formed relationships with African Americans eager to help in the investigation. For instance, an African American who knew Hays through some past work, William Trunbull, recommended that Hays contact Reverend Horatio S. Hill, who ran the Negro Religious Educational Centre in Harlem. Trunbull said he could provide "introductions to real people" better than any other. Similarly, Lillye M. Coleman, a relief worker living at the YWCA in Harlem, wrote Hays that she wanted to testify. She was "much gratified" to hear of his appointment, as she knew of his "work during the 'Sweet trial' in Detroit Michigan." She added, "I had the pleasure of meeting you in the home of doctor Edward Carter in Chandler Street [in Queens]." Adam Clayton Powell Sr., longtime pastor of the Abyssinian Baptist Church in Harlem and a force in the community, wrote to Hays: "Your presence on that committee will assure us . . . that the 'thirteenth Juror' [prejudice] which played such an important role in your very splendid book [*Trial by Prejudice*], will not have any influence on this committee." A second assurance was that "you will see that this committee goes to the bottom of the cause back of this riot. The incident at the Kress Store was only the occasion, the causes go back through several years." Powell went on to volunteer the help of Harlem pastors to the commission's task and, significantly, would line up witnesses for the crime subcommittee.[17]

Witnesses themselves stepped forward: most notably, Louis. F. Coles. He was an African American freelance journalist who wrote for out-of-town weekly papers. He knew both Hays and Villard. Villard had dined at his home, and Coles had corresponded with Hays on and off for some years (few of his earlier letters survive in Hays's records). Coles may have covered the Sweet trial, as he wrote to Hays that he recalled "very vividly how you handled" the case with Darrow. Coles wrote to both Hays and Villard, asking to testify about the general conditions in Harlem, especially how the merchants fleeced the customers and refused to hire African Americans. The mayor's crackdown on policy gambling and prostitution took "away from Negroes some of the means by which they made a livelihood." But what caught Hays's eye in his letter was that he was at the Kress store when the incident that provoked the riot occurred. He wrote directly to Coles: "As you were in the Kress Store at the time of the incident in question, we should appreciate it if you would be present to testify" at the first hearing.[18]

Both the government and radicals determined to overthrow it had information to share. At the start, some city officials were eager to participate. For instance, Charles Abrams, the legal counsel for the New York City Housing Authority and a Hays protégé, wrote to Hays offering the agency's resources. It had "large charts which would look good on any wall." He added that it had made "an exhaustive survey . . . on the slum and its relation to crime." This survey had found "that police bias was the one of the foremost obstacles to a healthy relationship between young blacks and city authorities. The survey report suggested that the police assigned to Harlem, all from outside the community, "took no real interest in the residents." Similarly, the Communist organizations active in Harlem responded to the call for information by providing a list of seventeen incidents, ranging from police harassment to a beating death, stretching back over several years. A documentary filmmaker friendly to radicals, Leslie Bain, arranged through Hays to screen her "Harlem Sketches" for the Commission.[19]

Two investigators did most of the research into police conduct for the subcommittee: Hyman N. Glickstein and James Tarter Jr. Hays brought Glickstein aboard; Glickstein had worked in Hays's firm before setting out on his own as a labor lawyer. He was an anti-Tammany Democratic leader who joined the fusion movement that elected Mayor La Guardia. He worked for the Commission through April, sifting the huge mass of material that came pouring in so it could be, in Glickstein's words, "presented quickly, efficiently and in as factual a manner as possible." In early April, he sent eleven letters to solicit information and records on police misconduct. The recipients ranged from Commissioner Valentine to Communists like Robert Minor. Glickstein also questioned witnesses at the hearing of April 6, 1935. He served as a liaison with the Unemployment Councils of New York and with ILD. Tarter overlapped with Glickstein in his work for the committee but he did much more of the field work: finding and interviewing witnesses, following up on grand jury and other official investigations, and even visiting the site of an incident.[20]

Starting a mere eleven days after the disturbance and continuing for almost eight weeks, the Subcommittee on Crime and Police convened five public hearings. Held on Saturdays in the courthouse on 151st Street, the hearings were well attended by journalists, activists, and the public: 1,850 people came to the open sessions. Commissioners not on the subcommittee also often attended. In all, more than fifty witnesses spoke at the hearings. Before the hearings began and in between the later hearings, subcommittee members and staffers investigated what happened in Harlem on March 19 and 20, sifting through official records, responding to the mail sent to the commission from people in Harlem, and interviewing more than a hundred people. These hearings, over which Hays presided, set much of the tone for how the commission was perceived.[21]

The members had plans for these subcommittee hearings, with finding the proximate cause that sparked the disturbance being the prime one. But the members were also interested in exploring how policing in Harlem built up resentments. For instance, a letter detailed an incident during which a magistrate dismissed charges and yelled at an African American policeman for arresting a white storeowner who fought with an African American customer. A subcommittee member noted it was "just the kind of a case we want to get hold of." The subcommittee was looking for evidence of police brutality outside the time of the disturbance. For instance, someone in the commission marked for Hays's attention the case of Thomas Aikins, which had been covered in the press and had been mentioned to the commission by the Communists. Hays in particular wanted to highlight the issues of police misconduct (he had hoped that a separate report on that issue alone would be written after the commission had delivered its findings). Some, like Hays, wanted to rebut District Attorney Dodge's pinning the violence on the Communists. Others wished to explore the systemic problems of life in Harlem, including discrimination by parts of the government, to explain the roots of the event. And during the hearings, the people of Harlem expressed their views about police misconduct and brutality, which also influenced the subcommittee's course.[22]

Expanding on the precedent of Valentine's investigation into the riot following the Scottsboro demonstration that allowed full press coverage and invited lawyers from all sides to cross-examine witnesses, Hays not only invited the Communists (through the ILD) to ask questions, but also allowed the audience to ask questions. This move proved controversial and distracted from the hearings' mission. Typical of the criticism was that of Leopold Philipp of the Uptown Chamber of Commerce. He asserted that the "free and easy manner" in which Hays conducted the hearings resulted in "a turbulent" sideshow that shed no light and only generated heat. Indeed, the hearings at times descended into shouting matches, and Hays struggled to maintain order. Some thought he did a good job. Villard praised Hays, saying he "presided admirably" over the hearings. Hays himself later downplayed the fractious nature of the hearings, writing in *City Lawyer* that the "tensity and excitement were reminiscent of a revivalist meeting." To Hays, the hearings gave the African Americans of Harlem a chance to "speak up and to grill the authorities who for years had dealt with them with little sympathy and often with brutality." Thus, while divisive, Hays's role as presiding officer proved key in allowing the people of Harlem to shape the agenda.[23]

Hays's civil liberties proclivities allowed people to express themselves regardless of who they were. For instance, Louise Thompson, a leading African American Communist famous for coordinating the 1932 trip of Harlem Renaissance representatives to the Soviet Union, testified. Hays showed awareness of her politics in that he asked her directly had she had anything to do with the production of the inflammatory leaflets, to which she answered no. Thompson's narrative of what happened inside the store, after Rivera had been moved to the back, made clear how easily the rumor of his being beaten was started and spread. Her testimony on the police behavior in refusing to answer questions, speaking rudely, and using force to empty the story was compelling. She helped establish the timeline for the Communist and Young Liberator leaflets appearing after the first windows had been broken and the speakers (including Gordon) stopped, arrested, and beaten. Her description of events inside the store made it into the subcommittee's report.[24]

Hays limited the scope of the hearings when witnesses or even commission members like Villard or Schieffelin opened up larger topics. When Joe Taylor (of the Young Liberators) began to talk about life and conditions in Harlem, Hays cut him off: "I can call over a hundred people in this room to give their opinion on conditions in Harlem but I cannot spend time on inquiring of their lives." Similarly, when a Communist wanted a police official to discuss Jim Crowism in restaurants in Harlem, Hays interjected, "We all recognize the discriminations. We all regret them very much. What I want to do is bring out facts as to what happened that day." At another hearing, when an ILD questioner wanted to establish that Harlem Hospital was too "overcrowded" to be effective, Hays responded, "We have a committee on hospitals." Let us "confine ourselves to crime, Negro and police on the night of March 19th."[25]

The hearings never went according to subcommittee script, as conflicting goals of participants channeled the course of the topics. The differing agendas were made clear at the opening hearing, as the Communists clashed with Hays. Taylor of the Young Liberators wished to use the hearings to spread their ideas, and Hays wanted to underscore that their actions exacerbated events. Both sides got a little of what they wanted. Taylor was able to explain that his organization of 140 to 180 members fought discrimination, while Hays was able to show that it operated irresponsibly that night. Taylor said he heard the story before 5:00 p.m. of a kid beaten several times from different people and therefore presumed it was true. He had tried to check, but the store was closed by the time he got there to inquire. In a revealing exchange, Taylor asked Hays, "if you heard thousands of people circulating rumors, would you believe it?" Hays responded, "I don't know." Taylor then pressed what he thought must have been an advantage: "Since 1930, it has been the common practice of the 5 and 10 cent stores to beat Negro boys and nothing has been done about it." But he had gone too far for a man who had defended the Sweet family and tried to intervene in Scottsboro. "Do you realize that your people suffer because of false rumors?" Hays asked Taylor.[26]

It was easy for the Harlem residents to shift the focus to highlight police violence and misconduct, as officials and other key parties did not participate or limited their participation. For instance, Jackson Smith, the Kress manager, had long attempted to avoid testifying, coming only on the day of the last hearing after much pressure was applied behind the scenes. Harlem hospital, pleading the press of duties, limited when its doctors and interns gave evidence. The refusal to participate in a meaningful way was led by the district attorney's office. At the opening hearing on March 30, Assistant District Attorney Alexander H. Kaminsky testified to the indictments that had been handed down for burglary and assault against police officers but refused to give the names of the indicted, save for those who had plead guilty. He would not give the names of those charged with unlawful assembly or explain why he withheld the names. Hays found the arrests for unlawful assembly suspect, as there obviously had been many such assemblies during the night but so few arrests for the offense. He wanted to know if they had been arrested for their political views. Kaminsky answered, "I am sure that the Grand Jury would not indict people for their political views." When Joseph Tauber of the ILD asked to cross-examine Kaminsky, Hays refused to allow it in the interest of speed, and Kaminsky added that "I refuse to be a party to a field day by irresponsible persons. So far this has been simply an occasion for police [baiting?]."[27]

The charge of police baiting was a loaded one. Led by the Communists and others in attendance, audience members had already sharply questioned police witnesses before Kaminsky testified. Hays and commission members had attempted to shut down the attacks, labeling them police baiting. When a Communist explained they wanted to ask Kaminsky about politically motivated police raids on Communist groups in Harlem, Kaminsky replied he knew nothing of them and that only police authorities might know. He was immediately contradicted by an ILD lawyer who said the raids were launched to get evidence to put before the grand jury and he had received a subpoena. Kaminsky then protested that he did not want to be questioned by anyone and asked that all questions be referred to his boss.[28]

After the first tumultuous hearing, District Attorney Dodge made the Commission's job harder. It had no subpoena power and had to rely on the goodwill of witnesses to come forward. While Valentine had promised police cooperation, Dodge wrote him and an investigator of the commission that officers who had testified to the grand jury or had cases pending in Magistrates Court or special sessions were instructed "not to reveal any of their testimony at any public hearing." Dodge extended the ban to assistant district attorneys, telling the commission that they "will not give you any information concerning any matters which are now under consideration." The police gained an excellent excuse not to appear or testify about the very things the committee wanted to investigate. Some officers did avoid testifying. Hays publicly blamed Dodge, saying that Valentine and his officers wanted to cooperate but were constrained by the district attorney. Privately he agreed with a lawyer who wrote him saying that Dodge's rush to indict Communists for inciting the riot and his restriction on testimony was not helpful; indeed, it stood in the way of "justice."[29]

The opening up of the hearing to the community meant that Hays, as presiding officer, interacted, over the course of several hearings, with three different African Americans participants in more depth than in his usual professional or activist endeavors: Louis F. Coles, Samuel Battle, and Charles Romney. Hays's most sustained contact was with Coles. Hays used Coles to establish important facts during the hearings. Thus, Coles, under questioning by Hays, clearly identified Rivera as the boy he had seen whose pilfering started the incident. He added details of the boy being taken to the basement and the arrival of the ambulance that upset people in the crowd. He testified that the attitude of the police at the riot, mostly white officers, did nothing to dispel rumors. When asked why the ambulance was there, he recalled, "One of the officers said it wasn't any of our business. That we had no right to ask questions." Coles also clearly remembered that the inflammatory pamphlets came after the first window was damaged.[30]

Hays's and Coles's interactions in the hearings and their correspondence throughout the hearings showed that their views did not always align. While Coles could praise Hays (Coles thanked him for the "fair way in which you presided"), he also disagreed with the direction of the hearings and differed as to the assessment of individuals. For instance, he suggested the commission look into the practices of the head of the Home Relief Bureau, Edward Corsi, as the "colored people have found him very cold toward them." Others were equally bad, and Coles provided a list of those who treated African Americans poorly, saying that "[District Attorney] Dodge has not been fair to us." In one letter, he characterized Valentine, Dodge, and others as "obdurate politicians, and they are trying to obfuscate the issue." In another instance, he stated, "You saw how the hospital [staff] . . . covered up [for] the police; no one could tell when a man was admitted, nor by whom."[31]

Hays was much more formal with police Lieutenant Samuel Battle. At the time of the disturbance, Battle was New York City's senior African American officer. He was a pioneer, being the first African American on the force, joining in 1911. He had been promoted to lieutenant in 1935 and served in Harlem. He was well known in the community. The scholar Stephen Robertson notes, "He and his wife appeared regularly in the society pages of Harlem's newspapers." In addition to testifying, Battle was charged with keeping order in the hearing room during sessions.[32]

Hays and Romney had more adversarial interactions than Hays had with Coles and Battle. Charles Romney was a Harlem resident, active in both the Young People's League of America and the Civil Rights Protective Association, who took it upon himself to look into various cases of police brutality. He would become a major figure in the hearings by exposing the abuses of policing. For instance, after one high-ranking police officer talked about the difficulty of policing Harlem, with its people of many "different nations," Romney challenged him. Romney pointed out that London's diverse population equaled Harlem's, and London police were popular and unarmed. The reply revealed police officers' fears: "I'd feel very sorry for the police of Harlem if they didn't carry weapons." The officer then revised his statement to include all of the city and added that he himself was still recovering from an injury gotten from when he arrested two "stickup men." Similarly, Romney challenged a police inspector, saying, "I've been to see you about discrimination" and he had done nothing. At a later hearing Romney challenged a doctor with the question, "don't you take [the] badge number" of an officer who brings in an injured man? The question implied laxness on the part of the hospital staff. But Romney's questions and comments could lead to side issue squabbles or into quibbles over the meaning of words and thus distract from rather than illuminate the point Romney was making.[33]

The open nature of the hearings did more than support the predilections of the commissioners. For instance, Hays and the subcommittee, following a liberal line that inclusion of more African Americans in the police force would forestall further problems, heard testimony contradicting that view. Taylor, in response to a question regarding whether African American policemen behaved the same way as white policemen, asserted neither treated "colored citizens" with respect: "They protect society by clubbing society." James Ford of the Communist Party replied to the question of whether "colored policemen" were more courteous: "There is no courtesy between police and people" and added that Harlem would be better off without police. "I have no faith in the police." The police did not contest this argument strongly. For instance, after Battle answered "yes" to a community member asking if he would want more African American officers in the police force, he then dodged Hays's follow-up question asking whether the riot would have run the same course if there had been more African American officers.[34]

But Hays and the subcommittee also would take testimony from people whom the subcommittee knew had views far different from theirs and use the statements to explain police and community relations. For example, the Communist Ford attempted to portray his group as the agent that kept the disturbances from turning into a race riot. He claimed Communists created their leaflet to channel the energy of the people into protest. While the commissioners were not persuaded about the Communists' role in preventing disorder, they chased after the idea that the disturbance was not a race riot. Lieutenant Battle reinforced this idea when he said that rioters had not clearly targeted stores that practiced Jim Crow—some stores owned by African Americans were also vandalized. Acting Police Captain Conrad H. Rothengast blamed "a hoodlum element. I believe the average man and woman in Harlem are decent, law abiding citizens and it was just a disorderly part of the community" responsible for the majority of the window smashing and rock throwing. He also denied, on the one hand, that the police mistreated Harlem residents and officers called people "Black Bastards" that night. On the other hand, he thought the violence was directed at the police and did not believe the people "were resentful because the boy was hurt, [the violence was because] the police are very unpopular." These ideas became central to the subcommittee's report.[35]

The exchange could be enlightening in the other direction. For instance, Villard got Police Inspector John De Martini to support one of his and Hays's ideas for a solution to policing problems. After an exchange where De Martini revealed that his community relations efforts in Harlem were quite limited and probably ineffective, Villard suggested, "Would it be possible for you to establish better relations with those in the community if a permanent advisory committee were formed and citizens were invited in to counsel with you?" De Martini responded, "I think it would be a brilliant idea."[36]

The subcommittee was sidetracked from its purposes by the claim that some other boy, not Rivera, was the boy at the Kress store or that Rivera was lying. The Communists and others pushed these ideas. They claimed that one witness (who never showed) would testify that Rivera was lying. Ray Dodd, who worked in the basement kitchen, said she had not seen a boy being beaten. Hays drew the conclusion no one was beaten in the basement, but Tauber of the ILD doubted her veracity as a six-year employee of Kress. The ILD also alleged that other African American witnesses were being kept away by the Kress store. This allegation was rebutted by Battle and by the appearance of one of the witnesses who testified that she was not kept away from the hearings by her employer.[37]

Hays, as presiding officer, took it upon himself to rebut the claims that Rivera was not the boy in question. "It is criminal that unfounded rumors should persist to the effect that Rivera was not the boy in question, and I think our first duty is to spike these rumors." Hays confronted both Coles and various Communists on the issue. Coles thought Rivera had been "gotten to" so he would say he had not been beaten. And Coles said he knew of two other witnesses to events in the Kress store. Hays's response was to request that they testify. This issue came to a head over the testimony of Alfred W. Eldridge of the Crime Prevention Bureau, part of the socialized court system. Eldridge, under questioning by Communists, revealed that Rivera "was under charges" for a minor offense and hadn't been sentenced yet. This fact opened the door to allegations that Rivera was a shill produced by the authorities. Advocates of this view said that he had always been under the officials' control, but Eldridge repeatedly denied it. Rivera confirmed Eldridge's account and repeated his statement that store workers threatened to beat him. That Battle agreed to the same set of facts did not sway those who refused to believe Rivera's account. After their questioning, Hays confronted the Communist Robert Minor and, asserting that they had a conflict between "evidence and suspicion," said, "Your crowd got out a circular that a boy was murdered. This statement was made without evidence." Today, Hays continued, they had evidence "of five people" that no beating happened in the store, let alone a murder. Minor refused to concede ground, nor would he and the other Communists back away from or apologize for their leaflets. That Hays was able to compile a record that disproved the rumor that Rivera was not the boy is evidence of his success leading the hearings.[38]

Hays, as presiding officer, could help cut through the self-serving evasions and lies of witnesses. For instance, the Kress floor walker, Charles Hurley, who initially confronted Rivera (and was one of two men bitten by the boy) denied that he had threatened him with a beating. He could not offer a convincing explanation for why Rivera grabbed onto a pole in the store and refused to be moved. Edward Kuntz, a lawyer for the ILD, through his questions clearly implied that Rivera was so afraid of the beating that he tried to keep himself anchored in the store in front of witnesses. Hurley admitted Rivera was terrified, and Hays pursued this: Why was he terrified, as logic said he should want to run and escape? The implication of the question was that Hurley was lying about not threatening the boy. Hurley's veracity was slowly undermined, but the deceit of some others was immediately exposed. For instance, after a police officer said he and his fellow officers did not use their clubs to break up a group around the time the first window was broken, Hays turned to Coles and asked, "Did you see anybody clubbed?" Coles answered, "Yes."[39]

The subcommittee examined police actions against individuals, some of which resulted in death. It did not limit itself to events that happened the night of the disturbance, as it had determined that policing over time had contributed to the disturbance. The subcommittee looked into five deaths (August Miller, Lloyd Hobbs, Andrew Lyons, James Thompson, and Samuel Laurie), three associated with the riot. They pursued furthest the instances of wrongful actions by police for which their investigators unearthed the most information. Thus, the beating of Thomas Aikins, which happened days before the disturbance, received more attention in the hearings than some of the killings. The committee had been made aware of these cases through many sources: the Communists, the Urban League, church groups, and even newspapers.[40]

The subcommittee looked most closely at the police shooting of the high school student Lawyer ("Lloyd") Hobbs. In the hearings, Hays curtailed exploration of other cases of brutality, saying, "Not at this time, I think the Hobbs case is most important." Indeed, testimony about the killing extended over multiple sessions. In the course of the investigation, Tarter spoke with hospital officials, copied hospital treatment records, spoke with an assistant district attorney, spoke with the Hobbs family, and interviewed the police ballistic expert as well as Inspector De Martini, who was in charge of Harlem. He also talked to officials at the Home Relief Bureau, spoke with witnesses to the shooting, and obtained two police investigation reports of the shooting. This was purposeful digging. After the subcommittee had heard the police version, Tarter conducted an investigation of the site of Hobbs's shooting. He sketched the layout of the stores and interviewed the owner of the stores. From them he found out that the windows of the stores had been broken between 8:30 and 11:00 p.m., a fact that would challenge the official account.[41]

The Hobbs hearings began with the official version. Rothengast testified that Hobbs was shot while committing a burglary, but when pressed about that claim replied that he was only saying what was in the official records. Not mentioned in the testimony was that hospital records described Lloyd Hobbs as wearing a tie and dress shirt when admitted, unlikely clothes to wear to a looting. Hays then called Russell Hobbs to the stand. Hobbs testified to facts that undercut the official account: He and his brother were coming from the Apollo Theater when they stopped to see what the "excitement" was about. They, and members of the crowd they had joined, fled when a horse-mounted policeman "ran up" on the sidewalk. The brothers ran in different directions, and Russell did not see Lloyd being shot.[42]

At the next hearing, Lloyd's parents, Lawyer and Mary Hobbs, made compelling witnesses. Lawyer Hobbs related that around 12:45 a.m. on the morning of the 20th, their son Russell told them that his brother Lloyd had been shot. The parents went to the hospital. "We found him lying on a cot. He said, 'Mother the officer shot me for nothing. I wasn't doing anything.'" The officer who shot him, Patrolman John F. McInerny, was in the room and said, "Why didn't you halt when I told you to." Lawyer Hobbs continued his testimony: "The officer said to me, "I told him to halt and he did not. I am sorry I shot your son." Lloyd died ten days after the shooting, and Lawyer Hobbs tried to file a complaint at the 123rd Street police station but received "no satisfaction at all." He sought help from the Urban League, but they did not intervene. Similarly, he said, the district attorney's office did nothing. Hays, summing it up, said, "[You were] in a peculiar predicament, the death of an innocently murdered boy."[43]

Before Mary Hobbs was called to the stand, Hays paused to impose some procedural guidelines and also said, "As soon as this [matter] came to the attention of our Committee we immediately investigated it." He said they would put other witnesses (whom Mr. Hobbs had located) to the shooting: Howard Malloy, Arthur Moore, and Samuel Pitts. Hays asked if anyone from the police department including Patrolman McInerny (who was there) wanted to ask any questions and said he would allow cross-examination at the next hearing. Apparently not caring that he was influencing the outcome, Hays began his examination of Mary Hobbs by framing her as a devoted mother, noting that both her sons had been in high school, and asking about the struggle to educate five children. These questions were designed to show the Hobbses as hardworking people worthy of sympathy from the public and government officials. Mary Hobbs reported that at the hospital "first they would not let us see him, they said he was a criminal." When the parents saw him, he said, 'Mother I am all shot up and have not done anything." McInerny told her, "I came up in the midst and fired and your son caught it." When she said Lloyd didn't steal anything, he replied, "That is what all mothers think. Their boys never steal." She told him, "Officer it looks awful to shoot to kill," and he replied, "He should have halted."[44]

James Tarter reported on his interview with Assistant District Attorney Saul Price, who said "his office was very much interested in the case," that his office "hadn't exonerated the officer who had done the shooting," and that Officer McInerny and Detective John J. O'Brien (who had investigated the shooting) had appeared before the district attorney. Tarter said the police claimed to have information indicating either that Hobbs was fleeing with stolen property or that the police at the corner were under assault by thrown missiles. Hays cut in to ask Russell Hobbs, "Did you and your brother go into any auto shop?" Hobbs replied, "No." Hays asked three eyewitnesses whether they had seen anything thrown at the police before the shooting. They also said no. Tarter added that despite O'Brien's report alleging that the supposedly stolen items were in police possession, when he queried the officer in charge about the items, he said they did not have them.[45]

Indications of police misconduct were strengthened by the testimony from three witnesses to the shooting whom Lawyer Hobbs, the father, had located. Howard Malloy, Arthur Moore, and Samuel Pitts lived near the site of the shooting, none knew the Hobbs family, and all testified to essentially the same points. Malloy had told his story to the *Amsterdam News* and had also searched out Lawyer Hobbs and told him. As the crowd was being dispersed by the police and running in different directions, Malloy said the "Hobbs kid ran into 128th Street west. When he was around 28 feet from the corner an officer stepped off the curb and made about two steps in 128th Street and he had his gun in his hand. He made one direct shot and kid crumpled and fell." He added, "I didn't see anything drop. He had on a lumber jacket. He was running like trainer." Moore corroborated Malloy's words: "The officer made one shot. He didn't say halt. He didn't shoot over his head. He just made one shot." The store that was looted, according to Malloy, had been looted an hour before when he passed it, and the crowd was in a "jovial mood." Moore added that "The kid" made two attempts to get up, and Moore heard him say, "I didn't do anything." Pitts testified that he was on the street trying to find out what the rumors about Kress were "all about," when "I got back to the 128th Steet side and along came a little boy running and the people said, run boy run. The boy was near the sidewalk. The boy [Officer McInerny] took a direct aim and shot." Pitts did not hear any cry of halt and saw no looting. Nor did he see the officer pick up anything. All three witnesses agreed that the police quickly put Hobbs in a patrol car (it would have been easy to bundle the five foot four inch, ninety-five-pound boy into the car), and it "drove off in a hurry."[46]

Poignant testimony came from Russell Hobbs's second appearance as a witness and from the police stenographer who interviewed Lloyd in the hospital on March 20. Russell Hobbs testified that as they fled from police whom they feared "would beat them up like they did on 128th Street," he heard one shot and someone told him, "They shot the kid that was with you." He looked for his brother, who had already been taken away by the police, and then went home to tell his parents. The stenographer for the Homicide squad, Detective Thomas J. McCormic, testified that he took a statement from Lloyd Hobbs at around 1:00 a.m. in the Harlem Hospital X-ray room. He told McCormic he was coming from a show at the Apollo and went to see what all the people were doing at 7th Ave. "Someone threw a brick into a window and I was shot by a cop."[47]

After Hays learned that the grand jury had failed to indict McInerny for Hobbs's shooting, he wrote to District Attorney Dodge, asking who had been called at the grand jury. "If there was any justification for the shooting, the public may know it." He reminded Dodge that "one of the most ominous features which emerges from the evidence we have taken appears to be a lack of confidence the people of Harlem have in the police, and their feelings that Negroes cannot expect justice," casting his inquiry to Dodge as an attempt to reassure the public. "In view of this you will realize the importance of my request." Dodge's reply merely listed the new witnesses, all policemen except for one doctor. He mentioned that McInerny had "signed a waiver of immunity and was willing to appear" at a future hearing, implying that his evidence would exonerate him. He added the unhelpful "We called all we knew of," which raised questions as to how thorough the investigation had been.[48]

Patrolman James V. Watterson's testimony was ineffective, especially before the skeptical person conducting the hearing (Hays had Tarter's material at hand and would use it to raise doubts about the police version) and a hostile audience. He maintained that McInerny's story was true, that Hobbs had entered the auto parts store through a broken window and was handing out items when the police car pulled up, and that he had fled. He did not answer a question put to him as to why anyone would break a window and rob a store with the police so nearby. He claimed that McInerny picked up the objects that Hobbs had dropped. He said McInerny called for Hobbs to stop. Under Hays's questioning, discrepancies between the police report and his memory came to light. The report said that missiles were thrown while McInerny was chasing Hobbs; Watterson said the throwing came after Hobbs's shooting.[49]

Detective John J. O'Brien, who investigated the Hobbs shooting, revealed himself to be either shockingly incompetent or engaged in a coverup, or both, while testifying. He admitted that he had not seen the items that Hobbs supposedly stole and that Officer McInerny was said to have in his possession that night, and O'Brien did not know where they were until after the boy died ten days later. He could not explain why the arrest record did not show the articles in McInerny's possession. He admitted the items had not been tested for fingerprints. He admitted to first learning the names of the witnesses to the shooting at the previous hearing. He admitted he talked to only one shop owner about the broken windows and that he had not interviewed the other shop owners in the area with broken windows. It became clear the police did not know which window was broken when. Hays pressed the issue of timing in Watterson's and McInerny's accounts: "It does seem strange that a police car came along and the police saw a boy get out of the window, take things out, does that seem [possible] all in a minute?"[50]

Malloy testified about his experience before the grand jury. He had told that body that Hobbs was empty-handed when shot and that he did not see the officer pick up anything. In a rare break from the discipline with which he had conducted the hearings, Hays asked if there any "Negroes" on the grand jury, and Malloy answered no. Hays turned to the audience. "Can anyone testify for the past 20 years that there were Negroes on the New York County Jury?' Three ILD lawyers all said versions of no. From the crowd came an interjection, a reference to Scottsboro that was probably not over anyone's head in the chamber: "Decatur, Alabama is ahead of New York City." A subsequent hearing revisited the items that supposedly tied Lloyd Hobbs to looting, which underscored that this evidence had at best an unclear provenance. Considering the items' importance in clearing Officer McInerny of wrongdoing, Hays's interest in the "mystery of the sudden appearance of the articles" indicated that he was not satisfied with the official story.[51]

The official story of what happened to Thomas Aikins fared little better during the subcommittee's investigation. Tarter had interviewed Aikins about his account that two policemen, David Eaghan and Eugene Cahill, had beat him so severely that he lost an eye. The arrest record justified the use of force on the grounds that Aikins's use of "loud and boisterous language" in a food relief line might have caused a riot. The subcommittee had Aikins's medical records from Harlem Hospital, and they had acquired two witnesses, "Buck" Brown and Ben Harlow (or Holloway), probably through the efforts of Aikens's lawyer, Eustace Densch. The commission had lined up its witnesses with care. Carter wrote to Hays that "Rev. Powell called to know when you want Mr. Aikins in reference to the . . . case today?"[52]

Aikins testified that he was beaten by the police several days before the riot. Aiken was on the bread line outside the 369th Armory on March 13, 1935. He had been in line for almost two hours, and he was standing where a gap in the line let people cross it to enter a building. Some men attempted to cut into line by filling that gap and were spotted by the authorities managing the line. Aikins was accused of being one of the line jumpers. A patrolman told him to get to the end of the line, and when Aikins loudly protested, "He smashed me in the mouth. I threw my hand up to protect my eyes. At that time another officer hit me in the head." He awoke on the ground being cared for by medical attendants. His sister, he said, was not allowed to see him in Harlem Hospital, as he was a prisoner—the implication being that his story of being attacked by police was being suppressed.[53]

As the police refused to testify, the rest of the story was rounded out by a bystander. Brown testified that he was behind Aikins in line and saw the dispute and assault. He made it clear that sending Aiken to the end of the line would have added an hour for Aikins to wait for food. Brown testified that after Aikins told the officers he had not cut in line, a white officer responded, "You black son of a bitch" and struck Aikins over the head. Another officer joined him and they both kicked Aikins, who had fallen to the ground. Officer Cahill struck Aiken on the head with a blackjack while he was down. They later dragged him into the armory; an ambulance arrived about twenty minutes later. Brown told the *Amsterdam News* this story because he was "indignant about what occurred." Neither Patrolman Eaghan nor Cahill testified, citing the district attorney's instructions to officers that they should not testify about pending cases or grand jury testimony. In this instance, it was the charge brought against Aikins for assault. They were invoking, without irony, the district attorney's words that to testify would "defeat the ends of justice."[54]

The damning testimonies against the police were, however, often overshadowed by belligerent comments from the audience. Perhaps the most disruptive moment in the hearings came while Officer Watterson was testifying about the Hobbs shooting. An African American Communist, Edward Walsh, shouted, "Will the dog bark a little louder, please." Hays confronted him and demanded that he should apologize. Walsh would not apologize and was supported by the audience in the crowded hearing room. Coles and Hays had a heated exchange over the incident. Coles interjected, "If you are going to ask people to leave, how are we going to get anywhere? You have always been absolutely fair." Hays's response was that insults would not help, because officers from the police or district attorney's office would not come to testify under such conditions. Coles spoke past him: "I believe the people here [in Harlem] are afraid of the police. They will not come [to testify] because of police brutality; they're afraid to be cut off relief." Hays did not comment on the import of Coles's point, saying instead, "You just bring those witnesses here." Hays declared a recess for ten minutes and said that if Walsh did not leave, the hearings would adjourn for the day. After the recess, Walsh said that he would leave so as not to hinder "the program of getting to the bottom of this police brutality." But he demanded an apology from the officer for thinking so "very little of the intelligence of the group." Hays, however, continued to insist he withdraw, which the transcript says he did, but some press accounts said he did not. Hays addressed the audience: "If the Committee is to get absolute facts we owe it to ourselves as ladies and gentlemen [that] if a man lies, or if he doesn't lie, to restrict ourselves to such language as to bring out those points without becoming abusive." His appeal to the African American audience as ladies and gentlemen rejected the racist rudeness that whites all too frequently employed toward African Americans, and his insistence that he was after light, not heat, apparently resonated with some.[55]

The nature of the hearings more than their substance often dominated the news. For example, the *New York Post* reported that the May 4, 1935, subcommittee hearing "encountered an audience so disorderly that it made little progress." There were more than 700 people in attendance. Only through "constantly threatening to adjourn" was Hays able to maintain "a semblance of order." Leftists and others spoke out, claiming they wanted to present evidence of intimidation of witnesses. From the floor, Romney repeatedly made charges of police intimidation of witness and claimed they tried to frame him for a crime to silence him. To cheers, he declared, the next time a policeman "interferes with me, my relatives or my witnesses . . . I am going to take the law into my own hands." On the other side, Battle shouted that this was a staged event and he would personally prosecute any policeman found to have intimidated a witness. There were calls to walk out when Hays proceeded to call witnesses to the cases of police brutality scheduled to be heard and witnesses who could clarify points about the incident at the Kress store instead of pursuing the intimidation charges.[56]

The investigation and hearings about the case of Samuel Laurie, who died at the hands of Officer Abraham Zakutinsky, encapsulated the dynamics between the investigators, the police, and the community audience. This was a case that had been brought to the attention of the subcommittee by the ILD, which claimed that Zakutinsky had "a record of brutal attacks upon workers in Harlem," including rumors that he "killed a young Porto Rican boy," and had been transferred to Harlem as punishment. His delinquency record, however, contained only reprimands for missing his posts when on "strike duty." The evidence was equivocal as to whether Zakutinsky had struck Laurie with his club, though the medical evidence was plain that Laurie died from a fractured skull. In his testimony, Zakutinsky claimed to have hit the falling-down-drunk Laurie only with his fist and denied using anything more than the required force to arrest him for disorderly conduct. The presentation of the evidence was interrupted by shouts from the audience that police brutality was being covered up by charges that the injured people had been drunk and fallen down. When Zakutinsky said that he had served on the force for three and half years, an African American woman shouted, "That's three and half years too long." After an adjournment, she apologized for disrupting the hearing. An African American man who identified himself as a police reporter with twenty years of experience called out to Hays, "You don't know what I do what the police do to witnesses in the back room." A condescending-sounding Villard lectured the man for being impolite and told him he had been a police reporter since before the "young man" was born. Coles wrote Hays after this hearing: "It might interest you to know that while many of the people may differ from your point of view they feel that . . . all of the Committee are doing all that is humanly possible to give an impartial hearing." He commented, perhaps ironically, that the May 4 hearing "was the most orderly hearing that has been held so far, this is due to the fact the witnesses answer questions frankly that were put to them."[57]

Hays's view of proper police behavior emerged clearly in the last hearing when new topics of police misconduct were aired. One new line of inquiry concerned the warrantless searches of homes and street stops. Robert Patterson said police entered his home without a warrant, arrested him, and held him for two days. The police had received a phone tip that he had committed a murder in Philadelphia. The man named as the victim had actually died in Harlem and had not been murdered. Two years previously, Patterson said, the man who had shared his apartment had died from natural causes. Patterson had been investigated at that time and cleared by the New York police. Detective Joseph Flinter in his testimony verified Patterson's story but asserted that the suspicion was enough to authorize the search. This statement prompted Hays to read the pertinent New York statute on arrests and inquire of the detective and other police officers in the hearing room, Lieutenant Battle and Inspector John De Martini, about their understanding of the law. When their answers did not conform to the statute, Hays lectured them on what the law required. The audience booed and hissed at the officers. Hays told

Battle that he should make sure such incidents never happened again. Romney came to Battle's defense, saying he should not be scapegoated. Other individuals testified about similar home invasions, beatings on the street, and stops of interracial couples on the street. Cyril Briggs of the *Daily Worker* testified that he was arrested while walking with an African American woman because police thought he was white. When it turned out that both were African American, he was released. That was the last bit of testimony given in the police and crime hearings.[58]

One intended audience to the hearings—the mayor—did not like developments, especially apparently the attacks on the police and the deflating of the idea that the Communists were responsible. After the first hearing of the subcommittee, La Guardia sent a memo to Chairman Roberts. It was attached to a copy of a one-page flyer of the Harlem section of the Young Communist League. touting how it was in the forefront of fighting for jobs for "Negro and white workers." It lumped La Guardia with District Attorney Dodge as "scared puppets of the bankers" who blamed outsiders for the violence. It asserted the police were the real outsiders, "brought in from all outlying sections to beat up and shoot the Negro people." The mayor's accompanying directive was ambiguous: "Please bring to the attention of the Hays sub-committee." [59]

An unintended consequence in conducting the hearings with a civil liberties frame of mind that allowed many to speak was that the Communists played a prominent part, especially in the early hearings. Moreover, that the hearings explored so many incidents that had been raised by the Communists gave credence to the idea that the Communists easily gulled the commission. But this idea is belied by many of its actions. Beyond his faulting the Communists for issuing lies that led to violence, Hays sought information from other sources. For example, the subcommittee used its investigators to "keep abreast" about policing and disturbances in Harlem while it was doing its investigation, never just trusting the allegations of the Communists alone. What the subcommittee did not do was automatically dismiss what radicals said. By being open to all voices, the hearings generated information that was used to reconstruct what happened on March 19 and March 20 and explain why it happened. Hays, in running the hearings, was willing to let people tell their stories, whether they were radicals, Communists, police officers, or ministers. Those, even if they were Communists, who could present their evidence clearly with supporting detail were prized. Thus, in Hays's handwritten notes of the testimony of March 30, at the top of one page, next to Louise Thompson's name, was the parenthetical comment "good witness." Her narrative of what happened inside the store was the only long quotation used in the subcommittee report where it made a case for police mishandling of the situation and contributing to the breakout of unrest.[60]

The civil liberties ethos made Hays alert to potential government attempts to suppress critics like Charles Romney. Romney distrusted Carter, the Urban League, and the Harlem Lawyers Association, and he thought all three were steering the investigation to their own ends. Beyond the crime hearings, he was a key player in the relief hearings; his questions and comments to Relief Commissioner Corsi revealed the extent of discrimination practiced by that office. In the last crime hearings, Hays refused to let Romney speak, which led to a later outburst from him decrying the commission's processes. When in the May 11 hearing he threatened to defend intimidated witnesses by taking the law into his own hands, his anger may have stemmed from the idea that the police were trying to "fix him up" to silence him. Romney had been arrested on a charge of disturbing the peace on April 11, 1935, after an incident at a cigar store. The dispute between the proprietor and Romney concerned the treatment of the boys who had broken the windows of the shop during the disturbance. At Romney's hearing on disturbing the peace, Battle wanted to offer testimony, but it was ruled inadmissible. After Romney's conviction, Battle told the judge what Romney "had said when testifying at the hearing of the Mayor's Committee about what he would do if the police interfered with him, his relatives, or his witnesses." Battle also told Romney's lawyer, "Your boy . . . is gone, I hope the Judge gives him 90 days. By that time the Investigation . . . will be over and we will be rid of him." Romney, however, received only a ten-day suspended sentence and continued to participate.[61]

Hays reacted to Romney's arrest as a civil libertarian concerned about government suppression of voices it did not want to hear. He thought it could be aimed at blocking Romney's participation, and he proposed bringing together a citizen's committee of figures in Harlem, including Adam Clayton Powell Sr., as an "impartial tribunal" to look into the matter. He abandoned this idea and asked Romney's lawyer to get the records of the court hearing and sought commission funds to get a transcript of the record of Romney's case. Nothing came of Hays's efforts, as others took up Romney's defense. He had strong backing from the Joint Conference against Discriminatory Practices, an umbrella organization begun by the Communists but supported by a wide range of different groups, including both Harlem Democrats and Republicans, and headed by Myles H. Paige. In a petition to the mayor, they concluded that there was "an attempt to stifle the entire investigation" and detailed harassment and persecution of Romney by the police (including by Lieutenant Battle) for trying to expose their brutality. They asked Mayor La Guardia to have the commission investigate, give him safe conduct to testify, investigate Battle, order that the intimidation of witnesses end, and stop police brutality "against the Negroes and other minority groups." Many of its requests became moot with the ending of the hearings.[62]

In the end, the hearings focused on the immediate cause of the disorder, centered on the disputes at the Kress store, and a few cases of police brutality (two of which had not even happened during the disturbance). It solicited testimony from a wide range of witnesses on each topic. The hearings rebutted the idea that the Communists were behind the disturbance, though the commissioners, especially Hays, made a case that the leftists' irresponsibility contributed to the rumors of the beating to death of a boy spreading widely and stimulating greater disorder. Testimony of police misconduct included beatings, racially insulting language used by police, harassment of interracial couples, and warrantless invasions of homes. The extent of property damage and the civilian-against-civilian violence that occurred were slighted in the hearings. But the hearing were ephemeral, and the commissioners hoped a strong report about crime and policing would prompt the city government to address the problems they had brought to light.

The subcommittee report on the disturbance of March 19 was written by Hays and Villard, and its conclusions as to the origins of the disturbance and the conduct of the police, as well as its recommendations, were incorporated into the report of the Commission. Immediately after the hearings on police action concluded, Hays began writing. Villard edited the draft, keeping almost everything in it that Hays had written. Villard reorganized Hays's draft and sharpened its focus on police misconduct. He expanded the recommendations. Throughout, he polished Hays's language and removed phrases like "a people peculiarly subject to emotional appeals" to describe the inhabitants of Harlem. Villard also removed a passage where Hays criticized an assistant district attorney, commenting, "better not to dignify that Assistant D.A. and give him the opportunity to come back and say he was outrageously badgered by irresponsible people." He urged Hays to "go over the whole thing very <u>carefully</u>, filling in the names and dates omitted and verifying every statement therein made either by you or by me, so that we shall have an absolutely copper-fastened report." In response, Hays added a section that tempered the indictment of the police and put in "a word for the mayor and the police." They planned to "discuss any suggestions or criticisms" at the next whole committee meeting, and Villard prompted Carter "to urge a specially full attendance of the Committee."[63]

Eight commissioners attended the meeting and made small alterations to the document. They downplayed the overall violence, strengthened the case against the officer who shot Lloyd Hobbs, and added language that would appeal to the mayor, reinserting "hooligans" in place of Villard's "criminal elements." Villard was happy: "I think between us we have done a swell report." He thought Hays's "addenda have added greatly to the balance and effectiveness of the report, and the treatment of the police is now beyond criticism." He worried, "Now how in the world can we get the mayor to release these reports? It is of the utmost importance." Villard asked Hays to "make sure that an adequate summary of this report is prepared and released when the mayor gives the whole report out. I don't think many of the papers will print so long a story. . . . As I am afraid that I shall not be here when the report comes out, won't you call any friends you have in . . . newspaper offices and see if you can't get editorial comment and special attention." In response to Villard's concern that the report would be buried, Hays inserted a new line to conclude the recommendations, underscoring their practicality. "Present economic conditions might make it very difficult to take action to remedy many of the conditions that exist, but fortunately no such obstacle exists to the carrying out of the recommendations suggested here."[64]

While Hays framed the May 29, 1935, "Report of the Subcommittee Which Investigated the Disturbance of March 19th" in liberal broad social and economic terms, he focused it on the events of that night and the actions of the police. The subcommittee concluded that "the outburst was spontaneous," that it was not a "race riot in the sense of it being a physical conflict between persons of the white and colored groups," that the Communists did not instigate it, but their "false and misleading leaflet" added to the disturbance, and that the "police made mistakes that contributed to the riot." Moreover, the "evils due to dreadful overcrowding, unfair rentals and inadequate institutional care" burdened people's lives. Underneath all of that was "the nervous strain of years of unemployment and insecurity" compounded by discrimination by stores, schools, and police officers against African Americans.[65]

The report declared: "Nothing more alarming has been developed in the hearings . . . than the intensity of the feeling against the police," which he had seen was "carried over into the hearings." This long-established feeling was a "grave state of affairs." In fact, "the inhabitants of a large section of the city have come to look upon the men in police uniforms as lawless oppressors who stop at no brutality or at the taking of human life." Nor was it limited by race: "The feeling expressed at our hearings was just as strong against the colored police" as "against the white." Critically, "the existence of intense hostility on the part of the law-abiding elements among the colored people toward the police is proof positive that there is something seriously wrong in the attitude of the officers toward the people." Given the people's attitudes, it was not surprising that they believed lurid rumors about the police. The importance of rebutting rumors posed a problem, which the report argued could be met by quick action to deflate them. The police department should devise "a system" to distribute "leaflets and placards" in the event of "any further happening likely to cause grave public disorder" to give "the public authoritative information from high officials." Deflating rumors "as soon as possible" could be achieved via the city and commercial radio stations.[66]

The subcommittee report praised certain police actions but concluded that the police were a major contributing factor to the unrest both in the incident that provoked the riot and in their everyday aggressive, arbitrary, and illegal actions. Commissioner Valentine, Inspector De Martini, and Lieutenant Battle were "sincerely desirous of changing the present unhappy condition of affairs," but that did not exonerate the police brutality. The police were faulted for failing "to answer questions adequately" before the violence broke out in the street. Nor did they form a "determined or effective plan of reassuring the public" of the boy's safety. The "attitude of the police indicated a desire to suppress the excitement rather than to explain the cause of it. People were ordered to get out of the store, groups were told to disperse, and crowds to fall back." When that failed, they used force. When asked what happened, an officers replied, "If you know what's good for you, you better get on home." In breaking up the "public meetings," the police may have acted properly "if the purpose of these meetings was further to excite the populace." But it was impossible to know, as the arrests for "unlawful assembly" came before the speaker "had an opportunity to say anything." The arrests were accompanied by racially "derogatory and threatening remarks." In jail, two of the arrested were denied counsel and mistreated. "The barbarity with which at least one of them was treated is shocking." The shooting death of Hobbs was "the most regrettable event of the entire disorder." After reviewing the evidence, the Report concluded that the police conduct was "inexcusable."[67]

The report detailed police abuses against the African American citizens of Harlem to illustrate the "state of mind of the people." It described how Patrolman Zakutinsky struck the drunk and "unsteady upon his feet" Laurie such a blow that he died from the blow. The case of Aikins was "equally shocking," as he was "mercilessly battered . . . that it was necessary to remove him to a hospital where the doctors were compelled to take out one of his eyes." The force used was unnecessary, as there "was no riot and no disorder" at the time. It noted the lack of a warrant when Patterson's home was entered and searched. The report declared that the campaign against policy gambling prompted hostility by Harlemites. "Various witnesses testify as to illegal searches of their persons and property by the police in quest of policy slips." After one such witness testified, Hays had asked for those who had similar experiences to stand. "More than twenty-five people arose," one who admitted to having the gambling slips. "Still another witness testified that he was arrested and taken to the police station merely because he was walking with a colored woman. He was held at the police station for some time until he could prove to the officer in charge that he was <u>a colored man!</u>" The report pointed out that there was "no law whatsoever to prevent persons of different sexes and races from walking together." The report maintained that "the large audience" at the hearings was "justified in shouting that the law is not being applied in connection with the arrests of Negroes." Indeed, the police abuses could all fit into the violations of the civil liberties principle of equal justice under law.[68]

The report offered a philosophical and practical primer on the need to restrain the police aimed at swaying Mayor La Guardia to make changes in the police activities in Harlem. With quotes from James Otis and Sir William Blackstone, the report stressed that the provisions of the Bill of Rights were "curbs on arbitrary power" needed to secure liberty, the end goal of government. Thus, police needed "thorough instruction in the law as to the limitations" of their use of violence. The report urged that this training be "coupled with an admonition that if any policeman 'musses up' an innocent citizen, however poor or whatever his color, he will lose his job." To the common assertion that police could not do their jobs if they "were observant of technical constitutional restraints," the report replied that an unlimited police might catch "a criminal who would otherwise escape," but the price was high, as it made "people regard the police as enemies rather than as helpful friends." Changing police actions would result in a "friendly" populace, and that would "gain more for the police in connection with the apprehension of criminals than they can gain by illegal tactics." And those changes "would make for far better police efficiency and morale." Color and poverty should make no difference in how police treated people: "The rights of the Negroes now flouted are as much to be respected by the police as are those of more fortunate citizens who reside in Fifth or Park Avenues." The invoking of equality of treatment, of course, resonated with La Guardia's championing of the city's poor, adding African Americans to the body of the people.[69]

The report praised La Guardia for being "a leader among liberals" and admitted that Valentine inherited a force animated by "wrong police psychology." It advised they take action to defuse the "resentment by people who have suffered injustices for many years." The behavior of the police in Harlem reflected "on the entire police force," handicapping the work of "kindly decent and well-disposed officers." No doubt "thousands of policemen in our city who carefully respect the rights of citizens and realize that their duty is to protect rights as well as to curb wrongs" were indignant at "those whose conduct is censurable." To allow those good officers to do their jobs, the mayor and commissioner needed to act, to embark upon the reforms already mentioned and to implement specific recommendations.[70]

The subcommittee report proposed three changes. First, the police commissioner should create a committee of from "five to seven Harlem citizens of both races to whom colored people may make complaint if mistreated by the police." The body envisioned would be volunteers beholden to no party or police domination who might function even as an advisory committee to the commissioner. "The members of this committee should have the confidence of the people of Harlem, and they should include in their number one or more men who are dissenters from established institutions and also men who are likely to have contact with victims of injustice." This rather idealistic vision of a police complaint board reflected a mixture of Mugwump sensibility, Darrow-like iconoclastic views, and social worker ethos. Second, officers who broke the law must be subject to the criminal law, not just to investigation and punishment within the department. It urged that every shooting by the police be investigated "by one of the highest officials in the Department" and the findings conveyed to the whole force so that they could learn the proper use of force. Third, to squelch rumors such as those that sparked the disturbance, the police department should implement a system to quickly distribute leaflets and placards as well as use of the radio to provide "authoritative information from officials in the Department as soon as possible" to the public.[71]

For its closing, it briefly left the narrow range of the police topic to say the situation in Harlem remained serious, with "wretched housing, inadequate and inefficient schools and other public facilities, unemployment, unduly high rents, lack of recreation grounds, discrimination in industry and public utilities against colored people, brutality and lack of courtesy of the police." It was fertile ground for racial and other propaganda. It was "futile to condemn the propagandists or to denounce them for fishing in troubled waters." Attempts to address "eliminate the evils" found in Harlem would be more useful. And the best first step would be to reform the police, as "the present economic conditions may make difficult the carrying out" of the larger reforms, but "here is one problem that can be solved without the expenditure of money."[72]

The report's treatment of the Lloyd Hobbs shooting indicated that this was a document meant to sway public opinion by showing the Hobbses as respectable people, rebutting the claim that force had been used only against hoodlum elements. It described the Hobbs boys (Lloyd and Russell) as "sons of a family of good standing and upright character." It asserted that sixteen-year-old Lloyd "had never been engaged in any improper activities." It concluded that it was unlikely that the boys had been looting. And Lloyd's flight was understandable, as a patrol car drove up and Officer John F. McInerny "alighted, brandishing a gun." Without warning, according to "reputable witnesses," McInerny fired once, hitting Hobbs in the back. The police story that Hobbs had been looting the auto parts store was discounted, especially in light of the claim of automobile accessories being found in the street near "where the boy fell" only being brought forward the day after Russell Hobbs testified at the committee's hearing about his brother's death. The report faulted the police action. Even if Lloyd was guilty of the crime alleged, there "was no public disorder at the time to call for violent action, a life should not have been taken for the offense." The officer at least should have fired a warning shot, or better yet pursued Hobbs on foot to capture him. The report pressed for further investigation by the police commissioner and noted that "proper warnings should be issued to the police not to use their revolvers unless thoroughly justified by the emergency and the character of the man they are pursuing." It balanced this criticism with a statement: "We are well aware that brave and humane officers have repeatedly lost their lives because gunmen and gangsters . . . have shot first." But "the risk all police officers run does not justify indiscriminate shooting, nor the killing of young boys. A policeman who kills becomes at once prosecutor, judge, jury and executioner."[73]

The policing report was sent to Mayor La Guardia on June 11, 1935, and by mid-July, Hays was fretting to fellow Commissioners Villard, Roberts, Ernst, and Carter that "there has been no action by the Mayor as yet." News of the subcommittee report had reached the community, however. Coles had apparently heard the rumors and wrote a letter in mid-July to Hays saying: "As was to be expected the Mayor's Committee activity have come to an abrupt close with nothing accomplished." Referring to officials who did not appear, he noted that "they ignored the mayor's request to appear before the Committee, and he did nothing as usual." He dismissed La Guardia as a "big wind bag and knows as much about running the city as a bull knows about running Wanamaker's store. Of course, he fooled you Liberal people." Hays responded that the "Mayor has our Report in connection with the police situation in Harlem, and I have a feeling that it will do considerable good. I have been waiting for him to make it public, and I hope he soon will do so." And that same day, in mid-July, Hays wrote a personal note to La Guardia: "I have been receiving many letters asking me about our Report. A letter just received to the effect that 'nobody expect us to do anything' rather got under my skin." He asked the mayor to "devote a moment to this or at any rate, let me know when we can give it out to the public?"[74]

After an inexplicable pause, the mayor released the subcommittee report on August 10, 1935. Following the press coverage, which did not print the full report, people asked Hays for copies of it. Hays began sharing mimeographs with friends, opinion shapers, and those who asked for it. The private reactions he received praised the report but also expressed doubts about how the government could solve the problems of policing Harlem. The white press ably summarized the report, though many papers (as the scholar Stephen Robertson notes) implicitly questioned its conclusions by noting that the members of the commission were liberals. The views of the African American press are mostly lost, as there are no extant copies of the *Afro-American* and the *Amsterdam News*. But the *New Age* thought the report's conclusions about the police captured the truth that it had long proclaimed. Fortunately, Hays kept a clipping of the *Amsterdam News* story of the report. It was the sort of reaction that the authors of the report probably wanted. Under the headline "Mayor's Board on Harlem Riot Blames Police," it quoted liberally from the document, hitting the highlights that the riot was spontaneous, that the Communists were not the inciters of the riot, and that police acted unwisely on the day and night of the riot. Police brutality was one of the many causes of citizen unrest. The *News* summarized the recommendations and underscored the conclusion that if something was not done, "Harlem would continue to be fertile field for radical propaganda."[75]

Coles, following the release, wrote Hays that, because the mayor had staffed the commission with men like Hays, Villard, and Randolph, it was a "monster that would rise up and destroy the Mayor. Well, it was his Frankenstein." The "conditions are just as bad, if not worse in Harlem than they were before March 19, 1935." Referencing the claims by some in the community that the police had withdrawn from Harlem and were treating criminals too lightly, Coles dismissed them as untrue. But policing was dirty business, and, quoting Kipling, he said police were no more "plaster saints" than British soldiers in India had been. He then cast that echo of imperialism into current racial terms: "Police on horses and motorcycles riding up and down the streets of Harlem . . . look worse patrolling Harlem than Mussolini's soldiers would look patrolling the fields of Abyssinia." In response to his comments, Hays sent Coles a copy of the subcommittee report, no doubt understanding that Coles would continue to press for reform.[76]

Others disparaged the report. One committee member who refused to sign the report publicly criticized it, asserting the one-sided hearings were "orgies of police baiting" dominated by Communists and led to the erroneous conclusion that the police were responsible for the disorder. Leopold Philipp of the Uptown Chamber of Commerce wrote to La Guardia attacking the "turbulent public hearings" of Hays's committee. They featured witnesses "wholly unrepresentative" of the community because the "hearing rooms were packed with radicals." The committee members "seemed to have preconceived ideas that the police and white business men of the community were to blame for the uprising." Police were "grilled by members" of the ILD, "by Negro attorneys who saw an opportunity to gain cheap publicity, and finally, by persons in the audience." It was an "atmosphere" that could not "develop any constructive suggestions or bring out the true facts" that contradicted the "views of radical lawyers and the mob." Citing the incident of the district attorney who was treated harshly by the ILD lawyers, Philipp was not surprised that they stopped attending.

Admitting that the abuse investigated by the committee might be real, he explained them away as being rarities and an outgrowth of the dangerous criminal conditions in Harlem. "Extreme police measures are required to curb these criminals so that the section will be safe." Philipp argued the commission should have heard from victims of the "holdup men, robbers, and thugs." Ultimately he argued that "closer investigation" would reveal that "the basis for the belief that policemen mistreat innocent, colored persons is as groundless as the false rumor which caused the rioting on March 19th." He ended with a call for more active policing in Harlem to control the criminal element and prevent further riots.[77]

Mayor La Guardia's answer to Philipp presaged the fate of the proposals of the subcommittee report and the final report. Portraying the Uptown Chamber of Commerce letter as "a well thought-out and fair presentation of the situation," the mayor said he would send it to the Police Department. He added "I am quite in agreement that taking a few isolated cases of improper police action does not represent the true picture of conditions." He reiterated his resolve that people in the city "must be protected against the vicious, criminal element." La Guardia said he emphasized "both of these conclusions to the Sub-committee when they filed their report with me." Then changing tone, the mayor declared that he was considering seriously one of the commission's proposals: "a Citizens' Liaison Committee" for the police department. "I would like to have your organization submit three names, from whom I can select one to place on this Committee." Both letters were shared with the subcommittee, making clear that their recommendations on policing faced resistance but were not yet ruled out.[78]

In face of the mayor's stance, in September 1935, Hays turned to Commissioner Valentine, writing him to inquire "whether anything has been done in connection with [the] recommendations" as well as several individual cases highlighted in the report. He listed the recommendations: giving the police thorough instruction as to the limits on their use of force, creating a biracial committee to hear citizen complaints of police mistreatment, prosecuting officers who violated the law, and developing a system to combat rumors. Hays asked whether anything had been done in connection with the cases of the shooting of Hobbs, the killing of Laurie, the assault on Aiken, and the arrest of Patterson.[79]

Valentine's reply to Hays either rejected the proposals out of hand or deemed them "impracticable." Valentine refused to admit the facts the commission had revealed that had prompted the recommendations.

He gave rather pat answers to the issue of the legal limits of the use of force and the prosecution of police who broke laws. Asserting that Police Academy probationary training had taught the force the limitations on their powers, he saw no reason to implement the suggestion that they be instructed on the limits. He declared that police officers charged with the commission of a crime "were treated exactly the same as any other accused person." He rejected the citizens complaint board as "unnecessary and impracticable." Valentine thought the printing of leaflets and placards "impracticable, because of the obvious impossibility of obtaining the large number of leaflets and placards that would be required, and the effective distribution of same, within a reasonable time after an unforeseen disorder occurred." He thought use of the radio more feasible but doubted broadcasts would reach "those responsible for the disorder" as they would be unlikely to be listening to the radio. This last example showed that even though he had three months to consider this proposal, he actually had done nothing about it. He likewise treated the four cases Hays asked about. The two homicides and the assault case had all been referred to the grand jury and no indictment handed down. In Valentine's words, the patrolmen were "exonerated." Patterson's arrest had "been thoroughly investigated by competent and appropriate officials of this department . . . , who found . . . that there was no cause of disciplinary action against the detectives involved." Valentine's position would not change upon receiving the fuller report of the whole commission.[80]

The task of drawing up the commission's final report devolved on Chief Investigator Frazier. He began sending sections of the report to the commission for their review toward the end of 1935. When Frazier delivered the section concerning the start of the disorder to the commission, Villard and Hays strongly objected to its tone and interpretation. Villard wrote Carter, "I must record my astonishment at the treatment given to the Communists therein." He objected to "the assertion that . . . the Young Communists League prevented the riots from being race riots." He sent a separate letter to Hays, who must have written to Carter to support Villard, as she replied, "I heartily agree with you . . . that Mr. Frazier's opening chapters contain misstatements as to the findings of the commission and create a totally incorrect impression of the results of the Communist activities in the events." Hays later reported, "I objected to some statements in the report which might be interpreted as approval" of Communist claims. He also objected to specific language such as "the capitalist system, communism, socialism, etc. or that used word like 'mass action," and others of the kind." Many other commissioners had changes, but the body felt pressure to have a full report to the mayor before the first anniversary of the disorder. Frazier was directed to revise the document, and Hays and Villard were appointed to check those revisions. Frazier did not make all the changes, Hays and Villard failed to make their checks, and some of the objectionable language remained in the final version sent to the mayor.[81]

The commission also revised the recommendations section. In the police section, a strengthening sentence about prohibiting interracial association was struck. "It should be impressed upon them that their private prejudices are no warrant . . . and that such interference will lead to dismissal from the police force." The commissioners also removed a recommendation that must have been added by Frazier: "Any entertainment venue that advertised itself as segregated by race was to be closed by the police." They likewise removed from the recommendation for the establishment of a police complaint and advisory commission a line that had come from the subcommittee report that the body should include "men who are dissenters from established institutions and also men who are likely to have contact with victims of injustice." They also eliminated a minor assertion that the vigorous investigation and prosecution of officers who violated the law would bring about efficiency in policing. They left unchanged the rumor battling recommendation.[82]

The wrangling over the report delayed getting it into the hands of officials. Hays proposed that a skeleton commission stay in place to keep pressure on the mayor to take action and maintain contact with the heads of departments, including Commissioner Valentine. Thus, in January 1936, Schieffelin and Hays wanted to meet with Valentine and get feedback on the section on policing. But not until early March did Hays send him the pertinent documents. Valentine's secretary responded a week later that Valentine looked "forward to reading" the material "at the first opportunity he has." There is no evidence he ever gave feedback to the commission. Many of the points, especially about the police, came indirectly from the people of Harlem, revealing the depth of the division between the community and the police.[83]

The commission sent the report in typescript (signed by ten of the thirteen commissioners) to the mayor on March 19, 1936, but he did not order it printed. No doubt the language of the report with its Marxist rhetoric was off-putting. But even if stripped of its tone, it called for liberal-style action most congenial to La Guardia, including preventing discrimination in city and public works employment, ending the biases in the relief system, enforcing the housing code and the building of public housing to limit overcrowding, improving health, education and recreational facilities to equal the rest of the city, as well as imposing limits on police action. It also criticized sharply some of La Guardia's officials. The heads of city agencies, when shown the report, harshly criticized it. Their reaction prompted La Guardia to commission Alain Locke of Howard University to evaluate the material. Locke found the report to be accurate, and in particular he agreed with the commission on the police. His confirming report found its way into print as "Harlem: Dark Weather-Vane," in August 1936. Still, La Guardia did not reprimand or dismiss his criticized officials and pigeon-holed the report.[84]

In face of the mayor's inaction, Coles wrote Hays: "I wish that the committee had been courageous enough to force the hand of the mayor and to make him receive the report fully as present[ed] at first." He argued conditions in Harlem would not improve until there was meaningful work on erasing discrimination in employment as well as other areas. He told Hays of a bright young boy who was being "down-graded" in school because of racial stereotyping. His letter prompted Hays into a rare admission that little had been accomplished. While he liked Coles's "spirit with which you keep interested," he noted it was "discouraging to realize what conditions are and to feel how little can be done or is being done." He even doubted that he could help the young boy: "Of course I am interested in the case of Mrs. Morgan's son and would be glad to see her if I felt that there was anything I could do, but I don't see how I could help." This admission of weakness and limits showed that Hays felt comfortable in confiding in Coles. Indeed, their whole correspondence indicated that Hays, who after all, had very strongly set views on policing, was willing to learn, to some extent, from the African Americans who were being policed in Harlem. And, in time, he also showed he shared Coles's spirit.[85]

As the year moved on through the spring, Hays and others of the commission pressured the mayor to release the report. Soon after Hays wrote to the mayor inquiring about its release, he learned from the mayor's office that various chapters of the final reports had been "referred to the departments they affect for study and report by the commissioners of those departments." The mayor also gave either the full report or sections to many of the mainstream newspapers in the city, framing the material in ways that highlighted the response of his administration to the criticisms of the report. When it came to the police critiques and recommendations, the mayor's views had been reinforced by Valentine's report, which rejected the recommendations wholesale. In June 1936, Mayor La Guardia held a contentious, two-hour private meeting with some of the commissioners. What leaked out concerning the policing parts of the report indicated the mayor discounted at least two policing topics. The first was "whether or not the police would 'interfere' with blacks and whites who were mingling in public." The second was the assertion that police unlawfully searched people in Harlem. Despite Chairman Roberts telling the mayor that he had been unlawfully searched by police on a number of occasions, that did not apparently change La Guardia's mind. In talking to the commissioners, and later others, he focused more on what his administration had done, such as fast-tracking a public housing project and appointing African Americans to positions in government. Eventually someone leaked the whole report. Various papers, including the *Amsterdam News* on July 18, 1936, published the whole report. The *Amsterdam News* had both the final version and the one with the recommendations sections as Frazier drafted and chose to print those recommendations, because they were "considered too hot, too caustic, too critical, too unfavorable by the mayor, and . . . [were] allegedly revamped by the commission to make it more to his liking."[86]

In September 1936, weeks after the report had been printed in the *Amsterdam News*, Villard took it upon himself to nudge the mayor about "his failure . . . to make our report public." Mayor La Guardia responded, "Owing to your sojourn in the country during the hot summer months apparently you have not kept informed about all that has been done in the Harlem situation." The mayor asserted the report had been available to the press for at least ten weeks, ever since it had been leaked to the *New York Post* (which Villard published) and *Daily Worker*. He added that he regretted that Villard had not been "not present at the last meeting of the Committee when they met at my office" and hoped to see him on his "your return to the city." The invoking of class distinction with its implication that Villard was out of touch, and the jab at the leaking of the report to Villard's paper and the Communist paper while overlooking the African American *Amsterdam News*, indicated that La Guardia was in no mind to follow the recommendations. Villard made the best of it by telling Hays, "The enclosed telegram having come from the Mayor I am notifying the Herald-Tribune, Times, World-Telegram and Sun that the Mayor has released the report." His list of establishment papers indicated that he hoped to build liberal opinion in support of the proposals for addressing the problems that had produced the disturbance. The city press apparently had been given the report and the city department heads' responses, and most of the mainstream press took their lead from La Guardia and emphasized how much the city had done to address the problems in Harlem.[87]

The mayor did take action to address the problems of Harlem. He often responded without ever admitting that he was responding. For example, La Guardia, in pushing for state aid on the construction of public housing in Harlem, sent the governor a copy of the preliminary report on housing. By 1940, that project, the Harlem River Houses, was done. Also in response, the city built the Central Harlem Women Pavilion at Harlem Hospital and two new Harlem schools. The city did more to integrate the staff of its hospitals and opened more civil service jobs to African Americans. And the Columbia University graduate and former football star Myles A. Paige was appointed the city's first African American city magistrate in 1936. Walter White strongly praised La Guardia's actions, and even the critical *Amsterdam News* thought that the mayor had tried to alleviate some of the problems that had prompted the disturbance of March 19 and 20 and that the Mayor's Commission had exposed.[88]

The salient area of inaction was in the policing in Harlem. No police officers were demoted or punished, no citizen complaint panel was created, and no extra training for police was made available. What La Guardia did do was apply his personal touch. Harlem now got his attention: He appeared at crime scenes to show that he would not neglect the people there. With no reform; and with the mayor, police commissioner, and district attorney all unwilling to embrace change, the law continued its course, and Hays was reduced to pleading for mercy for those caught up in its machinery. For instance, Harry Gordon, arrested and beaten by police for speaking at the street event outside the Kress store, was prosecuted for assault on a police officer. Upon Gordon's conviction, Hays wrote to the sentencing judge, referencing the subcommittee report, which he included with his letter. "I wish to say a word in his behalf. Gordon testified before the Mayor's Harlem Committee frankly and without reservation, even though cases against him were then pending. He is certainly not a criminal and he was exercising what he deemed to be his right of free speech." Hays continued, "I am somewhat surprised at the finding of guilt, but in any event I, together with many others, hope that the court will find it proper to grant a suspended sentence."[89]

Hays's immersion in Harlem in 1935 exposed him to the viewpoints of African Americans. From the surviving records, we cannot reconstruct

Hays's interactions with the African American members or employees of the commission. A year later, he was happy to supply a reference for Tarter, the investigator who did much of the legwork, but the letters exchanged were short and simple. Similarly, the letters between him and Carter are brief and formal. And while Chairman Roberts attended all the crime subcommittee hearings, he did not work with Hays as Villard did in crafting its report. We get some idea of his connections with witnesses and participants in the hearings. His series of letters with the journalist Coles were repeated, frank, and consequential—they often inspired Hays to take action. Like Thompson, Coles had Hays's trust as a fair witness. Hays wanted to make sure even someone as abrasive as Romney was not kept from presenting his views. Like everyone else, he deserved his freedom of speech.

In his only published account of the riot commission, Hays placed great weight on African American willingness to make clear what was wrong with policing in Harlem. In a chapter on progressive politics in his 1942 book *City Lawyer*, when talking about Mayor La Guardia, Hays segued to the disturbance and the commission (which he characterized as his only political appointment). Explaining how "little incidents stir up antagonism, racial feeling, and sometimes bloodshed," he traced the origins of the disturbance to the rumors, "the lurid circular" put out by "a colored Communist group," and "the stupidity of the city police." He explained that his "open meetings at a courthouse in Harlem" provided a venue for "colored people . . . to speak up and to grill the authorities who for years had dealt with them with little sympathy and often with brutality." The crowds at the hearings "made use of the opportunity" and "were thrilled to see democracy in action." He added that "Amens" from the audience sometimes made it sound like a revival meeting. He admitted that he had to threaten adjournment to keep control. "But the story of our Negroes and their treatment by the city was brought into the open." Passing over many other factors, Hays declared that "our report attributed the cause of the riots in large part to the stupidity of the city police. Why didn't they show Rivera to the first group that gathered instead of telling these people to go about their business?" Other conditions in Harlem had been improved for a time by the city under La Guardia, but Hays admitted that La Guardia had done nothing about police behavior. How Hays saw the issues of Harlem was revealed as to how he ended the Harlem section of his book: He did so by moving on to a discussion of the mayor's support of the third degree. The third degree was the police practice of harsh interrogation of suspects that often edged into torture and was an established worry of civil libertarians.[90]

Little changed in policing in Harlem (and in the city in general), with brutality continuing to be a problem. In 1938, Walter White of the NAACP drew attention to a particularly egregious example. In a telegram to La Guardia and Valentine, he protested the beating of an African American bootblack by a rookie cop that was stopped only when bystanders intervened. White called for the suspension of the officer and the mayor and commissioner to prohibit such actions. Instead, Valentine assured La Guardia that an internal investigation "disclosed that only sufficient force necessary to effect arrest was used" and thus there was no cause for disciplinary action. Moreover, the complaint had been withdrawn after the police interviewed the victim. Such police misconduct was so common that Adam Clayton Powell Jr., in his paper, *The People's Voice*, was relentless in detailing cases. Similarly, the *Amsterdam News* in the 1940s had a story of police brutality in every weekly issue of the paper.[91]

When a disturbance again broke out in Harlem in 1943 (begun by the rumor that a police officer had shot and killed an African American solider), Hays used the opportunity to call for the changes to police training and procedures that had been laid out in the subcommittee report. The disturbance was short-lived, the police action was restrained, and in another example of implementing recommendations from reports he disparaged, Mayor La Guardia toured Harlem on flatbed truck, saying rumors were untrue, and also spoke on the radio just after 1:00 a.m. to try to squelch rumors and restore order. After this disturbance, Hays wrote a letter to the *New York Times* recalling the history of the 1935 report and including a long quotation from the subcommittee report but implying it came from the full commission report. Hays pointed out that the 1943 disturbance, like the 1935 one, began with a mistaken assumption by the people of Harlem. He said the commission had concluded that "the long-time attitude of the police toward the people" was key in instigating the 1935 riot. "In Harlem the police are regarded as enemies." He reiterated that the report recited "violations of the civil rights of the people of the police and concluded, "The insecurity of the individual in Harlem against police aggression is in our judgement one of the most potent causes of the existing hostility to authority." He made four recommendations. "One, "that the police obey the law in the treatment of the residents of Harlem." Two, that they be "given thorough instruction in the law as to the limitations" on their use of violence. Three, that the commissioner of police appoint a body composed of people of both races "to whom colored people may make complaint if mistreated by the police." And four, that if a police officer broke the law, the district attorney prosecute the case "just as vigorously as where any other person" was charged with a crime. Hays added, "So far as I know recommendations along the above lines were ignored." And the "conditions in Harlem, the wretched housing, unduly high rent, lack of recreation grounds, and discrimination in industry" created "an emotional situation which might at any time cause a flare-up." And flare-ups would come again because of "a lack of proper treatment of the people by the police." He added, borrowing again from the subcommittee report, "The present economic conditions may make difficult the carrying out of many recommendations concerning Harlem, but here is one problem that can be solved without the expenditure of money."[92]

By not sending the letter to Mayor La Guardia, Hays revealed that he no longer thought the mayor would embark on reform without further pressure. Apparently too much time had passed and too little reform of the police had occurred. Moreover, crime fighting had proved a very successful electoral tactic for politicians; indeed, Thomas Dewey rode his crusade against gangsters (which was filled with police strong-arm tactics and questionable practices) to the New York governor's office. This letter shows what Hays valued as important. First, the letter downplayed the social and economic roots of the unrest in Harlem. Finding the root causes was fundamental to the liberal approach to the problems of Harlem. In the liberal view, if the problems of discrimination in housing, employment, medical care, recreation, and relief were addressed, the unrest would not be repeated. A comparison of Hays's letter with a much longer article by Villard, "The Slumbering Fires in Harlem," is instructive. Villard spends more than half of the article on the shortage and expense of housing, discrimination in relief, discrimination and inadequate medical care in the hospital, and the deplorable conditions of the schools. Hays had read the article in manuscript, yet he barely mentioned these topics. Second, his experience on the commission reinforced his already engrained distrust of the police. The African Americans who wrote him letters, testified, and jeered and hissed from the audience tipped the balance. That there were free speech potential issues in the police's first responses to the disturbances, and that charges of police misconduct were so prevalent and came from so many sources, shaped how he responded to the problems of Harlem. Third, Hays highlighted reforms that, while aimed at reducing racial discrimination by the police, applied to everyone. His argument was that equality of treatment would in itself do much to keep riots from occurring. This was Hay's civil liberties argument made as a civil rights argument, in many ways little different from what he had been saying for years. For example, he had the same overall prescription in his article "What the Jews Want from Hitler." The two stances were not mutually exclusive, but in Hays's mind one was fundamental. Thus, in the final analysis, his work on the Mayor's Commission showed Hays approached problems of racial discrimination as a civil libertarian.[93]

3

"What is a Negro?"

Cockburn v. Ridgway

In 1937, Arthur Garfield Hays represented Pauline and Joshua Cockburn in their efforts to stave off an injunction that would force them from their brand-new Westchester County, New York, home. The property was covered by a racially restrictive covenant prohibiting purchase and occupancy by Negroes and colored people. Such covenants were pervasive and exercised a tremendous effect in limiting where African Americans could live from the 1920s into the 1950s. While deploying a host of arguments to defend the Cockburns, Hays seized upon the case to advance an argument about the difficulty of determining race. Hays wanted to underscore that the policies of the color line rested on a shaky foundation of mere prejudice. Such prejudice had no basis in a modern scientific understanding of race and should not serve as a basis for legal policy. Hays argued that New York, and the nation, should not tolerate legal discrimination on basis of race, creed, or color. His actions in the case and his later recounting of the story made clear he saw this case a way to push the larger society away from its racialist predilections. His civil liberties ideology which rested on a foundational idea that all people should have full access to civil liberties—including the right to live where they chose—lay behind his taking the case. But it also built on his previous civil rights work, as the situation of the Cockburns derived directly from developments in property law that underlay the origins of the Sweet case.

Segregating housing by race began in the post-Reconstruction South as a part of the emerging white supremacy system of Jim Crow. It began with private behavior, but like other aspects of segregation was adopted into law. The shift into law was made easier by the expansion of regulation and urban planning during the progressive era. The basis had been there since the late nineteenth century, when governments began restricting property use for the betterment of the community. Prohibiting of use of property for certain purposes extended beyond noxious physical uses like a slaughterhouse to socially noxious uses such as a retail liquor store. The idea of zoning added to the development of segregating housing by law. Soon cities began segregating by ordinance. In an age that had seen race riots where whites used violence to remove African Americans from areas where they had settled, some saw the policy of separate districts as a way to preclude racial conflict. Southern and border state cities led the way in designating racial zoning by law. But even in the age of Jim Crow, such zoning was seen as a step too far by the courts. It was hard to justify laws such laws as conforming to separate but equal since the laws often stated that African Americans were not equal to whites and that the races should not live near each other.[1]

In the 1917 case of *Buchanan v. Warley*, brought by the National Association for the Advancement of Colored People (NAACP), the segregated housing district law of Louisville, Kentucky, was struck down by the United States Supreme Court. Melding a respect for property rights with the restriction put on government action by the 14th Amendment, the Court held that the law violated the due process of the citizen protected by the amendment. The opinion was not a defense of equality and even admitted that "racial hostility" was a "serious and difficult problem." But the solution to the problem of race hate was not to be found by interfering with property rights. The Court invalidated the law because it interfered with the right of property owners to sell their property without unreasonable restrictions. The unhampered alienation (sale) of land had been since the Revolution a key part of American property law, and imposing a racial limit on who could own land exceeded the power of government to regulate property in the public's interest. Seeing property rights as a fundamental civil right, one that was a foundation for other rights, the Court would not allow a government to take it away from one group of citizens based on race.[2]

Still, geographic exclusion continued. Cities responded to the *Buchanan v. Warley* decision by adjusting their laws in the vain hope that they could find a formula that would pass the constitutional test. In the deep South, towns either kept their existing laws or adopted residential segregation in planning documents, and these actions were never challenged in the courts. Other cities made zoning on other grounds result in the desired racial segregation: creating guidelines for single family housing districts with the price floor high enough that it effectively priced out African Americans. The most common and effective legal way to create segregated residential districts was through the use of restrictive covenants.[3]

The racial restrictive covenant emerged as an analogue to governmental regulation that limited the use of property. Instead of a government designating a use to be prohibited, a property holder upon deeding the land specified uses that would be prohibited in the future. Practically, property covenants worked best if they applied to not just one lot but to a group of properties. Thus, neighbors who had bought into a residential district would not wake up one day to discover their next-door neighbor had sold their property to a tanner. Such covenants would protect the value of the covenanted properties. No contract was self-enforcing, and so this method required that courts enforced the covenants. In the minds of their creators, racial restrictive covenants shifted from a noxious use to a noxious person. Persons of certain groups were cast as the equivalent of a use that hurt property values.[4]

Typical language for a restrictive covenant was direct: "At no time shall said premises or any part thereof or any building erected thereon be sold, occupied, let or leased, or given to any one of any race other than the Caucasian, except that this covenant shall not prevent occupancy by domestic servants of a difference race." Many were less sweeping, applying to "Chinese," "Negros," "those of Negro blood," "the Negro or African race" and "colored." Often "Negro" and "colored" were used in same covenant with phrasing that did not make it clear as to whether they were synonymous or separate categories. Very few covenants defined the racial terms they used. The society that recognized such covenants as legal was a society that was comfortable in allowing its white members to determine the race of others. In the age of separate but equal, commentators asserted that the covenants met the test, since African Americans could form their own covenants to keep out other races. There were a few examples of that, but the reality was that whites wrote most covenants; most were aimed at African Americans, though Asians, Jews, and other groups showed up in some restrictions. Covenants were employed for the "protection" of the white race from inferior races: Restrictive covenants were "Caucasian bulwarks."[5]

This tool for exclusion was slow to grow because it ran counter to important precepts of Anglo-American property law. From long before the American Revolution, English law had tended to support the relatively unrestrained sale and use of property. After the Revolution, United States law aimed to free the present from the "dead hand" of the past with fewer restrictions of the alienation or use of land. Before the twentieth century, these ideas of property law limited the use of restrictive covenants, but as planning and zoning arose, the antipathy toward restraints on alienation and the rule against perpetuities faded, with courts finding covenants reasonable and therefore enforceable. Even when courts ruled that racial restrictive covenants impeded the free alienation of property, they could uphold the bans by saying that while a person of the prohibited group could acquire the property, they could not occupy or use it. In general, the old rules were relaxed, allowing the racially restrictive covenants to stand and to significantly limit where African Americans could live.[6]

After the ruling in *Buchanan*, and spurred by the migration of African Americans out of the South, racial restrictive covenants became very common in urban areas across the nation, especially in places where the racial mores were not regulated by legal segregation. There were two types of covenants. The first type (more common in new developments) was placed as restrictions in the title deed. The second type (normally found in established neighborhoods) was an agreement among property owners to a set of restrictions recorded in a contract. The stated reasons for the covenants were to create or preserve property values and respectability. They went into effect either when the deed was registered or in the case of a community contract when a threshold of signatures was obtained. Both methods required notice alerting subsequent potential buyers of the limitations on the property. Since suing for damages would not reach the desired end (of keeping certain people from the property), the covenants relied on the Anglo-American's law predilections to allow property owners to seek equitable relief for harms. Specifically, the use injunctions barring sale or occupancy was the norm in enforcing covenants. As with any other contract, for it to be fully effective, the government's legal system had to be used.[7]

The involvement of an arm of the government in enforcing the covenants raised a constitutional point: Did such covenants—like segregated housing laws—violate the due process rights of citizens, or were they private actions? That private action was beyond the reach of the 14th Amendment was a doctrine adopted by the Supreme Court in *United States v. Cruikshank* in 1876 and given greater reach in the *Civil Rights Cases* of 1883. A late nineteenth-century district court case concerning a restrictive covenant against the Chinese, where the judge refused to enforce the covenant because it violated a federal treaty, said in passing that such covenants were not state action under the 14th Amendment. Seeing the covenants as a serious threat to the aspirations of African Americans, the NAACP adopted a test case in Washington D. C., *Corrigan v. Buckley*, to challenge that interpretation. Beyond the legal gain, the NAACP leaders saw the fight against restrictive covenants as a way to cement alliances with others, like Jews, who would fall afoul of covenants. In 1926, in refusing to review the *Corrigan* case, where a lower court had upheld an injunction to enforce a covenant, the United States Supreme Court declared that such covenants were private action and not state action and therefore beyond the reach of the civil rights amendments. With the seeming endorsement of the Supreme Court, the practice became entrenched in American life.[8]

The NAACP did not give up on challenging restrictive covenants. They read the *Corrigan v. Buckley* decision narrowly, noting that the Court had not settled the issue of whether judicial enforcement of such covenants was state action and, furthermore, that the section of the opinion that dealt with the 14th Amendment's due process clause was dicta (reasoning unnecessary to reach the decision made by a court, and therefore not binding precedent) because it applied to the states, not federal territory. The NAACP involved itself in numerous challenges to restrictive covenants in the District of Columbia and in the states. For almost two decades, however, the NAACP failed to get another case to the high court. While always raising the constitutional objections, the organization also pushed other arguments. One argument used in state courts was that the covenants were against public policy and thus not worthy of equitable relief—that would have the effect of killing the racial covenants in a state. Another approach was to invoke the technical aspects of property law against the covenant, which might result in a victory for their client but not end the practice. In some of these cases, the NAACP worked with real estate people or entities that managed real estate deals or made money from opening up areas for African Americans to live.[9]

The division between private and public policy making was not just ambiguous, it was also short lived. Zoning ordinances continued to be creatively used for racial housing segregation in the 1920s. The federal Commerce Department approved a model zoning law that used zoning to keep racial tensions under control through separation. Also, for protection of both developers and property owners, the federal government's 1931 conference on homeownership endorsed them. Promoters of private restrictive covenants circled back into government policy making. The National Association of Real Estate Boards developed a full range of justifications and templates for residential restriction by race through restrictive covenants. When the federal government during the New Deal entered into housing policy, the real estate developers and their ideas flowed into federal agencies and policies and shaped them. Thus, before the redlining by banks sanctioned by the Federal Housing Authority, the restrictive covenant was the tool of white racists in creating the African American ghetto.[10]

The NAACP's, and Hays's, familiarity with the saga of the Sweets (especially as it was conducted in conjunction with the *Corrigan* case) made clear the value of attacking restrictive covenants. If they were held to be illegal, then the limits on housing on African Americans would ease, and not just for wealthy ones who could afford to move to the suburbs. It was no small matter. For instance, around New York City, a survey of three hundred developments built between 1935 and 1947 in Queens, Nassau, and Westchester counties found that 56 percent had racial restrictive covenants.[11]

Pauline and Joshua Cockburn were enterprising and entrepreneurial and made the most of their opportunities after immigrating to the United States. Both were from seafaring families of the British West Indies. Pauline was born in 1896 in the Bahamas of a West Indian father, Ernest, who had been a mariner and inventor, and an Italian mother. The Bethel family name came from Scottish plantation owners who interbred with their enslaved workers before and after emancipation and divided their landholdings among all their descendants regardless of color. Her family relocated to England when she was young. The family was wealthy enough to have Pauline educated in private schools. In 1911, she married Joshua Cockburn in Liverpool, England. Joshua, born in the West Indies in 1877, joined the British Navy and rose through the ranks to be a ship's mate at the time of the marriage. In 1916, he commanded a support ship (the *S.S. Trojan*) in Great Britain's campaign against Germany in Cameroon. His crew had no white people. His service impressed British powers in Africa, and he was appointed to a colonial post in Lagos, Nigeria. Pauline was with him in Nigeria, and they had a son there. In October 1918, they left Africa for the Bahamas by way of New York. Joshua Cockburn served as third officer on the ship making the voyage; their son died en route and was buried at sea. Within a month of the Cockburns' arrival in the New York, news spread in Harlem that Joshua Cockburn was planning a pan-Africanist project. The radical and pan-Africanist newspaper *The Crusader* reported that Cockburn "was commissioned by wealthy Africans to purchase schooners for trading purposes." A month later *The Crusader* asserted that Cockburn brought "a message of hope from Africa," and that Africa was "the economic salvation of Negroes everywhere."[12]

Joshua Cockburn in July 1919 read of plans to start an African American–owned shipping corporation. The idea of a fleet was exciting to many African-descended people living in the New World as well as Africans in the Old World. The Black Star Shipping Line was started by the Jamaican-born, charismatic pan-Africanist leader Marcus Garvey, who had founded the United Negro Improvement Association in Harlem, which at its peak claimed to have more than two million members worldwide. Garvey preached African pride and uplift through self-improvement. In September 1919 Cockburn approached Garvey about joining the project. He appeared at a mass meeting in uniform as a sort of advertisement for the line. Garvey let Cockburn pick the first vessel for the line. The company overpaid significantly for an old freighter: the *S.S. Yarmouth*, with Cockburn receiving a significant kickback from the seller. It was quickly rechristened the *Frederick Douglass* but never made money on any of its voyages with Cockburn at the helm. Cockburn had earlier told Garvey that the line's voyages need not be profitable because they could make money by selling stock. Several voyages were disasters of bad seamanship and shoddy business practices. The ship was a stirring symbol, but mismanagement, breakdowns, and crew difficulties earned the ship a short history. Cockburn was paid a significant salary (the highest of any of Garvey's employees) and may have taken other kickbacks. When Garvey could not regularly pay him, Cockburn took the anchor from the ship. Garvey sued for its recovery and lost on the grounds that Cockburn had the right to attach valuable items from the ship as compensation for nonpayment of his salary.[13]

Seen as the embodiment of radicalism among African Americans, Garvey was investigated by the federal government, seeking evidence of illegal activities. Garvey's endless promotions edged toward hyperbole and allowed a prosecution for mail fraud. Significantly, Joshua Cockburn testified against Garvey in his mail fraud trial. But he refused to cooperate with the federal agents when they sought evidence that Garvey violated the federal Mann Act (which prohibited the transportation of women for immoral purposes) by his travels with his mistress. Garvey was convicted on the mail fraud charge and sent to prison and upon release deported. While his betrayal of Garvey was unpopular among Garvey's many supporters in Harlem, it did not hurt Cockburn with the African American elite, as figures like James Weldon Johnson and W. E. B. Du Bois despised Garvey.[14]

After the falling out with Garvey, and with Harlem booming, the Cockburns went into the real estate business, fixing their place among the elite of Harlem society. Their business was named the Pauline Realty Company and incorporated in her name. Later they also established the first post-prohibition liquor store in Harlem, which was characterized in the press as "flourishing." During the latter 1930s, Joshua purchased the Old Tree Inn in Yonkers with two female business partners. According to the 1940 census, Pauline Cockburn listed her occupation as "retail liquor." In any case, the liquor store business either meant that the Cockburns had no criminal associations—as license holders under the new state system were scrutinized closely—or that they had political connections who could get them the license even if they did not meet the strict criteria. Also, they had received a windfall of more than $50,000 on the sale of property to the Board of Education for the construction of one of the new schools in Harlem built in the wake of the disturbances of 1935. Since 1920, they had lived on 127th Street, and they became United States citizens in 1927. They appeared in the society pages of the African American press. They prospered, as can been seen by their donations. Joshua donated $5000 toward the construction of Cathedral of St. John the Divine in memory of his son who died at sea. He established a tennis tournament, first hosted in Harlem but later played at Lincoln University in Pennsylvania.[15]

That Pauline often seemed to operate as the front person for their enterprises was a significant but ambiguous fact. At his trial, Marcus Garvey accused Joshua of placing his realty business in Pauline's name because he had funded it with money stolen from Garvey. His accusation is only one explanation for using Pauline's name and not Joshua's on the business. They could have been carrying on the traditions of West Indian seafarers who often cooperatively pooled money and placed the funds under the control of wives, as they were ashore while the men were at sea. Also, as Pauline Cockburn was very light-skinned, while Joshua was dark, the placing of her name on the company might have secured several advantages in the business. Most notably, in 1920s America, some would be more likely to do business with a white person, and sellers often inflated the price for their property if they thought a purchaser was African American.[16]

Pauline Cockburn's name was listed as the purchaser of three lots in 1933, whether as an investment or as a site for a future home is unclear.

For instance, they could have been planning to sell all the lots in a rising market—though given the effect of the Depression on the market that was unlikely. Or they could have planned to sell the other two lots for capital when they built on the third lot. The couple commissioned the building of a house there in September 1936, valued at $20,000. Their house more than met the development standards, and that made it distinctly upmarket. To give some context, in 1936 the average family income in New York City was $1,745. They moved in on January 1, 1937, and Pauline Cockburn was served almost immediately with notice that a neighbor was seeking an injunction to bar their occupancy on the grounds that they had violated the covenant against sale and occupancy of the property by Negroes.[17]

That restriction was there because of the action of the of Max Held Realty Corporation, the company that developed the neighborhood. In the 1920s, the company developed suburbs outside New York City, in New Rochelle, Larchmont, and other nearby locales. The company acquired a large tract of land and subdivided it into large lots that became the Edgemont Hills development in the town of Greenburgh but with the postal address of Scarsdale. The lots were guaranteed to be exclusive because of deed restrictions on use and occupancy. As was the norm in this period, the building of houses was left to contractors who worked for the lot purchasers. Those builders were limited by the restrictions in the deeds: on cost of construction, size of the dwellings, and such. These restrictions were imposed for the "purpose of creating a high-class residential neighborhood." The Edgemont Hills restrictions specified that the cost of the constructed houses had to exceed $15,000, that business not be conducted from the premises, and that the dwellings meet a minimum size. Typical of the time, they also included a racial restrictive covenant on many deeds: "no part of the said parcels shall ever be used or occupied by or sold, conveyed, leased, rented, or given to negroes or any persons or person of the negro race or blood, except that colored servants may be maintained on the premises." The proprietor of Max Held Realty was Jewish, and the restriction did not apply to Jews. However, of the eighteen lots in this "general scheme of development," only fifteen carried the "negro covenant," including the three lots sold to Pauline Cockburn.[18]

Marion Ridgway was the plaintiff in the suit. She had purchased her lot and built her house after Pauline Cockburn acquired her lots but before the Cockburns built their house. She was the widow of a Manhattan doctor, and some press accounts say that she was originally from Mississippi. Ridgway explained to the press that she thought she had purchased a home in a "very exclusive neighborhood," meaning free, at least, of African Americans. Some accounts claimed she began her action immediately after seeing Joshua Cockburn outside his completed home, though other accounts say she was animated by seeing the Cockburns "with other colored persons inspecting houses under construction in the said tract and surrounding territory." An African American firm in Mount Vernon acted as a broker in the deals to buy the lots and build the house. Perhaps the appearance of African Americans in the area prompted someone to act against the Cockburns. Within a week of applying for the injunction, her lawyer, Francis A. Griffin, filed two affidavits in support of her action. Ridgway also asked for a temporary injunction to block the Cockburns from inhabiting their house pending the litigation. As this was an equity matter, the case would be heard and decided by a judge alone.[19]

The two affidavits were from Ridgway and Carlysle Held of the property developer company. Both showed the handiwork of lawyers in that they were aimed at covering the pertinent legal points raised by the action. Ridgway established her claim to the property and asserted she had bought her parcel and built on it because "a common set of covenants and restrictions" created by Max Held Realty guaranteed that it would stay "a high-class residential" neighborhood because of its "uniform scheme of development." Ridgway argued that if Pauline Cockburn was "permitted to violate" the racial covenant "as she is now doing, deponent will suffer irreparable loss damage and her property will suffer injury in fee and rental value." Held's affidavit affirmed that the racial restrictive covenant "was inserted for the purpose of preserving and appreciating the value of the tract as a whole and of the individual parcels" within it. Held swore that Pauline and Joshua Cockburn knew about the racial covenant when she bought the property. The Held affidavit raised the likelihood that the Cockburns may have bought the property after consulting a lawyer. If that is so, it may have been Hutson L. Lovell, who was listed on the brief in opposition. Any competent lawyer who examined the Edgemont Hills deeds would note that they were not uniform. Three lots in the development did not have racial restrictive covenants, which could mean that the scheme was not uniform and therefore not enforceable. Held further averred that Joshua Cockburn had told him that he planned "to build several dwellings" on their land "for use and occupations by negroes," and that "he, Captain Cockburn, was as good as any white man." Held was insinuating that Cockburn was trying to start a panic of white selling in the area, so that eventually he could buy lots at bargain rates and then either sell them at a profit or rent them to African Americans at the usually higher rates they paid. If Held's statement was true, Joshua Cockburn was like other African Americans involved in other cases, acting out of mixture of both civil rights belief and the quest for economic gain. Regardless of their goals, the threat of not being able to live in their newly built, expensive home prompted the Cockburns to seek more legal help, which brought them eventually to Hays.[20]

Hays's involvement with the Cockburn case was not preordained even if he was predisposed to engage with the topic as he knew the harm that the covenants caused and because he identified as a Jew and knew that they stemmed from prejudice. The connection between racial exclusions of African Americans and the racial exclusion of Jews was well known by Hays. His awareness of it from the very time he began work on the Cockburn case was shown by Laura Lyon's column in the *New York Post* on February 1, 1937. In it Hays mocked the prejudices against Jews and Negros in telling of an experience his daughter, Lora, had. She had written to "an inn upstate to make reservations for a skiing party," Arthur Hays told the press. "They took the reservation and wrote her everything would be hunky, and that no Israelites would be there. Lora replied, 'That'll be so nice for our party—because we cullud folk don't get along with 'em well either!'" Lora, and Arthur in his retelling, used the absurdity of a hierarchy of racial standing to confront an innkeeper who excluded Jews with the even more upsetting possibility that African Americans would be a customer. Beyond showing the linkages of prejudices, it also underscored that there were African Americans who could afford ski vacations and to stay at fancy inns, undermining the assumptions that African Americans were poor because they were less capable. Thus, the light-skinned, cultured, and British-accented Mrs. Cockburn offered another chance for Hays to attempt to undermine racial presumptions.[21]

Hays entered the Cockburn case with the support of the NAACP and shaped the response to the request for the injunction. The record is silent as to whether Hays was already representing Pauline Cockburn or whether the NAACP referred her matter to him. Whatever their provenance, briefs on restrictive covenants were sent by "the Association's Special Counsel Assistant [Thurgood Marshall]" to Hays, who entered the Cockburn case with the support of the NAACP and shaped the response to the request for the injunction. Hays added to the NAACP's brief a focus on racial definition, making it much more a case on racial identity and the difficulty of determining race. From there he drew upon expertise. His major role in the Scopes case had been to prepare the expert witnesses on evolution and the Bible for their testimony as to how science viewed evolution and how the Bible was interpreted in different ways. In the Cockburn case, the experts would be social scientists. The defense began taking affidavits of experts about racial categories. It was a fruitful area to exploit, as from the beginning of Jim Crow unclear racial categories were a problem for a functioning system of segregation. Homer Plessy, the plaintiff in the 1896 *Plessy v. Ferguson* case, appeared to be white, and that raised the question (ignored by the Supreme Court) of how a person's race was determined.[22]

Though never brought out in the litigation, Hays's point about the difficulties of determining race was exemplified by the different ways the Cockburns, especially Pauline, were characterized by officials who over the years took note of them: immigration officers and census takers. In a blending of "scientific categories" and common opinion, the Cockburns' race shifted by who measured it, probably by which member of the couple they saw and by which categories were employed. When Pauline returned to the United in 1919 from the Bahamas, she was first classed as "Italian" but that was changed to "West Indian." The latter category was one of the three categories of "race or people" recorded for passengers of this particular ship: "English," "West Indian," or "African." At first glance, she probably fit what officials were marking as "English," but her probable self-identification of the Italian heritage complicated that. In 1919, the immigration service distinguished between Northern and Southern Italians (as racial groups since the designation was not just geographic), but perhaps Cockburn did not know from where in Italy her family came and so her categorization was not certain. However, she also did not appear African. Therefore, they went with her land of birth—whether that was a racial category to the inspector or not remains unknown. In 1920, the census taker found Joshua Cockburn at his office in Harlem. Both Joshua and Pauline were marked as "B" for Black under color or race for that year. In this census, the colored categories were "For census purposes the term 'black' (B) includes all Negroes of full blood, while the term "mulatto" (Mu) includes all Negroes having some proportion of white blood." It is supposition, but it was likely the census taker presumed Pauline, who probably was not at the office, was as dark as her husband, which she was not. A similar situation may have happened in reverse in 1923. When the Cockburns returned to the United States from another visit to the Bahamas, both of their "race or people" categories were recorded as "British." The best guess was that the agent saw Pauline Cockburn and heard her accent and marked the form accordingly. This marking would make sense if Joshua Cockburn was not there and the clerk relied on Pauline's color and accent and assumed her husband matched her. In 1925, a New York State census enumerator who found the Cockburns at their Harlem home listed her as a black woman. Five years later the US census, which had grouped all people of mixed "white and Negro blood" as "Negro," classified her as Negro.[23]

The indeterminacy of race worked its way into the Cockburn's affidavits. Like the petitioner's affidavits, the Cockburn affidavits were shaped by the lawyers, especially Hays, though their combined efforts also show a bit more about their views than the other side's documents. Pauline's affidavit launched the attack on the meaning of Negro. She claimed that she had "no way of ascertaining what is meant by 'a person of the Negro race and blood'" in the covenant. The phrase was "too vague and uncertain" as the basis for any legal claim. She pointed out that she could just as easily claim to be "a white person with a small colored inheritance." She said she had been advised of the variation of different states in defining Negro and that in New York there was no definition, therefore it was impossible to say whether she and her family fit under the definition. She averred that only her husband was going to live with her, and they were "quiet and respectable members of the community, whose character has never been questioned, and who seek merely to enjoy the advantages of living in a clean suburban community." Their presence would not cause damage to her neighbor's property. Joshua pointed out that "Our home is without question the finest in the immediate vicinity," and he argued that caused the property values "to increase rather than to diminish." He denied the explosive allegations of Held that he was what a later generation would call a "blockbuster" and denied ever meeting the man. He traced the entire dispute to Norman W. Zaubler (sometimes the name appears as Zabler and in the case report as Zambler), head of Certified Home Corporation, a contracting firm. He had sought to build the Cockburns' house, but had not landed the deal. According to Joshua, Zaubler—who owned several properties in the tract—had refused to take the other parcels the Cockburns owned as partial payment for the job. But after the work was commenced by others, he approached Cockburn again with different business proposals, including going into the building of houses in the tract together or having Cockburn buy Zaubler's lots. Cockburn refused and, "shortly after," Zaubler "served the defendant with the summons and complaint" in Ridgway's action.[24]

The affidavits given by Pauline and Joshua Cockburn, besides telling their side of the dispute and raising the racial identity issues, demonstrated that they were not merely respectable, but "persons of refinement:" just the sort of people for whom Edgemont Hills was designed, if color were taken out of the equation. For instance, Pauline made much of attending (and boarding at) various private schools, in Liverpool, London, Leeds, Manchester, and Glasgow, in Great Britain, and her father's career as an inventor, saying that he had created "certain appliances used in cash registers, airplanes, folding beds and other things now commonly in use." Similarly, Joshua Cockburn established his educational attainments, pointing out that he had graduated from Manson's Nautical School in Liverpool and Rugg's Nautical Academy in London, receiving his shipping master's certificate in 1915. Moreover, he detailed his meritorious rise in the British Navy and noted his exemplary war record; he was "cited in dispatches"—meaning that his commanding officer thought he had done something worthy of notice by higher-ups. Joshua wrote under his signature on his affidavit that "We are Christian," making a clear assertion of their respectability.[25]

Hays, when he conceived of his approach to the Cockburn case, probably had Franz Boas in mind as the chief potential expert to explode the racial categories in the covenant. By 1937, Boas was widely regarded as the father of American anthropology and also someone who attacked the popular strains of racism in society: scientific racism, biological conceptions of race, and racial ideologies. At the time he was asked to participate, he had recently retired from Columbia University, where for more than a generation he had been training graduate students who would dominate the field for decades to come. He had become famous with his 1911 book *The Mind of Primitive Man,* and his 1936 introductory text *The Study of Man* was on its way to becoming the leading textbook in the field. But he was not just an expert among experts. Boas was "an eminence: one of the acknowledged greats in anthropology and a public authority on race, inheritance, culture, world affairs, and virtually any subject that a newspaperman, museum director, or average citizen might raise." A sign of his stature was that his photograph was on the cover of the May 11, 1936, issue of *Time* magazine. His attacks on modern racism (Nazi pseudoscientific and American eugenical ideas) probably made him known and very attractive to Hays as an authority. Boas laid out his credentials in his January 25, 1937, affidavit: "Professor Emeritus of Anthropology at Columbia University," two-time "president of the American Anthropological Society," an "honorary or corresponding member of the leading anthropological institutes and societies of Europe and America," and the "author of many books and articles on Physical and Racial Anthropology."[26]

Boas accepted that racial categories existed, but firmly rejected racial hierarchies. Boas roughly separated humanity into three different strains, Caucasian, Mongolian, and Negro. But, as much as he and his students and colleagues relied on the categories, their work showed that physical morphology was shaped much by environment. For instance, in a study Boas showed that head shapes changed between the first and second generation of immigrants to America. Racial types were unstable. There were no pure races; what set them apart was not as significant as the range of differences within the races. "The differences between different types of man are, on the whole, small as compared to the range of variations in each type." If there was no race now, there had been none in the past, and the differences between civilized races and primitive ones were explained not by biological differences but by historical circumstances. There was no path to rise to higher type, and assertions of that sort were cultural assumptions. Boas argued that the common markers considered as signs of inferiority were not necessarily so, pointing out that the thin lips of Caucasians were closer to human's ape ancestors than the fuller lips of Negroes. What mattered most were the individual's abilities, and Boas wanted people to move beyond the misguided "socially cultivated racial" categories that, driven by prejudice, led to discrimination. Boas in his works often took a common idea, said why it was attractive, explored how it might fit a society's expectations, then debunked the idea by drawing on data-rich studies to undermine it.[27]

Franz Boas's affidavit was brief and pointed. "A Negro is a person of full West or Central African racial descent, from those regions where no admixture of foreign blood has occurred. No one else can be accurately designated as a Negro." After summarizing the covenant with its use of both "Negro" and "colored," Boas concluded: "Despite my sixty years as a student of anthropology or perhaps because of them, I cannot tell what is meant by the words of this covenant." Perhaps because he was filing a legal paper, Boas was more restrained than he could be in correspondence or in popular forums. If the covenant had made a claim to racial inferiority or racial antipathy, or any other racialist idea, Boas might have been more expansive. On the other hand, his affidavit offered a small target that would not lead opposing counsel to explore the range of Boas's thought. One can only imagine the effects that could have been produced in court if the trial had examined his idea that the solution to "the Negro problem" was interracial sex and the production of mixed-race children. Boas's definition in the affidavit would be put to use in the brief filed before the hearing on the injunction.[28]

The brief in reply to oppose the temporary injunction against Pauline Cockburn shows that the points that would be made in both the hearing on the temporary injunction and the hearing on the merits were already fully developed at the time of the filing. The affidavits had already been taken, including that of the expert on race. The brief sent earlier by the NAACP has been lost, and it is impossible to know how much the brief in reply derived from its work. Logic suggests that the general constitutional arguments and the public policy arguments made in the brief came from the NAACP, and the arguments focused on New York public policy came from Hays (and others), as the NAACP had not brought any covenant cases in the state. Unusually for a Hays civil liberties brief, his partner, William Abramson, was also listed as an attorney. In addition, Hutson L. Lovell, an African American lawyer with a practice in Brooklyn, is also credited. He was a graduate of Fordham University Law School and had been in practice for more than a decade. The brief was divided into five defenses—the injunction was against New York public policy, was unconstitutional under the 13th and 14th Amendments, restricted the free alienation of property, was vague and indefinite, and was discriminatory and therefore lacking in equity—the lack of a definition of race (or the difficulty of proving determining Negro or other categories) appeared in several defenses.[29]

The Brief in Opposition declared (oddly stating in the negative): "It would be a bold man who would deny that the public policy of New York State opposes discrimination against citizens based on race, creed or color." This assertion rested on the state's civil rights laws guaranteeing equal treatment in public accommodations, transportation, and entertainment. Of course, this argument did not meet the challenge of the public/private distinction, and it was put forth only to "furnish a guide to the attitude which the Court should adopt in a matter involving the right of law-abiding citizens of the State to reside where they wish." To weaken the courts' long recognition of the other restrictive covenants, the Brief in Opposition pointed to the long-established ideas that some uses of property took away neighbors' "enjoyment of their own premises." It contended that the objections that were sustained in cases and by zoning statutes were to "the use itself": such as running a factory or a saloon. Here, the objection was "to the color of the skin of the person" using the premises it was not against the use, but the person. Unless Ridgway was contending that "colored citizens of the State of New York are themselves offensive nuisances," she could not use the "ordinary covenants" as analogous to support her position.[30]

Also, in the section on New York public policy, the Brief in Opposition put to good use the clause commonly included in these covenants allowing residence of colored servants and wandered into constitutional law to take on the reception of restrictive covenant in other jurisdictions. That colored people could inhabit the property only as servants was to "impose the badge of inferiority on colored citizens." The invoking of the phrase from *Plessy* was deliberate—it set up the rejection of the doctrine of separate but equal and contended that this clause added insult to injury and "set at naught" the "equalitarian policy" of the state." Citing *Buchanan v. Warley* as striking down the legislative power to segregate residents, the brief contended that it was "contrary to reason and sound public policy to permit a private group of land owners to impose the very discriminatory restrictions" prohibited to the state legislature. And since the power was forbidden to the state legislature, the courts through their equity power should not support a covenant "designed to reach the prohibited result." If upheld, there was nothing to stop all the landowners of the Township of Greenburgh—or, indeed, of the entire County of Westchester, or State of New York, "from following suit." This argument, stripped of its New York references, was the basic argument of the NAACP in restrictive covenant cases. But it was packaged here with a twist—by segueing to covenants against Negroes being legitimate to protect property values, the brief attacked the idea of the state approving of discrimination as "appalling." It pointed out (sounding themes Hays asserted often) that in "our short history many groups have been subject to prejudice—Irish, Italians, Jews" but such prejudice was "dissipated only when people, through neighborliness and association, come to know and understand other people. Striving toward the ideals of democracy, the State must refuse to pander to racial prejudice, however natural or profitable this may seem to be." With the guidepost of a policy that bars discrimination the brief urged the court to disregard decisions from "jurisdictions having a different and less enlightened public policy." Instead of following the segregating states, the court should follow the lead of the New Jersey courts, which refused to enforce a restrictive covenant against Jews, quoting the decision that said in a *dictum* that such covenants against African Americans were equally void. It concluded by pointing out that "Surely this Court will not feel disposed to assume the responsibility of telling half a million colored citizens of the State that they were mistaken in believing that they would enjoy legal equality within its borders."[31]

The Brief in Opposition's assertion that the covenant was unconstitutional was aimed less at convincing a judge than at making a case for an appeal. It put forth the arguments the NAACP had made in previous cases and would make in future cases. It used *Buchanan v. Warley* to establish the reach of the 14th Amendment over property and distinguished *Corrigan v. Buckley* (which the plaintiff relied upon "with calm assurance" that it settled the issue on their side) on a number of grounds. It asserted that the District of Columbia was not a state and therefore that the 13th and 14th Amendments had not been in play in the *Corrigan* case, as they were here (though in fact the brief did not invoke the 13th, a sign that the brief partially borrowed this from the NAACP's existing brief); that the case left open the question of public policy of a particular state; that New York had policies different from the District of Columbia; and that the assertion that judicial action was not state action in the decision was "mere *dictum*." It argued that the 14th Amendment protected acquiring and enjoying property without discrimination from the state, and that a judicial upholding by a state court would constitute state action. Its length and its connection to the other arguments about the police power of the state (what it had previously called the public policy of the state), the indefiniteness of the covenant, and "the position which should be taken by a court of equity" signaled that Hays and company were ready to seek an appeal.[32]

The Brief in Opposition also invoked the common law property law doctrine of unrestricted alienation of property. This argument would be attractive to a conservative jurist, or indeed any jurist trained in the common law system. However, it was poorly developed and failed to explain why this broad policy had failed to stop states from sanctioning restrictive covenants. Invoking the ancient statute of *Quia Emptores*, it declared, "It has been the unrelenting policy of Anglo-American Law . . . to frown upon the placing of restraints on the alienation of a fee simple." It quickly invoked the leading New York cases but then settled into a broad survey of the topic from many different jurisdictions, with lengthy quotations from cases far outweighing explication of the points. The point was made broadly, but the supporting case law showed that far more often the courts were setting bounds of reasonable limitations on alienation. Also, some of the quotations (for instance, from the California case of *Title Guarantee and Trust Company v. Garrott*) better supported other arguments made in the brief. The *Garrott* case imagined that a restriction on selling to those with "African, Chinese or Japanese ancestors" would become an unreasonable restraint on alienation when those classes became "so enlarged" that the restriction became "unreasonable." This idea allowed the introduction of evidence of the growth of the African American population of

Westchester and argued that public policy should not discriminate against their owning property in the future. While it did not discuss the cases that allowed restrictions despite the impingement on free alienation, it asked the court to dismiss them because they all came from below "the Mason and Dixon line" where there were "strong community tradition[s] of racial discrimination. Happily, the people of New York do not share in that tradition." Those "authorities were ones that "Courts of New York" need not follow. While the section in the brief did not address fully the questions between occupancy and ownership in the case law, it sought to secure Cockburn's right to occupy her property by quoting the language of *Buchanan v. Warley* that "occupancy is an incident" of the buying of real estate. It urged the court to "refuse to adopt the un-real distinction between covenants restraining alienation to negroes and covenants restraining the occupancy of premises by them." The argument on occupancy was aimed at averting a hollow victory where the restrictive covenants against purchase were struck down but the African American buyers were barred by occupancy covenants from dwelling in their property. But supporting this point, it used an example that did not fit the facts of the case. It asserted that an "individual of modest means" purchased "a small piece of property" in a "residential neighborhood" to reside there himself. The Cockburns were not of modest means, and there was sufficient evidence that they may have sought to build income housing in the neighborhood and did not just mean to reside there.[33]

The ideas of the experts worked their way into the brief in support of the argument that the covenant was a restriction on the rights of property holders to free alienation. While Franz Boas was the named expert cited in the brief, Professor Otto Klineberg would testify at the subsequent trial. A Boas disciple (he dedicated his 1935 book *Race Differences* to Boas), Klineberg was a social psychologist at Columbia University. His affidavit and testimony discussed the effect of education on the African American migrants to Harlem. His and others' studies had shown that African Americans living in the North did better on so-called intelligence tests than those living in the South. Racists explained that by asserting that the brightest African Americans moved North. Klineberg studied more than three thousand Harlem schoolchildren for a period of years, and he found that the lowest-scoring children were those who had arrived recently from the South. The relationship was "close" between length of residence in New York and better performance on intelligence tests. Further, the brief cited census data showing that in the decade ending in 1930, the African

American population of Westchester had grown to 4.4 percent of the total population and that "the county's colored inhabitants" showed a marked decrease in the percentage of illiteracy among African Americans over ten years old, falling from 4.7 percent to 3.4 percent. Though it did not say it directly, this bald statement asked the judge to draw the conclusion that a restrictive covenant would keep out better-educated African Americans or limit the opportunities to rise for those already there. It did say that the restrictive racial covenants' effects grew every year, as "the class against which it is directed is increasing in size."[34]

The argument on the impossibility of determining race was developed in the Brief in Opposition under the defense of the covenant being vague and indefinite, which would make it unenforceable and void. This section of the brief was, without a doubt, Hays's construction. It reproduced reasoning he had used in other contexts, which he would highlight when remembering the case. Leading off with the language of the covenant that it prohibited "purchase, lease or occupancy by 'negroes or any person or persons of the negro race or blood,'" the brief tossed up Boas's affidavit to question "Who is a negro? According to Dr. Franz Boas, whom there is no greater authority on anthropology, 'a negro is a person of full West or Central African racial descent from those regions where no admixture of foreign blood has occurred. No one else can accurately be designated a negro.'" As New York lacked a definition of Negro and other categories, Hays visited the variety of definitions from other jurisdictions—whose "lack of uniformity" was "striking." Dipping into well-known racial categories of "blood mixing" used in some states, the brief defined the half-blood mulatto, the quarter-admixture quadroon, and eighth-mix octoroon, admitting "we do not think that language has gone far enough even among those who are racially minded to give a noun for those who have less admixture." Pursuing the theme of indefiniteness, the brief asserted that if it meant to apply the prohibition to those groups, "it should have said so." Also, the phrase "the negro blood," if meant to cover such groups, was hopelessly vague, as it did not specify how much blood. It added no "certainty, as in the course of centuries, most of us have acquired an admixture of various kinds of blood." And how was the level to be determined? Adopting the rule of Virginia and Arkansas that "person of color included all those who have a visible and distinct admixture of African blood" begged the question, as "no admixture of blood is visible to the eye, and certainly, no layman should be obliged to guess what admixture any one has—even himself." Here the brief lost its focus of persuading a judge, as many white Americans then would have been profoundly upset to think of themselves as having Negro blood.[35]

Hays took on the "everybody knows a negro when he sees one" argument that he was sure would be the response to the contention that it was hard to determine who was a Negro. He attacked that argument with an analogy: "In Germany, where they apply principles of the kind sought to be enforced here, there is a general assumption that everyone knows a Jew." But really, such views were "held only by men who are very ignorant or very prejudiced, or both. No scientist shared them." And if the Cockburns self-identified their African heritage (which of course Hays knew that they had in the past), that only meant that they had pride. "From time immemorial, people descended, even in small part, from those of an oppressed or minority group, have taken the label or badge—not in shame but in pride—of the despised ancestor." It was "a perversity of mankind" that should "be honored." Thus, "the label means little—and often nothing—from a scientific racial point of view."[36]

Hays turned to the so-called markers of race: skin color, hair color, hair texture, the assertion that Negro and white fingernails were different. He demolished each. Pauline Cockburn was, "we venture to say, whiter than fifty per cent of those who are generally recognized as Caucasians." Josiah was "dark, but Black? No." And if they had children, of different hues, from white through "soft brown" to a "darker hue," which would "be denied the home?" Negroes could have blond hair, and "Scientific discoveries have taken kinks out of the hair of both whites and 'negroes.'" As to fingernails, that was refuted by the oft-told tale of Walter White, while passing for white to investigate racial violence, being informed by a stranger that he could always tell by the fingernails, yet this man could not see that White was a Negro, as his "fingernails differed from those of a colored man!"[37]

Hays asserted that determining race was difficult. Ironically he noted, "No one but a German Nazi can be certain about a race." And in the "melting pot of America" to carry on such an "endeavor to classify people of those with whom they associate" under legal penalty would be "unjust" and "contrary to democratic tradition." In a fanciful reach, Hays insisted that it would require Cockburn "to determine at her peril, every time that she invited a person to come on the premises, whether that person was or was not within the group excluded by the language of covenant." Taking away visitors, the covenant applied to purchasers, and its language was too vague to be implemented. New York case law demanded that injunctions be clear, and that applied to covenants as well. Beyond that, since restraints on alienations should be construed in an unrestrictive manner—unless someone was clearly within the specified categories, then it should not be applied. Rewriting the covenant to list "negroes, mulattoes, quadroons, octoroons, or descendants of the above, or anyone who is a descendant of any one who had negro blood" might make it specific enough to be enforced. But this is not such a covenant." One "drawn in that fashion we would respectfully suggest that an anthropologist be retained to assist" the court and landowner in determining race. If the court, were to decide, or let the plaintiff decide, they would "take the responsibility of deciding who is a negro." If they chose color as a determinate, that decision would strike at "Spaniards, Italians and all people of Southern climes. Facial and other characteristic lead to further perplexities." The indefiniteness of the covenant prompted this and could be avoided only by refusing to enforce it against the defendant.[38]

Similarly, Hays contributed the final argument in the Brief in Opposition, which attempted to show the absurdity of restrictive covenants and threw in various points that a judge might seize upon to avoid issuing the injunction even if he thought it justified at law. If construed to cover those with acknowledged African blood, it would exclude 10 percent of the nation's population. If Catholics and Jews were added, it would add another 20 percent. The list of the three groups was no accident, representing as they did the groups of people who were gaining political power in New York State. Conversely, if this covenant was legitimate, so would be one that would exclude Caucasian race or blood. Such limiting of the market was contrary to public policy, which favored competition. Hays stretched the circumstances to clothing, because after all, like housing, it was a necessity. He asserted no one would find a covenant to restrict buyers of clothing valid. Restrictions on the plaintiff's right to use her property would destroy the right to acquire it. It would "create a system of caste." Putting distinctions in the law "between white and black, Catholic and Protestant, Jew and non-Jew will arouse hatreds and passions which would shatter all that is noble and exalted in American institutions." Hays then enunciated a point he had made many times before in speeches, in articles, and in activism: "So long as people are equal before the law, and those who would discriminate are legally barred from effectuating their purpose, no American minority has reason to fear bigotry and prejudice." Free from legal discrimination, minorities could make their "own social fight." To go the other way would open the door to further divisions, the creations of the equivalent of the "Irish Pale," created by the British, the Russian "Jewish Pale," and policies like "the more recent familiar laws of Germany." Thus, if the court considered "the comparative burdens and benefits," it would see that it was "asked to deprive one woman of her home to satisfy the prejudice of another woman who lives some distance away." Ridgway "lives on the extreme end of this development—lot #18 of Block D." Her adjacent property was not part of the development and probably did not have "a similar covenant." Since she had not protected herself from the other side, the court should not enforce the covenant, as "the hardship imposed on the defendant would not benefit the plaintiff if negroes purchased property adjacent" to her property on the other side. "In a complicated civilization we must all take the chance that we may not like our neighbors." Yet the Cockburns showed no signs of being bad neighbors. Moreover, Ridgway had acted too late; she had not invoked it when Pauline Cockburn bought the property, but only after she built the house. The rule of laches (saying that those seeking equitable relief should act as soon as possible) blocked the issuing of the injunction. Indeed, Hays contended that the threat of the injunction was "a club to persuade Cockburn to engage in real estate activities" with the man who had served the summons and had earlier tried to do business with Joshua Cockburn. Ironically, that man had asked Joshua Cockburn to buy more property in the tract, in the very neighborhood he wanted to exclude him and his wife from.[39]

In the brief's conclusion, Hays presented a list of options for the court to refuse to issue the injunction. It also declared a preference for which of those it would like to see prevail in the case. And oddly, given how much effort went into the question of "indefiniteness" and the strength of some of the "technical rules relating to alienation of property," Hays wrote they would prefer a decision based on public policy because the restrictive covenant was "contrary to our American institutions" and with "the traditions and ideals of the people" of New York.[40]

The parties presented their arguments on February 1, 1937, at the hearing on the temporary injunction in the Westchester County courthouse before Judge Raymond E. Aldrich. Morris Orenstein, of nearby Mount Vernon, argued the case for Marion Ridgway. Like the developer Max Held, Orenstein was Jewish, which underscores a reality about restrictive covenants—that Jews were found on both sides of the issue. He asserted that Pauline Cockburn was in violation of the covenant because of her and her husband's race. To end the damage to Ridgway's property, the

Cockburns should be blocked from occupying their house. Hays focused on two issues, the difficulty of ascertaining any person's race and that the Cockburns were an asset, not a liability, to the neighborhood. Hays asserted that "No one but the Nazis of Germany can be certain about a race" and that "Certainly, in the melting pot of America, an endeavor to classify people—compelling them to determine the race of those with whom they associate, would not only be unjust but so contrary to democratic tradition that it is unthinkable." Admitting some "Negro blood" in both Cockburns, Hays also asserted that Pauline "was as white as I am." He pointed out the injustice of determining race by color by running his example of what would happen if the couple had children of different hues because it "would require the black children to move from the house" while the lighter ones would be allowed to stay. Hays also pointed out that, as reported in the *New York Post*, the Cockburns were "superior to their neighbors in intelligence, background and social graces." The point was made that if blocked from living in their home, the Cockburns would suffer real economic loss. This contention came through in the press, as nearly every article pointedly mentioned the value of $20,000 for the Cockburns' house. The press coverage in both the mainstream and African American press followed the lead of the defense and made the case about the question "What is a Negro?" Because of that question, the mainstream press recorded the markers of race color, leavened with social descriptors implying high status. The *Daily News* described Pauline Cockburn as an "extremely light skinned young matron who admittedly is of partial negro blood." Joshua Cockburn was described as her "dark-skinned" husband who was a realtor and "wartime commander of British navy ships." After arguments, the Judge said he would not decide the case immediately. While most papers held off making a prediction, the *Scarsdale Inquirer*, after it reported that the defense admitted both Cockburns had colored, blood forecast that the court would grant the injunction; in contrast, the *Afro-American* saw that Hays had challenged the legality of restrictive covenants and more importantly raised the question of their practical functioning: "whether white neighbors have the right to judge the amount or lack of 'Negro' blood in their fellow neighbors."[41]

Ten days later, Aldrich decided not to issue the temporary injunction. On April 10, 1937, he held that granting the injunction before the facts were established through trial on the merits would work a harm on the Cockburns, as they had invested heavily in their property. The judge said granting the injunction without a full hearing might be "a very gross injustice" to the Cockburns. A date for the hearing was not set. The *Amsterdam News* in reporting the story assumed that Aldrich would try the case and in the course of it would settle "the novel legal question asked by defense Attorney Arthur Garfield Hays, 'what is a Negro?' "[42]

After the preliminary hearing's decision was known, Hays wrote to Walter White of the NAACP to apprise him of his thinking on racial identity in the case. Putting the issue in personal terms, he declared, "you people call yourselves Negroes just like a lot of us call ourselves Jews, who come from a certain race and who belong to a minority group." He saw this as good, declaring that Jews and African Americans "are not willing to desert an oppressed group even if we have the opportunity to do it." On sticking by your group, he had made a similar point when recounting Darrow's confusion over race at the meeting when the NAACP recruited him for the Sweet case. But that was separate from the issue of pure race being a fiction. "As I said in my argument only Nazis know what pure races are. Nobody knows what a Negro is, even Negroes themselves, any more than anyone knows what a Jew is." The contrast to the Nazis was not just philosophical. Hays wanted the idea applied: "I'd like to be helpful in getting courts to do away with artificial distinctions among people of the human race." His choice of policymaking body was focused on the courts—either because he had little faith in legislatures and administrative agencies or because the courts were responsible for the recognition of racial categories in restrictive covenant cases. He also invoked a grand conception of humanity, "the people of the human race," that harkened back to the one blood theory of the era before the rise of scientific racism and also accorded with the conclusions of modern, Boas-shaped, anthropology.[43]

As part of its regular publicity efforts, the NAACP emphasized that the case relied on racial definition by releasing Hays's letter to the African American press. Between the denial of the temporary injunction and the trial, the heart of the letter later appeared in the *Amsterdam News*. The paper noted that Hays was a "Noted White Liberal" and that he had raised this question "What is a Negro?" so effectively in "the now famous Cockburn case in White Plains." Parts of the letter probably resonated with the intended audience. For instance, on the question of claiming identity, the readers of the *Amsterdam News* knew that Walter White could have easily passed for white, and had he chosen he could have easily downplayed his heritage. They would appreciate the part about sticking with your own group out of pride. And the hoped-for outcome was appealing. Beating back scientific racism would be a real gain. More was at stake than whether some relatively well-off people could live in a house in a tony neighborhood. That was what Hays and the NAACP wanted others to see.[44]

And they did. In particular, the *Pittsburgh Courier* reveled in the racial categorization challenges posed by Hays's argument. To the *Courier*, the case was one of a constellation of recent legal incidents pushing back against the color line. In a picture-rich story (one showing the outside of the Cockburn house and another of the eminently respectable Cockburns with their cat in their home), the paper declared the case was placing the court "on the griddle so to speak" by asking "Just what was a Negro?" As the headline on page one declaimed, the question was a "teaser." Noting that law forbade racial housing segregation, it said the case was asking for a ruling on the legality of restrictive covenants and more. "The grizzled sea captain has asked" his question "in the hope some light may be shed on the nature of the aversion which the whites profess to rubbing elbows with Negro residents." The paper linked the reaction of the whites of "the swanky residential section of Edgemont Hills" to that of whites when African American investors sought to buy the nearby "Sun Rise Golf and Country Club," which raised "a howl." It also linked the case to a recent effort by Harlem activists to stop the famous Cotton Club from excluding African American customers. The linkages in themselves made the point—the color line was pervasive and corrosive. The editorial that accompanied the news story took Boas and Klineberg at their word of being "leading anthropologists, who certainly ought to know" that given their definitions, there were few Negroes in the nation. Most people called that were "mulattoes of various colors," mixtures of various races. Classifying all as "Negro" had "produced all sorts of absurd situations." But it was done to "perpetuate the slave status for the descendants of slaves." Thus, the case had the potential to be important, and if it went against Cockburn, that was of little account. "The status" of "anyone whom white people choose to term" Negro "will not be materially altered." After all, that category was capacious, including "almost everybody with remotest Negro ancestry." If it was decided differently and they followed the Boas definition, "then the whole structure of American life is undermined." As for the term "colored," that was equally "questionable." It meant "precisely nothing, since there are no colorLESS people." Thus, the test was a step in the direction of taking the country to "the place . . . where there are just Americans."[45]

The African American press pushed the respectability angle of the case and the mainstream press picked it up. The couple's respectability was displayed in photographs of them, a constant reiteration of the value of the home by printing either its construction cost or a picture of it and mentioning that Joshua Cockburn was a captain. For an African American to have risen to such a rank was extraordinary in the United States. The price that the Cockburns said they paid for constructing the house, $20,000, was constantly mentioned in stories of the case. *Life* published a story that captured the racial and respectability points. Along with a photograph of their home, there was one of the couple—seated on a stuffed chair (she was settled on the seat, he was perched on an arm)—probably in their home. They are dressed in elegant, tasteful clothes. Her fine pumps are matched by his shoes with spats, her stocking-clad legs (an expensive piece of apparel in the pre-nylon period) matched by his neatly pressed, cuffless pants. His high collar and watch chain, her matching suit and finely coifed hair signal their prosperity. Printed in the "Private Lives" section under his name, the blurb accompanying the photographs declared incorrectly that he "was born in England, made enough money in Harlem real estate to build a $20,000 home in Westchester. This "outraged a neighbor: who invoked the covenant"—which the magazine implied was an old leftover from the past, as it had been "laid down by the settlers of Edgemont Hills." It "forbade any Negro from owning a home in the community." In fighting the injunction, "the Cockburns' counsel quoted the great anthropologist Franz Boas as saying that no one was Negro whose pure African blood had been tainted by an admixture of foreign blood. The court looked at Mr. Cockburn's black and dignified face, at Mrs. Cockburn's lighter skin, and took the case under advisement."[46]

Probably the most consequential development in case came with the seating of a new judge for the trial. Lee Parsons Davis had just been elevated to the bench after a long career in the Westchester courts, and *Ridgway v. Cockburn* would be his first trial as a judge. Davis was Hays's contemporary, graduating from Columbia University Law School in 1903. After a few years in private practice in New York City, he moved to Westchester and became a fixture of the courts there, first in private practice, then as assistant and district attorney, and again in private practice. In 1925, while Hays was defending the Sweets in Detroit, Davis was representing Alice Jones Rhinelander in a case that turned on her racial identity. The wealthy Leonard Rhinelander had married the relatively poor Alice Jones, who was from a mixed-race family and sought annulment of the marriage on the grounds that Jones had deceived him about her race. Davis denied that she could have deceived him about her race because of the visibility of race. When he announced this line of defense, he explained to the jury, "suppose I told you that a clear Chinaman was an American Indian or of pure white American blood, I represented that to you; well, that would be false, but you would not believe it. Of course, you would have to be blind, you see, to believe that." Thus, Davis argued, if Alice presented herself to Leonard as white, he could not have believed her. To prove this point, he had her show her unclothed torso and legs, to the jury: Her bodily appearance proved her race. Davis was not blind to race prejudice, he admitted, she was "branded openly now" as colored, and he had to be aware, as it resulted in some restaurants refusing to serve her during the trial. Given his views about race, Davis was unlikely to be swayed by Hays's contentions.[47]

The trial before Judge Davis focused on two issues: the question of determining race and the allegation that the injunction was prompted by malice. To make obvious the difficulty of determining race, Hays and the NAACP arranged that "on the day of the trial I had present in court for illustrative purposes a large number of light Negroes and equal number of dark Italians." The "light Negroes" had been gathered by the NAACP. A month before the trial, Roy Wilkins "wrote to a few New Yorkers to ask if they would act as 'exhibits' during the trial, explaining Hays 'would like to have in the court room a few 'white Negroes and a few 'dark white people.'" Where the Italians came from is unknown, but Hays's firm had a number of regular clients who were Italian or Italian-American. "My intention was to show that the color alone could not be the determining factor" in determining race and thus invoking the covenant. Prior to the trial, the *Amsterdam News* made the dealings with Zaubler central to the case. Its front-page article, drawing on the material in the brief and clearly other material that had been leaked, asserted that "behind Mrs. Ridgway's legal move there seems to be a white contractor." The paper declared he was "peeved because he tried but did not get the contract to erect the Cockburns' $20,000 modern eight-room home in this landscaped haven of space and flowers." Ridgway was just a stalking horse for Zaubler and acted only because he prompted her. The two foci were fundamentally different; the first aimed at a policy statement but the second was pointed at merely winning the case for the Cockburns on a technicality that the plaintiff did not have "clean hands" and therefore could not seek the equitable relief of an injunction.[48]

The two-day trial began on March 22, 1937, with the plaintiff presenting a case far simpler than the defense's. Orenstein, Ridgway's lawyer, established that there was a restrictive covenant. Ridgway testified that she owned a smaller but still substantial house in the development, which she had built in 1933, as she desired to live in a neighborhood that was "highly restricted." And the connecting piece in the argument was the race of Pauline Cockburn and her husband. The assumption, agreed to by all, was that Joshua would live in the house. As they had "Negro" blood, they could not occupy the premises under the covenant (except as colored servants), and they should be enjoined from doing so. However, Ridgway admitted that she had not brought the suit "until several months after she learned the Cockburns were building their home." That fact left open the question of whether she was acting out of malice, as action before would have spared the Cockburns considerable expense and preserved the neighborhood the way she wanted it. Hays argued, in his opening statement, that the covenant was unconstitutional, violated public policy, and (the point he meant to prove) that its terms were vague and did not "specify what constitutes a Negro."[49]

The race part of the Cockburns' argument developed through the testimony of both Joshua and Pauline as well as Klineberg experienced pushback from Judge Davis. Joshua Cockburn testified that he had "been called a 'man of color,'" and on occasion a "Negro." But he did not know what his race was. Judge Davis, according to Hays, "interjected, 'Don't you think he is trifling with the court Mr. Hays?' My answer was that I had discussed the question" with my clients and told them "A Negro was defined as a person with full African blood, and that I had advised the Captain to answer" the way he had, because he did not know. Pauline testified as to her mixed heritage and also averred she did not know her race. Upon questioning in cross-examination that she never denied she had "some 'colored blood.'" And in answer to a direct question from Davis, said, "she 'imagined' she was an octoroon." While the issues of how to determine race and the difficulties of doing so dominated the hearing, the mainstream press did not apparently notice Hays's stunt about the audience. Instead, for example, the *New York Times* reported "Residents of Fort Hill Road section of Greenburgh crowded into the court room." Maybe some of those people whom the reporter assumed were residents were "light Negroes" from New York City. The basis of this line of argument was, of course, the anthropological understanding of race, expounded to the court by Klineberg. He testified that "a Negro is a person of unmixed African descent." He defined "mulatto, quadroon and octoroon" as essentially admixtures of "blood" reflecting the contribution of African ancestry. He asserted that "Only 30 percent of the persons considered to be Negroes in the United States actually are true Negroes," and more importantly "skin color and other physical features" were "not conclusive evidence" of race. At the heart of the case, in his professional opinion, was that "Mrs. Cockburn is definitely not a Negro" and of Mr. Cockburn he added, "no anthropologist could definitely assign him to the Negro race."[50]

Negro or not, Joshua Cockburn was a "realty operator," or one who managed real estate deals. That tempted Zaubler to do business with him, which, when that effort failed, Hays said, prompted the suit. Because Ridgway had long delayed in seeking an injunction and Zaubler had delivered one of the summons for injunction, Hays argued, according to a local newspaper report, that "he would prove that it was Zaubler who inspired the ouster proceedings out of pique in failing to get the building contract and also in failing to get Cockburn to join with him financially in another real estate development he had in mind." But Hays's only evidence was Joshua Cockburn's testimony. Zaubler from the stand denied the accusation that he conspired with Ridgway to force the Cockburns to purchase additional property. According to the *Daily Argus*, Zaubler admitted that, "on learning the Cockburns intended to build on the property . . . , he negotiated to get the building contract, but failed." When pressed in cross-examination by Hays, Zaubler reported that Cockburn "threatened to put guns around his place if his neighbors persisted in trying to force him out." That dramatic statement of course invoked the memory of the Sweets in Detroit and made Cockburn into what people who believed in the color line feared: an aggressive rebel against the racial order.[51]

Judge Davis's decision and opinion in *Ridgway v. Cockburn*, issued on June 3, 1937, upheld the covenant and granted the injunction request to block the Cockburns from residing in their house. Davis thus rejected every one of the defense's points and steadfastly refused to admit that the case was anything but a contractual dispute governed by regular common law. Davis established the existence of a covenant prohibiting conveyance or occupancy of the property by "persons of the negro race or blood," with the exception of "colored servants." He also settled the Cockburns' racial identities. Pauline he wrote, "considers herself an octoroon" and "concedes that she belongs to the 'the colored race.'" Moreover, in the past she "called herself a 'colored person.'" As to Joshua, he was "concededly a 'colored man.'" Davis continued that the evidence indicated "that he has at least three-quarters negro blood. And then in a telling phrase as to how he saw racial categories (and ignoring the evidence of Klineberg), he declared, "In every outward appearance he is what would be called, in common speech, a negro." After an aside saying that they were "an entirely respectable couple," Davis dismissed Hays's argument that Negro should be defined scientifically and was limited to those with "unmixed African negro blood." Falling back on the rule that language in a contract should "be given its natural and ordinary meaning" and that the "intentions of the parties" was to control interpretation of contracts, Davis declared that the "word 'negroes' was used synonymously with the term 'colored persons.'" This conclusion was supported by the "internal evidence" of the covenant with its exception for colored servants. Since both husband and wife fell within the class of "negro, or a person of negro race or blood" of the covenant, it prohibited their occupancy of the property.[52]

Davis found that Ridgway had standing to seek the injunction. At trial it was apparently raised that Ridgway had no standing because the covenant was not part of a general scheme. This argument rested on the fact that only fifteen of the eighteen lots had deeds with the Negro covenant. But the testimony for Ridgway showed that the lapse of these three missing covenants was a clerical error and other variations between the deeds such as mandating an attached or separate automobile garage were determined by the size of the lots. Along the same lines, Davis made it clear that Cockburn was not a wronged party. "She was fully aware of the covenant. She consulted counsel, and was advised that the neighboring owners would be helpless to enforce it." She relied "upon this advice" to buy the land and "erect upon it a house of substantial value." In effect, "she defied the other owners to compel observance of the covenant." Thus, "she assumed deliberately the risk of being deprived of the use of the property if her opinion of the law was a mistaken one.[53]

No defense argument prevailed. Davis rejected the argument that the public policy of New York forbade discrimination housing based on the analogous statutory and case law on public accommodation. He asserted that "the public policy of the state must be found somewhere in the body of its law." And he concluded, "I know of no public policy which bars any group of individuals from contracting among themselves for the exclusive enjoyment of their own private property." The constitutional arguments of violation of the 14th Amendment received equally curt treatment. Davis cited *Corrigan v. Buckley* and declared, "It is sufficient to say that the United States Supreme Court has held that a covenant of this precise character violated no constitutional right. He rejected the indefiniteness argument, which rested on the idea of the difficulty of determining race and lack of specificity of how much negro blood made a Negro, by invoking the common understanding of "race" and his determination that the Cockburns were negroes. For the argument on the covenant being unreasonable and lacking in equity, Davis asserted that Cockburn had "voluntarily" assumed "an obligation" to obey a contract, while Ridgway only sought "merely to possess her property on the terms agreed." As to the defense of good faith, Davis denied the argument that Ridgway had first breached the property covenant limitation on structure height and that she was prompted into action by Zaubler. Davis also rejected the idea raised in trial that because Ridgway did not act when Cockburn bought the property, but waited until after the house was built, her action could be adverted by injunctive means.[54]

Davis took great pains to make this case seem an ordinary one of private contract rights—almost erasing that it was about race, or at least casting it as falling within the bounds of separate but equal. He wanted it known, "in view of certain arguments" that were "advanced by counsel," that "the issues in the case do not warrant the discussion of abstract social theories." This was a case of "contractual duty." As the contract was "valid . . . its wisdom is not a question for the court." He continued, "Under similar circumstances the remedy granted here is equally available to all litigants, regardless of race, or color." The equality of remedy, of course, rested on African Americans developing areas or creating community agreements with restrictive covenants against sale to whites. [55]

While the mainstream press reported the judge's decision by showing how it met Hays's arguments for the Cockburns, the African American press did more in exploring the decision's implications. *The Pittsburgh Courier*, in its subhead over an article on the decision, declared, "Ruling of Court Is of Vast Import to Negro Citizens In Cities Where Private Agreements Barring Negro Residents Prevail." Since the decision invited other places to duplicate the use of such covenants, the paper declared it was "inimical to the interest of Negroes everywhere." Mincing no words as to the root of the ruling, the paper said it was "patently a bow to local prejudice, inasmuch such covenants were held invalid by another State's court." It portrayed Davis's statement that this ruling was "no reflection whatever on the character of either the defendant or her husband" as an empty sop to their feelings. In an editorial a week later, the *Courier* reviewed the history leading to and from "the familiar Cockburn case," remarking that "these restrictive covenants are everywhere." Their increasing number and range would soon mean that African Americans would "find less and less desirous places in which to live." It hoped for a reversal on appeal. *The Afro-American,* the influential African American newspaper from Baltimore, also speculated that the Cockburns would appeal their case.[56]

As the case was making headlines, Marcus Garvey commented on it. The headline of his story in his paper, *The Black Man,* captured his view of Joshua Cockburn's struggle to occupy the property in Westchester and the assistance that the NAACP gave him: "How Foolish." At first hiding the subject of his editorial, Garvey summarized the case. "In one of the exclusive residential suburbs of New York an injunction was filed against a Negro the other day to prevent him from living in the district among white people, after he had purchased property there." Garvey asserted this "Negro . . . pleaded instead of his civil rights as an American Citizen to live where he likes, that black as he was, and colored as his wife was, they were not Negroes." On that point on the Judge "came to a quick judgment just by looking at the man and the woman, and declared undoubtedly one was of full Negro blood and the other had Negro blood in her veins." Garvey was sure that this man backed by the "financial resources" of the NAACP would appeal. He then revealed that Cockburn was "the Negro" and "Captain of the first ship of the Black Star Line—a man who professed then to be a true and proud Negro." He asserted that Cockburn "was then poor when he came to the Black Star Line. After he left the Black Star Line he became rich and a Real Estate Operator." At the same time, "the President of the Black Star Line had to spend two years and ten months in a Federal Prison for what others did to the Black Star Line." He blamed Cockburn along with others for its failures. Without their actions, it would have been "one of the most successful Steamship Companies to-day and the black race would be proud of themselves." But the rich Captain Cockburn was "trying to lose himself among the white people of New York. It is surprising that he is no longer a Negro. We never knew a person could change his race and skin so easily, but the peculiar anomaly is that the National Association for the Advancement of Coloured People is to collect money from Negroes to prove that a Negro is not a Negro."[57]

Garvey supporters in the United States pushed this race pride point. E. E. Berryman, a member of the Universal Negro Improvement Association in New Orleans, wrote to the *Pittsburgh Courier* to echo Garvey's views. She found the contentions of Cockburn to be "nonsense." Identifying Cockburn as "once a part of the Black Star Line Corporation" and now "considered as a poor truehearted race pride man," she claimed he had become, after gaining riches, something else. "Because he could not buy a piece of property in a white vicinity, he is no longer a Negro. Then what is he? Strange isn't it?" She continued, "Also the great N.A.A.C.P. is backing him up" in trying to prove he was not a Negro. She chided Cockburn to remember "what the scripture says about the Ethiopians skins and the Leopard's spots. If you ever happen to lose your money, the Negro race will forever brand you as a traitor."[58]

The Garveyites were right to recognize that Cockburn and the larger issue of restrictive covenants was a cause of the NAACP. But in taking on this cause, as in some others, the NAACP was merely riding the crest of demand for action from many African Americans. Reporting on a meeting in Chicago of "leading Southsiders" with national NAACP leadership, *The Pittsburgh Courier* explained that African Americans had to "organize to wipe out nation-wide restricted areas." Noting that the trade paper of a realty group was promoting model restrictive covenant language based on recent court decisions (including the *Cockburn* case), the paper advised that African Americans need to plan coordinated action. And indeed, with increasing tempo as time went on, that is what the NAACP did.[59]

Whatever the plans of the NAACP and other activists, an appeal of the Cockburn decision never happened. In 1942 Hays wrote, "My opponent knew that I would take an appeal from the adverse decision and that, if I were sustained on appeal, the result would be an invitation to colored people to flock to the section involved." With this consideration in mind, Hays reported, "our opponents never entered an order on the judge's decision, and the Cockburns are still living in Scarsdale." Exactly what grounds the two sets of opposing counsel thought were ripe for reversal were not stated. Nor can the grounds be inferred with any certainty from what Hays wrote. At least two lines of thinking would open the area to colored people. First, if the ruling was overturned on the grounds that there had not been a "uniform" plan of development as revealed by the lack of restrictive covenants on all lots or, second, if it was reversed on equity grounds that Ridgway did not come to the dispute with clean hands. If it was reversed on the larger grounds that restrictive covenants were against New York policy, that ruling would apply statewide and to all racial restrictive covenants no matter how worded. If it was overruled on the grounds of indefiniteness, then it would apply statewide but only to covenants with similar wording. In such cases, the first test might be in the area. Whatever the reason, the Cockburns stayed.[60]

Whether neighbors reconciled themselves to the presence of prominent people of color for the time that the Cockburns remained in the community is unknown. They could not overlook that Joshua was there, as he placed prominently in his yard a large ship's anchor. Joshua remained an important figure in Harlem. For instance, he was chosen to be vice chair for the committee to plan and develop the exhibits that would explore "a pageant of American Negro history" post-emancipation for the coming World's Fair. In 1939, Pauline hit a pedestrian with her car in Manhattan, and given her recent fame, the incident (which was ruled an accident with no one at fault) caught the attention of the press. The couple were listed by the United States Census for 1940 as living at the address in Greenburgh and being "Negroes." *The New York Age* in 1941 noted that they had hosted another African American society couple at their Westchester home. In 1942, Joshua died. Four years later the town sought to acquire a corner of the property to construct a sewer line. Pauline Cockburn asked for a high price for the parcel and after some back and forth, the town secured an easement. In 1949, the town took the Cockburn home for nonpayment of taxes.[61]

A few years after the culmination of the case, Hays reflected in his book *City Lawyer* upon its importance. The passage is short and part of a chapter titled "Pictures on my Office Wall," where he pretended he was talking to a visitor about cases that he had memorialized through photographs or documents on the wall of his office. Hays did not mention the role of the NAACP in his recounting of the case, only the matter of determining race. In his account, he re-created his first encounter with the woman "who had originally come from the Bahamas." Her mentioning of a restrictive covenant caught him by surprise, "and led me to ask Mrs. Cockburn if she were a Negress, for she was of a light color." When she said yes, Hays inquired as to how she knew, and she replied, "she had always taken this for granted, and had always associated with colored people." This reply prompted Hays to reflect on the Southern states' definitions about certain percentage of blood making someone a Negro but that there was "no such definition" in New York law. "It occurred to me that the question of whether or not one is a Negro depends upon scientific definition." To Hays, that scientific definition came from Professor Franz Boas, the distinguished anthropologist of Columbia University," whose affidavit declared "that a Negro technically was a 'human being with one hundred per cent African blood.'" Then he continued that to enforce the covenant, "the court could not grant an injunction unless it was able to define just what a Negro was." Moreover, if an injunction was issued, it would prohibit "my clients" from living "in their own home."[62]

That personalization of the issue on how to determine someone's race continued as he treated the trial proper. "On the day of the trial I had present in court for illustrative purpose a large number of light Negroes and equal number of dark Italians." This was a living exhibit meant "to show that color alone could not be the determining factor." He placed Pauline Cockburn on the stand and when asked whether she was a Negress, she answered, "I don't know; it depends upon what you mean by the term." Hays pointed out that he had schooled both Cockburns on the point. Hays made the point even stronger by detailing the triangular exchange among him, Joshua Cockburn, and Judge Davis, where Davis asserted that Cockburn was "trifling with the court" by saying he did not know his race. This retelling was Hays's way of again making an important point to a larger audience, as he had not convinced the judge. Hays concluded the story by saying, "I did not succeed in my contention but I did win the case," relating that he prevailed because of his opponent's fear of losing an appeal, and the opening of "the section" to "colored people" kept the plaintiffs from enforcing the judge's decision. His noting the Cockburns were "still living in Scarsdale" stood in stark contrast to his account in his earlier book of the Sweets' house in Detroit standing empty.[63]

Hays's version was tailored to pound home his point about how hard it was to know race. In his account, he slid over anything problematic about the Cockburns. For instance, he did not say that they were experienced real estate investors, so likely to be well aware of restrictive covenants. Hays recalled Pauline learning that her property "was covered by a covenant prohibition sale to Negroes or tenancy by Negroes" after "she had built a beautiful and expensive house in Scarsdale." Similarly, Captain Cockburn's service for the British naval forces was highlighted, but his role in the Star Line and his testimony against Garvey were not mentioned. They were, to Hays, "cultured, pleasant people." He streamlined the story too, dropping Klineberg's testimony and focusing only on the Boas affidavit, which he also simplified: omitting the geographic African regions of Boas's statement and making it even more limiting. Nor did he mention that the very question "what is a Negro" was something that he was willing to let fall by the wayside if the court ruled that New York public policy prohibited such covenants. Most interestingly, it was in this vignette that Hays retold the story of the recruitment of Clarence Darrow for the Sweet case and his confusion over the race of Walter White, Arthur Spingarn, and Charles Studin. In Hays's view, the events separated by a dozen years were linked, because it was in that conversation of 1925 that the germ of the idea of the difficulty of determining race was planted in his mind.[64]

There is another level to Hays's view of race in this account, and that is that individualism trumped race. Hays never said this explicitly. But in his recounting of another Darrow story, he implicitly made the point. He told of Darrow being "At a meeting in Chicago held to protest against colored people moving into a white neighborhood." When asked about "a certain Negro," Darrow "drawled," according to Hays, "I think he's a pretty nice fellow. He had me over to his house to dinner the other night and if you treat him right, he will probably invite you too." Darrow reveals here that he has punctured one of the strongest of racial taboos, socialization across the color line, and he is urging the audience to do the same. Race did not matter, the character of the individual did. Moreover, if others recognized this and treated him right, then the man would show his quality. But also notice that Hays has used colored and Negro interchangeably here, or at least subsumed Negro under the larger category colored. How was it determined? By the common "judgment" of the common language, lumping all colored and Negroes? Or, given almost all he had written about race, could this also come around to individuality and agency? The "certain Negro" might have been one of those many people with African ancestry who proudly seized upon the label—they were, after all to Hays, people worth admiring—worth sitting down and having a meal with and enjoying an interesting and meaningful conversation.[65]

There is a subtext to this aspect that was implicit from Hays's first encounter with Pauline Cockburn, and that was the questioning of the fundamental assumption of white supremacy that underlay the case. When the Cockburns insisted that they were respectable, when they proved they were as well off as their neighbors, when their house was arguably the best in the neighborhood, when Joshua's nautical achievements were touted, they gave the lie to the assumption driving restrictive covenants, redlining, and other manifestations of the color line in property law: that the presence of colored people lowered the value of an area. When Hays agreed with them, the contention had to be noticed. Thus, Davis declared, "There is no reflection whatever on the character of either the defendant or her husband, nothing to indicate that they are anything other than an entirely respectable couple." Such a statement—even when Davis tried to cover up his ruling as being only simple matter of breach of contract, actually exposed the reality that prejudice drove the creation of the restrictive covenants and that the color line enforced a racist order.[66]

Hays's focus on the indeterminacy of race had weaknesses. Hays's use of experts was just a fallacious appeal to authority. In the brief (and his later account), he established Boas's standing and used his definition of Negro to argue the indefiniteness of the covenant, but he did not test the ideas. Ironically, this tendency was matched by Davis's citation of *Corrigan v. Buckley* in ruling that the covenant was not a violation of constitutional rights. Neither man probed the reasoning behind their authorities' pronouncements. Davis overlooked doubts that the assertion of the court about the covenants being a private action beyond the reach of the 14th Amendment was binding. Hays did not see that Boas's definition of Negro was based more on assumption than empirical evidence. Asserting that there was more variation among the three groups into which he divided humanity—Negro, Caucasian, and Mongolian—Boas assumed that they were separate, but on what criteria was unstated. And Hays's trusting of the anthropologists could backfire. In fact, it did in this trial, as Klineberg's estimation that Joshua Cockburn had three-quarters Negro blood was used as evidence by Davis in addition to his ordinary language judgment. Also, Boas's undermining of the previous racist categories and the assertions of racial ranking of races was incomplete. There were plenty of textbooks, teachers of anthropology, and laypeople who subscribed to the theories that Boas had refuted. Conceivably, a jurisdiction might empower anthropologists to determine someone's race for governmental purposes. There was case law to that effect. And Boas, in supporting a case for a man's immigration in 1925, himself testified that Armenians were Caucasians, not Semitic, implicitly ratifying the categories. Such a development would have been very unlikely in the diverse New York, especially in light of the reactions in the state to what was happening in Germany. And after all, though Davis had not mentioned it, the Supreme Court in the *Ozawa* and *Thind* cases demonstrated how easy it was for a court to slide between scientific and lay judgments on race in upholding racist policies.[67]

Still, the argument on the indeterminacy of race that Hays interjected into the restrictive covenant cases had enough appeal that the NAACP and others adopted it in their ongoing struggle to end the practice. Challenges to covenants continued to bubble up in American cities, and the NAACP continued to bring a constitutional challenge before the Supreme Court, arguing that judicial enforcement of covenants was state action that denied African Americans equal protection of the law (not due process) under the 14th Amendment. Cases in Washington and Michigan that would become part of the constellation of cases that made up *Shelley v. Kraemer* used the argument that race was impossible to determine. Experts—both anthropological and medical—bolstered the argument by proclaiming that the common markers, like skin color, did not determine race. And the briefs asserted that only experts could determine a person's race. They sounded not surprisingly like Boas and Klineberg from the Cockburn trial. At trial, lay witnesses' statements as how they determined race often dissolved into vagueness and ambiguity. The difficulty of establishing race could also be used as a tactic. Most notably, Charles Hamilton Houston of the NAACP at a 1945 conference on how to pursue challenges to the covenants advised other attorneys to use racial indeterminacy to challenge the signers of racial community contracts as to whether they were white. However, in its brief to the Supreme Court, the NAACP downplayed this theme and emphasized different sociological arguments on the effect of the covenants in blighting African Americans' lives by limiting where they could live. The Court held that enforcement of a covenant was state action and thus prohibited by the 14th Amendment in the states and Civil Rights Acts in the District of Columbia. While there was resistance and attempts to keep restrictive covenants alive, those too fell to constitutional challenges.[68]

Hays's actions, as a white lawyer who embraced the causes of the NAACP and his willingness to talk about the issues, led the organization to call upon him as a speaker; a letter from Roy Wilkins to Hays in June 1937 revealed the nature of the relationship between Hays and the organization and what they denoted as important in his work against the color line. Wilkins invited Hays to address the opening evening session of their next national conference, to be held in Detroit. In a short note of reply, Hays, pleading the pressure of work, passed on the opportunity. But Hays had been not the first choice as a speaker, and he was invited only seventeen days before the event after an unexpected withdrawal of the original speaker. The lateness of the invitation and an admission that he was a fill-in indicated a somewhat close relationship, on one hand. The organization could call on him in a pinch; Wilkins knew "that you are too familiar with the work of this association and with the esteem in which it holds you to believe other than that we are always happy to have you as a speaker for any of our meetings." And they knew he would be a draw, as Wilkins asked for a quick response so they would "have the advantage of the advance publicity which the announcement of your name would give the conference." They were even willing to cover his travel costs by plane if necessary. On the other hand, he was not the original headliner, and he was invited by letter, not a telephone call, which revealed that the relationship was not that close.[69]

Equally revealing were the ways that Wilkins positioned Hays's possible participation. Wilkins took pains to explain that Hays's work in "the Cockburn case, in view of your investigation in Puerto Rico [of civil liberties and rights there], and in view of your association in the famous Sweet trial," as well as his "long service" on the national legal committee of the NAACP, would make the speech very welcome. Behind Wilkins's framing was the idea that it was important for the members and those who followed the news of the organization to see a white ally. Also, Wilkins wanted to enlist Hays, a noted anti-fascist, to broadcast that the organization opposed the fascist states, especially because much of the organized anti-fascist activity in the United States was conducted by the Communists, who thus gained support from African Americans. He pitched Hays as an example of working across the color line to defeat the color line and illiberal forces. His appearance would give "inspiration, not only to colored people, but to the liberal minority striving to preserve our civil rights in a constitutional democracy" facing the spread of "fascist ideas." Hays, Wilkins thought, could "help to orient more firmly the viewpoint of the colored people" toward combating fascism so as "to promote our civil liberties."[70]

That focus helps explain why Hays had no further known connection with the struggle against restrictive covenants. Indeed, in the next few years he sometimes passed up other civil rights work. For example, in February 1938, Robert Marshall of the US Forest Service asked the ACLU for help on figuring out whether the service could do anything about the private resorts built on forest lands that discriminated against Jews in the West and African Americans in the South. Marshall wanted to insert nondiscrimination clauses into future contracts. Roger Baldwin of the ACLU wrote to Hays, prefacing his remarks with the admission that "I asked Mr. Charles Houston of the NAACP to get me the answers to the enclosed questions from Bob Marshall, but he's tied up with the lynching fight and may be slow. Perhaps you can give me the answers quicker." Hays never responded and was apparently not involved in the memo the ACLU produced laying out a course to follow.[71]

Hays's disengagement with racial matters came in part because his civil liberties work and events were taking him in other directions. Even before the decision in *Cockburn v. Ridgway*, Hays had traveled to Puerto Rico in May 1937 as part of a fact-finding mission about civil liberties and rights on the island, prompted by the Insular Police shooting peaceful Nationalist protesters. That topic would continue to engage him on and off for years. Deep involvement in both the flag salute campaigns of the Jehovah's Witnesses campaign and the struggle to end the restrictions on speaking in Mayor Frank "Boss" Hague's Jersey City occupied him. His writing also picked up. After the *Cockburn* decision, in the summer of 1937 he was on Martha's Vineyard working with his ghostwriter on revisions of the second edition of *Let Freedom Ring*. He was very involved in defending the radical writer John Strachey in the attempt to ban him from speaking in the United States. World events impinged also, reorienting his focus on fighting fascism to advance civil liberties. On one level, the rise of the fascist states and their actions prompted Hays to write his only non–legal-oriented book, *Democracy Works*. He then moved on to begin writing his account of his career, *City Lawyer*. Moreover, the world debates reshaped the ACLU, as red-baiting prompted a recasting of the governing board, brought about its antitotalitarian pledge, and eventually caused the purge of the Communist board member. In 1938, his great hero Darrow died, and to honor him Hays increased his work for the American League to Abolish Capital Punishment that Darrow had headed. At the same time, Aline was diagnosed with a serious illness that would upend their home life. Thus, for a plethora of reasons Hays did not involve himself in work against the color line for a number of years. That would change with World War II.[72]

4

"The effective moment to shoot the gun"

The Campaign Against the Color Line
in the American Bar Association

In April 1943, soon after he had publicly resigned from the American Bar Association (ABA) because of its refusal to admit African Americans, Arthur Garfield Hays wrote to someone who had applauded his action. He had considered doing so since at least 1938, but now "was the effective moment to shoot the gun."[1] In 1943, Hays was the most prominent of the members of the ABA who pressured it to end its ban of African Americans. While scholars have delineated the story of the establishment of the color line in the bar, its ending has received less attention. Starting in the 1920s, African Americans and liberals (often Jews or Catholics), who were discriminated against in the profession, began urging an end to the color bar in the ABA. As civil rights activism began to bear fruit, opponents of the exclusion of African Americans from the ABA increased their efforts. Their efforts in the late 1930s saw no success, but in the World War II era they prevailed. Hays played an important role in the final push to end the color bar in the ABA.[2]

The attack on the color bar in the profession of law was part of the well-known alliance between African American and Jewish activists. Jewish civil rights lawyers were important to the early African American civil rights struggle, especially in the National Association for the Advancement of Colored People (NAACP). This alliance was cemented by the convergence in outlook between elite members of both groups. Jewish lawyers like Hays were important in ending the discrimination against African Americans by the ABA, opening up opportunities for them in the legal profession.[3]

Legal segregation, though it existed in only part of the United States, cast a large shadow over the entire nation. It empowered racial discrimination against African Americans in many areas of public life, including the legal profession. Given the importance of lawyers to defining and enunciating a system of civil rights and liberties, the existence of a color bar in the largest and most important legal professional organization had tremendous ramifications. At the time of the fall of the color bar, the ABA was "a center of power and influence, not only in legal circles but in political circles as well." It was the preeminent professional organization for lawyers that existed alongside more than 600 local, regional, and specialized bar associations. The ABA was not a mass organization; "only 3 percent of American lawyers belonged to the ABA in 1910, 9 percent in 1920, 17 percent in 1930." Yet as one of the few lawyer groups with national membership and as one of the oldest, the ABA emerged as the leading voice of the bar. Its influence was felt widely in the courts and legislatures across the nation. It consolidated its power when the corporate bar came to dominate the association.[4]

In the beginning decades of the twentieth century, the large hierarchal-ordered law firms with owners (partners) and journeymen helpers who ideally would become partners (associates) came to dominate the profession of law. These firms met the legal needs of big business and were often called Wall Street firms, even if their offices were elsewhere. Their regular corporate practice supplied them with wealth and power. Protestant men, often of Anglo-Saxon origins, staffed the elite firms. They moved in the social circles of their clients. They stood in stark contrast to the majority of the profession, who worked alone or in small partnerships and depended on a flow of clients who usually hired a lawyer for a single task. The corporate lawyers led the way in creating a stratified profession: of the elite bar and the rest. And the precepts of that profession were promulgated in the ABA's Canons. They set a professional model that privileged service to the private client, banned advertising, and discouraged the use of the contingency fee to preserve the honor of the profession. The Canons—forms of which were adopted by many state and local associations—became the means for self-policing the profession along the lines that the corporate lawyers favored.[5]

The profession, under elite guidance, reflected the racial and gender ordering of the larger society. Working in concert with the Association of

American Law Schools, the ABA labored to limit entry to the profession from groups it deemed suspect: African Americans, women, Jews, and Catholics. From the turn of the twentieth century into the 1930s, barriers against women and African Americans entering the legal profession "were extremely high," and the few who were "admitted to the bar had virtually no hope of a job in a [corporate] law firm." As the large firms set the tone for the bar, their exclusion kept them from becoming leaders of the profession. However, for men of Catholic and Jewish decent, the barriers were not as high. In particular, "Jews flocked to the legal profession: they made up 26 percent of the freshly admitted lawyers in New York City between 1900 and 1910; and an amazing 80 percent between 1930 and 1934." However, Jews were overrepresented among those in single practice, and those were dependent on a flow of one-job clients. As their numbers grew, resistance to Jews in the profession stiffened; for instance, from his position on the Harvard Law School Faculty, Felix Frankfurter lamented the near impossibility of placing his Jewish students in leading firms.[6]

Jews and Catholics, mostly excluded from the leading firms dominated by Protestants, formed their own firms composed of members of their own groups. Some of these firms rose to prominence, and their members joined the ABA and emerged as leaders of the bar. Samuel Untermeyer and Louis Marshall were the preeminent corporate Jewish lawyers of the era. Also, among Catholics and Jews there were always a small handful who gained entry to the elite firms and entered the ABA. And, in response to the rejection by the ABA and local bar associations, African Americans and women established their own local organizations and nationwide bar associations: the National Bar Association (1925) and the National Association of Women Lawyers (1899). The existence of such other associations did not preclude membership in the ABA. Indeed, in 1918, the ABA admitted its first woman member. But African Americans were a different matter.[7]

In the decades since it was founded in 1878, the ABA apparently assumed no African American lawyers were eminent enough to join the organization. Membership was open to lawyers "in good standing," but in practice that meant those who were better off, served in government, or had high social standing. Given the realities of the larger society that denied African Americans the paths to wealth, power, and social prestige, the ABA did not have an official policy to bar African Americans lawyers from the organization. After the turn of the twentieth century, as corporate lawyers came to dominate the association, their vision of professionalism left little room for African American lawyers. But just enough: three African Americans (all with records suitable for membership) had been admitted to membership. This discovery in 1912 prompted a flap. The membership chairman said admission of African Americans raised "a question of keeping pure the Anglo-Saxon race," and white Southern members sought the African Americans' expulsion from what they called a social organization on the grounds that they had not disclosed their race in applying. One of the African Americans was an assistant attorney general, and in response to calls for his expulsion, the attorney general of the United States threatened to resign, asserting there was no color bar and the man met the standards for membership. While calls for expulsion were rejected, the door was shut to future African American applicants. A resolution passed in the 1912 meeting decried the admission of "three persons of the colored race" to the association because "it has never been contemplated that members of the colored race should become members."[8]

The resolution reflected the racism built into American law and society, where separate but equal was established and resting on the bedrock idea of racial difference and white superiority. Building on older ideas of ethnic difference arguing that cultural differences came from biological differences, scientific racism flowered. Scientific racism gave weight to the social prejudice. For instance, the popular works of Madison Grant and Lothrop Stoddard saw nations rooted in the racial composition of their populations and urged various public policies, ranging from segregation, through anti-miscegenation laws, to immigration restriction to preserve American civilization. Indeed, the Progressive Era saw an intensification of racism beyond black and white. In Progressive-Era New York State (but in fact merely reflecting the larger society), a key aspect of society "was a set of racist beliefs that certain ethnic and religious groups, notably WASPs [White Anglo-Saxon Protestants] were better suited than others, especially southern and eastern European Catholics and Jews to participate in American civic and economic life." Given such a climate, it would have been surprising if in 1912 the ABA had allowed the integration of African Americans into the organization.[9]

The 1912 meeting also developed the means to enforce a color bar. It declared that when local councils of the organization submitted names for nomination in the future to the executive council, African Americans be identified as such. With knowledge of who was applying (one African American newspaper later claimed that the ABA "immediately placed race-identification spaces on its applications" forms), those in the leadership of the national organization (often Southerners) could block membership. And they did so. The mechanism varied over the years, as the governing structure of the ABA evolved. But the result was clear: The ABA "committed itself to lily-white membership. . . . It had elevated racism above professionalism."[10]

Liberal members of the bar protested the practice, but it continued for over the next twenty years, supported by the common racialist thinking of the day. For instance, Hays's co-counsel of the ACLU, Morris L. Ernst, was "for decades . . . a vocal crusader against" the ABA's "long standing policy" of "not accepting black membership." In 1929, he wrote an unsigned opinion piece in *The Nation* arguing that the association should apologize for the 1912 resolution and end its limitation on membership. When he received a recruitment pamphlet, he recalled in his 1945 autobiography, he wrote the association asking if they accepted "Negro members" and in reply was told, "Sorry, we did not know you were a Negro." Indeed, racialist thinking was prevalent in legal circles through the 1920s. For example, the important legal scholar Henry Wigmore responded to the gift of Hays's *Let Freedom Ring* this way: "You and I are at opposite policies in most public matters. But we have one thing in common besides mutual respect, viz, we are emotional. I wonder if you are Irish extraction?" Given such thinking, and with segregation so well entrenched, it is no surprise that the ABA continued to exclude new African American members.[11]

By the late 1930s, the walls of segregation were beginning to show their first cracks. The NAACP in cases before the Supreme Court challenged the functioning of segregation at both ends of the social and economic structure. At one end, the Supreme Court began to rein in the excesses in Southern courts in treating African American defendants, trying to limit the effect of mob pressure on juries, asserting that defendants should have adequate counsel, and stopping the wholesale exclusion of African Americans from juries. At the other end, the Supreme Court made it more difficult for Southern states to exclude African Americans from graduate and professional education by invalidating a Missouri law that paid out-of-state tuition to African Americans of the state who sought graduate or professional education because there were no graduate facilities in the state for African Americans.[12]

And a number of African Americans were rising in the profession. For instance, with the development of the New Deal, professional African Americans were "playing unprecedented roles in federal administrative agencies." At the same time, the support of white mentors encouraged the legal careers of African Americans such as Raymond Pace Alexander and Thurgood Marshall. Significantly, the contacts between white and African American lawyers came through specific legal work—not through shared participation in professional organizations or social interactions. Indeed, in the elite firm of Davis Polk, success stemmed from social connections that extended professional associations, proving the common assumption of the early twentieth-century bar: Professional associations mattered.[13]

Given the changing legal landscape and the rising prominence of African Americans, their exclusion from the ABA seemed all the more pointed by this time. The logic of exclusion had also eroded since the creation of the color bar. For instance, women had entered the profession, as the ideas that had kept women out weakened across the society. Some of them became prominent in the profession, though not in the Wall Street firms. An indication of how closed corporate practice was to women is shown by the fact the Association of the Bar of the City of New York waited until 1937 before admitting women even though they had been in the ABA since 1918. Thus, by the late 1930s, the prohibition on African American membership seemed anomalous to some.[14]

Hays was one of those who wanted to end the practice. It fit with the general range of his causes. His understanding of the way the profession worked (after all, he headed a Wall Street firm) and his awareness of the many discriminations that limited African Americans prompted him to act. He worked with, and admired, the leading African American lawyers of the period. Thus, in the late 1930s, Hays and others moved to break the color bar using the same techniques that would later prevail: nomination of suitable candidate and eventually mounting a publicity campaign to prompt change. Before the 1938 ABA annual convention, Hays proposed nominating Charles Hamilton Houston for membership. Houston, in Hays's words, was "an eminent colored member of the Bar." Houston was, of course, the Harvard Law School–trained human dynamo who transformed Howard Law School from a failing institution into one that received ABA accreditation and was able to join the restrictive American Association of Law Schools, and who at the time of this proposed nomination headed the legal branch of the NAACP. Hays sought to have Houston's nomination "seconded by a large number of well-known lawyers."[15]

Three things stand out about this first nomination. First, it is important to note that Hays, in picking Houston (and then the later candidates he supported) as a test case, was following the exclusiveness tendencies of the ABA. Houston and the others were exceptional. They stood out in terms of education, professional attainments, and social standing. In some ways they were the African American analogues to the Jewish lawyers who had made good in the profession and been admitted to the ABA. They were by no means reflective of the overall African American bar. The realities of the profession for African Americans are chronicled in the chapter "Inching Along" in Pauli Murray's autobiography, about breaking into the profession; and in the chapters "Teething at the Bar" and "On My Own" in Conrad Lynn's autobiography. Second, the effort came when the ABA had seen a downturn in members and the rise of a new national professional organization for lawyers, the National Lawyers Guild. The ABA suffered a loss of members during the Depression decade. In 1936, it had fewer than 30,000 of the nation's 180,000 practicing lawyers. Also, the guild was an appealing alternative to the ABA. Founded in 1937 by liberal and radical lawyers (including the ACLU's Morris Ernst) with a constitution that proclaimed the importance of human rights over property rights, it had very a low dues fee and opened its membership "to any member of the bar in good standing regardless of color, sex or political beliefs." It pushed an openly progressive political economic agenda and a new code of professional ethics that emphasized the lawyer's responsibility to society. In the heady New Deal era, the guild quickly gained members. Third, the proposed Houston nomination was private, an inside-the-organization affair, as Hays did not raise the issue publicly or pursue a press campaign.[16]

Hays wrote to the president of the ABA, Arthur Vanderbilt, about the exclusion of African Americans. Vanderbilt had a long career as legal reformer and law professor as well as an active private practice that subsidized his civil liberties work—he represented the striking Patterson silk mill workers and was involved in the fight against Mayor Hague's repression of speech in Jersey City. Vanderbilt, while admitting the "the issue existed," asked Hays "not to make a point of it at that time." Hay later recalled that Vanderbilt "hoped the matter could be cleared up within the Bar Association. He pointed out to me that the real difficulty was that the members of the Bar from the South would resent the admission of Negroes." Vanderbilt argued, according to Hays, "that it was necessary to bring them [the Southern members] around before anything could be done. I thought perhaps it would be better to wait, and I did wait." But not for long, as an opportunity to make the struggle against the color line in the ABA public presented itself within a year.[17]

Later in 1938, Frank Hogan's elevation to the presidency of the ABA came when the organization was attempting to escape the image it had created of itself as the bastion of economic conservativism and as the ally of the Liberty League and thus revive its falling membership. At that time, led by Grenville Clark, who argued that civil liberties were worth defending, as they were a conservative cause larger than economic rights (one that could preserve all liberty), the ABA created the Bill of Rights Committee. The ABA's role in defending legal tradition during the Court-packing fight, prompted by President's Franklin D. Roosevelt's plan to reorganize the Supreme Court, followed by the Supreme Court's shifting jurisprudence on governmental regulation of the economy, as well as the saber rattling of totalitarian governments of Germany and Italy, helped to prompt the founding of the new committee. The effort to change its image gave Hays the opportunity to get the association to confront its color bar.

Hays opened this public campaign for an ending of the ABA's color line by latching onto a request by the ACLU for cooperation between the two organizations on civil liberties. On August 10, 1938, he wrote formally to the new president of the ABA. Hogan had risen on Thomas E. Dewey's coattails. He was one Dewey's hand-picked special prosecutors dedicated to rooting out corruption in New York. Hogan, like Hays, was a believer in the Bill of Rights, and his elevation to the rank of president of the organization signaled its shifting stance on public issues. Hays wrote to Hogan on ACLU stationary to pass on the ACLU's praise for the move (provided it was not just a cloak for economic conservatism) and to ask that the two organizations work together. "We welcome the American Bar Association's long delayed recognition of its responsibilities in this field and trust that its work too will be conducted on behalf of all minorities without discrimination. As a first step we urge the committee to lift the ban against Negroes in the Bar Association." This "first step" was the only specific request in the letter. And while Hays was writing on behalf of the ACLU, he added a personal statement: As a member of the ABA, "I intend to resign unless some action" was soon taken "so that Negroes may be admitted to membership. I hope that such an example on my part will be followed by many other members."[18]

Hays's threat to resign and to try to take others with him was not an empty one. The strong links of some of the ABA's prominent members to the Wall Street elites and consequent opposition to the New Deal weakened the ABA's appeal to the profession. Also, the National Lawyers' Guild was a viable alternative to the ABA at this point. Indeed, the ABA's effort to found a civil liberties committee was a step toward remaking its image and keeping its position as the predominant national organization of the bar. Hays threatened to tarnish that rebranding as it came out of the package. In addition, Hays apparently leaked this letter to the press. Ten days after the letter was written, the *New York City Age*—an important African American newspaper—published a story about Hays's warning, "Hays to Resign from Bar Association because of Jim Crow Policies." The article summarized Hays's letter, quoting its lines about "conducting the work on behalf of all minorities without discrimination" and "lifting the ban against Negroes" as well as his intention to resign and inspire others to do so. Others, maybe having read the *New York Age* (for no mainstream paper published a similar story), took up the cause. For instance, New York lawyer Joseph C. Thompson sarcastically suggested that that the ABA change its name to the "American White Bar Association" if it continued to refuse to admit African Americans, while another attorney lobbied members on the issue.[19]

Hogan responded to Hays's short letter with a three-page missive; it covered the importance of the Bill of Rights work, denied the organization had a color bar, and discussed the potential for ABA and ACLU cooperation and ended with a plea that Hays not carry out his threat. Hogan talked about how he had for years sought to "arouse interest" in defense of rights and how he regretted that "individuals and groups were inclined to be aroused when their rights were infringed, but to be quiescent . . . when the rights of others, who did not hold their own political, economic, or social views were trampled upon." He praised the ACLU for its advocacy of the defense of all. This call particularly appealed to Hays, as that was his long-standing and much-advocated-for position both within the ACLU and in his writings and speeches. Hogan wrote that the "Junior Bar Section" comprising 6,000 lawyers under thirty-six years old had recently praised the ACLU for its all "all-inclusive" approach to defense of civil liberties and rights.[20]

Hogan, in denying the ABA had a color bar, asserted "neither in the Constitution nor in the By-Laws" was "there any such ban." There was no "test based on race, color, or creed." He referred Hays to the bylaws, which he quoted at length, showing that any person of good standing at the Bar of any State was eligible, that each state membership committee by majority vote nominated a candidate for membership, and that all nominations were then voted on by the Board of Governors. "Two negative notes in the Board of Governors shall prevent an applicant's election." Though he did not say it, the last bit was the fly in the ointment, as the Board of Governors included one member from each federal judicial circuit.

Two of those circuits were composed of Southern states that mandated segregation and conscribed the lives of African Americans and could be depended upon to vote no on any African American applicant. Instead, Hogan asserted that the system was a selective system that sometimes erred but was not a discriminatory system; significantly he suggested no remedy in changing the rules that would accomplish the goal sought by the ACLU and Hays.[21]

Hogan, however, then suggested a different course. He implored Hays to understand that "the members of our profession ought not to adopt the attitude that 'we won't play, but will go right home' unless everybody else plays just as we wish them to." He compared resignation to opposition to government policy by himself and Hays. When confronted with a policy they did not support, "we did not pack up and leave the country; we worked for the view we believed in, in the rank and file of citizens." And he asked Hays and others who shared his mindset to stay within the organization. Seek the changes "on the inside reasoning and voting, rather than on the outside throwing rocks." Hogan begged, "Don't resign. I have just started, and want an increased and not a decreased membership." It would be counterproductive, he asserted: "there would be something peculiar about the announcement that 'American Bar Association actively takes up defense against violation of the Bill of Rights, and Arthur Garfield Hays thereupon resigns.'" From that little piece of flattery, Hogan segued to saying that he had forwarded the ACLU letter to the Bill of Rights' committee chairman, Grenville Clark. Clark, a fellow Wall Street lawyer, was an advocate of international law and the sort of conservative with whom Hays could work. Hogan closed on a personal note: "How many years has it been since we crossed from Havre to New York on the same boat and you conducted the auction pools [for distance covered in a day], and I lost with disheartening regularity?" The personal touch reinforced the call for change from within.[22]

Hogan's appeal to bring about change from within, and his flattery, worked to some extent. In a response sent two months later, marked "personal," Hays relented. "You have persuaded me that the thing to do is to stay in the bar Association and there raise the issues on the question of the admission of colored lawyers." He asked for Hogan's advice as to how to go about it in general and what Hogan thought of a particular course of action: "My thought is to propose the name of one of the outstanding lawyers of the colored race, with a number of prominent seconders—men who are far more respectable than I am—and then make a fight on the proposition. Don't you think this is a way to go about it?" Hogan apparently did not respond, and Hays let the matter drop.[23]

A year later, according to what Hays had proposed, the nomination of "one of the outstanding lawyers of the colored race" was implemented. In 1939, William Hastie was put up for membership in the ABA. If there was an African American with the ideal resume for the ABA, it was he. A child of the middle class, he was valedictorian of the famed Dunbar High School in Washington, was elected to Phi Beta Kappa at Amherst College, and was valedictorian of his graduating class. He graduated from Harvard Law School and was lavishly praised by Felix Frankfurter as being one of its best. He worked in private practice in Washington and later was a lawyer for the federal Department of the Interior. And in 1937 he was nominated as the first African American federal district judge (for the territory of the Virgin Islands) in the nation. While his confirmation was marred by race-baiting, he was confirmed and proved an able judge. Yet the ABA leadership continued to seek to put off ending the color bar. Grenville Clark in a letter to the NAACP "questioned the wisdom of pressing for his admission at that time." Not surprisingly, as his biographer notes, "While on the federal bench in 1939, Hastie himself was rejected by the ABA!" Hays apparently had no role in the Hastie nomination and never referred to it. It is not clear why the efforts to integrate the ABA in the late 1930s failed. It might have been that the internal pressure for change within the organization was not strong enough. And it could have been that a private campaign that relied on goodwill was not the right tool to overcome the established racist policy.[24]

The movement to end discrimination in the profession was not just focused on the ABA. Benjamin A. Hartstein of the Federal Bar Association (FBA) pushed this organization toward a more racial inclusive profession. The FBA represented the growing number of lawyers in federal government service. When the FBA was created in 1925 it had a clause in its constitution that limited membership to white persons. Despite this, in the early 1930s, some Northeastern state chapters of the FBA had begun to admit African Americans. The national organization refused to follow suit and even took the step of disaffiliating a chapter that had admitted African Americans. Still other chapters not in the South ignored the color bar; throughout the 1930s, other African Americans were proposed as members of the national organization. These applications might have been possible because the language limiting membership to whites only had probably been removed from the organization constitution and replaced with a clause modeled on the ABA's bylaws. According to Frank Coleman, who was working to tear down the color line in the profession, members of the FBA justified their denial of African American applicants because "admission of Negroes to membership might jeopardize" the relations between the FBA and ABA, as it was understood that the ABA had "long followed the definite policy of excluding Negroes." All the attempts in 1930s to open the doors of the FBA to African Americans failed. Starting again in 1942, various FBA members, particularly those serving on its Bill of Rights committee, challenged the practice. There were rumors that United States Attorney General Francis Biddle had threatened to resign from the FBA over the matter. Like the Hastie effort, Hays had nothing to do with this campaign against racist exclusion in this professional organization.[25]

Indeed, from the end of 1938 to 1943, Hays was silent on the ABA's refusal to admit African American lawyers, and this silence was probably caused by tribulations in his personal life and turmoil in the ACLU. In the early and mid-1930s, the Hays family was close. Arthur and Aline were intellectual and social partners. They entertained together, went out together, and vacationed together. Aline was more radical than Arthur and had her own interests and causes that she pursued, as well as those she shared with him. Arthur's adult daughter Lora was close to her stepmother and her stepsister, Jane. But in the fall of 1938 Aline became seriously ill, probably with cancer. And though she had a period of recovery after an operation, her good health was precarious. For instance, in the summer of 1941, Hays, Aline, and Jane vacationed on Martha's Vineyard. Between tennis and boating, he wrote drafts of his last book, Aline painted, and Jane enjoyed the company of the children of their close circle of friends. But the illness strained the marriage over time, so much so that one of Hays's friends, C. Fulton Oursler, asserted that toward the end of her life Aline was not speaking to her husband. She would die on June 3, 1944.[26]

The years 1938 to 1942 were hard on the ACLU. Bad publicity, first an attack in H. L. Mencken's *American Mercury* magazine and red-baiting by the congressional committee headed by Representative Martin Dies (which would evolve into the House Un-American Activities Committee), resulted in much internal conflict as to how to respond. Eventually the organization brought in new board members to balance the many radicals on the board. Divisions in the board between the anti-Communists (who included Socialists, liberals, as well as conservatives) and those who tolerated the Communists escalated. Eventually the anti-Communist members, aided by both Morris Ernst and Roger Baldwin, engineered the purge of the Communist Elizabeth Gurley Flynn from the board. After the restrictions on speech that emerged after the United States joined World War II, the national organization was paralyzed. It refused to intervene in the massive federal sedition trial against American fascists in Washington and was slow in responding to the forced removal from the West Coast and subsequent internment of American citizens of Japanese descent as a war measure. Hays was deeply involved in the internal struggles over all these issues, which consumed much of his time.[27]

Also, Hays may have hoped that the growth of the National Lawyers Guild, and its welcoming of African American members, might have pushed the ABA to change. But by 1940, the guild had split into bitter factions, with its more moderate members accusing the more radical ones of being Communists. and it was soon red-baited away from any chance of growth. Key liberals, including Morris Ernst, Ferdinand Pecora, and Robert Jackson, left the organization when it refused to take a strong anti-Communist position. Its once robust membership roll had shrunk to about a thousand members by 1940. It could not be a countervailing body to the ABA that could force a change of the status of African American lawyers within the profession.[28]

It should not be thought that Hays slacked in his activities during this period between the first aborted attempt to leverage his prominence into prompting the ABA to change and his resignation from the organization in 1943. Besides his firm's work (which included a Spring 1939 trip to France to drum up business) and the near endless controversies in the ACLU, and also the work done there, Hays wrote two more books. Beginning in 1937, he assembled a team of researchers and writers including McAlister Coleman to produce his only book unrelated to law, *Democracy Works*. Much of the final writing of this book took place in the summer of 1938. At this point Hays was very worried about the rise of totalitarian states and their threat to liberty. Thus, this book was aimed at a popular audience and was meant to undercut the much-bandied-about idea that the fascist and Communist states were more efficient than democracies. At his own expense, Hays sent out 153 copies of *Democracy Works* to friends and influential people. Its release was overshadowed by the outbreak of the war, and it sold poorly. And on the heels of that work, again working with Coleman, Hays wrote much of *City Lawyer*. By the end of 1941, he had delivered to the press the manuscript of this semi-autobiography containing sketches of some of his important causes and cases and a distillation of his philosophy. He then embarked on publicity work to promote it.[29]

Even if there was a gap in his attention to the issue, Hays never abandoned hope that discrimination against African Americans by the ABA could be ended. Perhaps Hays's determination stemmed from both his experiences in the university and his later work on behalf of the "non-sectarian" fraternity. In both settings he saw the importance of social connections. In his own life he knew that the bonding with classmates in extracurricular activities opened opportunities to him, and that presumption also lay behind the desire to form Pi Lambda Phi chapters. Exclusion from such social connections limited a person's professional attainments and thus was not just a social slight revealing the prejudice of others but a restriction that harmed people. A democratic society should not allow exclusion where not all could strive equally. Also, the death of Clarence Darrow in early 1938 might have motivated him to keep up his work against segregation. Hays greatly lamented the death of Darrow and remained tied to the other issue in which Darrow had involved him, opposition to the death penalty. He went to the memorial held by the American League Against Capital Punishment, where Darrow had served as the figurehead president and participated in finding his successor. Three years later, in yet another effort to secure a commutation for a federal prisoner he thought unjustly convicted, Hays admitted, "It seems to me like pretty raw case. I wish Darrow were with us. I know he would move heaven and earth to prevent this boy being sent to the electric chair." It is likely then, even with the tumult and disruption, that Hays harbored hopes to continue to work against the color line and was waiting for an opportunity to intervene.[30]

In these years, Hays certainly knew that African American attorneys faced more than polite ostracism. For instance, he was familiar with the attack on Leon Ransom, which took place in February 1942 when Ransom was punched by a former deputy sheriff while leaving a Southern courtroom. Another white man, as the scuffle was ending, brandished a gun and threatened, "we are going to teach these northern Negroes not to come down here raising fancy court questions." Thurgood Marshall prompted the ACLU to act on the matter and drafted a letter aimed at the Tennessee Bar Association that was sent to Hays for his input for the final version that would be sent out under his name. The letter stressed the fraternity of the bar. "The Bar is indivisible; we are all practitioners of the law and brothers in our profession. Attacks such as the one occurring here are to be most seriously condemned." Hays barely changed the wording and sent out in his signature. Incidents like this and the obvious gap between the rhetoric of a war against Nazi racialism and the preservation of segregation in America would prompt Hays into action. First, in 1942, he began representing Winfred Lynn, who was challenging his induction on the grounds that the draft was segregated by race and violated the antidiscrimination clause of the Selective Service Act, and, second, Hays acted on his latent interest in the ABA color line.[31]

After the 1942 nomination of Francis Rivers, an African American lawyer, to ABA membership seemed to be failing, Hays reentered the struggle against the association's color bar. Jonah J. Goldstein, with William B. Herlands as co-sponsor, nominated Francis Rivers for membership in the ABA. Goldstein had previously nominated Rivers but he had been passed over, and Goldstein convinced Rivers to try again in 1942. Rivers attend Yale College (where he was Phi Beta Kappa) and Columbia Law School. After his graduation from this top-flight law school, he had trouble finding a job until he was hired by Goldstein and Goldstein. He moved from that firm to another Wall Street firm, then started his own. He impressed some leaders of the New York bar, and, backed by leading figures Louis Marshall and Underhill Moore, he broke the color line of the New York State Bar Association. A little bit later, the most important local bar association in the nation, the elite Association of the Bar of the City of New York, admitted him as its first African American member. He served a term in the New York Assembly as a Republican. Rivers was, like Frank Hogan, hired by Thomas Dewey to be part of his team—one of two African American lawyers among the staff of seventy-four. When Hogan succeeded Dewey as district attorney, he publicly promoted Rivers and raised his salary.[32]

His main sponsor, Jonah J. Goldstein, like Hays, was an active Jewish liberal legal professional. Goldstein was an immigrant success story, and his role is emblematic of the Jewish–African American alliance of the early civil rights struggles. Arriving on the Lower East Side of Manhattan as a five-year-old child, he obtained a good education, became a leader in social organizations assisting Jewish youth, and then went to New York University Law School. His firm, unlike most, hired both African American and women lawyers. In 1931, Goldstein was appointed to the city Magistrates Court, where he was active in pushing juvenile justice measures. He was elected to the County Court in 1939. He continued his racial equality practices there. In 1940, as a judge, he appointed for the first time an African American lawyer to defend a white man accused of homicide. At the same time, he was in every way a leader of the bar.

Herlands, also Jewish, was not as prominent as Goldstein, but he had been active in the anti-corruption campaigns that brought down Tammany Hall and was Mayor La Guardia's commissioner of investigations.[33]

Yet the application of Rivers languished, and in April 1943 Goldstein wrote a contingent resignation letter to the ABA. He began by pointing out that he had been a member of the association for twenty-nine years. He would "continue my membership if I can do so without stultifying myself." He could not be a member of "a professional organization which bars Negroes from its membership." To do so would "be contributing to the perpetuation of bigotry. This I refuse to do." Then in a line that made the resignation contingent and also pushed the ABA to respond, Goldstein wrote, "Unless I receive concrete evidence that the association is not pursing this discriminatory and un-American practice, you may regard this letter as my resignation." To make his action have impact, Goldstein gave the letter to the press, which mistakenly reported that he had resigned.[34]

The press story had immediate effects: prompting resignations by others and most significantly stimulating Hays to renew his efforts against the color bar by resigning from the ABA. For example, Rivers's co-sponsor, Herlands, echoed Goldstein's stance, saying he would resign if Rivers was not accepted. And on April 8, 1943, Hays wrote a letter to the ABA stating that "I wish to follow the lead of Judge Jonah J. Goldstein in resigning from the American Bar Association because of its failure to admit into membership Mr. Francis Rivers, a Negro, who stands high at the bar in the City of New York." Hays continued, "I am hopeful that the resignations of Judge Goldstein and myself may lead hundreds of right-thinking men to follow our example." While he did not say it in his letter, Hays intended to, and did, pursue a publicity campaign to pressure the ABA into admitting African Americans to membership. As he explained in the middle of the campaign, "Knowing no other way of doing this than by publicity," he resigned "and likewise notified the newspapers of my action." Hays more than anyone was responsible for making the color bar a public issue in the press, and not just in the African American press, but in the major metropolitan dailies. And press coverage brought about immediate resignations: For example, after learning of Hays's action, Herman Hoffman, the president of the New York County Criminal Courts Bar Association, also resigned.[35]

When Hays resigned, he sent Goldstein a copy of his letter, writing: "Good for you! Please note the enclosure. Years ago I raised this question but was asked to wait a while in the thought that the American Bar

Association would straighten out the situation." Goldstein's "personal and unofficial" reply, in stronger terms, reiterated the reasons for his stance. He began: "It is indeed a sad commentary on existing conditions that my action should call for congratulations." But "Self-respect, and American principles of democracy, gave me no alternative other than to take the action which I did." He pushed for an end to exclusion on the grounds of justice: "I am always mindful of the last words in the salute to our flag, 'with liberty and justice for us'—all means ALL. The individual or a minority group may be singled out for injustice—never for justice. Justice is only assured when it is meted out to all." Nothing in his letter to Hays dealt with the mechanics of pressuring the ABA or proposing how to change its rules to bring about the ending of the color bar. In short, Goldstein importantly set out the principle, and others found the means to implement it.[36]

Those others were not African Americans. By necessity, their role as applicants to the ABA for the most part silenced their direct words. Their sponsors, members of the organization, spoke for them. But there is no doubt that there was a meeting of minds between the sponsors and applicants concerning means and ends. Without a doubt, the applicants had to be willing to endure the likely rejection by the ABA, and while there are no surviving records of discussions between these applicants and sponsors, it certainly was always done with the applicants' permission. After agreeing to allow their names to be put forward, the applicants usually let their sponsors and those who wanted to change the rules to do the talking. For example, in applications to break the color line of the FBA, the sponsors and applicants worked in concert. As one sponsor wrote, "We were inviting him to join us in a battle which would most certainly be embarrassing and possibly costly to him while the other of us risked nothing by our endeavor. . . . [He] expressed himself as fully willing to participate." However, Rivers would be different; he would comment to the press during the controversy.[37]

Hays's connections to a wide circle of lawyers mattered when he resigned from the ABA. Some indication of the extent of his circle of contacts is revealed by the practice of the ACLU using him to recruit lawyers to do work for organization. In the late 1930s the "legal secretary" for Baldwin—a lawyer in the organization tasked to handle the legal matters for Baldwin—wrote to Hays: "Mr. Baldwin wishes to add some more attorneys to our list and believes that a few good Irish Catholics would be most useful. He tells me that you know some of these gentry and suggests my writing to you to get the names." It is not just that he knew the rank and file, but Hays was friendly with some of the most important government lawyers of the day; he was connected. For instance, when Francis Biddle was solicitor general, Hays wrote to him to discuss the extent of free speech in time of war (as a private citizen, not as an ACLU officer) following a Biddle speech, but he also invited him and his wife to visit him. "Aline and I were talking of you and Katherine last night. We wondered if it would not be possible for you to pay us a little visit on the shore. We are at Sands Point, Long Island, for the summer, right on the water, and with sailboat in the backyard—the yard being the Sound." And Hays also was admired by some of the titans of the conservative bar. For instance, working with the ABA Committee on the Bill of Rights as it began cooperating with the ACLU on free speech cases, Grenville Clark wrote: "You are a veteran in this subject and I am a comparative newcomer and amateur." Hays had nurtured that relationship by sending Clark a revised edition of *Let Freedom Ring* in 1938. Thus, when Hays resigned, the profession noticed.[38]

Notably, Hays's decision to resign and to do so publicly was a tactic. He could and did resign from other organizations without making it public. For instance, he quietly slipped out of the National Lawyers Guild and later in life allowed his term on the Executive Committee of the American Council for Judaism to expire, in effect silently resigning. In each case he differed with the direction of the organization; with the Lawyer's Guild it was their economic policies, and with the Council for Judaism it was because they had embraced a religious mission he did not share.[39]

In 1943, the news that he had resigned brought responses. Hays's action won him immediate praise from his liberal friends and encouraged him to push forward. A Hays associate in the ACLU, John Haynes Holmes (a noted pacifist and co-founder of both the ACLU and NAACP), wrote to laud the action and Hays. "My heart gave a leap of joy when I read of your action in resigning from American Bar Association in protest against the denial by the Association of membership to a Negro lawyer. Of course, this is just the thing that you would naturally and inevitably do." Alice Dunn, the chairperson of the "International Committee" of Manhattanville College of Sacred Heart, after reading the *Chicago Herald Tribune* story about Hays's resignation over Rivers's languishing application, characterized it as a "magnificent stand." Similarly, Walter White of the NAACP informed Hays that the Board of Directors had passed a motion of appreciation for Hays "for the magnificent stand you have taken regarding the refusal of the American Bar Association to accept Negro lawyers as members." Fellow corporate and international lawyer William H. Wadhams merely wrote, "Dear Art, Bully for you!" Lawyer and banker Richard Welling tartly noted, "I almost wish that I had been a member of the Am. Bar Assn. So that I could join you in resigning." Robert D. Abrahams of a five-man law firm in Kansas City said that a few years earlier he had been asked to join the ABA by letter. "I replied that I could not, in good conscience do so, since I knew that Negroes were not accepted as members. At that time, I stated that I would be glad to join, if at any time the Association changed its policy. I never received any reply to my letter." Thus, Hays's action "delighted" him. Jerry Finkelstein of the *Civil Service Leader* (the newspaper of the Civil Service and War Jobs) wrote, "That's a fine fight you are carrying on for Frank Rivers." He added, "Mr. Rivers will appear in our 'Merit Man' column next week. Merit men are usually picked from outstanding civil servants." Indeed, the praise was mixed with anticipation of action. Holmes hoped that others would follow and that the ABA would face the "vital issue."[40]

In a response to Holmes, Hays explained, "For years I have had in mind the idea of resigning from the American Bar Association because of its attitude toward Negroes. I waited, however, until there would come an opportunity for my resignation to mean something." The judgment that the issue was vital in the minds of many and this was the time to act came from the circumstances of the war. The struggle against Nazi racism raised serious doubts about long-standing American practices. As one lawyer wrote to the Association, concerning Rivers: "In these days when so many of his race are in the armed services of the United States, it is definitely wrong, I believe, for an association of members of our learned profession with 'American' as part of its name to, to exclude fellow Americans solely because of their race." Another wrote to Hays telling him he planned to resign immediately if the facts, as he read in an article in the *Chicago Sun* that had carried Hays's letter, were true. He added, "I notice in the same edition of the *Chicago Sun* it is stated that 75,000 Negroes are already overseas. . . . If the American Bar Association has no clearer idea of what we are fighting for than to discriminate along Fascist lines . . . then the sooner the fact is known and acted upon, the better." Hays's story certainly "had legs," especially in the African American press. So much so that the Continental Features and News Service that provided stock biography and photographs to the press wrote him to request a new picture of him, as "A number of the Negro newspapers that we service have requested the same and this week's story in most of them will be around your splendid action in behalf of fair play." Significantly, the mainstream metropolitan papers also carried the story. They reached a far larger audience than the African American press, and some of those readers were members of the organization. This development provoked the pressure on the ABA that the opponents of the policy sought, bringing it into line with the views of many African Americans.[41]

The strong reaction by the African American press underscored the popularity among African Americans of the ideas enunciated by Hays. The arguments used by the supporters for ending the color line certainly coincided with views of Francis Rivers about the meaning of the war against Nazi racism. In 1942, Rivers told the Non-Sectarian Anti-Nazi League convention that segregation "copies the worst features of the Nazi system." Pointing to segregation in both the armed forces and the defense industries, he called for the league to lead the nation in the fight against Nazism at home, helping to establish "a country free from discrimination." But it was more than shared ideas. That members of the association threatened to resign in protest, showing they were willing to make a sacrifice to end discrimination.[42]

The press coverage of resignations from the ABA caused others to seek information, allowing Hays to continue to recruit more supporters to the campaign. For example, Wilber G. Katz from the University of Chicago Law School wrote Hays asking for more information. Similarly, on the same day, Benjamin Levin, a member of the ABA from the rising Boston law firm of Mintz, Levin and Cohn, wrote to Hays, saying he was "a little disturbed over this situation. However, before doing anything, I would like to get the facts from both sides and would therefore appreciate a letter from you giving me the facts as you know them." Hays wrote nearly identical responses to Katz and Levin. He stressed that "the Rivers application was before the Bar Association for some time and that they stalled to the point where Judge Goldstein resigned." He also related that he had "raised the same issue in a letter to Arthur Vanderbilt, who, I think was then president. . . . I then threatened to resign but Mr. Vanderbilt asked me to hold up the matter in the thought that a more liberal policy might be followed in the future. He stated that there were a number of Southerners in the bar Association and their agreement would first have to be obtained." Change had not come, and when he "read in the papers that Judge Goldstein had resigned, it seemed to me that if enough of us followed his example we might make the Bar Association sit up and take notice." If others followed, the ABA would "end this disgraceful attitude."[43]

And others did continue to follow. For example, Victor House, "a member of the American Bar Association for a good number of years," wrote to President George Morris to say he was "unequivocally opposed to the continuance of a policy" and that the "only reason which would persuade me not to tender my resignation . . . would be my conviction that one can usually more effectively oppose bigotry. . . . from within an organization than from without." Along the same lines, Socialist and lawyer Marion L. Severn, who had previously resigned from the New York State Association in 1942 over "a gratuitous insult to the Negro race," was inspired by the resignations to write to the ABA and say that unless they offered an "acceptable explanation of the incident," she would resign. She shared her letter with Hays, who in turn urged her to release her letter to "the newspapers so that the attendant publicity may lead others to follow our example."[44]

The public resignations also prompted Benjamin A. Hartstein of the FBA to take action. Hartstein had been named chairman of a special committee of the FBA to investigate charges of discrimination against Negroes in the profession. The struggle to open this association to African Americans, which stretched to 1945, prepared Hartstein to pressure the ABA. He wrote directly to the president of the ABA decrying the situation. He wrote that "snobbish aloofness has no place . . . in a democracy." He urged that Rivers be "acted on"—meaning be admitted. If he was not, Hartstein declared, then he would come to the Chicago convention to "give expression to my views and ask for a clear declaration of policy." Hartstein spoke to the press, saying that if the ABA continued to interpret its requirement that a lawyer must be of good reputation to be eligible for membership as applying to whites only, that made "a mockery of democracy." Hartstein sent a copy of his letter to Hays, who shared it with the African American press.[45]

And that press was interested in the story, and controversy intensified when the ABA responded. Harry S. Knight, the secretary of the ABA, in a letter to Hartstein denied that it barred African Americans from membership. He asserted that there was nothing in the organic law requiring the "exclusion" of African Americans. Knight added that Rivers had not yet been rejected but that his case was pending. In fact, he asserted that Rivers had not yet been formally nominated to the national organization, as the

New York State Committee on Admissions had been "disrupted" by loss of members to war work. Knight maintained that the ABA had at least one (and maybe more) African American members, referring to those admitted in 1912 and one from West Virginia admitted in 1929, probably because the ABA did not know he was African American. Taken as a whole, the letter implied that the resigning members were overreacting. Knight also released this letter to the Associated Press—one of the major news wire services. The publication of this letter in the *Chicago Defender* prompted Rivers to speak out. He said that Knight and others who asserted that he was not being rejected because of his race were "kidding no one but themselves." Rivers said that he had been previously denied admission, and he quoted the 1912 resolution of the ABA convention that said it had never been "contemplated" that "members of the colored race" could join the association to explain why. He pointed out that it never had been repealed and that "it speaks for itself."[46]

Hays's and others' resignations over Rivers's application brought action by bar groups and others. The membership committee of the New York Bar Association appointed the anti-corruption investigator Samuel Seabury to see if Rivers's application had been derailed by race discrimination. This committee also gained the backing of the Association of the Bar of the City of New York and was staffed with leading legal figures closely connected with important political figures, including Henry Taft (brother of the late president), George Medalie (Thomas Dewey's mentor), Joseph Proskauer (a close associate of ex-Governor Alfred Smith), and Basil O'Conner (President Franklin Roosevelt's former law partner). The resolution creating the committee said that if it discovered the claims were true, "steps be taken immediately by the Bar Association to abolish this discrimination and thus accord equal rights and opportunity to all members of the legal profession." Hays was at the meeting that created the committee and said to the press that eight lawyers had sent him copies of their letters of resignation to the ABA. He added that several others had written to the ABA asking if the organization did bar African Americans. At nearly the same time, the Bronx County Bar Association appointed its own committee headed by Matthew Levy to cooperate with the Seabury-headed investigation.[47]

The other bar associations urged the ABA to end its discrimination, and Hays saw this momentum. In response to a single practitioner from Boston who questioned the course of resigning and advocating working within the organization, Hays explained how he came to resign, why working from within alone would not work, and how he thought his campaign would bring results. He explained that he had tried to work from within, but that had failed. Indeed, President "Vanderbilt pointed out to me that there were many Southern members . . . and it was difficult to make them see the light." Thus, within the ABA the "matter has since been at a standstill." So, Hays admitted he seized upon Goldstein's action to spark "a rebellion within the Association [that] would force a change." But, to be "effective" many members would have to do it; "resigning in its self" did not "count for much, but the newspapers should be notified of any resignation" to increase the pressure on the ABA to change its "constitution." Hays added "It looks as though the action of the NY County Lawyers may help" move the ABA to this end.[48]

Also, after learning of the wave resignations, Percival. E. Jackson, a Wall Street lawyer, legal reform advocate, and former counsel to a Senate Committee investigating bankruptcy proceedings in the federal courts, wrote to Morris to declare that "It seems to me that if there is such a policy, these and similar resignation would be wholly justified." He urged the creation of "a clear statement of principle by the Association" against such discrimination. He sent a copy of his letter to Hays, who cheered him on and laid out a plan for further public action to pressure the ABA. "Good for you!" Hays added, "I think, however, you should give the matter some publicity so that a lot of other fellows follow your example." He stressed that "now is the time to bring the matter home to the Bar Association, and I am hopeful that a lot of other men will either write them in protest or resign, so that the Bar Association will know that something has to be done about the matter." The gender-specific nature of Hays's conception of the association and the profession is clear from his choice of words. His statements underscore two things: First, the social (even fraternal) nature of the profession, and second, that individual action mattered. Thus, Hays's ideas reflected the ABA's own vision of the bar as being composed of individual professionals and the association being a fellowship.[49]

The ABA responded to Jackson, and he passed their letter on to Hays, who then continued to press the issue. As the president was away, another officer wrote to Jackson. After referring to the press coverage of the controversy, he wrote that Rivers's application was not yet before the Board of Governors, but that when the president returned, the board would act on the committee report. Hays immediately asked Jackson to seek more details. He requested him to "write to Bar Association asking for the facts, to wit; when was the Rivers application received; what has happened to it; how does this compare with the usual procedure where men are nominated to the Bar Association?" Whether Jackson did this or not is unclear; what he did do was begin lobbying for change within the organization. He wrote to a candidate vying to be his state's delegate to the ABA to say that "before I vote for you I must ask, 'have you taken any position in the recent controversy concerning the admission of Negroes?'" Jackson was advocating change from within to "make it impossible for those who have racial prejudices to bar the admissions of Negroes." Jackson received a firm statement the next day from the candidate asserting that he did not think that ABA "should discriminate because of race, color, or creed." Any "lawyer in good standing, endorsed by local and star bar," should be admitted without any such discrimination.[50]

Among the flurry of correspondence, a letter from a non-member revealed the mechanism of how the color bar then currently worked in the ABA; it would lead to the development of the means to break it. John Beardsley, an active member of the ACLU as well as a superior court judge in Los Angeles, on learning of Hays's resignation, wrote to him to pass along what the president of the ABA had written him about how African Americans had been barred from the organization. Beardsley wrote that a few months previously President Morris had written him asking him to join the ABA. He reported that he had replied he would be "glad to accept if the association would wipe out the color line which keeps out those brother lawyers who are Negroes." Morris's long reply laid himself and the association wide open. He explained that in 1936, the governing structure of the ABA was changed so a Board of Governors ran the organization, including admission to membership upon recommendation of state bar associations. That body was composed of a figure from each federal judicial circuit, numbering, at that point, ten, as well as officers of the association. He further wrote that the constitution of the ABA provided that at least two members of the Board of Governors had to come from the circuits in which the "Negro racial problem is deemed to be of great importance," and the bylaws provided that two negative votes in the Board of Governors could block such a nomination. In Beardsley summation of Morris's view: "nothing further was to be done." But Beardsley, who was, at the time of the Rivers's controversy, recovering from an illness, thought differently: "Now maybe (is) the time to make a nation-wide fight on the matter." He drafted a letter to Morris, which he shared with Hays, proposing a change of the rules to stop the practice.[51]

Hays thanked Beardsley for his "valuable" letter and sketched out a plan of action. He told Beardsley that his letter gave him information long looked for as to how the color bar worked. Though Hogan had essentially given him the same information (that the two negative votes were enough to stop a nomination) in his letter in 1938, Hays seems not to have appreciated its importance then, failing to realize that it explained how—in the absence of any explicitly discriminatory rules in the ABA's constitution or bylaws—the color bar operated in practice. This time around, however, Hays fully exploited the information provided by Beardsley to further his campaign and provide it with a focused goal. He decried that the ABA, did "by indirection what it would be ashamed to do directly." Moreover, he added, "I have taken the liberty of repeating these facts to the press. I hope you don't mind. I assume the letter to you was not marked confidential and you said nothing in your letter to me to that effect." Hays explained the mechanism to the African American press. Moreover, in replying to Beardsley, he passed on the information he had learned from Jackson. Hays explained, "The position now taken by the ABA is that the Rivers [sic] application has not yet been passed upon." But the matter was more important than Rivers. "Rivers will probably be admitted, with the hope on the part of the ABA that the agitation dies down. Of course, that would not go nearly far enough to suit me." Hays pressed for an active antidiscrimination clause: "My proposal is that the constitution be amended to the effect that there should be no discrimination against men because of race, religion or color. Then if a man is improperly turned down by the vote of any of the governors, that member of the board should be subject to removal." Hays requested a copy of the final letter to Morris, but none is in Hays's papers, though Beardsley agreed that "acceptance of Rivers would in no way meet the demands of the situation. When I get back to court, I shall do what I can."[52]

The revealing of the mechanism of how African Americans were kept out allowed the development of means to stop the practice without admitting that the ABA was discriminating. Hays's proposal would of course not have done that, because it would have first announced a nondiscrimination policy and then punished board members if they violated it. It was unwieldy and unworkable. But by July 1943, a modification of the bylaws proposed a remedy even as the ABA insisted it was not discriminating on the basis of race. The nature of the fix was revealed in correspondence between Seattle lawyer Edward F. Stern and the president of the ABA. Stern, like Beardsley, in the wake of press reports concerning the failure to admit African Americans to the association, had considered resigning. Before he did so, he asked President Morris for "some explanation" so that "definite and immediate steps should be taken to change the polices of the association." Morris responded supplying a summary of the facts. Rivers's application had been delayed by the "departure of one of the members into the armed services" of the admissions committee for New York. That vacancy lasted several months, and in response for a request for delinquent dues, Goldstein wrote back that he intended to resign because he construed the delay as racial discrimination. Hays, hearing about it, did resign. River's application had come through "in due course" and was pending before the Board of Governors at its next meeting. Morris denied that there was a bar against "person of any color, race or religion" either in its bylaws or "unwritten law. He wrote rather disingenuously that "There are Negro members of the Association now," referring to surviving members admitted before 1912 and the man who had slipped past the rules in 1929. He stated that only two negative votes were sufficient to reject a nominee but said an amendment had been proposed for the next meeting that would require a majority vote of the board for admission. That would "make easier admission to the Association." Stern shared a copy of this letter with Hays, asking if the facts were true.[53]

Hays assured him that they were, save that discrimination was real and ongoing. He told Stern about his failed nomination of Houston and how the then president had hoped to bring around white Southern members to the position that African Americans could be admitted. Hays said he knew that "no negroes have been admitted for several years." He explained the rule that two negative votes given by the board would reject a candidate and "that there are at least two southern judicial districts," which "meant definite discrimination against negroes." It worked as "a practical bar." Hays said he then seized the opportunity of the Rivers application to stir "up public sentiment so as to cure the situation." He was hopeful change because of the publicity. He advised Stern to write President Morris to say that he, Stern, favored "the new amendment and hope that that will end the 'unfair' aspersion on the American Bar Association that it would discriminate against men because of their color."[54]

Stern agreed with Hays that the bylaw change would probably work to "end the discrimination." But instead of writing a cheeky letter to the ABA president, Stern mobilized support the for the amendment change by writing to other members urging their support to "assure the passage" of the amendment to the bylaws requiring that "A majority vote of the Board of Governors shall be required to elect a nominee to membership in the Association." For example, he wrote Hays that he had contacted W. G. McLaren, "a highly respected lawyer of this city [Seattle] who has long been active in the affairs of the American Bar Association and who is attending the annual meeting this year. I am sure he will give this matter his wholehearted attention."[55]

During the August 1943 annual meeting of the ABA in Chicago, the body ended the color bar. First it passed a general resolution, declaring that membership was "not dependent upon race, creed or color." This was not a change to the constitution of the organization, but rather a statement of principle, which of course without saying so replaced the 1912 resolution. Second, it passed a bylaw amendment originally proposed by Joseph C. Thompson (who in 1938 had gone on record saying that if the policy was not changed, the ABA should add "white" to its name) to loosen the grip of white Southerners on the membership admission, raising the required negative votes to block a candidate from two to four. This new bylaw did not require a majority vote, but it accomplished the goal of ending the practical exclusion of African Americans from ABA membership.[56]

Following that, the board of governors elected Judge James S. Watson of New York, an African American, to the membership, but denied the application of Francis Rivers. Newly elected president Joseph W. Henderson did not explain why Rivers was not let in. But a report in the press asserted that other board members said that they needed to investigate his case more closely. In response, Rivers told the *Pittsburgh Courier* that he was not surprised by his application being "pigeonholed . . . for future consideration," adding that he would "not accept membership before all the distinguished members of the bar who resigned in protest against my inadmissibility to the association because I happen to be a member of the colored race—are invited by the Board of Governors to withdraw their resignations . . . and are accepted to full membership." His statement adroitly threw that matter back on the ABA. It also underscored that if the ABA was punishing him for being outspoken, he was not cowed into silence. In September 1943, Governor Dewey nominated Rivers to fill a judicial vacancy in New York City. Certainly this was an action designed to court the African American vote, but it also increased the pressure on the ABA by adding to Rivers's credentials. In October 1943, the City Bar Association of New York accepted the Seabury Committee's report declaring "that considerable progress had been made toward ending discrimination" in the ABA. It noted the change in membership admission rules and the admission of James Watson "and expressed hope that acceptance of the application of City Court Justice Francis E. Rivers, also a Negro would follow." The Seabury committee was to be continued "to check further on the situation." Not surprisingly, given the continued pressure, Rivers was admitted to membership in March 1944 well before the annual meeting. [57]

White Southern ABA members (and some others) continued to resist. After the admission of African Americans to the ABA, Southern members "were profoundly upset." A former ABA president complained about the ending of the color line in the profession. A white Southerner complained that the ABA would not be able to recruit new white Southern members if more African Americans were admitted. The Dallas, Texas, Bar Association asserted that membership of African Americans reduced "the dignity of the bar" and unsuccessfully called for reconsideration of the new ABA bylaw. However, those who disagreed with the ABA's opening up to African American members did not want to abandon the organization. One opponent to the changes "urged his Southern colleagues to remain in the association lest Eastern Jews come to dominate it." This comment showed that at least some of the proponents of the color bar recognized (and resented) the role of Jewish lawyers in ending it in the ABA. Their resistance, however, failed. The course was set for the profession.[58]

Because of the ABA's leading role among bar professional organizations, most other bar associations followed its example. Also in August 1943, the National Association of Women Lawyers at its own Chicago convention admitted three African American lawyers to its membership and adopted a resolution that opened membership to qualified lawyers (in good standing with a state bar association) without regard to race, creed, or color. At the same meeting, the presidency of the organization passed out of the hands of Marguerite Rawalt, who had opposed African American entry. She took her fight to the FBA when she was named its president in the same year and led its opposition to integration in that organization. The FBA finally integrated in 1945 after Rawalt's stint in office ended. Also, bar associations in large cities, like that of Chicago in 1945, ceased discriminating against African Americans. In short, the ABA's ending of its color line made it harder to maintain racial prohibitions in the profession.[59]

The course of the campaign against the ABA's color bar from 1938 to 1943 revealed that World War II reshaped the ideological landscape of American racism. In 1938 and 1943, the agitators for change (mostly liberal and especially Jewish lawyers) had remained the same, and the qualifications of the African American lawyers who had agreed to function as test cases in the two campaigns were equally impressive. In fact, in some respects the 1940s should have been a harder time to effect change because the threat of a strong new bar group in the shape of the National Lawyers Guild had failed to materialize. What made the change possible in 1943 was that the racist ideas that were the foundation of the color bar had come under serious attack as a result of the war. That opposition to Hitler's racism was part of the war effort "nurtured the development" of an "ideology of equality, liberty, and dignity" among many legal professionals. And lawyers and judges used that ideology to reshape the law in a host of areas, jettisoning the racial order that had previously prevailed. The new constellation of ideas also worked well with the shift in tactics for those opposed to the color bar. When two members of the ABA went public with their critique of the racism in the association's membership practices (and as their story appeared in both African American and mainstream press), their message quickly resonated with others in the organization, generating a change in the rules.[60]

In October 1943, Hays had written that while confident that "the furor raised" by his action would "end the discrimination," he feared that "it may well be that when the situation changes I shall apply for read-mission to the American Bar Association. It may also well be that I'll get turned down." His concern continued after the fall of the color line and may have been heightened by the initial rejection of Rivers's application. In October 1943, a lawyer who had followed "the action taken by you and Judge Jonah Goldstein" and "terminated" his membership in the ABA "until such time as they would end discrimination" wrote to Hays asking whether the actions of the convention were sufficient enough to allow him to rejoin, as he had just gotten a dues bill. Hays replied that he was happy he had resigned; "apparently, they are ready to take you back and I don't see any reason why you should not rejoin. In time, I shall, myself, again apply for membership. I hate to do it immediately because I have an idea they might keep me out." Hays's letter indicates that apparently he had not gotten a dues letter. But he did not end on a pessimistic note. Instead, he concluded simply and clearly, "In other words, I think we accomplished the purpose."[61]

As Hays knew, admission to the professional organizations would probably not bring about significant change in the professional lives of most African American lawyers. Indeed, Hays surely knew that African

Americans were only a tiny percentage of members of the profession. In 1930, there were only 1230 African Americans among the nation's more than 160,000 lawyers. Rather, admission to the bar associations was a recognition that they were equal. Like any other lawyers, African Americans would have to make their way in the profession, and that was not easy. For example, Hays knew the difficulties of making ones' way in the profession through his contact with refugee lawyers in the 1930s. At the prompting of Baldwin and others, Hays would welcome refugee lawyers fleeing the Hitler regime into his office. But there were real limits on the firm's ability to take them on, as their training did not prepare them to practice American law. In telling Baldwin that he could not help another, Hays confessed, "I get very much discouraged as to what is going to happen to German lawyers in this country." But he admitted that if they could not be full lawyers, their resourcefulness would allow them to cope. "The only encouraging feature of the situation is that somehow these men do seem to adjust themselves": One used his language skills to help in the patent law field, and another who "had been a tax expert in Berlin and is making a thorough study of our laws so that he might be of value in the tax field." Thus, to see truly accomplished lawyers be denied the recognition that they had earned simply because of their race likely galled him and prompted him to action to increase chances in the profession for others.[62]

Hays knew that lawyering was a business and one that a would-be lawyer had to master, regardless of that person's race, religion, or color. The business aspect of a firm was a reality in Hays's practice. Unlike that of Goldstein's (or his co-counsel in the ACLU, Morris Ernst), Hays's firm was not noted for hiring women or African Americans. His partners tolerated Hays's activism, but few of them shared it. As corporate lawyers, they hired accordingly. The prejudice of clients certainly raised an impediment to hiring African American lawyers. For instance, Hays once sent an article of how to combat prejudice against Jews to Irving Bush, the president of Bush Terminal Company, a longtime client with whom he was friendly. He received a revealing reply: "I agree with the principles which you lay down," and in general Bush said he supported democracy. But he had reservations: "I am a little in doubt whether there should not be some restriction based upon intelligence to the right to vote. If this course were adopted we would probably end up by being governed by the Jews." He supported opening Palestine just to Jews, even though it was just "race discrimination," but then they would move there instead "of anywhere they damn pleased." On the other hand, after all, Arabs "may not be the most comfortable neighbors." Bush reserved the strongest sentiments for African Americans. "So far as the negroes are concerned, I have no objection to their color—except that they sometimes smell. I am afraid, however, that if I lived in a southern state, I would object to having my political destinies controlled by a large group of uneducated colored people." He closed with a joke, saying the answer to these problems would be to elect Hays president, "Mrs. Bush, Vice President. Possibly you might appoint me Secretary of the Treasury so I could run the mint." Hays did not reply to the letter, but such views no doubt influenced his firm's hiring practices.[63]

Hays's answer to the prejudice of clients was to share his knowledge of how to prosper in the profession with those who were likely to suffer from discrimination. He was seen as a mentoring resource by some. For instance, in 1941, he was the attorney whom Clarice F. Brows, who had filled in as staff counsel at the ACLU, sought to speak to about her job hunting after the ACLU (in the words of Lucille Milner of the national office) "thought necessary to have a man in the place." Hays had worked with Brows on a number of briefs and seemed pleased with her work, and he probably agreed with Milner's assessment that she was "far better qualified for the work than most of the male applicants." Milner said that Brows wanted to speak with Hays because she "values your advice and suggestions above anyone else's." Sadly, there is no record of the conversation. Brows went on to work for Associated Gas and Electric as staff counsel. It was not just personal mentoring, though. In 1952, Hays addressed an assembly at the Benjamin F. Butler Law Club of New York University. According the organizers, it was the largest extracurricular organization at the law school, with 150 "men," including fifty alumni. Significantly, in this club, "No person" was "denied membership because of race, color or creed." The group advocated for changes in the law school curriculum to have it be "supplemented and integrated with free play of ideas on vital issues of day." Encouraging lawyers to be involved with ideas and to deal with the issues of the day appealed to Hays. Yet when he addressed them, he talked about the business of being a lawyer. His talk focused on "building a practice." He returned to the club in 1953 to discuss the same subject. He knew these idealistic lawyers of various colors, creeds, and races would need to have professional success before they could be welcomed into the ABA and other prestige organizations even if the color bar was gone.[64]

5

"The educational effect would be worth the investment"

Lynn v. Downer

The night before the court hearing, when he was to represent his brother on the charge of draft evasion, Conrad Lynn received good news. "I received a telephone call from the great Arthur Garfield Hays," who said "he would be happy to appear with me in the federal court." Conrad's brother, Winfred Lynn, had refused induction into the segregated military. Hays joined the case in late 1942 and continued to work on it through 1944, making it the only legal challenge to the segregated military that reached the United States Supreme Court during World War II. It is revealing of Hays's character that he took this case while others refused. It also exposed how difficult it was to manage cause litigation and how easily opportunities could be squandered. Hays and Lynn's other backers failed to make the most of this chance.[1]

The *Lynn v. Downer* case deserves to be better known for the light it sheds on the role of the war in the long civil rights movement. For many years scholars thought that the war liberalized American social values, but this understanding has changed over time. Reflecting current consensus, Kevin M. Kruse and Stephen Tuck point out that while the war did "reshape the battleground and tactics of the black freedom struggle," it did not bring swift change. "It empowered black activism at the same time it constrained" civil rights accomplishments. And although African Americans leaders like A. Philip Randolph and white liberals like Hays

171

worked together to leverage the ideology of the war to bring down segregation, they failed.[2]

The African American activists and their white allies who brought the case thought that it should be an educational effort—a lever to change public opinion about segregation during World War II. But they lost in the courts and failed to build public opinion against segregation in the military, partly because they did not use Hays's considerable public relations skills to good effect. How the case unfolded explains why they failed and why a war fought in part against Nazi racism did not reshape the attitudes of white Americans on segregation of the races. Public opinion polling showed little change in white attitudes about race during the war, and an Office of War Information report on racial attitudes in March 1943 reported that 90 percent of whites surveyed supported a racially segregated military.[3]

We do not know much about Winfred Lynn, and much of what we do know comes from his more radical brother, Conrad. Winfred Lynn was the eldest brother of seven children in a family that had come North near the turn of the twentieth century. The parents, Joseph and Nellie, had been employed by the extraordinarily rich Belmont family in the South and had followed that family to Newport, Rhode Island, but later resettled in Rockville Center, New York. Joseph worked as a landscape gardener on the lavish estates of Long Island while Nellie did domestic work in the mansions. The children attended integrated public schools and took private music lessons. Conrad, and probably Winfred, did work for their parents' clients while growing up. Later, Winfred (Winnie to his family) worked as a car mechanic in a local filling station. For an unknown reason, in the 1920s Winfred ran away from home. He returned home, married, but soon divorced.[4]

Following Nellie's death, Joseph took up with another woman who banned his children from her house, and Winfred took over raising the younger Lynns. The youngest, Samuel, was placed with an aunt, while the unmarried children lived with Winfred. The Jamaica neighborhood in Queens, where they lived, contained a vibrant African American community. It was second only to Harlem in terms of its numbers of African Americans in the state. The African American homeowning population had expanded dramatically in the area during the 1920s. It was a place that fostered "an active organizational life" with property owners' associations, a large National Association for the Advancement of Colored People (NAACP) chapter, and "an active chapter of the Communist Party."

Indeed, this African American community had a tradition of challenging the existing racial order.[5] Winfred Lynn added to that tradition.

At the time of his conscription at age thirty-six, Winfred Lynn was a landscape gardener and possibly had his own firm. According to his brother's later account, "Winnie supported no political party, but he distrusted the economic premises of communism . . . and held the position that a person who really wanted to make it could get ahead." He saw segregation as an impediment to his economic progress and an insult to his human dignity. The war brought about a new affront; according to Conrad Lynn, the Lynn family, including Winfred, "had very strong feelings about the government's humiliating conscription practices." Apparently the siblings discussed the treatment of their race in the Army "and were particularly offended by the contemptible roles assigned to black men." As a contemporary account of his motivation put it, Winfred Lynn "couldn't make sense out of the contradiction between the theory of a war for democracy and the fact of a jimcrow [sic] army."[6]

Thus, upon receiving his notice declaring his classification as 1-A in June 1942, Winfred Lynn wrote to his draft board: "Please be informed I am ready to serve in any unit of the armed forces of my country which is not segregated by race." Unless promised this, Lynn claimed, he would "refuse to report for induction." In an August 16 meeting with the draft board, he repeated his determination, and they referred him to the United States Attorney's Office in Brooklyn, which likely informed him that he would be ruled a draft delinquent and subject to arrest. On September 8, he received an order to report for induction by September 18, 1942. "To contest the validity of the induction order based" on a racially segregated requisition, Lynn refused induction and became a "draft delinquent." He was arrested by the FBI (Federal Bureau of Investigation) and jailed in Manhattan. Through his brother, Conrad Lynn, he sought a habeas corpus to contest his incarceration and the segregated draft.[7]

Conrad, at the time of the *Lynn* case, was a political radical with an extensive public record. The second-born son of the family, Conrad at first followed his father's religiosity and Republican politics; he also shared his father's pride in the exploits of the African American New York–based regiments of the First World War. His mother's aspirations that her children achieve, his own drive and willingness to sacrifice, as well as the assistance of family friends carried Conrad through Syracuse University. At the university, he was exposed to a multitude of people and ideas; he went from wanting to become a minister to wanting to become a lawyer. He was strongly influenced by a professor, Candace ("Pan"—after the Shakespeare character) Stone, and a fellow student, David Dworsky. Lynn found Marxism, which Dworsky espoused, appealing, and in 1928 he became a member of the Young Communist League. Not surprisingly, his radical politics caused him some trouble in law school, but nevertheless he graduated in 1932, resisting the pressure of the Communists to quit and take up work as a Party organizer. As an African American law school graduate with a history of radicalism, Conrad faced bleak prospects looking for work during the Great Depression. Winfred, with whom he was living in Jamaica, refused to let him take up other work, paid his bar examination fees, and subsidized his job search.[8]

In New York City, Conrad's commitment to radicalism continued even as he struggled to make a living and find an institutional home for his activities. After he landed a clerkship in a Harlem law practice, he supplemented his income with a Works Progress Administration job. He continued to labor for the Communist Party. However, he also befriended other non-Communist radicals and formed an intimate relationship with Gene Phillips, a white woman. Phillips was, like Lynn, a protégé of Pan Stone. His differences with Party orthodoxy deepened as he developed interests in anticolonialism and pacifism. In 1937, Conrad was expelled from the Communist Party for his refusal to conform to its dictates on the plans for autonomy for the part of the American South that was predominately African American, and that the anticolonial struggle for freedom be subordinated to the needs of the Soviet Union in world affairs. Nevertheless, he retained his Marxist views. In 1940, when summoned before a New York legislative body investigating Communists in the Works Progress Administration, he refused to name names.[9]

Even as his radicalism continued to define him, Conrad Lynn became associated with many different groups through his social connections. For instance, Phillips was a Socialist and, like Stone, a supporter of Norman Thomas's Workers Defense League (WDL). Formed to combat injustice against workers in the name of socialism, the WDL was involved in trying to improve the lot of tenant farmers in the South, which carried over into confronting the problems of segregation. Lynn was enough of a presence at the WDL that the FBI thought he worked for them. Also, as he later recounted, some of his friends infiltrated "conservative and respectable Negro groups" to build a popular front to address the problems of capitalism. At the same time, he had established himself well enough in the profession (eventually he had an office in the same building that housed the headquarters of the Brotherhood of Sleeping Car Porters led by the African American Socialist A. Philip Randolph) that he could drop his other jobs. He began associating with pacificists in Harlem, where he came into contact with Bayard Rustin and the Reverend John Haynes Holmes. Lynn's activism focused on improving the situation of African Americans in the United States; he was active in A. Philip Randolph's March on Washington Movement (MOWM) and became counsel to the Jamaica branch of the NAACP.[10]

Winfred Lynn's case hinged on the antidiscrimination clause of the Selective Service Act of 1940, which, on its face, seemed to contradict the military's insistence on racial segregation. Military service for African Americans was limited and defined by racial segregation and negative racial stereotyping. African American volunteers and draftees were ushered into a racially divided military service. A racially divided military service, based on the legal doctrine of separate but equal, meant in reality that African Americans were made into second-class soldiers and sailors. In the 1930s, the policy of the military was to not mingle "colored and white enlisted personnel" when they accepted African Americans at all. In 1940, the Air and Marine Corps blocked African Americans from joining. The Navy consigned them to jobs as cooks and stewards; the Army designated African Americans as labor troops who would support and supply the white combat troops. That African American non-commissioned officers and officers would never command white troops revealed the ideology of white supremacy that pervaded the military's plans.[11]

In the 1930s, many African American leaders to begin to stress the "connection between fighting fascism and opposing discrimination." Thus, established civil rights organizations, the African American press, and new organizations focused on the issue of ending racial discrimination in the armed forces and mounted campaigns aimed at the Democratic administration of Franklin Roosevelt. Their efforts were contradictory and conflicted. NAACP lawyer Charles H. Houston in October 1937 appealed to President Franklin Roosevelt to end racial discrimination in the armed forces. His public letter was the start "of an intense campaign by the black press" led by Robert L. Vann, the publisher of the largest African American newspaper, the *Pittsburgh Courier*. Vann at first called for 10 percent African American personnel in the Army on a non-segregated basis, two spaces for African Americans for each West Point entering class, and an all–African American Army division commanded by men of the same race. After polling his readers and finding they feared that full military integration would fail, he reversed himself and called for an increase in the segregated military so African Americans could serve their country in the same proportion as their percentage in the population. These shifting demands did not help the attempts to pressure political leaders into embracing antidiscrimination in war preparedness. Nevertheless, the movement's voice grew louder as war became more likely. In May 1939, the Committee for the Participation of Negroes in National Defense was founded by the *Pittsburgh Courier*. Led by the World War I veteran, activist, and scholar Rayford W. Logan, it aimed to end discrimination in industry and the armed forces. In 1940, leading African Americans, including Logan, appeared before the House of Representative's Committee on Military Affairs to advocate for an increase in African American personnel in all branches of the military. Yet, in the late 1930s, as white Southerners became more and more important to the governing coalition that was the Democratic Party, it became hard to achieve any civil rights goals. Thus, discrimination in the armed forces, which in some people's estimations had replaced anti-lynching legislation as the chief legislative goal of African Americans, remained "a potent political issue in the forthcoming election."[12]

In June 1940, Democrats in the House and Republicans in the Senate introduced bills calling for the first peacetime draft in United States history. It was an unpopular measure; "arrayed against the draft was a potent combination of isolationists, pacifists, liberals, gold-star mothers, educators, and youth groups." The bill was debated and amended for some time, with opposition led by many anti-intervention Republicans. Northern, white liberal Democrats, following the suggestions of their African American allies, introduced amendments adding nondiscrimination clauses, but these amendments were voted down. The military was particularly vocal in its opposition to these antidiscrimination proposals because they contradicted the War Department's plans (rooted in the leadership's entrenched racism) to keep the military segregated. Late in the summer, Wendell Willkie, the Republican nominee for president, announced that he supported the peacetime draft. His position took the conscription act out of the presidential campaign and moved it toward passage.[13]

The act, signed into law on September 16, 1940, passed with a new antidiscrimination clause introduced by arch isolationist Hamilton Fish of New York. In introducing the amendment, Fish said he did so at the suggestion of key figures from the Committee for the Participation of

Negroes in National Defense, including Logan. The act authorized the registration of all men between the ages of twenty-one and thirty-five. Section 4(a) of the act stipulated that, "in the selection and training of men under this act, there shall be no discrimination against any person on account of race or color." While some interpreted this language to mean no segregation, "in the course of the debate on selective service . . . Southern Congressmen made it clear that they did not expect this to mean end of segregation." Indeed, the act had other language concerning acceptability and training, such as that no man would be taken into the military "unless and until he is acceptable to the land or naval forces for such training," and "no men shall be inducted for such training service until adequate provision shall have been made for . . . [their] shelter." But "acceptable" and "adequate provision" were left undefined. During previous debates on earlier versions of the bill, various congressmen had declared, based on these clauses, that the antidiscrimination clause in selection and training would not disturb segregation in the military.[14]

The War Department used this language in the act to limit the anti-discrimination clause. The clauses backed up its barring African Americans from the Air Corps and Marines. As the Army was segregated (and the Navy did not use the draft until 1943 and followed the Army's practice), the military insisted on limiting the number of African Americans called. The Army asserted that segregated training was efficient and necessary. It required that the Selective Service segregate the draft by race. When pressed about the obvious disparity between the principle of being conscripted without discrimination and the practice, General Lewis B. Hershey, the director of the Selective Service, blamed the military. He explained that the "Men who make up the army staff have the same ideas as they had before they went into the army." Their belief in white supremacy meant that they "insisted on maintaining segregation in service, training, and conscription." The result was, in Hershey's words, "simply transferring discrimination from everyday life into the army."[15]

The military's insistence proved a problem for the Selective Service. Selection was supposed to be random to guarantee fairness within the classification ranks. The Selective Service had thus drawn the first names to be conscripted out of giant "goldfish bowl" in a blaze of press publicity. Nevertheless, the service found a way to comply with the letter of the act as it also obeyed the War Department's directives. First, it used the racial classifications of white and Negro on its basic registration card. Thus, when a name was drawn it knew the man's race. The Selective Service drew the names from a common pool, sorting them into separate lists by race after they were drawn. It argued there was no discrimination in selection because men were selected randomly, without regard to race; then the military delayed the induction of African Americans until there were spaces in the segregated training camps. Thus, draft boards with sizable African American populations in their districts kept separate lists for whites and African Americans out of necessity because the separate training facilities might not be ready for one race or the other. The New York City Headquarters of the Selective Service basic form reads "Requisition for Examination—Induction," indicated how it worked: "1. Your Quota for this Call is the first ____ White men and the first ____ Negro men who are in Class I.A."[16]

As the Army did not build segregated training facilities quickly enough, the bureaucratic sleight of hand produced another problem. The delay between selection and induction (which normally was a short furlough to allow men to make arrangements before they left civilian life) stretched for months for African Americans. In New York State, before the United States entered the war, the time gap between selection and service grew even as the number of African American men conscripted increased. For instance, 900 African Americans drafted in January 1941 were told to expect induction in February but were not called up until months later. The problem continued to grow: 27,986 African Americans had been drafted but not inducted by September 1941. By 1943, the number had reached 300,000.[17]

By late 1942, this conscription system with its functional segregation reflected the state of race relations in the war effort. African American organizations pressured the Roosevelt administration to improve the role of African Americans in the military and war industries. Thus, the Roosevelt administration promised to recruit African Americans in numbers representative to their percentage of the population, but it also insisted they would serve only in segregated units. The administration also appointed an African American civilian aide to the secretary of war (William Hastie), appointed an African American reserve officer to the Selective Service (Campbell Johnson), and promoted the nation's first African American general (Benjamin Davis) and promised to begin training of African Americans for the Army Air Corps. These beachheads into the lines of white supremacy were followed by integration of officer candidate school and the limited acceptance of African Americans into both the Navy and Marines. Segregation remained the norm within the military, and the Army continued to relegate African Americans to work battalions. Their deployment overseas lagged behind white units. Progress had also been made on employment of African Americans in the war industries through an executive order establishing the Fair Employment Practices Commission (FEPC) in June 1941. Significantly, the FEPC was brought about by the threat of a mass protest by the MOWM: Civil rights activists had prompted the government to change entrenched racial policies and practices. But there had been no organized movement against the draft.[18]

In 1941 and 1942 a few African Americans in Northern states refused conscription, and the first resisters did so on the ground of being pacifists. If a draft board accepted their status, they were assigned non-military service duty (for no pay) in Civilian Public Service camps, but if they refused that they were prosecuted as draft evaders; more than 2,200 were jailed. With tepid support from African Americans, their organizations, and their press, the draft resistance movement failed to grow. The Selective Service noted how few incidents of draft resistance occurred. It asserted, considering the low "morale" of African Americans confronting a segregated military, that the small number of resisters was "little short of phenomenal." Certainly the high penalties imposed by the courts (three-year prison sentences were the norm) on those who were prosecuted as draft evaders discouraged others from the tactic. This penalty did not deter Winfred Lynn; as he later recounted, "I was determined to make the sacrifice of going to prison . . . rather than submit to the mockery of fighting for democracy in a jimcrow army." His brother searched for ways to keep Winfred from prison while they challenged segregation in the military.[19]

He would have difficulty in obtaining support. Efforts like Winfred Lynn's challenged the "Double V" campaign: the idea that African Americans would fight, in the words of the *Pittsburgh Courier*, "for freedom" in a "two-pronged attack against enslavers at home and those abroad who enslave us." The Double V was eagerly taken up by African Americans at all social levels. Lynn's refusal to be inducted ran counter to one of two parts of that effort: the idea that African Americans should fight against America's foreign enemies. The ideology of double struggle, however, was ingrained in how African American organizations responded to the war at the start of the *Lynn* case. Thus, Lynn's refusal to serve questioned a basis of African Americans' willingness to serve, a key part of the Double V campaign.[20]

The changing race relations during the war and his own recent experiences primed Conrad Lynn to do more than bring a narrow case. He looked for legal assistance and ways to leverage his brother's action into a larger protest. In the face of the spread of the world war, and growing "racism and bigotry" on the home front, Conrad Lynn briefly embraced pacifism and chose to "witness for justice." In particular, Lynn felt betrayed when Randolph, who created the MOWM, called off the March on Washington after FDR issued the executive order establishing the FEPC. He thought it a "typical Socialist trick to avoid 'revolutionary confrontation,'" which he would have welcomed. His dismay deepened when the FEPC did not significantly reduce the discrimination against African Americans in the workplace. At the same time, he was also repelled by the Communists' insistence that all radicals should ally with the opponents of fascism to aid the Soviet Union. He joined an interracial group of pacifists, including the Reverend Holmes (who was a mainstay of the ACLU), in walking from the Harlem YMCA to the White House to deliver petitions to ask for action on ending discrimination in employment. The march took place between Winfred Lynn's telling the draft board he would not be inducted into a segregated military and his arrest. Conrad came away from what he called a "pilgrimage" thinking it had accomplished nothing toward opening up jobs for African Americans. Thus, it is likely that this experience primed him to try different tactics when confronting the segregated military: a legal case that would be linked to mass appeal. He sought aid from the groups he was familiar with: the MOWM, ACLU, and NAACP.[21]

With little assistance, Conrad petitioned to file for a writ of habeas corpus. Indeed, Milton Konvitz (who became involved in the case) noted that "I know that no responsible civil liberties lawyer advised Lynn to make a case. Neither the A.C.L.U nor the N.A.A.C.P. advised him to go into court." Conrad Lynn's application questioned why the government held Winfred Lynn in custody and challenged the legality of his induction based on the antidiscrimination clause of the 1940 act. The hearing date was set for December 4, 1942, and he sought help for that hearing and more. He met with representatives of the MOWM on November 11 and "urged that the March on Washington Movement go on record as opposed to the quota system." While focused on trying to develop a civil disobedience strategy, the organization committed to help Lynn. But it was poorly equipped to manage a legal challenge. Thus, Lynn also solicited help from the NAACP and ACLU. The NAACP, which had not aided men who challenged segregated conscription and was reorganizing its legal efforts (spinning off the Legal and Education Fund,), refused to aid Lynn with his habeas corpus hearing. But he was given the assistance of volunteer counsel (Milton Konvitz) by the ACLU.[22]

During the war, the ACLU committed to ending segregation in the military, a stance it had been prompted into by the NAACP. After receiving a report from Thurgood Marshall, in March 1942 the national ACLU board formed a committee to "conduct a vigorous campaign against race discrimination in the armed forces, in cooperation with other interested agencies." The committee saw itself as "a coordinating agency, enlisting the support of other agencies for specific projects in the campaign." With the help of Edward Bernays (a pioneer of opinion surveying and making), it gauged attitudes about race and the state of race relations through 1942, noting the rampant discrimination in the military and war industry workplaces. It also concluded that by January 1943, that there had been "some improvement in situation," with more African Americans receiving military training, the creation of the Tuskegee squadron, and increased use of African American workers in war industries. It also found that among the organizations it hoped would act against segregation in the military, only African American organizations were "doing any effective specialized work." And that work focused on education—alerting the public to the extent of the problem and trying to build support for ending segregation in the military and war work. Recognizing that the NAACP, Urban League, and MOWM were "limited" in being able to influence the military and the president, the committee hoped to launch "an intensive education campaign under the auspices of an organization composed of influential whites." The committee was willing to entertain court challenges to discrimination. However, its ambitious plans were stillborn, as there was neither the money nor the will in the ACLU to undertake the program. Indeed, the NAACP had determined by this point—given the division in African American ranks and the risk of being accused of thwarting the war effort—not to launch a test case against the segregated military. Thus, the "ACLU publicly called for an end to segregation" but did not actively seek plaintiffs for a test case.[23]

Not surprisingly, when Conrad Lynn offered his brother as a plaintiff, the ACLU vacillated. At first, as was expressed by Pan Stone, Conrad had "received valuable cooperation from" the ACLU through the efforts of "Professor Milton Konvitz of the New York University law school." And he would have been "glad to continue were it not for delicate relations with the NAACP." Indeed, Conrad Lynn later asserted that Marshall interceded with the ACLU to persuade it not to take Winfred's case. When Conrad Lynn physically went to the ACLU to ask for help, its representative "reluctantly admitted that they had an informal understanding with the NAACP not to take a case involving black people if the NAACP disapproved." And so, without assistance, the brothers faced the weight of the government. Before the hearing, Colonel Johnson, aide to General Hershey, head of the Selective Service, approached Conrad Lynn to attempt to persuade him to drop the case. Lynn refused, and on the night before the hearing, he received a phone call from Hays.

Hays told Lynn that Stone, Conrad Lynn's mentor at Syracuse, had urged him to take on the case, as Winfred Lynn was not a draft dodger, but willing to serve his county as long he was not "discriminated against on account of his color." Lawyer members of the ACLU could, and did, take cases dealing with issues in their private capacities as lawyers, and thus Hays was able to join the case, not as counsel for the ACLU, but on his own. Hays stepped in, perhaps believing that by taking a case of value outside the ACLU, he could lead his organization to follow. To that end, he kept the organization informed of what he did on the case.[24]

When Conrad Lynn arrived at the Brooklyn courthouse, as he recounted later, Hays was "already there. . . . He read my file very carefully and at 10:30 A.M. he was ready." The government was also ready, as it was well represented by military lawyers; according to Conrad Lynn, "the courtroom glittered with brass." Lynn described Hays as "a man of enormous dignity and impeccable credentials," but the judge would not look at him. Instead, Judge Mortimer Byers declared, "I have before me the petition for a writ, the writ of *habeas corpus*, the return to the writ. Writ dismissed. Next case!" Hays, moving with the aid of his cane, limped to the bench and lectured the judge on the issues behind the case, declaring that "he thought we were sending soldiers into battle against the Nazi superman philosophy because we were committed to the proposition that all men were created equal." It was a "disgrace" and "mockery . . . to refuse to listen to a young black man who asked only that the government live up to its own professed beliefs."[25]

Hays reported to the ACLU that he appeared before Judge Byers and that the case was dismissed, but he left out of his account the key point: that in an exchange with Hays, Judge Byers opened the door for the case to continue. Byers ruled that Lynn had not submitted to induction so he had not suffered discrimination, prompting Hays to ask, "If the prisoner goes into the army . . . will you issue another writ?" Hays, and press reporters covering the case, came away with the idea that he would. So, as Winfred Lynn later said: "I accepted service on the advice of counsel in order to make a legal test case against military segregation of Negroes." He was freed on a bond of $1,000.[26]

Hays, along with Conrad Lynn, carried the case forward under government scrutiny. After the case failed to be quashed at the first hearing, the FBI began investigating Conrad Lynn. Hays's and Lynn's first step, after Winfred Lynn was inducted, was to seek a new habeas corpus from Judge Byers. "The only difference" between the first and second application was that the writ was now directed at "Lynn's colonel, instead of his jailer." Conrad Lynn brought the petition for the writ to the judge's chambers, but the judge refused to either sign it or speak to him. According to Lynn, Hays was "indignant. He felt the judge had double-crossed him." After releasing this story to the press, they approached Judge Matthew T. Abruzzo, who issued the writ. Conrad Lynn may have personally served it upon Colonel Downer, commandant at Camp Upton on Long Island. The hearing was set for the last month of 1942.[27]

Hays and Conrad Lynn (with Lynn continuing to do most of the work) prepared a brief, which in the words of author and editor Dwight Macdonald did "not confine itself to legal technicalities, but cuts to the heart of the issue, arguing in broad social and historical terms." The brief ranged far beyond usual legal sources, for example drawing in material from the *Encyclopedia Britannica*. It launched an attack on segregation itself. The brief compared segregation to the imposition of restrictions on Jews by anti-Semitic governments, arguing that by its very nature segregation was discrimination and that the Selective Service Act of 1940 did not provide for classification by race and in fact forbade discrimination. It argued that principles of democracy and efficiency in conducting the war demanded that segregation be abandoned. It asserted that segregation of troops allowed racists "to humiliate" African American soldiers in "myriad ways," weakening their morale generally. It explained away the Supreme Court rulings that upheld segregation by asserting the Court was only refusing to interfere with "the exercise by the individual states of their police power." It argued that the national policy did not include racial segregation and pointed to examples where integration was the policy, including the creation of the FEPC. It contended that Lynn was harmed by being denied equal treatment before the law, which was protected by the 5th and 14th Amendments. And as the unconstitutional action of the Selective Service did not "command either obedience or respect," Lynn was entitled to be discharged from custody, as he was held illegally.[28]

Lynn and Hays appeared for Winfred Lynn against lawyers from the Justice Department and from the Judge Advocate General's Office. The government lawyers argued that the draft procedures were necessary because of the military's policy of segregation, that the prohibition of discrimination by race did not extend to segregation, which was legal, and that Winfred Lynn had suffered no harm as he was conscripted later because of the practice. Hays argued that the theory of conscription "was that it was a privilege to serve and that there was discrimination where men were chosen out of their turn, which selection depended somewhat upon color." He pointed out that the 1940 act "particularly provides that there should be no discrimination for or against men because of color." But Judge Marcus Campbell dismissed the suit. In Hays's words, the court "took the position that we had not shown that Lynn suffered any damage." Indeed, he was in fact a beneficiary of the system because he was called later rather than sooner. Moreover, Campbell also questioned whether Winfred Lynn was affected by the quota, as he was conscripted as a draft delinquent. In saying so, Campbell ignored what prompted Lynn into his delinquency and that the delinquency charge had been dropped on the same day that the habeas corpus was issued from the court to Colonel Downer.[29]

After the ruling, Hays wrote to the ACLU describing what happened at this hearing. Most importantly, he related that they had established some clear facts, including that the state director of the draft admitted that the total quota of draftees was broken down by race, as "men were chosen, not serially and in order, but to some extent because of color." The local draft board in Jamaica, following the policy of the Selective Service, called up ninety white men and fifty Negroes, noting their color, "instead of choosing the first 140 men who were eligible." Hays concluded that the case should be appealed and asked for up to $300 from the ACLU to support the appeal. The governing board of the ACLU agreed, even though "nobody thought there was a chance of success in the higher court. But they felt that the educational effect would be worth the investment." Considering the ACLU's desire to launch an educational campaign against segregation, the board seized upon the *Lynn* case as a way to start such a campaign. It also indicated that it did not intend to lead that educational campaign or conduct the case, leaving it mostly in the hands of Hays and Conrad Lynn.[30]

Following the defeat before Judge Campbell in December 1942, and after receiving assurances from the ACLU that it would contribute funds for the appeal, Hays and Conrad Lynn planned to split the appellate work. Promising to go over Lynn's work, Hays asked him to file a notice of appeal and to prepare the record and brief for the appeal. However, on January 15, 1943, Conrad Lynn was inducted into the Army by conscription. Lynn said he planned to invoke the training part of the antidiscrimination clause of the 1940 act when he arrived at a segregated training camp. After induction at Camp Upton, he was sent to Madison Barracks along Lake Ontario in upstate New York. The Army thwarted his plan to challenge segregated training by sending him (in Lynn's words), to "the first unsegregated training unit in the American armed forces!"[31]

Thus, Hays and Gerald Weatherly, acting for the ACLU, took over management of the case. In truth, the ACLU did little. Weatherly did try to keep track of where the military posted Winfred Lynn, advising the Army that he should not be sent overseas as his case was pending. The military did not agree to this limitation. Lynn was transferred to different stateside bases and eventually posted to duty in the Pacific Theater of Operations. Colonel Downer retired. Surprisingly, Conrad Lynn was not fully removed from working on the case. Through the intercession of his commanding officer, in September 1943, he was given leave for a week to help in the "arguments of Winfred's case in the United States Court of Appeals for the Second Circuit." But before the case was heard, it became incorporated with organizations' and individuals' struggles against segregation.[32]

Considering the opportunity the war provided for challenging American racism, it is not surprising that opponents of segregation became interested in the *Lynn* case. For them, Hays became the "face" of the story. Other African Americans sought Hays's assistance in similar cases. Beyond potential plaintiffs, opponents of segregation noticed Hays's involvement. Thus, the Public Affairs Committee of the National Board of the YWCA, at the time of the District Court arguments, sent Hays a letter praising his "association" with the *Lynn* case. It hoped for his "success in your prosecution of it" because it challenged not only the segregated draft, "but the whole philosophy and tradition" that sustained racial segregation. An African American professional driver, in a letter to Morton May of May Department Stores, praised Hays's action: "He espouses the cause of those who are not fortunate, regardless of race, creed or color. Only this morning did I drive him . . . to the Court House in Brooklyn, where he is pleading an important issue for the colored people." The reference to

Lynn's case is fleeting, but the author rightly underscores how important the matter was to those seeking change in the racial policies of the nation.[33]

Interest in the case motivated opponents of segregation to involve civil rights organizations to support Lynn's case. Brooklyn activist Wilfred H. Kerr, shortly after Judge Campbell's decision, attempted to persuade the executive secretary of the NAACP, Walter White, to take up the case. An African American Socialist who was also a member of the Brooklyn chapter of the NAACP, Kerr wrote that Hays and Conrad Lynn were handling the appeal and pitched the case as a good "weapon in our struggle" for a "non-segregated army." A "mixed"—that is, integrated, Army—with African Americans commanding white troops would send a message of uplift "to the depressed hearts of the [colonized] people of the world." But the message could only get out if a leading organization would broadcast it, as the "people have not been thoroughly awakened to the meaning and possibility of a non-segregated army." He offered to bring both Hays and Conrad Lynn to meet with White to further persuade him. White did not respond, and the NAACP did not directly involve itself in the case yet, but Kerr was not alone in trying to interest other organizations into backing the case. One would step in.[34]

Ashley Totten persuaded the MOWM to use the case to attack segregation in the military. In February 1943, at a meeting of the New York branch of the MOWM, Totten, the national secretary of the Brotherhood of Sleeping Car Porters (the man who had recruited A. Philip Randolph to the leadership of the union), argued that the MOWM should make Lynn's case, a "rallying point for a nationwide struggle against racial discrimination in the armed forces." It probably helped that Hays had a good relationship with Randolph; he had worked with him on the Mayor's Commission in 1935 (see chapter 2), and in 1941 Hays had been made an honorary member of the Brotherhood of Sleeping Car Porters. The MOWM in turn became the midwife to a new, focused organization, the Citizen's Committee for Winfred Lynn. At its birth, it claimed it had the support of the ACLU and WDL. Totten also attempted to gain the support of the national office of the NAACP, with little initial success. He had more success among white radicals.[35]

Nancy Macdonald and Dwight Macdonald, white supporters of the WOWM, quickly took up the case. As the *New York Times* archly observed in Nancy Macdonald's obituary, "the union between Dwight Macdonald and Nancy Gardiner Rodman seemed made in establishment heaven . . . both were descended from prominent families, he from the Dwights of old

New England, she from the Gardiners of colonial New York." Her money and commitment to left-wing causes backed and informed his editorial ventures, first the influential intellectual journal *Partisan Review* in the 1930s and later *politics*, founded in 1944. Dwight Macdonald placed the story of Lynn into a leading nationwide liberal periodical, *The Nation*. In his article, Macdonald presumed that the case was destined for the Supreme Court and declared that it raised two fundamental points. First, he asserted it presented the question: Was segregation in itself discrimination? Second, he contended the case raised the issue: Could a war fought for "democratic aims" be conducted with a "Jim Crow army?" But in passing, Macdonald also underscored a key problem with the Lynn case: It was mostly unknown beyond those who read African American newspapers. Only the African American press covered the story in ways that highlighted its importance. Thus, the *Baltimore Afro-American*, commenting on the planned appeal, said the case would "answer the questions: Is a jim-crow army compatible with a war alleged to be fought for democratic aims? And, Is segregation in itself discrimination?" Linking the Lynn case to the struggle against the Nazis, it continued, "an adverse decision would open the legal way to a separate Jewish army too, if prejudice in America increases to that extent.[36]

The Citizen's Committee for Winfred Lynn took some time to organize and begin its work. The most active members—Kerr, Nancy Macdonald, and Dwight Macdonald—were friends. In building the organization, they asserted they wanted "the widest possible support" for the case. The committee included a mix of mix of civil libertarians, Socialists, and other interested citizens, some African American and some white. Equally significant, the Communist Party was not part of this organization and would denounce it. Roy Wilkins of the NAACP was a wary addition, and while A. Philip Randolph backed it, he was not directly involved in the committee. Kerr became its chairman. They were more earnest than informed, as was indicated by their sending a standard recruitment letter in late May 1943 to Konvitz, who had been involved with the case from before the first habeas corpus hearing and was now working for the NAACP Legal Defense and Education Fund. It was probably through the Lynn Committee that Albert C. Gilbert (an African American lawyer, educated at Harvard University and New York University Law School who practiced in Harlem) joined the legal team.[37]

The Lynn Committee would raise funds to pursue the appeal and attempt to use the case to launch a public crusade against the segregated military. Working through the MOWM (the committee was housed in the same building as the MOWM), it held a mass meeting on April 22 in New York City. More than 750 attended and heard eight different speakers, including the lawyers Hays and Gilbert, major civil rights figures Randolph and Wilkins, as well as the key figures from the committee. The audience included many members of the NAACP branches from Brooklyn and Long Island, even though the national organization had not adopted the case. The MOWM considered having Winfred or Conrad Lynn address its national conference to be held in the summer of that year, though such plans were fruitless, as both were in the Army. In May 1943, the MOWM brought out a pamphlet produced by the Macdonalds, *Jim Crow in Uniform*. It covered the full range of issues concerning segregation in the military. After introducing the facts of the *Lynn* case, it appealed to people to join the committee and support it financially. As late as the fall of 1943, supporters of the committee were writing letters to the African American press imploring readers to support the committee with donations. The MOWM was conflicted as to what it wanted to do with the *Lynn* case. At the late June–early July 1943 MOWM National Convention, some pushed for developing a grassroots mass movement to have men do what Lynn had done and follow "the law," refusing segregated military service. Others aimed at a legal strategy, asserting that the organization planned to take Lynn's case to the Supreme Court. If the Court failed "to rule in favor of Lynn, then the Negro has no recourse to the courts of the United States." But if it ruled in his favor, "then the War Department would have to abandon its Jim Crow Policy." This statement captured the view of Lynn's key backers: A legal victory or an awakening defeat would shape their view of what sort of brief should be written for the case.[38]

Just as the educational campaign was slow in developing, the hearing of the appeal was delayed and the preparation of the brief also languished. Those working for Lynn lost focus on the case. In September 21, 1943, instigated by Randolph, they regrouped. Hays, Gilbert, and Weatherly met with key figures of the Lynn Committee and the MOWM: Kerr, Randolph, and Pauline Meyers. Hays and Gilbert, according to Meyers (the executive secretary of the MOWM), "were sincerely interested in forwarding the fight on the case, but both . . . had been handicapped by the tendency" of the ACLU to " 'buck pass' on the case by passing the blame for the lack of activity on first one attorney and then the other." The ACLU also apparently wondered whether this was the case to bring to court, as Lynn could not prove injury. Weatherly for the ACLU prepared to meet that challenge by offering a sociological section to the brief that would assert that African Americans were injured because they could not get into the Army, where they could earn a decent wage. Meyers was scathing in her attack on this position, calling it a "misrepresentation of the Negro's position," as the "real problem . . . was that of the indignity of jim crow." Hays asserted he saw no need for the sociological approach since the goal of the case was to prove "that the discrimination violated a citizen's rights." Gilbert interjected that perhaps they could secure the aid of Charles Hamilton Houston, who had "a peculiar gift of presenting the sociological case of the Negro on the basis of a purely Negro analysis." He stated that unless they could get him to join the suit, the sociological line should be abandoned. It was unlikely that Houston could be brought in, as the case was scheduled to be heard soon, in November. In a meeting right after this one with Gilbert and the committee, it was proposed to keep Weatherly out of the preparations. With Weatherly's proposed contribution now nixed, Hays "left the committee under the impression" that the ACLU would be "left out of the case from now on," as he and Gilbert would deal directly with each other in the future. Hays and Gilbert promised to prepare the records and briefs as quickly as possible. Instead, Gilbert would be dropped from the team. Randolph must have been pleased with Hays's stance and performance, for two months later he asked him for assistance on another matter, and so it is possible that Hays also later expressed an interest in keeping the ACLU involved.[39]

Immediately after the legal meeting, the Lynn Committee was reformulated, with the MOWM taking greater control of it. The original committee proposed that it be recast as the national committee, but Randolph and other members of the MOWM scuttled that idea and created a new national committee, with the original committee now being designated a local committee under the new national committee's direction. But continuity and good relations were fostered by elevating Kerr and Nancy Macdonald to the national committee. A plan for forming a broadly based national committee of prominent figures was made, money was pledged for immediate operations, and organizations and individuals were listed to solicit for further funds. Solicitations extended beyond civil rights organizations to labor, fraternal, church, and women's organizations. The goal was to create an active organization that would "give the case national significance." The newly formed committee was named the National Citizen's Committee for Winfred Lynn and headquartered in the same building as MOWM. It was significant that neither Nancy Macdonald nor Dwight Macdonald attended either meeting, as that meant that the persons in charge of the educational campaign had little interaction with counsel preparing the case. The new committee was immediately asked to participate in a planned MOWM and WDL mass meeting that would discuss the *Lynn* case, among other things. The National Committee later in 1943 published a pamphlet, "The Story of Winfred Lynn," that succinctly presented the issues of the case and tied them to the larger goal of ending segregation in the military, not just in the draft. The committee portrayed the ending of the Jim Crow Army as a way to avoid more race riots like the one in Detroit that had broken out in June 1943. Service together in the military would promote "a better understanding" between the races. It prominently listed its supporting organizations as the ACLU, MOWM, NAACP, National Council for a Permanent FEPC (started by Randolph but affiliated with the Congress of Industrial Organizations), and WDL to establish that theirs was a legitimate organization and effort. It concluded that a democratic America after the war was possible, if Jim Crow in the Army was ended. It implored people to "fight Jim Crow in the Army" by joining the organization or contributing.[40]

After the new Lynn Committee formed and became active in both recruiting and trying to educate the public about the case, the NAACP changed its stance and the government responded. Ever vigilant to competitors to its position as a leading organization of civil rights advocacy, the NAACP now began to show interest in becoming actively involved in the case. At the NAACP national convention in October 1943, the organization adopted the position that it supported Lynn "in his effort to be recognized as a conscientious objector to serving in a segregated army." Their framing of the case turned Winfred Lynn into a conscientious objector, but it also indicated that his protest was acceptable to many African Americans. Wilkins wrote to Hastie, who had resigned in protest from the War Department, to add a personal appeal to the formal request by the Lynn Committee that he serve on it. Wilkins did not urge Hastie to serve but said the NAACP supported the case and if he had questions he should write to Hays. Hastie did join the committee. This growing organized action to promote the case possibly inspired the military to try to cut it off by offering to send Lynn to the "Army's Officers' Candidate School for the Chemical Warfare Service" if he would "dissolve the Lynn Committee." The offer was particularly astute, as officer training schools were where the military had integrated training. Winfred refused the offer.[41]

In early December 1943, the United States Circuit Court of Appeals heard the case. The Hays, Gilbert, and Weatherly brief contended that Winfred Lynn had been inducted through the use of a racial quota, which constituted discrimination in violation of the Selective Service Law prohibiting such discrimination. It expanded on the District Court brief's treatment of what was considered discrimination by presenting a long list of different dictionary and commonsense definitions. It also argued that the lower court had erred in rejecting this claim that Lynn had not been part of the "Negro quota." It rebutted the idea (raised in the lower court) that Lynn had benefited in that he was called later than he might have been if there had been no separate lists, or that that the separate lists made no difference in when he was called. Ultimately, it dismissed the harm argument to stand on principle: The law prohibited discrimination by race, and every man (including whites) categorized by race was thus discriminated against. This argument was an implicit attack on separate but equal, and so the brief argued that previous cases upholding segregation as constitutional only applied to the states, not the federal government. The United States attorney countered that Lynn had suffered no harm and indicated (building on the claims of uniform reach in the petitioner's brief), if the court granted Lynn his habeas corpus, that it would open the gates to thousands of African Americans to leave the service.[42]

While the decision was pending, the National Lynn Committee increased it activities. It made repeated appeals for funding and support and placed his story before the public. It probably asked for action from groups interested in racial justice. New York City's WEVD radio station, between the argument and decision in the Court of Appeals, broadcast a thirty-minute story on Lynn's challenge to the segregated draft. The Lynn Committee press release for the broadcast declared that the "full story" of the *Lynn* case would be "heard on the air for the first time." It portrayed the *Lynn* case as "the dramatic fight of one Negro against the status of second-class citizenship to which his people have been relegated, the Lynn case has come to be known as 'the 20th century Dred Scott case.'" It said its participants would show the connection between military segregation and discrimination in civilian life as the nation entered an era of heightened racial strife marked by riots and fears about the shape of the postwar era. In December 1943, the Jewish fraternal organization, Workmen's Circle, through a number of branches in New Jersey and New York, wrote to federal officials asking that Lynn be released from the service and that the draft be reformed to prohibit separate lists by color. While showing full familiarity with Lynn's experience, the letter made the larger point that the draft as constituted created "two classes of citizenry." Their interest was more than matched by many African Americans. In February 1944, Winfred Lynn was put on the "honor roll of race relations" for 1943 "for his fight through the courts to abolish Jim Crow from the armed forces." This list of a dozen African Americans and organizations and a half-dozen white people was put together after a nationwide survey of African Americans by the Schomburg Collection of the New York Public Library. Lynn's actions clearly resonated among African Americans.[43]

The Circuit Court delivered its decision in early February 1944. The majority opinion, written by Judge Thomas Swan and supported by Augustus N. Hand, brushed aside the lower court's ruling that Lynn had been admitted as a draft delinquent and therefore the process by which he was chosen no longer mattered. The majority opinion admitted that Lynn was inducted as "a member of a Negro quota." But it denied that Lynn had suffered any harm by being drafted in this manner. Indeed, ignoring the arguments in the Hays, Gilbert, and Weatherly brief, the majority held that Lynn had benefited because he probably was inducted later. The majority opinion justified the practice of a segregated draft by reading the legislative history of the antidiscrimination clause in the conscription act through the filter of previous federal laws and practices that sanctioned "the Army's history of separate regiments of whites and Negroes." The court argued if the Congress had wanted to end segregation in conscription and training it should have said so more clearly.[44]

Significantly, Judge Charles Clark dissented. His reading of the legislative intent of the Congress in adopting the antidiscrimination clause went further into the record to show that the very clauses that the military used, the acceptability and training facilities clauses, were not designed to continue racial segregation. He ignored the few statements of the congressmen who had said these clauses supported segregation to point out that the aim of those specific clauses was to prevent the induction of unfit people and placement of draftees in unsafe facilities. Replying directly to the majority opinion about the meaning of the law, he wrote: "I find it difficult to think of more apt language to express the Congressional intent." No discrimination meant no segregation in conscription or training. Lynn's willingness to serve under the law exposed the Court's premise that he benefited from a delay (implying that "avoidance of service is to be desired") unpatriotic, "unsound," and "contrary to the whole spirit of the Act." Clark, following the reasoning of Lynn's brief, then turned separate but equal against the government by asserting that that doctrine required "equal calls to service." He discounted the idea that deciding in Lynn's favor would open the door to African Americans already in the service to leave the service, as they had not raised their objection at the proper time, when they joined. He kept Lynn's protest within the confines of supporting the war effort when he concluded, "However undesirable the colored people may regard service in segregated units, they are justified in asserting that it is less degrading than no service at all or service delayed, if not belittled, in the light of their available man power."[45]

A divided court raised the potential of appeal to the United States Supreme Court and renewed interest in the case. The *New Journal and Guide*, a Norfolk, Virginia, African American paper, said the case was a "ticklish one . . . since to decide in favor of the defendant would have branded the whole discriminatory structure of draft induction as illegal. . . . But in deciding against Lynn the court had to place some very peculiar interpretations upon plain facts, plain law, and plain justice." Four days after the Circuit Court ruling, Hays announced for the ACLU that the case would be appealed to the Supreme Court. The ACLU expressed "gratification that the issues have been squarely met by the court, thus affording an opportunity for an appeal on the merits of the case." If the chance of victory was slight, the risk of taking the case to the highest court and receiving a catastrophic ruling upholding segregation was not high. The Supreme Court had recently shown in higher education, transportation, criminal procedure, and voting rights cases a willingness to alter the established racial regime in American law and life. And, as the war progressed, the suit became more popular with civil rights activists as the hesitancy of challenging segregation had declined within African American circles. For instance, in the *Pittsburgh Courier*, the prominent African American sociologist Horace Cayton wrote that the Army's assertion in the *Lynn* case that segregation was not discrimination was both a dodge and a straw man. "[W]hat we're kicking about is both." Indeed, both undercut "the entire ideology of the war" and weakened "the heart of our democratic structure. It is important especially at this time when we are fighting racialism to see that the Federal government is not in any way officially and formally upholding policies of either discrimination or segregation." The importance of the case now made it imperative that the NAACP become involved. Beyond that, the NAACP's Legal and Education Fund had become established and expanded its staff. Thus, Marshall wrote to Hays that "we are likewise very anxious to do whatever we can to help in this case and would appreciate an opportunity to do so." By January 1944, the NAACP supported the case fully: "in our opinion the case is a worthy one although in Mr. Hays' [sic] words, it is 'new law' in a fresh field and the chances of losing it are just as good if not better than the chances of winning it."[46]

The Lynn Committee quickly went to work to raise money for the ACLU's handling of the case before the Supreme Court and to increase the salience of the case in the public mind. It did not wait for new stationery but rather repurposed some from the old committee, with "national" added to the name, with changes in the leadership and its address added through strikeouts and typing in new names, and adding at the bottom of the page, "The 20th Century Dred Scott Case." The slogan was meant to inspire fear and hope: They argued that an adverse decision in the case would be "as equally catastrophic" as *Dred Scott* had been to African American citizenship in 1857. But they also framed it as part of the forward march of history: "<u>Slavery was historically outworn in 1857, and second-class citizenship for the Negro is outworn in 1944</u>." They sought donations to fund the appeal and to spread the message. The letter admitted that the case was known "TO RELATIVELY FEW PEOPLE. WE WANT YOUR HELP IN MAKING IT KNOWN TO EVERY DEMOCRATICALLY MINDED AMERICAN!"[47]

Two briefs were submitted on the petition for a writ of certiorari from the Supreme Court, one from the Lynn, Hays, and ACLU team as counsel and one from the NAACP as amicus curiae. They had to contend with the majority opinion of the Second Circuit, which had held that segregation was the Army policy and drove the selection and training of men, and the antidiscrimination clauses did not intend to end segregation. The government's brief relied on these points. The petitioner's brief argued that Winfred Lynn had been inducted through the use of a racial quota, which constituted discrimination in violation of the Selective Service Law's antidiscrimination clause. It portrayed the case simply: The law prohibited discrimination by race, and all men (including whites) categorized by race were thus discriminated against if they were not inducted randomly. It deliberately kept its focus on the draft and did not go into the practice of segregation in the military. The focus on the civilian nature of the draft was a strategic choice. If their argument did prevail, it would establish a precedent that did not rest on the war powers, which would end with the war. In oral argument, Hays conceded that racial segregation in the

Army might be justified on grounds of military necessity, but that did not reach to the selection of men because they were civilians at the time of selection. Even this limited argument was an implicit attack on separate but equal. The NAACP brief, written after the Lynn, Weatherly, and Hays brief, was crafted by Konvitz and Leon Ransom, a graduate of Ohio State University Law School and then acting dean of Howard University Law School. Ransom had been an active attorney for the NAACP in some of the leading cases of the 1930s. The brief took on directly the claims of the Circuit Court that segregation was established and legal practice in the military by asking the court to construe the act on its face. More reaching, the brief used the recent case of *Hirabayashi v. United States*, which upheld the curfew order against people of Japanese ancestry, to assert that distinctions between citizens by reason of color or race without the imperative of a "critical military situation" was "<u>beyond</u> the brink of constitutional power of the Federal Government."[48]

While the lawyers worked well together, the interactions between the organizations were not marked by close cooperation. For instance, in February the NAACP issued a press release touting its filing of an amicus curiae brief in the *Lynn* case. Significantly, they failed to mention that the Lynn Committee was handling the case. Also, in February, Dwight Macdonald, who had launched his new magazine *politics*, in its first issue reprinted the original Conrad Lynn brief before the District Court. He did so in the first installment of his regular column, "Free and Equal," to promote the idea that the case was presented to the courts through a "social brief" that would address "broad social and historical" issues. He only mentioned the National Committee's role in promoting the case. Acting on the assumption that they were working toward the same goal, the National Citizens Committee asked Konvitz at the NAACP for a list of names and addresses of the NAACP's National Legal Committee so literature could be sent to them. Konvitz asked Wilkins, who responded that while he did "not favor releasing this list," Konvitz should check with Marshall. While it is unknown what Marshall decided, the exchange shows that Wilkins did not want to share resources with the Lynn Committee. The NAACP national office's keeping the Lynn Committee at arm's length caused confusion and delay. For instance, the NAACP Baltimore branch had collected $53.00 for the Lynn effort, "encouraged our members to attend the meetings of the local Lynn Committee," and even "had some of the secretarial work of the committee done in our Office." But these actions stretched the branch's resources, and so it wrote to Wilkins asking what was "expected of the NAACP Branches in support of the Winfred Lynn Case." Until they heard from the national office, they would "withhold further action." Such limited cooperation hampered the development of an effective campaign to generate public interest in the case.[49]

These smoldering tensions between the groups went public when in April 1944 Dwight Macdonald publicly scolded Hays for his approach to the case and Hays and Konvitz responded. In his magazine, Macdonald chastised Hays's approach, which he characterized as being "in the narrowest legalist tradition" avoiding the "big social questions" raised by the case. He declared that Hays had "expunged all general social considerations from his consciousness that he scarcely seems interested in the fact that Winfred Lynn's segregated quota had something to do with the color of his skin." Macdonald dismissed this approach as a mistake because it did not focus on the "whole principle involved." He lamented the focus on the draft because it thus did not challenge segregation in the military. He asserted that a sociological brief that directly challenged segregation would, even if it brought "an adverse decision . . . have been a politically educational document." Macdonald saw the case in Marxist terms. Hays's approach was not materialistic but legalistic and guided by his liberalism and support for the New Deal. He wished to avoid real conflict that would bring about real change. Macdonald also made no mention of the NAACP brief, which was more in line with his own strategy. Hays's response, printed following the article in the same issue, defended his course, saying that if he had argued the case as a segregation case it would have been "summarily thrown out of court." So instead he worked to "establish a principle which also is important" of no discrimination in selection by civilian authorities. If the court ruled in Lynn's favor on this point, it would allow a further attack on segregation when it could not possibility be justified by exercise of the war powers. What Macdonald deplored as the slow legalistic approach, Hays saw as the essence of law—that it "moves step by step." Macdonald shared the exchange by letter with Konvitz, who also rejected the criticism of Hays. He agreed with Macdonald that selection and training were linked in the act and that Macdonald's argument thus was logical. But "if it was only a matter of logic, there would be no need to study law." Konvitz thought Hays correct in believing that the court would not declare segregation unconstitutional "in a case involving the armed forces. If a beginning is going to be made, it will probably be made in a case involving segregated educational facilities." He reminded Macdonald that Hays had come to

Conrad and Winfred's aid at a critical time and had stayed with the case despite his doubts of winning it. He added that Hays would "see it through for whatever it is worth." He particularly thought Macdonald had been "unfair" to Hays in saying he was defending the existing economic order. He characterized Hays as "a true civil libertarian and [one who] considers the Bill of Rights of much more importance than any other part of the Constitution." These exchanges revealed a depth of difference between the groups in both their starting philosophies and tactical choices.[50]

Even where they had worked well together in the crafting of legal arguments, their efforts were in vain. The US Supreme Court on May 29, 1944, following a hint put forth by the solicitor general in his brief, refused to grant certiorari in the case. The Court seized upon a technicality to avoid the case. The writ was denied "on the ground that the cause is moot, it appearing that the petitioner no longer is in respondent's custody." Since Winfred Lynn had been transferred out of the custody of Colonel Downer as part of his duties, the suit was dismissed. Of course, Lynn had not been in the custody of Downer at the time of the Circuit Court decision. Nor had this objection to the suit been raised at any earlier point. And as was pointed out by commentators at the time, this evasion overlooked the "established procedure of substituting respondents" in such cases—that is, on petition to a court that Lynn's current commander be substituted for Downer. The Selective Service was pleased with the outcome. General Hershey wrote the attorney general on August 25, 1944, to thank him for the help from the lawyers from the Department of Justice in handling the case, saying the Supreme Court's denial of certiorari was a "most satisfactory solution."[51]

On the other side, Winfred Lynn wrote from the South Pacific "that nothing fazes me." His brother, Conrad, called the decision "hypocritical evasiveness." Lynn's supporters immediately decided to petition for a rehearing. The effort was led by the lawyers; Hays and Conrad Lynn discussed options and at least Weatherly and Konvitz met on May 31, 1944, with Weatherly committing to move forward with a petition. The next day, Konvitz sought Marshall's approval to submit an amicus curiae brief in support. Marshall doubted the course. "Is it not a waste of time, effort, and money?" he wrote. "There are loop-holes in the Lynn case big enough to drive trucks through." But he relented, though he thought there was nothing new to say. Konvitz immediately wrote a memo to Wilkins. In it he outlined a press release, reviewing the case, explaining the Court's reason for denying certiorari. He stated that the petition for a rehearing would focus on the issue of the respondent officer and saying that if the Court's ruling followed in other cases, it would block any other use of habeas corpus against the military, as the government could transfer the petitioners "from one camp to another," changing the person who held them in custody. By June 10, 1944, the rehearing plans were appearing (attributed to efforts by the Lynn Committee) in African American papers. The *Cleveland Call and Post* said the Court had found the case "too hot to handle" and quoted Kerr, saying that "the Negro and the Progressive people of this country want to know why segregation is not discrimination and what is the meaning, if any, of the clause against discrimination in the 1940 Draft Act."[52]

By necessity, the briefs focused on the issue of the respondent and that a writ of habeas corpus should not be defeated by technicalities. The lawyers fruitlessly explored other options; for instance, Hays, acting as counsel for the ACLU, wrote to the secretary of war arguing that the military had made an implicit promise not to transfer Lynn abroad and thus out of the jurisdiction of the court—presumably trying to set up an argument that the case should be reheard on the ground that the military had broken that agreement. But the adjutant general's office produced documentation showing that it had in fact made no such promise in Lynn's case in correspondence with Weatherly in February 1944. This gaffe showed how poor coordination had been between parts of the Lynn litigation team earlier in the case. The rehearing briefs argued that the particular officer did not matter; rather, the jurisdiction of the military mattered. But as the commander in chief could not be sued, Downer had been used, and when Lynn was transferred from his custody, then Lynn's current commander should have been substituted for Downer and the case reviewed by the Supreme Court. The ACLU brief also made an impassioned argument that technicalities should not be used to sidestep the "precious safeguard of personal liberty." The actions in filing the petitions were covered by the African American press, which used the occasion to advocate for ending the segregated draft.[53]

The Lynn Committee took a different route. In response to the failure of the Supreme Court to hear the case, the Lynn Committee reconstituted itself and stepped up its educational effort. First it changed its focus, broadening its ambit to ending all racial discrimination within the military. Its new name said it all: "The Lynn Committee to Abolish Segregation in the Armed Forces." Second, it championed the case of some African American members of the military who had been subjected to dishonorable discharge following their protests against discrimination, but it did defend men who sought legal representation in their cases against the segregated draft. Third, it planned, according to Macdonald, "a publicity campaign" to change minds. Its publicity campaign, however, quickly morphed into an attempt to bring segregation in the military into electoral politics. In July 1944, the Lynn Committee asked candidates for federal office four questions: Did they support racial segregation in the military? What did they think was meant by the no discrimination clause in the 1940 draft act? If elected, would they help abolish segregation in the military? And did they have a proposal of their own to remedy the injustices "now being done to hundreds of thousands of American boys now serving in the armed forces?" The four questions were also put in a petition and sent to Lynn Committee supporters, asking them to get signatures and find other groups (including unions and churches) to sponsor the effort. The letter emphasized the goal that by ending segregation in the military, "our young men and women in the services, colored and white, will learn to understand and respect each other," which would be a "tremendous step in the struggle for racial democracy." However, their effort did not generate any political traction in the 1944 election.[54]

While the Lynn Committee followed its educational and political path, the ACLU narrowed its focus on legal developments. It was concerned that the military had found a way to avoid constitutional challenges by transferring people out of the jurisdictions and that the ramifications reached beyond this single case. The pleading in the rehearing of Lynn, according to an ACLU attorney in Washington, prompted the Supreme Court to ask "the War Department for a memorandum in the case of Winfred Lynn to explain why they removed him from the jurisdiction of the original court and evidently there is some idea of reviewing the case if the answer is unsatisfactory." At the same time, the case of Mitsuye Endo was before the Court, challenging the legality of interning loyal United States citizens of Japanese descent, where a similar tactic had been used and a similar request was sent concerning her case to both the War and Interior Departments. "It would appear that the Court has attempted to meet the jurisdiction problem not by changing any rules, not by a decision, but by getting commitments from the administrative departments." Endo's case was resolved when the Court held the internments unjustified. But Lynn's petition did not receive a similar favorable result. On January 2, 1945, the Supreme Court denied the request for a rehearing in his case.[55]

The war ended in August of 1945, but the segregated military continued prompting the Lynn Committee to carry on and Randolph to form a new group: the National Committee to Abolish Segregation in the Armed Services. Part of the impetus for this new organization might have been Randolph's determination to have African Americans lead their own organizations. This was a position that Kerr saw as separatism and strongly disagreed with, driving a wedge between the organizations. Randolph's plans for the organization were overly ambitious, and it failed to gain much support. The two organizations cooperated to some extent. Randolph continued to allow his name to be used for fundraising by the Lynn Committee and agreed to a change in the new organization's name to avoid confusion. Thus, it is not clear who arranged a hero's welcome for Winfred Lynn in Harlem later in the year. While honorably discharged, Lynn came home "with no medals for military achievement. His title of 'hero' was won in another war—to abolish segregation in the armed forces." He spoke to "an audience that packed and jammed the auditorium of the Public Library." In his talk, he "spoke from personal experience on official an[d] unofficial methods employed by commanding officers to enforce second class status on negroes." The African American press that covered the event called the Lynn case "famous" and said that it "struck at the heart of military bias."[56]

After the war, the Lynn brothers continued to work against segregation in different ways. Conrad Lynn's activism shifted focus. During his service he was active in battling segregation and ill treatment within the military. His and his brothers' time in service were apparently monitored: James Evans, who replaced Hastie as assistant to the civilian aide to the secretary of war, later noted that all the Lynn men had been involved in pushing against segregation while in the military and that Conrad, in particular, "did not find military service arduous when he was inducted." After his discharge in October 1945, his commitment to Marxism caused him to drift away from his old friends, including Dwight Macdonald, who was still active in the Lynn Committee. He turned to fighting segregation policies by direct action, participating in one of the first freedom rides of the postwar era. Samuel and Winfred Lynn persisted in activism against the military. Samuel, who had "served with the Army Air Forces," was in 1947 "actively pressing his application as a candidate for a commission in the Regular Army," pushing against the military's desire to shrink the number of African Americans in command. Winfred participated in a public forum on segregation in the military. Eventually he returned to private life, using his GI Bill funding to pay for training at Cornell University in the use of herbicides and insecticides to modernize his gardening business.

His commitment to the cause continued as shown by where he chose to live: Rochdale Village, the integrated, co-operatively owned housing venture built in Jamaica.[57]

Postwar activists mostly focused on ending segregation in the military itself, not discrimination in the draft. The position of African American service members declined after the war ended as opportunities for training and advancement fell. However, facing bleak economic prospects, African American men "flocked to the military in record numbers" before 1950, prompting the military leaders' attempts to limit their numbers and advancement. The issues became somewhat known to the larger society because of a number of lawsuits brought by African American soldiers and because the mainstream press covered the discriminations against African Americans troops in Germany. Nevertheless, activists knew that the issue was not salient among most Americans. Indeed, an educational pamphlet put out at this point by one group (which was intended to reach a mass audience, as it had a preface by the popular cartoonist Al Capp and illustrations by the famous WWII illustrator Bill Mauldin) was titled "Nobody Knows."[58]

As the Cold War deepened, however, the issue of the segregated draft returned with the proposal of plans for universal military training and then a peacetime draft. A segregated military determined to keep African Americans at about 10 percent of the force would result in a segregated draft. And because the conscription act of 1940 with its anti-discrimination clause had expired, there seemed little legally that would stand in the way. Randolph reacted to the proposed revival of the draft by launching the Committee against Jim Crow in Military Service and Training in November of 1947, aiming it to use the political process to stop segregation from being part of any new draft law. He and his allies publicly announced plans to create the "League for Non-Violent Civil Disobedience Against Military Segregation," promising to urge mass civil disobedience by inductees to a segregated draft.[59]

In the end, a burst of activism and a changed political and media climate desegregated the military through executive order. The creation of the league and the resultant publicity its leaders and other African Americans received in the mainstream press made the segregated military a major national issue. Moreover, the unity shown by African American organizations and leaders over their refusal to countenance a segregated military any longer meant the compromise path used in WWII, the expansion of African American roles within the military, would not be tenable in the Cold War era. This point was underscored by the recommendation of the President's Commission on Civil Rights: that the military needed to be integrated. The advocacy of civil rights in the Democratic administration of President Harry Truman prompted a revolt of the Southern conservative leaders. The defection of the Dixiecrats and their voters from the Democratic Party required Truman to strengthen his electoral appeal to African Americans and those whites who were sympathetic to ending segregation. Thus, in 1948, he issued an executive order desegregating the military. The death of segregation in the military was not quick or easy, but its formal demise immediately put an end to the practice of the segregated draft that lay at the heart of Lynn's case.[60]

The *Lynn* case says much about challenging military discrimination during the war years. It shows us that mobilizing action against racial barriers was difficult. The government (especially the military but backed by civilian leadership) was very resistant to change. Civil rights organizations were hesitant to challenge the segregated draft. In 1942, when the case started, the NAACP rejected the case and the ACLU offered weak help. If Lynn had not been first represented by his brother, and if Hays had not decided to act as an independent agent, the case would have ended in the district court at the first hearing. After that, the MOWM kept the case alive. The new and rather limited Lynn Committees managed the litigation in its first stages through the hearing before the Second Circuit Court of Appeals and mounted an educational campaign. Even after the ACLU and NAACP joined with the MOWM in supporting the case, the litigation effort failed. From drafting the briefs, through the application for certiorari, the Supreme Court's rejection, and the petition for a rehearing before the Supreme Court, tensions and divisions between the groups and individuals involved bedeviled all their work. They did not see the implications of Lynn being shifted in his military assignments that in the end proved fatal. Since legal victory was never the sole goal, the failure of the educational campaign—the litigation as protest—was more significant.

The educational campaign carried out by the Lynn Committees and their allies did not capture the national spotlight. At times they did break through and get the story covered in mainstream newspapers, but an established campaign never emerged. One problem was that it failed to use Hays in their campaign. This was a real missed opportunity. Hays was a dynamic and popular radio presence in this period. Hays's experience on the radio was extensive. He had spoken on many different shows, including on "Wake up America," which was on the blue radio network carried on more than a hundred stations across the nation. Hays had mastered talking for the radio. He sounded natural over the air, a result of the process he followed: "I find that writing out a speech clarifies my thought, but I hate under any circumstances to read a speech. And my own experience is that particularly over the air one is more effective if he forgets his manuscript." For instance, after he participated in a radio event for the General Federation of Women's Clubs, the head of their Radio Committee reported to him that they had gotten good follow-up coverage in the *New York Daily News*, adding, "I would rather have a write-up like this in the 'News' than in the 'Times' because it is the masses we wish to reach." After one broadcast, the organizers wrote to him: "we had some telephoned comments afterward which indicated that both your information and manner of delivery had hit the mark." For another broadcast, a station received 105 letters about Hays, and the station declared, "They constitute a great tribute to you. . . . I congratulate you on being compared to both Will Rogers and Honest Abe." Moreover, since Hays tended to go off the scripts he had prepared, it was likely that any address he gave would have reached the larger points that he scrupulously avoided in his brief to the Supreme Court, but which Lynn's backers wanted to get out to the public. But that was a lost opportunity, as Hays did not participate in the one radio broadcast in early 1944 on a New York City station.[61]

The print media campaign did not reach the masses either. The *Lynn* case was, as one historian aptly put it, "virtually ignored" by the "news media." Or, as another scholar declared, the "case generated almost no press coverage." Most of that campaign ended up being carried in the African American press, and even there the *Lynn* case was lightly covered. Moreover, the stories that did appear in the African American press originated from the Lynn Committee. The papers did not aggressively follow the story. At first, the problem of fitting the case into the existing popular Double V campaign probably made the papers shy away from it. The African American newspapers' reliance on the NAACP press releases for much of their information on legal matters, and that organization's failure to adopt the case early, had a secondary repercussion of reducing press coverage. Also, the decision by Hays, and the other lawyers, to focus on discrimination in selection, an obtuse strategy difficult to connect clearly to the crusade against racism in the military, might have limited press coverage by the African American press.[62]

Thus conscribed, the Lynn story had little chance of reaching the greater society. Very few white Americans read African American newspapers. In general, the mainstream media was just not interested in most racial stories other than race riots, which they inevitably blamed on African American militancy or Communist agitation. Only very few white publications covered the topic of racial discrimination in any depth: *Common Sense*, *The Nation*, the *New Republic*, and *PM*. As the mainstream press almost ignored the Lynn case, it did not reach the ears or eyes of most white Americans and thus had no chance to educate them about racial segregation. This effort to change the attitudes of white people about segregation failed.[63]

Even with its inconclusive end, the *Lynn* case says much about how Hays involved himself in civil rights matters, the level of his commitment once he began, and how others perceived his activism. He apparently took the case because Stone convinced him, in Conrad Lynn's words, that "Winnie was no mere draft dodger but an opponent of racial discrimination." He stayed on the case even though there were many exit points, such as when Byers refused the revised writ or the adverse decision by Judge Campbell, because he thought it could achieve something. He pulled the ACLU fully into the case, which eventually brought the NAACP on board. Moreover, after it was over, but while the issue of the segregated military was still alive, Hays participated in two public forums hosted by Randolph's organization to draw attention to the discrimination. From all that survives of the interactions between him and Randolph, Marshall, and Wilkins, they found him a good working partner. Most significantly, the Marxist Conrad Lynn, who had little good to say about any of the others involved in the case, was effusive about Hays. He characterized him as "one of the finest and most compassionate attorneys in the world." Lynn said that for his brother, Hays gave "the best extemporaneous court argument I had ever heard." Lynn judged that "it was impossible not to be impressed and filled, just a little, with awe." Conrad Lynn portrayed him as a hero, but, unlike mythic heroes, real-life ones did not always prevail.[64]

6

Prejudice

The Limits of Hays's Racial Liberalism

In February 1945, while submitting an article idea, Arthur Garfield Hays wrote: "I should want to add to it somewhat—a reference to the Ives-Quinn bill as the kind of law that will lead to the bootlegging of prejudice." Ives-Quinn would become law and establish a New York State body dedicated to rooting out discrimination in employment like the wartime federal Fair Employment Practices Commission (FEPC). The FEPC was one of the signal achievements of African American activists during the war, and creating a permanent FEPC became a key part of the liberal agenda in the postwar period. The NAACP and ACLU supported local, state, and federal versions of the FEPC. While defeated at the federal level, various fair employment practices laws were enacted by states and cities. Hays's opposition, expressed in a phrase not original to him, "bootlegging prejudice," or people hiding their prejudice, encapsulated his view of governmental efforts to end discrimination in employment. It stemmed from his belief of what he thought were the limits of acceptable government in a democracy. His view had tangled roots in the negative example of alcohol prohibition and censorship of books, fears of arbitrary government, so-called indefinite laws (ones that created agencies whose regulations functioned as law), and group libel laws that criminalized speech attacking people for their race, religion, or color. In this area, Hays thought that it was both philosophically and tactically better to leave these matters in the private, not public, sphere. His stance put him at odds with his own organization (the ACLU), with people with whom

205

he had worked in fighting the color line (like A. Philip Randolph), and with former employees and associates (most notably Victor Rotnem and Will Maslow). Significantly, more than any other topic tied with African American issues, fair employment linked to Hays's fixed view on how anti-Semitism should be combated. His opposition to fair employment practices laws occurred ironically as Jewish and African American organizations came together to work on the behalf of civil rights, helping to elevate fighting racism as a key part of post–World War II liberalism.[1]

The FEPC was one of the major achievements of African American activists during the war, and creating a permanent FEPC became a key part of the liberal agenda in the postwar period. The NAACP and ACLU supported local, state, and federal versions of the FEPC. New York created the first permanent state government agency dedicated to promoting fair employment practices, and the federal FEPC is considered the first nationwide policy promoting equality for African Americans since Reconstruction. It is regarded as the significant civil rights achievement of the Franklin Roosevelt administration. Fair employment was also a policy that came about from the efforts of a figure with whom Hays worked closely, A. Phillip Randolph. The FEPC and other government bodies created to root out workplace discrimination were charged with addressing discrimination against race, color, religion, and national origin. As an early academic proponent wrote, "the rights of Negroes have been the touchstone for the rights of all minority groups in this country. The affirmation of their rights has meant the affirmation of the rights of all minority groups, indeed of all Americans." That statement shared Hays's oft-stated idea about fighting discrimination, that fighting for one meant fighting for all, and should have predisposed him to support fair employment policy. Yet his opposition emerged soon after the proposals for government agencies to fight workplace discrimination developed and persisted through 1945.[2]

It is almost impossible to overstate the extent of entrenched employment discrimination in the United States at the inception of World War II. Employers, unions, and governments all discriminated, with African Americans suffering the worst from practices that locked them out of jobs and whole industries. In the legally segregated states the situation was bleakest, but it was little better in the rest of the nation. A common attitude was expressed by Standard Steel of Kansas City, Missouri, when it explained to the Urban League, "We have not had a Negro working in 25 years and do not plan to start now." Companies in defense industries like the aircraft industry (including New York's Republic Aviation) proved adamant in prohibiting African Americans in skilled manufacturing jobs, even in the face of personnel shortages. Many American Federation of Labor unions were closed to African Americans. Federal and state employment agencies in general cooperated with employers who discriminated. In *The American Dilemma*, Gunnar Myrdal noted that the proportion of non-whites in the leading industries necessary for the war fell from 5.4 percent to 2.5 percent from October 1940 to April 1941.[3]

Established African American civil rights groups and individuals sought to use the emergency of the world war to leverage change in employment. Their efforts through traditional lobbying and activism accomplished little. Any progress that did occur did not approach the hopes raised by the jobs boom brought by rearmament and ideology of the war years. In response, A. Philip Randolph created the March on Washington movement, which planned to bring a huge number of African Americans to the nation's capital to march for an end to discrimination in defense employment and in the military. Fears of violent reaction by white residents to the march pushed President Franklin Roosevelt into negotiations with Randolph. Receiving strong backing from Walter White of the NAACP and having carefully crafted demands that could be met by executive action, Randolph agreed to call off the march in return for the creation of the FEPC. Executive Order 8802, promulgated on June 25, 1941, declared that "there shall be no discrimination in the employment of workers in defense industries or government because of race, creed, color, or national origin." The order made it the "duty" of employers and of labor organizations "to provide for the full and equitable participation of all workers in defense industries." It established the FEPC to "receive and investigate complaints of discrimination" and take "appropriate steps to redress grievances." The action was extravagantly praised by African American organizations and the African American press. Indeed, African American support proved key in the history of the FEPC as it developed.[4]

The FEPC had an unstable institutional history and few allies in government. What was called the FEPC was actually two separate bodies: The one created in 1941 declined into insignificance and was placed in the Office of Production Management, then moved to the War Production Board, and later, in June 1942, settled under the War Manpower Commission. It was resurrected in May 1943 by Executive Order 9346 and housed in the Executive Office of the President. And from the creation of the first FEPC until the demise of the second FEPC, many in government (led by the leaders in the White House) saw it "in part as a tool to reduce, deflect, and absorb discontent" of African Americans. The significant resistance in the government to the FEPC carrying out its mission with zeal came from the belief that the United States could not both win the war and change American society at the same time. More often its efforts were stymied, not supported, by other agencies.[5]

The first FEPC was a "tiny government agency." It spent only $80,000, hired only twenty people, had no local or regional offices, and its committee members were all unpaid volunteers. For a long period, it relied on the staff of other agencies, who did not report to the commission. Without enforcement powers, the first FEPC could only delineate "a set of policies for fair employment." It engaged in a tour of key cities to shed light on the prevalent discrimination and exclusion, not just of African Americans but also Jews. At the same time, it also put out materials making it clear that discrimination hurt the war effort. Even this educational program prompted resistance. White Southerners denounced it in the strongest terms, prompting the head of the commission to announce that it had no intention of overturning segregation. An attempt to investigate the exclusory practices of Southern railroad companies, especially the requirements added to contracts by whites-only unions and accepted as legitimate by another federal government agency, ended in a prolonged impasse. The head of the War Manpower Commission postponed the hearings for more than nine months, and when they were held, the companies and unions refused to participate in them. The impasse led to the appointment of a special presidential commission that continued investigating while a lawsuit seeking to declare the union practice illegal worked its (eventually successful) way through the courts.[6]

If white Southerners, business, and unions resisted, African Americans sought to make the agency effective. African American leaders and organizations lobbied for the appointment of people to the body (especially African Americans) who would actively pursue workplace equity. They did not prevail in all cases, but where they did those members made a difference. The African American members were more aggressive than their white counterparts on the commission. Not only that, but African American workers turned to the FEPC to seek redress for the exclusion and discrimination they suffered in all areas of the nation. Many African Americans gave testimony at the Southern railroad hearings, revealing that they thought the government would be amenable to their aspirations. However, Victor Rotnem, the head of the Civil Rights Section of the

Department of Justice, asserted that the FEPC pandered to the "professional Negro" and fueled "Southern rebellion" and judged it "a political mistake . . . liable to explode at any moment." Yet the FEPC, if politically tenuous, was necessary for the war effort, and thus after being reduced to almost insignificance in the War Manpower Commission, a concerted campaign by influential African Americans (spearheaded by Randolph) and the African American press to "save the FEPC" prompted the creation of the new FEPC.[7]

Rotnem, under the direction of Attorney General Francis Biddle, assisted in the reorganization, which strengthened the FEPC. Central among the ideas pushed by the Justice Department was a way to move the FEPC's focus away from education (which was wrongly seen as stoking racial strife and tensions) toward being able to investigate and enforce its own findings. In this effort, the Justice Department contingent was looking back toward revitalizing the Reconstruction-era legislation and amendments. The second FECP was granted autonomy, allocated a larger budget, and given expanded authority to conduct investigations—though in practice it mostly responded to complaints. It had an executive secretary, who drew a salary, and opened an office in each of the twelve manpower districts in the nation. It continued its practices of open hearings and thus suffered more public resistance from companies and unions to its work. At the same time, it fielded more than 8,000 complaints and settled about a third of them. It gained the full backing of the president when a rogue union attempted to stop an FEPC-arranged employment of African American street car conductors in Philadelphia. Their wildcat strike shut down a major war production city and was broken by the use of federal troops to run the transit system. This headline-grabbing action seemed to indicate that the federal government was poised to take real action against workplace discrimination.[8]

The creation of the FEPC raised a new area for action on civil rights. Conservatives in Congress were hostile to the FEPC in all its forms. It was denounced as the opening wedge of social equality by white segregationist Southern congressmen. The funding for the second FEPC was precariously passed by only two votes in the House, and a House committee undertook a hostile investigation of the agency. As the war was winding down in the summer of 1945, Southern senators tried to pass a series of amendments to its budget authorization that would have severely restricted the FEPC. While they failed, they set the stage for its reduction. Congress cut its budget in half and ordered its termination in 1946.[9]

Despite the FEPC's weakness, the lack of commitment by many in government to its goal, and resistance by some business and unions, African Americans made significant gains in employment in the later years of the war. For instance, by one account, between January 1942 and January 1944, the percentage of African American workers in defense industries rose from 3 percent to 8.3 percent. At the same time, the quality of jobs improved, expanding from the menial jobs to which African Americans had long been confined. Also, the number of quality jobs held by African Americans in the federal government increased.[10]

Liberals, organized labor, and African Americans thought the FEPC a success and envisioned the creation of a permanent FEPC. Toward the end of 1943, Randolph and other African American leaders began pushing for a permanent FEPC; they cast this movement as a war aim: preserving freedom through freedom of economic opportunity. Soon there was an alliance of organizations that embraced Fair Employment legislation composed of civil rights groups, including the NAACP; civil liberties groups like the ACLU; religious groups, most notably the American Jewish Congress: and labor, especially the Congress of Industrial Organizations (CIO). Its proponents separated belief from action—that is, they said employers could be prejudiced; they just could not discriminate on the basis of that prejudice. Calls for a permanent FEPC that would function like the National Labor Relations Board (NLRB) became a key component of liberalism (and its main opponents were segregationists and business interests), so much so that when running for reelection in 1944, President Roosevelt called for a bill creating a permanent FEPC. Bills were introduced but did not move forward with the other economic acts that came at the end of the war. In 1946, a bill promoting fair employment practices was defeated by a Southern filibuster in the Senate. That a filibuster was necessary showed that the idea had become popular; indeed, both parties embraced the idea in the 1948 presidential election. One of the reasons why both parties supported a permanent FEPC in that year was that the Republican candidate Thomas Dewey had overseen the creation of a state FEPC in New York when he was governor.[11]

New York's policy of fair employment practices predated the first federal FEPC by two months. The Democratic Governor Herbert Lehman created a Committee on Discrimination in Employment, commonly known as the Governor's Committee; staffed it with more than two dozen prominent New Yorkers; and announced it would redress the problem of "discrimination in employment." New York policymakers had long known about the widespread job discrimination. They had read about it in the 1935 interim Harlem riot report and findings of the 1938–1940 Governor's Commission that had examined the problem. That commission had drafted ten different bills to address discrimination in the workplace. The Republican party (which controlled the Assembly and Senate) smothered the bills. But war preparations gave a new reason to expand labor regulation further in the state, prompting the creation of the Governor's Committee (under the New York State Council for Defense), and three weeks later a Republican-sponsored, CIO-backed law, the Mahoney Act, passed into law. It made it a misdemeanor for a defense contractor to deny employment on account of race, color, or creed. Even though they had a law, the Governor's Committee thought it would be better to educate the public and persuade them to embrace fair employment practices than prosecute offenders.[12]

Under the direction of public relations pioneer Edward Bernays, a committee member, the Governor's Committee undertook a very extensive campaign of education before moving on to investigation and persuasion. The campaign stretched from school programs, through direct mail to print media and religious groups, to radio broadcasts, to the public. It stressed fairness and fair play as necessary for democracy to work well and have a chance to defeat fascism. The title of a three-day radio campaign carried over twenty different stations in early December 1941 captured the essential point: "National Defense Through Democratic Employment." In early 1942, the Governor's Committee opened field offices, hired staff, and began seeking voluntary compliance with the Mahoney Act. They targeted the employers pressuring them to adopt fair hiring practices. Its staff of twelve and its budget almost matched that of the first FEPC. By June 1945, it had undertaken 2,000 investigations covering about one-third of all New York firms engaged in defense work under contract. While Lehman was still governor, bipartisan laws passed the legislature, adding "national origin" discrimination to the Mahoney Act and expanding the committee's powers of investigation, including the granting of subpoena powers. Significantly, at this time, the National Jewish Congress joined with the Urban League and the CIO as a strong backer of the expansion of the committee's power and fair employment policies in general. Still, they did not prosecute firms but rather engaged with them and persuaded some through repeated pressure to open their doors to African Americans.[13]

The ascension of Republican Thomas E. Dewey in 1943, however, endangered fair employment policies in New York. Dewey at first refused to restaff the committee. The business community lobbied against the Governor's Committee after it began its enforcement-through-persuasion campaign. Budget-cutting considerations by the legislature led to attempts to eliminate it. But after the Harlem disturbance of 1943, Dewey quickly filled the committee, making Alvin Johnson the new chair. And with Dewey's support, Johnson began drafting a bill that would create a permanent fair employment agency for New York. The bill that emerged, the Wicks bill, was similar (though broader in terms of scope and stronger in penalties) to the later bill that became law, but it got caught up in Dewey's presidential ambitions, and he had his legislative agents suppress it to curry favor with Southern delegates in the Republican party. At Dewey's urging, the legislature wrote and passed a bill creating a joint commission against discrimination. Dewey then faced a backlash from the liberal elements of his own party, African American organizations, labor leaders, and religious groups; in response, he worked again with Johnson, who had been moved over to the temporary commission to draft a new bill. Working with liberal Republican Irving Ives, Johnson helped to hammer out a bill to create a permanent agency with the power to investigate upon complaints, whose decisions were appealable, and which could impose moderate fines. Its jurisdiction was limited to those who employed more than six workers, employment agencies, and labor unions.[14]

Support for the bill was demonstrated through the appearance of more than 200 organizations and individuals testifying on its behalf in five regional hearings on the legislation held by the Joint Committee in November and December of 1944. Among those who supported the legislation were the ACLU, NAACP, League of Women Voters, New York State Council of Churches, American Jewish Congress, Urban League, and CIO. Business organizations were conspicuous by their absence; they began their vigorous lobbying against the measure when it was jointly introduced by Assembly Majority Leader Ives and Senate Minority Leader Elmer Quinn. Business organizations and the New York Bar Association came out against it in public hearings, but they were overwhelmed by the broad coalition of supporters. The bill became law on March 12, 1945. The New York agency's preferred means of enforcement was through informal pressure of meetings with agency staffers and businesses. At its prompting, discriminatory clauses were struck from application forms and want ads across the state, and in just two years from the law's enactment, the percentage of African American women employees in clerical and sales jobs quadrupled. Public utilities hired Jews for the first time. New York, in creating the State Commission Against Discrimination, became the state pioneer of antidiscrimination legislation. Others followed quickly; by the end of 1945, New Jersey and twenty-eight cities from Phoenix to Chicago had passed fair employment laws.[15]

Fair employment policy became one of the issues that defined the liberal movement of the postwar era. It melded together advocates from religious, labor, civic, and civil rights organizations. It gave "stimulus . . . to the movement for permanent FEPC legislation." As Will Maslow saw it in 1945, "not since the Civil War has there been so much local interest in preventing racial or religious discrimination in employment; forty-nine different bills have been introduced in twenty states this year." And pushing for the legislation were two organizations, the American Jewish Congress and the ACLU. Maslow, from his position in the Commission on Law and Social Action in the American Jewish Congress, worked with the ACLU to develop model state civil rights laws, starting with outlawing discrimination in employment. Maslow was convinced from his time in the NLRB that a strong law with enforcement power was needed to gain leverage to make change. He denounced laws adopted without enforcement provisions as "counterfeit measures." Moreover, the Pennsylvania law that the American Jewish Congress backed allowed third-party complaints to prompt investigation, and in Philadelphia in 1948 the American Jewish Congress brought the first case. Beyond action on jobs, the alliance of the ACLU and American Jewish Congress extended the prohibitions to public accommodation and labor unions. The commitment to ending job discrimination was an important transformation for liberalism as "civil rights headed the liberal reform agenda." Yet one of America's leading liberals, a man who had challenged the color line in various guises and a power in the ACLU, stood against it.[16]

Hays's stand against laws prohibiting employment discrimination based on race, color, or religion emerged soon after the policy emerged and continued to 1945. Hays made three critiques against Ives-Quinn and, by implication, the permanent Federal FEPC as well as city and other state proposals. First, he said that they regulated people's thoughts, something the government should not do. Second, he argued that regulating private business relations was a step beyond what the government should do. Third, and most importantly, he thought that such laws would actually stir up the very hatred they were designed to overcome. These criticisms grew from Hays's foundational ideas: his preference for keeping government from intruding too much into people's lives, his restrained resistance to the burgeoning administrative state, and most importantly his view of how Jews should combat anti-Semitism. He put together his opposition to fair employment legislation under one term: prejudice.

For Hays, opposition to the FEPC and Ives-Quinn began with a "philosophical" stand born of his experience. In 1940 the publishing house Dorrance and Company asked Hays to come up with "Ten Commandments for Liberals" for free speech, free press, and the like, which they planned to place in a mass circulation magazine. Hays produced the list for Dorrance by the summer of 1940. The list appeared with some modification in his 1942 book, *City Lawyer*, where Hays mocked his own dogmatism by setting them out as coming from "his own Sinai." His "Ten Commandments of Civil Rights" came out of his own experiences in battling for civil liberties. Most of them were rooted in preserving an individual's autonomy, like the "right to obey your conscience," allowing you to "refuse to take oaths, salute flags, to drill, or to kill. You also have the right to be killed. This is illustrated by the demand of our Negroes for military equality with whites." In this reference to the recent *Lynn* case, Hays parenthetically noted that "The Supreme Court doesn't wholly agree." Among those rights that Hays declaimed was one to have "personal prejudices." He phrased it this way: "You have a right not to like or to employ Protestants, Jews, Catholics, Negroes, Communists, Nazis, or men with red hair. You have a right to reveal your ignorance and bigotry." Significantly, the "ignorance and bigotry" sentence had not been in the 1940 original form and underscored that Hays wanted to show he did not think such prejudice was good. But he also gave a real-world application: Employers had the right to exercise their prejudices in choosing their workers. In April of the next year Hays repeated these ideas in a speech before the American Jewish Congress.[17]

This "right" prompted a very strong editorial, "A Dangerous Doctrine," in the opinion-shaping African American newspaper *The Chicago Defender*. Quoting Hays's words, "The right to prejudice is a civil liberty. We can't have a free society unless people have a right to their prejudices," the *Defender* asked its readers to guess who could have said this; maybe it was an arch segregationist, like Senator Theodore G. Bilbo? "Or even Hitler or Goebbels?" Maybe it was "some of our Southern liberals." But no, it was Hays, a "liberal of the n-th degree" and "director [sic] of the American Civil Liberties Union." It decried that Hays had made "racial prejudice a right." It wondered if he wanted to take it further and enshrine it in the Constitution or make it one of the new "Four Freedoms": freedom to racial prejudice, freedom to lynch, freedom to collect poll taxes, freedom to peonage." Thankfully, there were others "more sensible than Hays with his distorted sense of liberalism that has led him to defend civil rights for fascists and Dixie Bourbons who when given power would take away from the people the very same civil rights Hays is so anxious to protect." It concluded, "Hays' crackpot philosophy is dangerous doctrine."[18]

Hays responded to this editorial, defending his stance, extending his argument, and explaining how it fit in with his own work against racism. His letter of reply added to his position, saying to be complete it needed to continue, "you have a right not to like or to employ Protestants, Jews, Catholics, Negroes, Communists, Nazis, or men with red hair. You have the right to reveal your ignorance and bigotry." While he believed this, Hays also asserted, "At the same time I approve wholeheartedly the Defender platform for America, 'American race prejudice must be destroyed.'" He differed over means, asserting: "You cannot destroy prejudice by law." Indeed, "as soon as you tried, you would have a gang of snoopers, GPU and Gestapo men on the trail of everybody." The invoking of both Soviet and Nazi secret police was vintage Hays and fit with his views on the many dangers to societies that favored liberty. Hays aggressively pushed his point on the extent of prejudice across human society. "You yourself are aware of prejudice among colored people one for another" over skin color that "you deplore." He asked, "what law would you pass to prevent this?" Whatever one you did pass would "stir up more animosity than you would dispel." Hays argued that race prejudice could only be undone "in the course of time" as people "come to realize that a man's worth does not depend upon the color of his skin." As individuals in society, "we should condemn prejudices and try to influence people toward an intelligent attitude." But law should not be used, for "after all" it was "force, the result of which would be to emphasize prejudice." Hays then underscored that he thought that the prejudice written into current law was wrong. "One reason why I object so thoroughly to segregation in the army is that it seems to me we have lost a very great opportunity for white men and Negroes to mingle together. We tend to lose our prejudice as we get to know one another." He asked for solidarity: "We should fight against all influences that tend to divide people or keep them from getting to know one another." He ended his letter with words from Darrow (the closing argument in the second Sweet trial, though Hays did not say so): "I would advise patience; I would advise understanding. I would advise all those things which are necessary for men who live together." That he invoked Darrow showed the roots of his ideas and also emphasized how important they were to him.[19]

Just because Hays did not want to use law against prejudice did not mean that he was willing to tolerate it. But for him, it presented a difficult problem for social relations: At what point did one stand on one's rights against others' prejudice? Hays worked out a rough standard in the aftermath of the Sweet trial. In his closing statement of the first trial, prosecutor Robert Toms had tried to meet the argument that the Sweets had (as Hays put it) the "right of free residence as well as . . . self-defense." Toms asserted "that people have many rights which they voluntarily waive." To Hays, conformity to a social practice, such as a man yielding his seat on a streetcar to a woman, was the type of right that could be voluntarily waived. In Hays's parlance (paraphrasing Toms), you granted others the privilege of their prejudice. But other rights were impossible to surrender without becoming "a slave"—giving up freedom itself. These included "the right to live, and the right to refuse to be intimidated." A person can decide whether to conform to social practice. "If I'm a decent man, I'll give many as a matter of courtesy. But I'll assert my rights—when they're important—so that people may never forget that I have them." Hays illustrated with the common example of restaurants that refused service to Jews. "As a Jew, I wouldn't go into a restaurant . . . where I wasn't wanted—unless I was very hungry and the demand for food on my part made it more important for me to eat than to regard the prejudices of other people." And the calculus extended further. "Were my wife hungry, I'd have less regard for those prejudices." And "were my child hungry, I'd have no regard for those prejudices." As a Jew, however, in contrast to many African Americans, he may never have needed to assert his right, "yet I would fight with all the energy that life permits, that the State guarantee it so that under the law I and my race should be equal." This conception that in the private sphere one could, if there was equality in law, protect one's own rights was at the heart of Hays's idea of liberty.[20]

Hays assumed that prejudice was individual (in the above example and in his statements about it in general), and thus he did not trust individuals (like a powerful commissioner) to have too much power in government. In this he was an inheritor of eighteenth-century American republicanism, reinforced by nineteenth-century liberalism, but it mixed with his expanded notions of liberty. A small example can be seen in his reaction in 1937 to a proposal in a bill to remove the court review of the power vested in the New York City License Commissioner to close theaters. Hays wrote to Governor Herbert Lehman urging him to veto the bill: "I wish to join with many others to voice my opposition to the amendment of Section 11401 of the Penal law, which would permit revocation of theatre licenses at the will of one man. This is censorship gone wild." Hays tied censorship struggles to the idea of capricious government power, making it part of the civil liberties struggle. He extended this linkage in a larger critique of "personal" government during World War II. In late 1943 and early 1944, Hays was one of the supporters of an effort led by the ACLU to protest, in a seven-page letter, Mayor La Guardia's "growing tendency to resort to arbitrary administrative action and other summary methods in dealing with public agencies, labor relations, indecency, gambling and crime."[21]

A more important source of Hays's critique of the fair employment legislation stemmed from his unease over the development of the administrative state, which had been growing since the Progressive era. Like many lawyers, he saw it as a threat to liberties. Lawyers pushed to include due process and detailed recordkeeping into the administrative process to protect liberty against government, often for business activities. Hays raised those points and often added a civil liberties gloss to the critique. He also helped convince the ACLU to join him in calling for limits on what were then labeled "indefinite laws."[22]

Early in the New Deal, Hays began to enunciate the idea that indefinite laws were limiting liberty. These were the many federal laws that created agencies whose regulations had the force of law. In a draft article, Hays railed against the Securities and Exchange Commission. Hays opened by pointing to "the danger to civil liberties arising from indefinite laws and judgment by commission instead of by court." He then held up the Securities and Exchange Act as an example of the trend. While not defending Wall Street's abuses, he stressed capital markets as necessary to capitalism under which, "in spite of its defects, mankind has made the greatest progress in the history of the world." He found the falloff of new capitalization from the period of 1923 to 1932 to be very worrying and ascribed some of its decline to stifling regulation. He did not like the registration aspect of the new securities regulatory system. Because the law was indefinite and the regulations were vague, "honest men" did "not dare to do legitimate business." They feared "the interpretation of the law by some political commission which endeavors to show its usefulness by constant and useless inquiry." Selling or buying a good deal of stock prompted questions from the regulators that impeded "the normal processes of trade." At the same time, the requirements for organizing a new business and issuing new stock had become extensive and onerous. Instead of such "snooping and spying," Hays wanted "stringent laws penalizing fraud" in the stock market and vigorous enforcement "of violators in the courts." Under the "Reign of Terror on Wall Street" by "an agency which acts as legislator, investigator, prosecutor, judge, jury, and administrator," markets would not, he feared, rebound, and the Depression would continue. This over-the-top treatment spoke as much to Hays's frustration with loss of business early in the Depression and being forced to adapt his legal practice to new realities as to a deep and abiding suspicion of regulation—and he had fit his irritation with regulation into his embrace of civil liberties, though with no real specificity.[23]

The idea of indefinite laws being a danger crystalized after the NLRB, in a sweeping 1937 order, limited the Ford Corporation's ability to use propaganda to push an anti-union position. The NLRB ordered Ford to stop distributing anti-union literature. In the context of the bitter and violent struggles between Ford and unions, the ACLU's Committee on Labor Rights saw Ford's literature not as protected speech but as coercion directed at the workers. But Hays, like others on the ACLU's national board, saw encroachment on freedom of speech. He crafted the ACLU's new position on government regulation by administrative agencies when it touched upon speech. The larger cease-and-desist order for other actions was seen as legitimate, but the NLRB was asked in a letter to "clarify" whether it really meant to curtail Ford's expression of opinion, which was protected speech under the First Amendment. Thus, the ACLU asserted that administrative agencies were limited by the Bill of Rights.[24]

This opposition to commission governance became part of Hays's idea of liberty from government. In his prose ode to democracy and capitalism, *Democracy Works*, published in 1939, he expressed his view in some depth. This work was, in part, a defense of the New Deal as well as an attack on the idea, shared by both the right and the left, that freedom had to be sacrificed in the quest for economic progress. However, in a section labeled "misgivings," Hays discussed his fear of indefinite laws. He worried about the creation of a bureaucracy that *"for all practical purposes* will be more powerful than Congress or the courts." The "safeguards against governmental tyranny which are provided by Anglo-Saxon tradition" did not apply to many agency inquiries. Using the SEC as an example (though prefacing it with a disclaimer "that the representatives of the Securities and Exchange Commission in New York are an exceptionally able, considerate and courteous group of men"), he wrote that they had the power to raise a question, examine evidence, take testimony, and render a decision. Hays did not want to do away with regulatory agencies but wanted to extend due process protections of the courts to their procedure. He found particularly galling the restrictions that the government put between private parties. He illustrated this with what he probably thought a farcical example. His showman client Billy Rose consulted him about a group of his "chorus girls" who may have wanted to unionize—and Hays and Rose doubted that the chorus girls wanted to form a union. The union that said the chorus girls wanted to be represented refused, under the National Labor Relation Board's rules, Hays's (as the employer's lawyer) a request to find out the women's position toward joining a union through a secret poll. The union's lawyer insisted that Hays's request was an attempt at undue influence by the employer. Hays, sticking with his view that employers had the same free speech rights as lawyers, fruitlessly protested, asserting the civil liberties distinction between speech and action, the line that had become ACLU policy.[25]

He generalized this position and sought action on it. The "government boards, whether they be the Federal Trade Commission, the Securities and Exchange Commission, the National Labor Relations Board or any other," acted, he thought, with procedures that lacked due process protections for those who were brought before them. "There is a tendency in our complicated society toward trial by commissions instead of trial by courts." Men's reputations were ruined and people needed the same protection as before courts, as commissions' actions amounted to "censorship on business, which is just as bad as censorship over literature." He pushed the ACLU to consider these indefinite laws that empowered agencies like the NLRB and the SEC to make rules and enforce them. He knew that other groups were working on related issues. Even though he thought it might "be too huge a job for the Union," he wanted to enlist the aid of various other groups in developing a meaningful corrective, including stock exchanges, "various bar associations," and even the National Association of Manufacturers, as well as Wendell Willkie "and men of his type." He predicted that "some of our members will at once object to our communication with the National Association of Manufacturers, but I think they may have a great deal of data on this point."[26]

His commitment to clarity and due process for administrative law became a touchstone for Hays. In 1940, it prompted him to work (unsuccessfully) with the Association of the Bar Association of New York to develop regulations for the NLRB. He floated some ideas of potential ways to make the law more "definite," such as making discrimination against union men "a violation in which event the employee should have a right to damage consisting of back pay." When the Federal Power Commission (FPC) began a prominent investigation of Mississippi Power and Light Company in 1942, Hays wrote to George Slaff, who was on the staff of the FPC and whom he knew. He hoped Slaff would give honest answers to his questions. "Should companies have the right to have counsel present during testimony of all witnesses? Could the witness have counsel? Should the hearing be public if the investigated want it so? Should transcripts be made available afterwards to the parties?" Hays was driven not by formalism but by a desire for basic fairness. "After all, the rights at trial" had "developed through many generations . . . because they are recognized as necessary from the point of fair play."[27]

Hays's misgivings about the regulatory state did not mean that he eschewed connections within it. Most significantly, Will Maslow, who had once worked closely with Hays, went to work for the government. A Russian-born Jew, Maslow immigrated to the United States as a child. Educated at Cornell and Columbia Law School, he had worked for Hays's firm and the New York City Department of Investigation. Hays wrote him a glowing letter of recommendation when he sought a position in the Justice Department's Anti-Trust Division. "He is a man of unusual ability, conscientious, a hard worker, attractive personally, and would . . . satisfactorily handle any work." Hays added that Maslow "had entire charge under my supervision of the Wendel will case," which was Hays's most lucrative single case, and Hays attributed his success in the case to Maslow. In 1937, he became a trial lawyer for the NLRB, and by 1941 he was a trial examiner for the same body. From 1943, he was director of field operations of the second FEPC. Similarly, Shad Polier, who had been associated with the ACLU for a while (where he introduced Hays to a miscarriage of justice case of Emerson Jennings that Hays would devote years to), moved on to the NLRB before he was called up for military service in World War II. Also, after the war, Hays pressed his partners to open a Washington Office in conjunction with Victor Rotnem and his partner that would deal with administrative law matters. But neither his personal ties nor his adherence to the New Deal could deter Hays from pressing his critique.[28]

Thus, as he wrote *City Lawyer*, Hays again took aim at administrative law. As it was being polished, both the editor Quincy Howe and ghostwriter McAlister Coleman expressed skepticism of Hays's treatment of administrative agencies, with Coleman suggesting a weakening of Hays's "exuberant hallelujah for the Street's essential integrity." Yet Hays rejected their criticism. His chapter "A Page from the Book of Wall Street," which was mostly accounts of practices and strange happenings in the stock exchanges, contained critiques of the SEC—and the administrative state as a whole. In addition to the regulators not being experienced in the field, as they were "a group of young lawyers in Washington," Hays lambasted a process that combined investigation, judgment, and penalty in the hands of one agency. "I resent the humiliation of asking some lawyer at Washington what *he* thinks a law means. . . . I have been in the business long enough to understand what a law means, that is if it is clear." Unclear laws "do not belong on the statute books of a democracy. Indefinite laws give men in government too dangerous a power." He added, "I object to laws the purpose of which is to save people from themselves," and he put the Securities Act in such a category along with censorship of books and prohibition of alcohol. He carefully explained he did not want to do away with the New Deal, especially in its efforts to guarantee each individual, food, shelter, and opportunity.[29]

His views drew some notice and comments from those who were or had been administrative agency regulators. For instance, Herbert A. Cone of the SEC wrote to Hays that he was interested in his "comments on Government agencies" and sought clarification of his argument and asked for elaboration of his proposed remedies for the problems he identified. Polier wrote to Hays to complain about the administrative agency critique in *City Lawyer*. "I was disappointed by your abrupt and, I thought, unfair condemnation of administrative law." Despite the pushback, Hays persisted in his view of indefinite laws.[30]

In 1943 in a letter to *American Magazine*, responding to an article by Senator Harry F. Byrd attacking President Roosevelt and his use of executive orders, Hays put a full foundation under his view of indefinite laws. He laid the blame at the feet of Congress, which had embraced "a new philosophy of government" that favored the passage of indefinite laws. Such laws "from time immemorial have been a favorite weapon of tyrants." Invoking fondly the *Lochner*-era jurisprudence, where the courts were particularly active in striking down progressive legislation, Hays declared, "There was a time when any law that was indefinite was held to be unconstitutional" as a violation of due process protections. Beyond that, they went against the prohibition on ex post facto laws because "until after trial no one can tell what the law is." Indefinite laws encouraged government "of men rather than law." And where men with power in government could discriminate because the law was indefinite and bendable to their will, "tyranny follows." Indeed, in such conditions, if "the government wants to 'get' a man, the course is easy." In light of the ongoing war, the letter is sprinkled with references to fascism and tyranny, but it also contained his established critique—sometimes in the same terms of administrative agencies slowing business, requiring visits to Washington "to get the opinion . . . of some cub lawyer in a government department," and minimal due process protections. To Hays this was not the "traditional democratic system" of definite laws and judgment by court." He admitted modern civilization might be too complicated for the "old procedure," and that it might be impossible to frame definite laws on some subjects. "But where that is so, the government must perforce let us alone." To that final point, he quoted Justice Louis Brandeis's famous construction of "the right to be left alone,—the most comprehensive of rights." Hays had clearly linked indefinite laws to his embrace of individualism (the individualism to be economically active) and to belief in a zone of privacy where government action was inappropriate.[31]

His concept of indefinite laws also had other roots. Hays kept up on issues of the use of law to oppress radicals, including African American radicals. Thus, when the Supreme Court struck down Georgia's sedition law, he wrote the Communist paper the *Labor Defender* to praise the ILD's and conservative lawyer Whitney Seymour's work on the case. "The Angelo Herndon victory was a significant step in the fight for civil liberties. Vague, general statutes have been, for generations, the simplest method for governments to 'get' a man whom they want to put out of the way. . . . It is about time that a 'sedition' statute was thrown out on the same ground." He also disliked the ease by which people in government could misuse law against people whose ideas they did not like.[32]

Part of the solution to arbitrary administration was, in Hays's view, more due process. The ACLU began looking into the treatment of enemy aliens during World War II, separate from the Japanese internment under Executive Order 9066. Hays wrote, "I know of no lawyer who has represented an unsuccessful alien brought before one of these boards who hasn't been outraged by his lack of ability or opportunity properly to present his client's case." For example, counsel could not cross-examine. Hays thought the answer "to some extent" was "to follow decent trial practice" in such boards. Then they would be less inquisitorial and more in line with American traditions. He did not just express himself philosophically on the need for due process in administrative matters, but advanced specific proposals for reform. A starting place he suggested would be to devise a system where all administrative tribunal decisions were "subject to review both on the facts and the law."[33]

The rise of Hitler (and the growth of American fascist groups) made the need to preserve liberty more pressing and would lead Hays and the ACLU into serious debate over how to respond and still stay true to the mission of protecting civil liberties. Sparking the original debate was a Roger Baldwin–supported study of the European laws that prohibited fascist propaganda, banned their marches, or banned speech that promoted race and religious hate. It concluded that such restrictions were necessary against totalitarianism. In the original debate and subsequent ones, Hays was among the strongest voice for the position that the ACLU should defend the free speech rights of American Nazis. And like his co-counsel Morris Ernst, he also spoke in various legal and public forums on behalf of their free speech rights. After much wrangling, the ACLU took a public stand, asserting that it would defend the Nazis' right to free speech. It made its declaration in a 1934 pamphlet, *Shall We Defend Free Speech for Nazis in America?* Changing world and domestic circumstances would again renew the debates, resulting in minor revisions of it.[34]

Spurred by Jews and Catholics who had risen to power in a number of states, American jurisdictions began to consider and pass "race hate" or "group libel" laws, and Hays was at the forefront of the ACLU's attempt to block their passage or challenge them in court. New Jersey's 1935 law was the first, and New York considered a similar law in 1937. It prohibited speech "advocating hatred, abuse, violence, or hostility against any group or groups of persons by reason of race, color, religions, or manner of worship." The ACLU represented the first person charged under the New Jersey statute, a Jehovah's Witness who had distributed anti-Catholic leaflets. The case was dropped, and the New York bill died in the legislature. And later the ACLU (with deep involvement from Hays) would challenge the New Jersey law in court, on behalf of the German American Bund who were prosecuted for possession of anti-Semitic literature. In 1941, the ACLU's brief carried the day in the state's highest court.[35]

From 1935 to 1941, group libel laws were particularly contentious subjects among American Jewish organizations and public figures and still within the ACLU. Group libel laws were popular in many circles. For instance, with the fall of France to the Nazis, *The Nation* endorsed them along with a congressional committee to investigate subversive and fifth column organizations. It thought the times so dire to warrant some relaxation of adherence to robust policies of free speech. Such a development was anathema to Hays, and he was deeply involved in the public and private debates. These debates fixed for Hays what he thought of using law to change people's minds.[36]

In late 1937, Hays wrote an article, "How Shall We Meet Nazi Propaganda," that laid out some of his ideas against restriction laws on Nazi speech. He admitted it was "much easier to suggest what not to do than it is to suggest what to do." But the United States should resist the impulse to use law and force "to suppress it." To do so "would be an attempt to use Fascist methods to prevent the growth of Fascism." Once the laws existed they "would likewise be used against other groups first, so-called Communists, then radicals, then union men, then all dissenters." He continued, "the only safety for any group from methods of repression is our insistence upon the rights of all." Practically, if American jurisdictions did not prosecute Nazis, it would deprive them of a cause to rally around. Hays said anti-terror laws, prohibition of armed drilling, and bans on marching in uniform—as long as those laws applied to all groups—would be effective. This formulation had no reference to religious or ethnic groups and was expressed purely in the realm of past free speech struggles. The American concept of "competition of ideas" leading to truth would "give them enough rope in the hope that thereby they will hang themselves." When he turned to examples, he brought in religious conflict, pointing to the negative example of the New Jersey group libel law and the prosecution of a Jehovah's Witness whom Hays said "was arrested on the complaint of a Catholic." Segueing to race, Hays warned that "laws like this make all groups self-conscious and do more to arouse racial antagonism than could ever be done by word of mouth."[37]

Hays took care to explain combating Nazi propaganda should not become a "Jewish proposition." That would be the "worst thing in the world . . . nothing would do more than this to stir up prejudice against the Jews." He continued, "Jews should urge not the right to be free from attack"—which is how Hays interpreted group libel laws. Rather, they should urge "civil liberties both for the attackers and themselves." The struggle against fascism "should be on the ground of civil liberties in general and not on the ground that any one group needs protection." As for those who were concerned about communism in America, "it should be pointed out vehemently that the most effective way of arousing Fascist spirit is to engage in red-baiting." It promoted a "hysteria which arouses admiration for those tyrannical forms of government which in the name of order deprive their people of liberty." Hays said this is how fascism rose in Europe. And balancing it by trying to repress both communism and fascism would strengthen both. Allow free speech, and that would prevent "the growth of underground movements," as it would deprive the Nazis of attention and guarantee that the government would not make martyrs for their cause.[38]

The outbreak of World War II did not change Hays's thought that it was a mistake for Jews to only attempt to fight for their own legal rights and to legislate against anti-Semitism. He included a manifesto-like statement in his book *City Lawyer*. It prompted Dr. Hugo Marx (a judge in Germany before the rise of the Nazis), who was associated with the World Jewish Congress, to write to Hays to criticize that point. "With regard to the Jewish question you write . . . : 'The safety of the minority groups in the United States lies in the fact that all minorities taken together constitute the majority. So long as all minorities have equal rights under the law they can take care of themselves.'" He continued: "Have you ever contemplated the problem what can happen if one minority is the object of the same discrimination from the side of all other groups? Just this is the situation of the Jews all over the world." Hays responded, "A great many of my friends feel as you do. I think that so far as America is concerned, you are wrong. My point is that when an attempt is made to discriminate by law, each minority group realizes how dangerous that might be to its position." He skirted Marx's point by focusing on the United States pushing intergroup minority solidarity through action on other groups' behalf: "at present I think the best fight made for the Jews is the fight on behalf of the Jehovah's Witnesses." He continued, "Neither we nor anyone else can expect more than equal rights under the law, and my experience is that whenever there is an attempt to discriminate against any minority group all other minorities fight against such laws."[39]

The ACLU's policy on libels against race and religion was laid out in an April 1939 document. It cautioned that "the greatest danger to free institutions" came from "precedents that maybe be established . . . to strike at groups with views widely feared and hated." It reviewed the existing laws and cases both criminal and civil. Framing the efforts in light of the clear and present danger rule, it declared that the criminal statutes "entirely ignore this test in their sweeping limitations." Proposed civil libel laws "not only pervert the historical purposes of actions for libel and slander" (which were to protect individuals) but also conflicted with "the basic principles of freedom of expression." Besides, they were unnecessary, as published falsehoods were covered by general criminal libel laws. The ACLU asserted that "law imposing penalties on expression of views usually defeat their own purpose by developing conflicts where none existed before . . . heightening prejudice." It gave as an example the prosecution in New York City recently "of one [Robert] Edmondson for criminal libel because of vicious and continuous attacks upon the Jewish race by pamphlets" as "the right attitude to" such suits. It noted the briefs filed by the American Jewish Committee, the American Jewish Congress, and the Human Relations Committee of the National Council of Jewish Women joined with the ACLU in opposing the prosecution. The policy paper quoted from the judges' ruling in the case. It was better to let the lies and defamatory material be circulated than risk suppressing honest criticisms. And granting the power to limit expression of opinion "put into the hands of every court and jury the power to determine what views are true or fair." The ACLU also pointed out that anti-masking laws, foreign agent registration laws, and anti-military training laws fit the spirit of the clear and danger test and were sufficient. It concluded that using the means "of repression which these very groups espouse" was a mistake. "Racial and religious intolerance cannot be cured by suppression. It must be combatted in the open with the weapons of democratic propaganda." The ACLU's faith in democracy caused it to believe free speech itself was sufficient defense "for civilized people, under all circumstances and everywhere." These ideas echoed Hays's attacks on group libel laws and carried over to other topics he categorized as being essentially the same in their function. [40]

Group libel laws continued to be advocated both among Jews and within the ACLU, and Hays continued to argue against them. Thus, Hays responded to an article by leading Conservative Rabbi Robert Gordis that appeared in the intellectual *Menorah Journal* in the spring of 1939. Gordis had advocated expanding the law of libel to cover groups, not just individuals. Hays's published response in the next issue, silently borrowed from the ACLU policy paper on the topic (which he had helped to develop), pushed the idea of a free market in ideas. Hays argued that group libel laws would do more harm than good. "Prosecutions and lawsuits attract public attention and cause group conflicts on matters which otherwise remain comparatively quiescent." That was the exact language used by the ACLU document, and indeed the whole Hays letter follows the document's argument closely, though often making the language more personal. For example, Hays asserted, "A man like Edmondson belongs in jail. We forget that making a martyr of him might have disastrous effects. No propaganda speaks so loudly as that which emanates from prison walls." The danger of unleashing repression of speech was made clear by plunging into the potential questions that would arise in a trial of a man who said "the Jews killed Jesus." "What is the issue to try? What is the question of fact?" If you used the law against the radio priest Father Coughlin, who preached "vicious nonsense," you unleash a whirlwind. "And have you ever realized how a lawsuit against Coughlin, instituted by Jews, would publicize his propaganda, would stir up discussion through the land, would line up people on one side against the other, would make antisemitism a burning public issue, perhaps a political issue?" Since we all tend to "express our views largely in reference to groups and classes," the laws would reach to anti-fascists too. "I would not trade my right to attack the Nazi Bunds for their right to attack my group or race." Since he was aiming this discourse at fellow Jews, Hays added to his reply his stand on equal rights under law. Given that "we Jews can take care of ourselves" to fight anti-Semitism and "intolerance in general, whether directed at Catholics, Jews, or Protestants, Negroes or Japanese, the C.I.O. or the A.F. of L., the American Civil Liberties Union or the Liberty League, socialists, Communists, democrats or republicans." As waves of prejudice rise and fall, there was hope that this wave of anti-Semitism would fall; after all the KKK "at one time had millions of followers" but now was defunct. Hays also faulted his people for not having come to the aid of others in the past. To him it "was significant that during the years of attack against Catholics, Orientals and Negroes, we Jews were never excited about passing laws to protect them." Asking for protection seemed a retreat from emancipation to hide behind the protection of special laws. He concluded restrictions that "would keep people from freely expressing their opinions about races or groups" were "more dangerous than the propaganda to which we object." To close, he confronted the elephant in the room: "free speech was not the reason for Hitler's rise in Germany." Hays would do more than just proclaim his views; he would act against group libel proposals.[41]

Within the ACLU, Hays battled members wanting to fight anti-Semitism by weakening its stand against group libel laws. The reconsideration was started by Professor Jerome Michael of Columbia University Law School and backed by many influential figures within the organization. In December 1939, Michael submitted to the ACLU draft bills, and a subcommittee was appointed by the board to consider it. ACLU Staff

Counsel Jerome M. Britchey considered Michael's effort, "by far the best proposal," but the subcommittee summarily rejected it. Michael asked for a written report. The subcommittee was expanded and the bills again considered. Michael also shared with the ACLU a bill that would use the federal commerce power to try to ban such propaganda from interstate commerce. Significantly, only two members of the subcommittee, including Hays, disapproved of "group libel bills in principle. The other six members of the committee" believed "that some sort of legislation is required to meet an increasingly serious problem." But each of them thought parts of Michael's proposals unworkable, with objections ranging from restricting the libels only to false documents to shifting the burden of proof to the state. The proposals and objections were reduced to a memo and sent back to the board with an indication that the subcommittee was divided evenly over Michael's proposals. Hays missed the meetings, but he stopped the proposal from moving forward within the organization. This development was made clear when the ACLU came out against a 1940 bill for revision of New York libel law to include group libel, using the 1939 policy statement as the basis. The memorandum against the New York bill was prepared by a member of Hays's private law firm for the ACLU.[42]

While debates over group libel continued within the ACLU, Hays's views prevailed. In 1944 the Board of Directors revisited the policy, especially focusing on the idea of supporting proposals that would mandate the disclosure of the names of members of organizations that spread race or religious hatred so that the disseminators of such propaganda could be known and better combated. The development of disclosure policies and laws as a means to combat propaganda was vigorously advocated by Ernst and opposed with matched vigor by Baldwin and Hays. By 1944, the ACLU reaffirmed its position against group libel laws, praising the veto of one bill in Rhode Island and the ruling of the New Jersey law as void by that state's supreme court. Similarly, criminal libel penalties were found to be rarely used and ineffective. Civil libel suits had been uniformly dismissed, usually on the grounds of no provable injury. As for requiring of the "disclosure of information concerning the publishers of literature inciting racial or religious prejudice," the ACLU thought such laws were impossibly vague, prone to likely abuse, and easily avoided.[43]

Outside of the organization, Hays responded to attacks on his opposition to group libel and advocacy of prejudice as a civil right. Ben Halpern, a staff writer for the *Jewish Frontier* (a leading Zionist paper), wrote an article calling for group libel laws, asserting that the state can require "standards of civil morality not only with regard to acts but also expressions arising from basic attitudes." He argued that certain ideas were beyond the pale and Hays was mistaken that people had a right to their prejudices. Hays responded with his standard attack on the laws, citing the Edmondson example and saying that the laws would tend "to line up people as Semites and anti-Semites," promoting the evil the laws were "intended to prevent." He confessed he could not follow Halpern's arguments concerning moral and intellectual rights: It all seemed "confusing to me but perhaps that may be because I do not understand those who advocate 'free speech, but—'" Hays rested his defense of prejudice on freedom. "There can be no freedom if one man is denied the right to hold or to preach what some one else may regard as unjustified moral views or erroneous intellectual views."[44]

For Hays, freedom of speech was tied to minority rights. The war made Hays aware that his ideal of the minorities acting in each others' interest and thus preventing the oppression of any one group was under threat. Besides the ongoing wound of racial segregation, the war through the internment of citizens of Japanese descent opened the door to further persecution. Hays expressed this clearly in a letter to Minoru Yasui, then in the Multnomah County Jail in Portland, Oregon. Yasui, a lawyer who deliberately broke the military-ordered curfew that applied to people of Japanese descent, was a plaintiff in one of the four cases that eventually reached the United States Supreme Court challenging the treatment of Japanese-American US citizens during the war. While admitting he was not conversant on the intricacies of Yasui's case, save that the district court judge "wrote an opinion condemning the application of these Executive Orders when they referred to American citizens," Hays expressed his "horror" at the developments. "That any American citizen, whatever his ancestry, should not have a right to his day in court and to his freedom unless he has violated," a law was an outrage. This was "the first time in American history that any distinction has been made against men because of their blood or ancestry, and to me it is an extremely dangerous precedent which at any time can be used against any minority group." It was misguided in Hays's view given the "loyalty of our citizens of Japanese descent." Despite the "hysteria," Hays hoped that Yasui's "experiences will emphasize" to him "the importance of democratic government where men are free from executive control and are entitled to the due process of law." These events confirmed Hays in his civil libertarian principles. "In fact, the more we depart from American principles, the more certain I am of

American ideals." He continued, "Whenever anything is done that seems to be wrong, I always feel that that is an illustration of how horrible totalitarian methods are and is further proof that those who believe in democracy must continue to fight for it."[45]

Beyond proclaiming the precedent of Japanese-American wartime discrimination as a threat to liberty, Hays's reply to Yasui embodied many of his ideas. It is important to note how Hays stressed the danger of executive action and held democracy as the shield. In this he is very much echoing the positions of his previous book, *Democracy Works*. By democracy he did not just mean elections or the people's right to rule, but rather a system like that asserted in Holmes's *Abrahams* dissent where the freedom to express ideas was sacred. By 1942, as the war again was leading people to justify restrictions on speech to protect the nation, Hays renewed his commitment. To Judge Julian Alexander of the Supreme Court of Mississippi, who worried too much freedom would lead to national suicide, Hays elaborated his "confidence in democracy. In my judgement, the people have too much good sense to commit suicide." Americans, Hays thought, were not seduced by Communism and there was no security reason to suppress Communist speech. But he admitted that there were limits, noting where the government had restricted religious freedoms. "It seems to me that the real question" was not whether the American people are "fit for democracy" but rather "whether one has faith that they are. I have such full confidence in a democratic system that I am not fearful of dissenters of any kind." In short, Hays's conception of democracy was tied to freedom of speech."[46]

Hays's letter to Yasui also referenced a mythic American past to draw attention to the gravity of the situation, asserting this was the first time the United States had discriminated against Americans based on ancestry. As someone who had long been involved in the civil rights struggles of African Americans, he knew better. Like the early free speech fights of the ACLU, Hays pretended there was a better past. Moreover, Yasui's letter had not come out the blue; the national ACLU had bitterly debated how far it wanted to go in supporting the Japanese Americans and others in their protest against the war policies. Hays was for full involvement and was on the losing end of those debates. He had kept up on developments and constructed arguments against the removal and internment policies. These were rhetorical arguments, aimed at moving those in the ACLU and in the larger society to action. For instance, in a letter to a friend, Dr. Percy Friedenberg, he wrote that holding all individuals responsible because of their group was contrary to notions of fairness that held individuals responsible for their actions. By pretending there was a better past, Hays made fighting policies that treated people by group even more important to fight, as a precedent had been established. Hays worried "what that may mean in the future if it should so happen that other groups are regarded as dangerous. The real protection of minorities is recognition of equal rights under the law, and I am fearful of any precedent to the contrary."[47]

Others who were as worried about discrimination thought that legislation could address it, especially employment legislation—and the leading organizations in drafting the bills that became law after the first FEPC and Ives-Quinn were the ACLU and the American Jewish Congress. And a key figure in this movement was Will Maslow. Maslow, who had been a Socialist in his youth, was red-baited as part of the attack on the FEPC. After the FEPC was defunded, Maslow landed a job as the director of the Commission on Law and Social Action of the American Jewish Congress. This department, created right at the end of WWII, used both legal and social means to protect the rights of all Americans. It represented a shift in strategy of the Congress from trying to educate anti-Semitic prejudice away to eliminating discrimination. Significantly, it did not limit its activities to only advocating for Jews, but established links with other groups, especially African Americans and other organizations, especially the ACLU. At the same time, Congress members steadfastly sought to maintain their identity as Jews. Building a pluralistic society that respected each group's civil liberties and rights was the goal. Maslow was a perfect fit for the organization, which saw law as its major tool. Legislation, administrative action, and litigation all had their place, and together were the "means for casting both behavior and attitudes toward minority groups in an egalitarian mold." As Maslow later said, "law itself is an educational device." In the immediate postwar era, they partnered with the ACLU to develop model state civil rights laws, outlawing discrimination in public accommodation, employment, and labor unions.[48]

Hays challenged the notion of fighting prejudice through law. He began his opposition about a year after the first FEPC was born in 1941, after New York had created its Maloney law, and continued it through the debate over the creation of a permanent FEPC and the debates over the Ives-Quinn bill in 1945. He first expressed his views privately and then sought to bring them to the public. Once he stated his views, he was drawn into debates with proponents of fair employment practices legislation, most notably with Maslow. In late August 1942, Hays wrote a belated letter of assessment of a manuscript to a lawyer who had sent Hays his work on "Civil Liberties in War Time." Hays opened up with his opposition to legislation prohibiting discrimination in employment. While praising the man's approach and thinking it "an excellent piece," Hays disagreed "with the conclusion where you say, 'the solution of the problems lies in individual tolerance, mass education and governmental legislation'" and gave as a positive example the New York law "outlawing" racial and religious "discrimination in employment." It was the last item to which Hays objected. "I think legislation along these lines always works out badly, that is if it is restrictive in any sense." He added, without explaining his reasoning, that he did "not think this policy works any more than does the policy expressed in the New Jersey law making it a crime to say things which would stir up hostility against groups." The group libel comparison indicates the taproot of Hays's view of fair employment practices legislation. But Hays expressed another aspect that in many later speeches and writings was glossed over. He did not object to "persuasive" laws—laws that set a policy but did not penalize. It was the element of force that Hays in particular objected to when it came to this issue. For Hays, this related to the state not policing people's minds.[49]

In November 1942, Hays went public with his misgivings about fair employment practices law in part of a radio address on another topic. Hays proposed to the producer a discussion between him and a proponent of such laws. The producer wrote back to say he was "intrigued with your slant on racial prejudice as outlined last evening. As you know we have quite a whopping syndicate 7 and ¼ million for our weekly debate in print . . . and the racial prejudice angle would be a fine subject." He continued, "I can dig you up a good opponent who believes that racial lines should be abolished by any method needed to do the job." The national radio show and published debate apparently never occurred, but Hays expressed his ideas in speeches to various groups.[50]

Thus, people in fair employment agencies became aware of Hays's critique and wanted to know more about it. For instance, Bernard Gittleson, a statistical analyst with the New York Committee on Discrimination in Employment under Alvin Johnson, wrote Hays "a personal request." Johnson had tasked Gittleson with going through the public record to gather information about views on the fair employment. Gittleson wrote: "During my research of quoted statements in the newspapers I ran across statements made by you at the Waldorf-Astoria on April 15, [1943,] before the American Jewish Congress, Manhattan Women's Division." The liberal tabloid *PM* had quoted Hays as saying, "the right to a prejudice is a civil liberty. We can't have a free society unless people have a right to their prejudices." The article said that Hays declared he was "against all legislation . . . against discrimination in employment." Gittleson asked, "I wonder if you would . . . advise me as to your reasoning." He sent Hays "an analysis of the laws prohibiting discrimination in the State of New York," meaning the Maloney law and probably older laws against discrimination in public accommodation and service.[51]

Three days later, Hays responded by letter, clarifying his position on Fair Employment Practices laws. He noted that *PM* had gotten the quote correct, but that "the statement that I was against all legislation which would be against discrimination employment is far too broad." Hays asserted that he approved "of legislation preventing discrimination in public works or where people have contracts with the government; in fact where ever the government plays a part." But he added, "I am against legislation which would affect private employment." His public sphere is quite capacious though—not just direct government employment and contracts but business where government plays a part. His conception almost reaches to the established constitutional idea of a business "affected with a public interest" and might have been inspired by Gittleson sending him the current New York statutory law. He transitioned to his reasoning behind his stand by his fuller statement about prejudice as a civil right from *City Lawyer*, adding that people had right to their personal prejudices. "You have a right not to like or to employ Protestants, Jews, Negroes, Catholics, Communists, Nazis or men with red hair. You have a right to reveal your ignorance and bigotry." Hays argued, "I think you emphasize prejudice if you try to use compulsion." Before he explicated this point, he made an aside. "Beside this, there are prejudices for as well as prejudices against. I don't see why one should not associate with people of his own choice." (This was a common pattern in Hays's thought about this subject, which he never explained more fully, but its repetition indicated its importance to him.) Returning to origins of his view, he wrote, "My experience in civil liberties is that force defeats its own object."

He illustrated this point in his reply to Gittleson by discussing the New Jersey group libel law, which made "it a crime to say anything that would stir up religious dissention." He underscored that the purpose of the law "was to protect the Jews against the Friends of New Germany" who "had big organization in the vicinity of Union City." However, the first case that "arose was that of a member of Jehovah's Witnesses who was charged with passing around a pamphlet that attacked the Catholics." The consequence was that "immediately people in the locality were lined up into Catholic and anti-Catholic." He added that the case was dropped but did not say that the group libel law movement prompted a vigorous debate and clarification of ACLU thinking on free speech. He stayed focused on the local result: "there was more religious dissention in the town than there had been for years." Hays added without explaining further: "Along the same lines was the Edmondson case in New York," not cataloging, as the ACLU had earlier, the number of Jewish organizations that opposed the prosecution. Hays thought it a safer course that people be left to their prejudices, as "practically everybody has one kind of prejudice or another." This reality did not mean that Hays thought that such prejudices were good; he knew they were pernicious and affected religious, racial, and ideological minorities. "Fortunately, the minorities in the United States are so much bigger than any one majority that we have continual shifts and changes. So long as minorities have equal rights under law, I believe they can take care of themselves." Taking care of themselves was done in the private sphere, and law should only reach as far as equal rights—which, while he did not say it here, did not include segregation. He ended that if the law outlawed prejudices, it would only "emphasize prejudices by trying to compel people to ignore them. Human nature doesn't act that way." Hays's description of human nature was on one level not flattering, as people were held to be ignorant and bigoted. But many previous statements, and indeed his whole career as public figure, told a different story. People could be educated and moved to be more knowledgeable and tolerant. In sum, Hays preferred moral suasion to legal suasion.[52]

This focus on force explains why the he supported some ACLU positions on racial and religious discrimination. For instance, when the second FEPC encountered open defiance in Philadelphia, Hays supported the agency's actions for the ACLU. In this case it had worked out an agreement with a public-serving union and business and was thwarted by a wildcat strike of a separate union. Hays wrote a letter to Malcolm Ross of the chairman of the FEPC, praising its work and urging that it take even further action. "We, of course, supported and approved of the decisions and orders made by your committee when the case was pending before it. In view of the important precedent . . . we trust that this challenge will be met in a clear and forthright manner." In 1943, Hays, for the ACLU, defended from censorship the Randolph-inspired campaign for a permanent FEPC. The ACLU had long battled against the arbitrary power of the postmaster general to ban things from the mail and supported legislation to limit the power of the post office to act as a censor. Randolph's organization had created stickers to put on mail that declared, "Make FEPC Permanent for Jobs and Justice," and the third assistant postmaster in Washington ruled them "controversial" and banned them from the mail. Hays wrote to him to inform him that pulling the stickers was beyond his power (as had been determined back in the 1920s) and asked him to withdraw the ban. For Hays there was no conflict between his view on the permanent FEPC and stopping censorship, as the policy being suppressed did not matter when defending against censorship.[53]

On a broader note, which gives some indication as to where Hays's view on how fair employment legislation fit with the rest of his agenda, the ACLU continued to build on its work against race discrimination in 1944. Two examples that Hays supported show the ACLU's commitment to the cause. First, in a parallel action to what had been raised by Winfred Lynn's case against the draft—that segregation was discrimination—the ACLU sought to use the same argument in New York. Thus, Hays wrote to the New York Attorney General Nathaniel L. Goldstein saying that the ACLU was "intending to bring some actions to enforce Sect 43 of the New York Civil Rights Law." Hays asked him "whether segregation is discrimination under that provision. There is as you know, no direct reference in statute to such practices, and we should, therefore like to have the attitude of the State on this issue." However, Goldstein refused to answer the question, as he thought it would be in effect rendering an advisory opinion, which was not permitted. In response to the refusal, Hays requested that if Goldstein "had rendered an opinion to any agencies, department, or officer of the state on this or related questions," would he send it to the ACLU. This request remained unanswered. Second, as postwar demobilization began to be planned, liberals, including the ACLU and Hays, joined in the call and pushed for inserting a no-discrimination clause in the demobilization bill so that when employers let go of workers from defense industries they would not return to the infamous practice of letting minorities go first.[54]

Both his following the ACLU lead and his differing from it caught people's attention. For instance, in August 1944, civil rights advocate and close associate of A. Philip Randolph, Arnold Aronson wrote to Hays about the demobilization bill. "Some time ago I had the pleasure of corresponding with you with respect to legislation prohibiting discrimination in employment. At that time you expressed yourself in opposition to such legislation." Press reports that the demobilization bill would "have bar on discrimination against any persons on account of race, creed, color, etc." raised a question in his mind. "I shall be most grateful . . . if you will kindly inform me of the intent of your amendment also whether this amendment indicates any modification in your view with respect to such legislation . . . for a permanent FEPC." Indeed, when earlier in 1944 the ACLU sent a telegram to the Democratic party urging the adoption of a plank in its platform supporting the creation of permanent FEPC with strong enforcement powers, some assumed Hays supported the stand. The telegram listed Hays first as a sender, and the chairman of the Democratic Convention, Samuel D. Jackson, responded directly to Hays, presuming he supported the policy because, Jackson wrote, he had "read your book with a great deal of interest and especially your analysis of the generic phases of the Negro question." He added, "I passed its contents on to the platform committee," and they adopted such a plank.[55]

A bill to combat anti-Semitic propaganda prompted Hays to write his fullest statement of opposition to a strong FEPC, exposing how connected it was to his stand on how Jews and society should respond to anti-Semitism. First introduced in 1943 by a Democratic congressman from New York, Walter A. Lynch, the bill regularly reappeared in the postwar era. It proposed to penalize sending through the mail all materials that were defamatory and false and would "tend to expose people characterized by race or religion to hate, contempt and ridicule." Significantly, the 1943 bill had gained the support of the American Jewish Congress and also the CIO. Hays, in an exchange of letters with Nathan Pearlman of the American Jewish Congress (a former New York Assembly member, former congressmen, as well as a judge of the New York Special Sessions), had stated his and the ACLU's opposition to such legislation, thinking it wrong in principle and difficult in application. After reviewing how the ACLU had battled against censorship by the post office and thus was not inclined to give the office new topics to censor, Hays turned to the reach of the law. He wondered if the literature of the Jehovah's Witnesses, which continually attacked the Catholic Church, would be banned from the mail. "Take books on the Crucifixion of Jesus, the Judgment of the Sanhedrin, the appeal by Pilate to the mob. I presume this stirs up prejudice . . . yet how can you meet his prejudice by banning stories of this kind?" Moreover, how would falsehood be proved? Hays repeated his view that "the worst danger" came from how prosecutions would stir up the issues further and offered his standard answer, that with equal rights under law, Jews could "take care of ourselves."[56]

The pressure for passage of such a law even reached into the Department of Justice. In early 1944, Rotnem, the head of the Civil Rights Sections, wrote to the ACLU inquiring whether the Department of Justice should support the Lynch bill. A Harvard Law School graduate who had worked for Jerome Frank in the legal division of Agricultural Adjustment Administration before the purge of liberals from that agency, Rotnem was "a crusader" for social and legal change. He was also a protégée of Francis Biddle and would after his time in government work for the ACLU and become friendly with Hays. Baldwin replied for the organization that it was "opposed to all such legislation," including the bill to ban "from the mails such matter." Baldwin pointed out that many failed efforts had been to made to draft an acceptably narrow statute that would not be "open to abuse." He pointed to how civil and criminal libel statutes could be invoked in limited degree against offensive literature. And of course, anything that crossed into action was subject to law. Baldwin misleadingly asserted that only Jewish groups supported the Lynch bill—overlooking the support of the CIO—and ascribed their advocacy to "a reflex of the tragedy of the Jews in Europe," rather than developments in the United States, where he thought anti-Semitism was in decline or stable. And significantly, he added, "In the field of employment, the Fair Employment Practice Committee has a limited jurisdiction and similar statues can be passed in the states." That last point underscored the divergence between Hays and the ACLU on fair employment practices legislation and policy.[57]

Hays's stand against a ban of anti-Semitic material from the mail caused G. M. Cohen, the editor of the *Jewish Post* ("A journal for Indiana Jewry" published in Indianapolis), to commission an article on the topic. Cohen asserted that his paper had "a pretty wide reading public" and was "the only Jewish paper that feels that the Lynch Bill won't get anywhere or us anywhere, and that being so I wonder if you could set down on paper again your stand in the matter." He wanted a reply "to the many articles in the Anglo-Jewish press criticizing your stand." Hays jumped at the chance, writing, "I am unalterabl[ly] opposed to the Lynch Bill and bills of that kind," and asked for the form and length of the proposed piece. Cohen told him that length was of no consequence and that they will "print everything you write." Within a month Hays had delivered the piece, "What Shall We Do to Be Saved?," saying that it was "longer than I intended and probably longer than you expected." He added, "Would you mind letting me know as soon as possible whether you can use it, as otherwise I should like to send it elsewhere." Cohen told Hays he was going to use it in full; "however, I am calling out all our storm troopers this Friday to protect our office from irate readers."[58]

The piece in the *Jewish Post* proved to be Hays's longest and most elaborate statement on prejudice, what he thought the proper approach was to fight anti-Semitism and how he saw fair employment laws as the wrong approach. Opening with a vignette of sharing a cab with two women, Hays recounted that the driver launched into a rant over his house being robbed "by a couple of 'niggers' who threatened his wife and child." The driver continued, "The next time I catch a nigger . . . I'm going to beat him up." Hays interjected that it "was wrong to blame colored people in general because of the acts of individuals" and said that was like "the Nazi philosophy to excuse persecution of Jews." This statement prompted a reaction from one of the women. She "glowered at me, 'How dare you compare Jews to Negroes?" This vignette launched Hays into a philosophical exploration of the root of prejudice, of the "ordinary" human desire "to draw a circle around himself and his kind" dividing the world into "we" and "they." A "disgraceful act" by the "we" group was individual: He was a bad man. But a "they" group action prompted the reaction "That's the kind of people they are." Fear also arose from the thought that "they" would "would infringe" upon the "we" group. "This fear, not unnaturally, leads to hate," like anti-Semitism.[59]

Hate had a long history in America, but Hays was optimistic it could be defeated. He traced the waves of prejudice from the eighteenth century through the Second Ku Klux Klan of the 1920s; it rose and fell and shifted targets—Jews, Catholics, African Americans, and Jehovah's Witnesses. Hays also highlighted how initially German-descended established Jews greeted the influx of Eastern European Jews in America with prejudice but how through interaction the prejudice declined. The right way to combat hate was to defend all groups, as defending one group benefited all. For example, when the NAACP was "successful in court, principles are laid down which rebound to the benefit of all minority groups." There should be no acceptance of discrimination, no "'hush-hush' policy of not talking about it, but action made "against intolerance in general," as a "fight against a specific prejudice gives an undue preponderance to that one prejudice." Thus, laws that attempted to criminalize stirring up racial or religious hostility were bad ideas, because they would defeat their own purposes. Prosecutions would "cause group conflicts on matters which otherwise remain comparatively quiescent." Lifting liberally from the ACLU policy document, he reviewed the New Jersey group libel law, taking it from its first prosecution through its being ruled unconstitutional on the grounds of being vague and indefinite, and used the case of Robert Edmondson to underscore the danger of free speech in the use of libel in this way. Hays raised the problems of proving malice or claims of truth and warned that to go down that path would allow juries to decide what was "true or fair." And if juries were not to be trusted, then putting this power in the hands of one official, as in the proposed Lynch bill, which would allow the postmaster general to decide whether to ban material because it stirred up religious or racial hate, risked even more. "When these things" were determined by "court, jury, or administrative agency," the different parts of the public would be inflamed by the airing of charges and countercharges. He imagined that some despicable group might even recast itself as a religion to gain protection of the law. He drew on a recent decision of *Cantwell v. Connecticut*, which established a high standard of "fighting words" before suppression of speech could occur even on the volatile topic of religion.[60]

From speech, Hays shifted to discussion of employment. "There is another kind of legislation that has popular appeal particular among Jews": that which "would prevent discrimination in employment even by private industry or private individuals." His framing was of private workplaces, a silent admission that he supported fair employment practices for public employment. To Hays, such legislation ran against "prejudices for," harking back to his statement to Bernard Gittleson, and he shifted immediately to the topic of prejudices against. "I see no reason why any state should compel me to employ a man against whom I may be prejudiced whatever may be the cause of my prejudice." He ran the examples of dislike of a man with red hair or "a pimply face." Would the law force explanation as to the root cause of the "dislike," which might be irrational? "Am I not to be permitted to choose?" he asked. Revealingly, Hays refused to engage with real workplace discrimination in this discussion, and while he mentioned industry he envisioned a personal face-to-face firm. The personalizing of the issue clearly put it in the realm of private in his account. He continued, "one must recognize anyhow that such laws are unenforceable." Echoing his previous point on race-hate laws, he added, the "mere attempt to enforce them would stir up the very controversies and evils of which we seek to dispose."[61]

Hays ended the piece with his philosophical speculation of the origins of prejudice in its once probable utility of allowing for the "avoidance of things you do not know." He again condemned it when that "prejudgment becomes ineradicable," which turned it into "ignorance or bigotry." He repeated his solution that the only way to fight anti-Semitism was to fight "intolerance in general." But in doing so, "not to rely too much upon law except to insist upon the legal right to express yourself." Speaking to his audience, Hays declared, "We as Jews need no protective laws." What Jews needed were "equal rights and the Bill of Rights. We are safe only in a free society where all of us have a right to our prejudices to be ourselves, to think and say what we please." Thus, restrictions on free speech, "even when intended to help us," acted "as a boomerang and exacerbate the evils which we deplore." He ended with "We need a fair field but no favor." As much as Hays cast this argument about the needs of Jews, shining through that covering was an argument for individual freedom. Thus, his civil libertarianism directly shaped his fair employment practices opposition.[62]

Hays's optimism in "What Shall We Do to Be Saved?" about anti-Semitism was misplaced, though it may have been hard for him to judge. During all of his public life, anonymous cards and letters sent to Jews expressing hatred were common, as was street violence against Jews. For instance, in 1939, anti-Semitism reached one of his vacation retreats. In previous years, Hays, Aline, and Jane had spent part of the summer on Martha's Vineyard socializing with other off-islanders who also summered there, including McAlister Coleman. In 1939, they did not make it to the island, and Coleman, in writing to Hays in passing, said, "With the exception of your absence this was the happiest Summer we've had here despite a nasty free speech fight against anti-Semitism which has been raging round Edgartown and has now got to the point where someone is sending anonymous post-cards to the Jewish families at Menemsha." Anti-Semitism in the United States reached a high tide during World War II. Jews were commonly seen as shirkers from military duty and blamed for the war. Physical attacks on Jews in urban areas (including New York City) were common, and "grossly negligent police" rarely attempted to aid the victims. In 1943, an investigation headed by William B. Herlands, Mayor LaGuardia's commissioner of investigations, looked into the wave of anti-Semitism in New York State. Also in 1943, Hays helped a family of Jews who had suffered an assault at Bear Mountain Park and were fined for attempting to prosecute their assailants. Under the pressure of such developments, some Jews even took to hiding their identity, such as when a law student at Columbia chose to change his name to disguise his identity to improve his prospects.[63]

Among Hays's friends the piece was well received, so much so that Cohen brought it out as a pamphlet. Hays required some editorial changes:

"I would not want to have it entitled 'The case against the Lynch bill,'" and suggested changes including, "one of your subheadings reading 'Against the F E P C Also.' This is not correct. I am not against the F E P C. It is clear from the article that my argument applied only to private industry or private individuals." Hays, who bought 300 copies of the pamphlets, reported that he had shown it to his friend Oswald Garrison Villard, co-founder of the NAACP and reform-minded publisher, who "expressed high approval of it. Hays's friend Newman Levy, upon reading it, wrote, "It is one of the best presentations of the case I have seen and as you know, it coincides pretty much with my own views. During the past few years I have seen a lot of proposed legislation to help fight against anti-Semitism but I have yet to see a bill that would not do more harm than good." Jim Luitweiler of Bendix, Luitweiler & Co., a Wall Street banking firm, another friend, added, "I consider it the best that could be said with respect to the wave of anti-Semitism in this country." He added that his wife and children would read it, and friends of his "who advocate legal protection will read it too." His great friend C. Fulton Oursler wrote to say: "I am sure you know that it will not be universally approved—the breadth of vision in it must ultimately prevail." And he concluded, "The piece is trenchant and wise and again, or as usual, I am proud of you."[64]

The praise received prompted Hays in 1945 to try to make his case against special protective laws for Jews (including fair employment practices laws) to a larger public. With the help of his friend Coleman, he revised the *Jewish Post* article "What Shall We Do to Be Saved?" and sent it to Oursler, then an editor at *Reader's Digest*. In a cover letter he said he would want to go more into how fair employment laws like Ives-Quinn fit into his view of just pushing prejudice underground. A fellow editor at *Reader's Digest* agreed with Oursler that it was not for their publication, as it had "too much dynamite." Probably that "dynamite" was the article's discussion of religion: the Passaic Board of Education had sought to end its subscription to *Reader's Digest* over an anti-Zionist article. But the "material bearing on anti-discrimination laws, which I marked on the final page," had potential. The editor asked Oursler to "sound" out Hays "a little more about this (privately and personally) and find out just what his ideas are in more detail. . . . I wouldn't encourage him with the thought that there might be an article for us." But if Hays and Oursler discussed it, it did not inspire Hays to elaborate his views.[65]

Hays was not the lone liberal voice opposed to Ives-Quinn. Charles C. Burlingham shared many of the same views. A leading admiralty lawyer and an important judicial and civic reformer who was a friend of Mayor La Guardia as well as past president of the City Bar Association and longtime head of the city school board, he reached out to his establishment connections whom he believed agreed with him on the issue to speak out against the bill as it was pending in the legislature. Like many established elite lawyers, he distrusted administrative agencies. He thought the law the wrong tool to use to fight prejudice and hoped at first to have a cross-section of figures including "a Negro and a Jew and a Labor man" to join him in signing a public letter against the bill. He failed to get either an African American or a labor leader. However, he obtained the support of Villard. Burlingham privately expressed the view that Villard was "equivalent to a thousand niggers." The slur demonstrated that many fighting prejudice did not extend their theories on civil rights for all to personal action.[66]

The Burlingham letter, published by the *New York Times* on February 13, 1945, advanced a host of arguments against the Ives-Quinn bill. It argued that extending an anti-discrimination law to the private sphere was a step too far. Public and semi-public employment like utilities were already covered by existing law. Using the "expensive" and powerful machinery of an administrative agency (which could easily be corrupted by machine politicians) to that end would be wasteful, especially as public education efforts had brought about improvement in employment for African Americans in the state. It contended that the "remedy was worse than the disease": an administrative agency would be predisposed to see and prosecute discrimination, maybe where there was not any. It attacked the "inquisitorial process" of the bill and worried about business owners' motivations for hiring being second-guessed because they were hard to ascertain through the process. It would lead people to hide their views. "Prejudice will become a commodity to be *bootlegged* with all the evil consequences which followed our attempts to control drink by law." It thought the actions of the earlier Governor's Committee and Federal FEPC had been a better approach. Instead of force, education should be used by "fair-minded men and women of every race, color, creed, and national origin" to guide public opinion to make discrimination unacceptable.[67]

The print debate that ensued tilted heavily in favor of the supporters of the Ives-Quinn bill. Burlingham's hopes for rallying opposition, even printed opposition, to the bill were dashed. There was one short letter written in support that argued that law was never the answer to prejudice, a position that went beyond the Burlingham letter writers' stance, which recognized that law was appropriate in some instances. Additionally, Jack R. McMichael, the executive secretary of the Methodist Federation for Social Service, in reply pointed out that prejudice and discrimination were different things. One was internal and one external to the person, and the external could be controlled by law, preferably one "with teeth." McMichael said the comparison with the Federal FEPC was false, as it engaged in some of the same methods outlined in the bill. Indeed, strong legislation was "not an enemy of education but an aid to it." Moreover, the bill had the strong support of minority group organizations who had felt the sting of discrimination, and their voices should be heeded. A letter signed by ten people involved in fair employment matters, including Alvin Johnson (chair of the Governor's Committee that drafted the bill), argued that the analogy to Prohibition was false, as support for discrimination was nowhere near as entrenched as love of alcohol had been. They pointed out that the creators of the law expected it to work not along the draconian lines Burlingham's letter laid out, but much like earlier state and federal efforts. Finally, Osmond Frankel, one of the most important lawyers in the ACLU (identifying himself as writing on behalf of the New York Committee of the ACLU), pointed out many flaws in the argument and asserted the benefits of the proposed legislation. He wrote that the legislation would decrease discrimination, which would have the educational effect of showing how groups could work together. To the claim that existing law was sufficient, he maintained that the existing antidiscrimination laws were dead letters because there was no agency to enforce them. And he denied that the FEPC educational style was sufficient because Burlingham overlooked that it was backed by the president's wartime power to cancel contracts. Moreover, he found the Prohibition comparison ridiculous; "one does not bootleg a state of mind." Nor would smuggling of prejudice generate the profits that smuggling alcohol had, and thus it was unlikely that corruption would arise as it had under Prohibition.[68]

Hays's familiarity with the debate is shown by his adopting the phrase "bootlegging prejudice" from it. The term had not appeared in his writing before the letter. And while the letter writers saw the corruption of prohibition in the bribery of officials and defiance of the law by the masses, for Hays the bootlegging was more the idea of government overreach, touching on people's personal preferences. Hays did not embrace many of the other ideas of the Burlingham letter. He did not worry much about expense of regulation or the possibility of machine politicians staffing the agency with their friends. But he ignored important points made by the proponents of Ives-Quinn in these letters. A permanent FEPC and Ives-Quinn allowed the employers to hold their views; they just could not harm others by discriminating against them by not hiring them. Hays failed to see this distinction between prejudice and discrimination. This lapse was particularly striking because the analogy to free speech law and the standard of clear and present danger was implicit. To put it in terms of Hays's favorite argument for free speech, American Nazis could denounce Jews in their publications but could not beat up Jews on the street or engage in speech that likely would imminently provoke an attack. Hays could not adopt this view. But the stance of so many liberals and some of their arguments might have had some effect: He neither wrote the *New York Times* to voice his support of the Burlingham letter nor appeared in hearings to testify against Ives-Quinn.

Shortly after Ives-Quinn became law in 1945 Hays reiterated his basic position on fair employment legislation before a particularly hostile audience. The text of his speech is lost, but *PM* reported on his comments. Under the headline "Hays Opposes Anti-Bias Laws," the liberal tabloid stated that "He told a group of the American Jewish Congress, yesterday that while he opposed such discrimination as un-American and undemocratic, he felt that, 'The right to a prejudice is a civil liberty. We can't have a free society unless people have a right to their prejudices.' " He apparently said that he could support legislation that prohibited discrimination in government employment and by companies with government contracts. As a major promoter of fair employment practices legislation, the American Jewish Congress through a spokesman said "that it was opposed to Hays' [sic] view and that it would continue to seek legislation which would end such discrimination by both public and private employers." This report caught the eye of Maslow. From his office as director of field operations for the second FEPC, he immediately wrote to his former boss to ask him about his comments.[69]

Unfortunately, Maslow's first letter and Hays's response to it are lost, but from Maslow's later comments it is likely that he asked for clarification and Hays repeated what he had said to Gittleson in 1943. Maslow then sought further elucidation from Hays. He admitted that "from your letter" he could not tell "whether you object to entrusting any FEPC with coercive powers or whether you merely believe these powers should not include criminal sanctions." If his objection was limited to not giving the FEPC criminal sanctions, Maslow agreed with that position. He pointed out that the bills pending in Congress for a permanent FEPC did "not make discrimination or the violation of a Commission order forbidding it a criminal offence." Rather, they "merely provide for administrative orders forbidding such discrimination." On the other hand, if Hays thought that "mild" coercive powers were "unwise," Maslow disagreed. Saying his experience at the second FEPC, created by Executive Order 9346, showed that having "the vast and undefined war powers of the President" in reserve gave the Commission leverage. It was able to settle successfully most cases through persuasion, marking real success. "Yet many of its most important cases are still pending because of recalcitrant employers or unions." He wrote that 500 of 2000 cases had been transferred to the central office and implied that only coercion would lead to resolution on them. Maslow shifted from coercion to the broader topic of the limits of law in ending prejudice.[70]

Admitting that "prejudice cannot be curbed by law," Maslow argued that what the FEPCs "attacked" was "not prejudice but discrimination, its evil byproduct." He backed up this assertion by reviewing some of the steps taken by the Brotherhood of Locomotive Fireman to drive African Americans from the position of firemen, including contacts that ban the employment of new African Americans and restrictions on the seniority and promotion rights of existing African American workers. Using a rhetorical question, Maslow posed, "Is this mere prejudice or a matter of 'of private concern?'" And the answer was that the United States Supreme Court had ruled against the union on these points in the previous year, saying they were in effect of public concern. Maslow went broader to ask, was "'prejudice a civil liberty when it compels Negro college graduates to work as Pullman porters and Mexicans to get less pay than Americans for the same work?" Prejudice allowed "the doctrine of white supremacy" to thrive and stifled civil liberties, so that "even a pamphlet like the 'Race of Mankind' is barred." This short pamphlet was created by Columbia anthropologist Ruth Benedict, a disciple of the anthropologist Franz Boas, with the help of lecturer Gene Weltfish, who in 1943 compiled some of her many observations debunking the popular misconceptions about race. The Army planned to use *The Races of Mankind* as an educational tool to explain the war against Nazi racism, but some passages praising the Soviet Union's racial policies sparked controversy. The pamphlet was attacked as Communist propaganda. The United Service Organization (which saw to troop health, morals, and morale) banned it. The Army dropped it and the FBI investigated the authors. In response to the reaction, civic groups and churches embraced it, placing orders for at least three-quarters of a million copies. Thus, Maslow drew on his greater knowledge of examples of egregious discrimination and used the government's reaction to *Races of Mankind* to argue against Hays's argument: Prejudice endangered civil liberties.[71]

Maslow also disagreed with Hays's on the tactical points. "You talk of stirring up prejudice by cases coming into court," he wrote, referencing the analogy that Hays had repeatedly drawn to group libel laws. "On the contrary, publicizing prejudice kills it." Maslow supported this assertion with the most famous FEPC enforcement action, the Philly transit strike. "On the lines of the Philadelphia Rapid Transit Company Negro motormen are now working and recently a Negro was elected a vice-president of the CIO union. Was prejudice stirred up here?" Segueing to education and persuasion, Maslow argued they were "certainly desirable and indispensable." He believed that "any administrative FEPC would no doubt dispose of 90% of its cases at the regional and informal level if it could." But returning to his opening point, "such success by persuasion is only possible where the threat of sanctions lurks in the background." Besides, one should not "underestimate the education value of a coercive law. Most people are law-abiding. If discrimination is declared illegal, they may not drop their prejudice but they will stop discriminating." He closed by trying to take the sting out of the exchanges by framing them as comparisons of "our experience[s]" and offering to continue the conversation.[72]

In his reply, Hays dodged more than he engaged. For instance, when it came to coercion, he wrote: "The only point I have made is against penalties or sanctions where the matter has to do with private employment. Government employment is quite a different thing; so is employment by a public utility or a railroad; so is the right to join a union. In private business, however, I am all against coercive measures of any kind. Am I wrong about this?" All the other points raised by Maslow he left unaddressed. Signs of his thinking are found in his copy of Maslow's letter of March 31 where the phrase "coercive powers" is underlined. Also, Maslow's passage beginning with the firemen and oddly running to the discussion of college graduates working as Pullman porters, Mexicans earning less money for the same work, and the *Races of Mankind* is underlined and marked "Public Service." How he thought all these fit under the private/public distinction is unclear.[73]

Maslow, in his reply, called the private/public division an "artificial distinction." He thought the "concept of private employment" was "outmoded, certainly for corporations employing thousands of persons." Even allowing for Hays's conception of public extending to "employment by a public utility or membership a trade union," Maslow argued that limiting fair employment legislation's coverage to government employment was not enough when "private" decisions by large employers had society-wide effects. When "private" employers assigned "Negroes to menial or low paid jobs then society has a vital stake in the problem." Social and economic costs rose because of such discrimination: "the growth of a master race or white supremacy doctrine; the disproportionate numbers of Negroes on relief, with criminal records, illiterate or diseased." All that contributed to racial tension, which "erupts into race riots." Even during the war, the practicing of hiring whites only in the textile mills of the South significantly depressed production of canvas because an available workforce that constituted "one-third of the population" was not utilized. "Try to convince soldiers without tents that this is a private matter." Maslow also pointed out that "you and the ACLU rightly believe that discrimination by unions is a public matter." That raised an important point: "a union cannot discriminate unless the employer is a party to its restrictive practices. Why then regulate the union and let the employer alone?" Of course such regulation should reach to large employers: "I concede that small employers should be exempt from a regulatory statute." He added that all current federal bills followed the New York State law example of excluding employers of five or fewer employees.[74]

Maslow ended on the point of education. He was convinced that it "cannot do the job." He pointed out that from 1910 to 1940, "The Negro's lot actually deteriorated . . . in many industries, [as] segregation in the South became more pronounced." He added emotional weight to this political economy argument: "Hitler did not invent the notion of park benches marked 'Jude'; many southern towns have used 'colored' in the same way." His point was that prejudice against African Americans "developed in part because the Negro was poor, illiterate, ill-mannered." Thus, "he was deprived of jobs." If you reversed that, the prejudice would be undermined. "Giving him a decent job tends to end illiteracy and uncouthness and poverty. Thereafter, as the Negro advances up the economic scale, prejudice against him decreases." Maslow had asserted that taking the step toward job fairness would have multiplier effects, reaching even to changing people's minds. He implored Hays to join him. "All we need to do, therefore, is to start the ball rolling."[75]

Hays's speaking and writing opposing strong fair employment laws ended with his and Maslow's conversation. Perhaps Maslow's arguments prompted Hays to reconsider. Yet, given Hays's views and reasoning, getting him to change his mind would have been difficult. His opposition to strong fair employment agencies was tightly linked to his approach to combating anti-Semitism, which was rooted in his conception of civil liberties. Thus, why Hays stopped talking and writing about the topic is open to interpretation, but it could not have been because the efforts to pass such laws ended.

There was much action in the states. As Maslow noted, state laws were an important goal of liberals after the 1946 Senate filibustering of the permanent FEPC bill. Proponents hoped that progress in the states would give them leverage to pass a federal law. State laws passed in Massachusetts in 1946 and in Connecticut in 1947. In 1949, New Mexico, Oregon, Rhode Island, and Washington also enacted such a measure. Fair employment laws were debated in many more states. There was a slowing down of passage of such laws in the early 1950s. Chance of a federal law faded and then ended. In the 1952 presidential election, the Republican candidate Dwight Eisenhower strongly opposed the creation of a permanent FEPC, and the Democrat Adlai Stevenson reluctantly supported such a measure. Eisenhower's election ended the hope of a federal law, and resistance by business stiffened and blocked passage of laws in the states until 1955, when Michigan, Minnesota, and Pennsylvania passed them. However, Hays, who was active as a speaker until his death in December of 1954, did not engage with the issue.[76]

It possible that Hays might not have noticed the actions in other states, but he could scarcely ignore what was happening in New York both in the state agency and in the groups that pressured it to do more. The New York State Commission Against Discrimination created a dozen community councils—in the urban and suburban counties of New York and all the boroughs of the city. These councils engaged in education work, conducting forums on discrimination and sending out speakers (especially targeting schools). The commission assumed "that the creation of an informed and sympathetic public opinion is one of the necessary conditions for ultimate success." To that end, in 1949 it distributed 318,082 copies of thirteen different items, including 100,000 posters. It arranged for the production of a "March of Time" film, which by 1950 was shown to a million people in 354 different movie theaters across the state. It moved on to hearings in October 1949 and its first cease-and-desist order in October 1950. It had success, and there was "no doubt that the outward and more obvious manifestation of discrimination—discriminatory advertisement and questions as to race and religion on employment registration blanks" decreased in New York, and areas of employment previously closed to African Americans and others were opened. By contrast, in Chicago, which had a city law (with no enforcement mechanisms), a study found that 85 percent of contractors for the city used discriminatory application forms. The newspaper voice of New York liberalism, the *New York Herald Tribune*, on March 28, 1949, declared that since 1945 the Commission's "achievements have been many." And because of its "tactful" approach, previous business opponents like the Bronx Chamber of Commerce and the former president of the State Chamber of Commerce came to support it or a permanent federal FEPC. On the other hand, there was evasion "through the use of subtler methods." And to keep the pressure on, the Commission on Law and Social Action of the American Jewish Congress repeatedly surveyed employment agencies in New York City from 1945 to 1949 and found numerous violations. And actions of the agencies and advocacy groups did result in some anti-Semitic attacks by enemies of the policy. Moreover, the American Jewish Congress asked the Commission to investigate discriminatory advertising by New York's resorts. Clearly there were many of opportunities for Hays to have entered the debate, yet after 1945, he did not.[77]

What Hays did talk and write about mostly was the accelerating effect of the second Red Scare. President Truman's building of a security state, the excesses of the House Un-American Activities Committee, the rise of Senator Joe McCarthy, and states' policing affiliations of civil servants all presented serious challenges to civil liberties. And Hays spoke, wrote, and acted in opposition to the threats he saw to civil liberties. Hays's focus in his last years can be seen in the short statement he gave to the *Brooklyn Barrister*: "the activities of the Dies and Thomas Committees, the President's loyalty investigation, state investigation of the same character, the screening by private corporations, books [like] the RED CHANNELS, the ravings of McCarthy, the Feinberg law, municipal ordinances against Communists, loyalty oaths, have led to fear on the part of even our most outstanding citizens of saying or doing anything or joining any movement." Moreover, he actively challenged McCarthy's claims, defended teachers who ran afoul of New York's Feinberg law that banned membership in subversive organizations, and debated the need for Red hunting in general. For instance, when he appeared on the nationally syndicated radio program "Wake Up America" on October 27, 1946, it was not to debate fair employment practices laws but rather the topic "What do we mean by un-American Activities?" Also in 1946, he worked with Coleman not on perfecting the fair employment article but on articles attacking HUAC and the penchant for organizations and individuals (on both the right and left) to publish lists damning people by association. Even more revealing, in an October 1949 address to the New York chapter of the American Council for Judaism, an audience that would have been receptive to his argument against strong fair employment agencies, and where he repeated both stories (the cab ride) and topics (group libel laws were wrong) from his *Jewish Post* "What Can We Do to be Saved" article, he did not mention fair employment. Where he had in the past article discussed fair employment, he now talked about a recent controversy of threatened boycotts of a new film version of Oliver Twist over its anti-Semitism.[78]

At the height of his actions against racial discrimination, from 1942 to 1945, Hays also opposed one of the most consequential policies that was aimed at combating racism: employment discrimination laws. His opposition had many roots; it grew from Hays's conception of the limits of government, his unease with the growth of the state, his commitment to a distinction in the treatment of the public and private spheres, and his view of how anti-Semitism should be fought in a heterogeneous society. His expressed views against strong FEPCs stood in contrast to those of many of his associates and allies. His stance put him at odds with the ACLU, which worked for the creation of such laws. It pitted him against Randolph, whom he worked closely with during the *Lynn* case, who spearhead the creation of the FEPC and the later calls for a permanent FEPC. It prompted his former employee Maslow (who came to make such laws a key part of his organization's campaign against racism) to challenge his views in private correspondence. Hays had repeatedly shown that he would take and hold stands even if those close to him pushed for the opposite goal. And sometimes his stand had carried the day, as it had with group libel in the ACLU. But liberalism had changed, and Hays could not carry others with him on this point. He was out of step with the times on this topic. His stance against strong fair employment laws revealed the limits of his liberalism (rooted of his civil liberties values) when it came to race.

Conclusion

In 1945, the *Pittsburgh Courier* ran a series, "Americans of Good Will," written by its New York–based correspondent Evalyn Coppoc, who interviewed prominent supporters of African American rights; its July installment featured the "incomparable" Arthur Garfield Hays—characterizing him as "a human dynamo." Coppoc found Hays both an easy and elusive interviewee: "he refuses to talk about the good he has done"; indeed, "unless one is persistent" one "will be left with no more knowledge than the fact that the questioned is just Arthur Garfield Hays." She sketched out the basics of his extensive private law practice, his successful writing career, admiration of Darrow, and associations with organizations: the ACLU, the League to Abolish Capital Punishment, and the NAACP. Coppoc saw that it was not the organization or a specific cause with which he was involved that mattered. Hays found "happiness in defending the oppressed." He refused to be pinned down as to where this determination to fight for the oppressed came from. He was more open about his view (expressed as early as 1928) that prejudice was normal among people and grew from lack of familiarity: "that prejudice against new or strange things or people has often like fear served as a protective shield for the human race." But "once you get to know people an understanding is effected thereby prejudice for those persons is lost." He said his work during the Sweet trial "as an associate of Clarence Darrow" was the "first opportunity he was given to know Negroes personally and socially." He admitted (as he had done previously) that he was self-conscious at first and tried to balance formality with forwardness. He asserted he had "no great intolerance against people who have prejudices because he knows that prejudice is usually due to ignorance, a feeling of inferiority or lack of experience." Hays either stayed away from his more provocative phrasing about the right to prejudice, or Coppoc refused to reproduce it. Coppoc listed some of Hays's race work: the Sweet trial, efforts on behalf of the Scottsboro boys, and "the famous Lynn case." She portrayed them as part of his larger mission in life of "fighting" for the "insulted and injured."[1]

From the time of Sweet trial, Hays fought the color line in various ways and was guided by his larger view of what would create a better society. His work against race discrimination emerged naturally from his work with the ACLU and his association with other civil liberties organizations. Thus, the ACLU's work on policing issues brought him to the Mayor's Commission on Harlem. But he also made a reputation, at least among African Americans, as someone who fought racism, which led the Cockburns to seek his help in their restrictive covenant case. During WWII his struggles against the color line peaked. The failure of the national ACLU to act as aggressively as Hays wanted on Japanese internment and in the Washington sedition trial opened up time for him to engage in other work. At the same time, the anti-racialist ideology used to justify the war stimulated Hays and others to act and predisposed some to respond favorably to those actions. Thus, the Lynns involved him in the challenge to the segregated draft, and Jonah Goldstein's resignation from the ABA prompted Hays's campaign against that organization's color line. While the *Lynn* case was a defeat at law and in shaping public opinion, the drive to end the exclusion of African American lawyers from the ABA was a success because the war's fight against Nazi racism proved an effective rallying point. But the possibilities opened by the war also exposed the limits of Hays's racial liberalism, as he came out against strong fair employment laws. While his opposition had little effect, the movement for effective government action against employment discrimination stalled.

Postwar, Hays carried on pretty much as he had for decades, continuing to practice law both for fee-paying clients and for causes. As he done after WWI, he traveled to Europe to reestablish international clients. Until 1951, when he resigned as counsel, he was active in the ACLU. Much of his attention was focused on battling the second Red Scare, which he saw as a dire threat to American liberties. He continued giving speeches, but his writing fell away. He never again attempted another book after *City Lawyer*, and the number of articles he produced declined. But when he advised Victor Rotnem to think about writing his own book, Hays revealed what his writing had meant to him. He told Rotnem "to keep copious notes of your work in the Civil Liberties Union because, after the war there will be a mighty good book there. This will also keep you on the right path as you will want to live up to your memoirs."[2]

He embraced new causes. For instance, in 1944, J. J. Singh, of the Indian League of America (which advocated less immigrant restriction and allowing the naturalization of people from India), thought the widely syndicated columnist Drew Pearson had slandered him. He went to the ACLU, who referred him to Hays because of Hays's flourishing libel practice. Hays approached Pearson, who both publicly apologized and retracted his earlier statement. Hays then wrote Singh, expressing his outrage at the racism of America's immigration system. "There never was any reason why the Nationals of India should not have been permitted to become citizens of the United States. The bars to their naturalization reflect discredit not on them but on us. It is about time that we removed this discrimination against one of the most highly civilized and cultured people on earth." Hays ended up serving on the advisory board of India League of America.[3]

He also continued with race work. Indeed, through his connection with A. Philip Randolph, Hays stayed active with the movement to end segregation in the military. For instance, in 1949 he served as the national counsel for "Commission of Inquiry into Wartime Treatment of Negro Servicemen," an endeavor sponsored by Randolph's organization, the Committee against Jim Crow in Military Service and Training. This commission was organized to expose the problems of the segregated military: It was structured like a government investigatory body and held public hearings, taking testimony from a range of individuals, including Senator Jacob Javits, Colonel Campbell Johnson of the Selective Service, and various soldiers and sailors who had suffered discrimination. The group held hearings in Washington, DC; St. Louis, Missouri; New Orleans, Louisiana; Los Angeles California; and New York, New York, to build support for completing the integration of the military. Hays presided over the hearing held in New York City in June 1949. At that hearing, a witness testified as to how, during the war, Miami Beach, Florida, denied of the use of many facilities to African American soldiers, that it prohibited them from being in town after sunset, and that these restrictions by the town were enforced by the military police. Hays expressed shock: "It is amazing that there has never been a test. What is the matter with the NAACP or the Civil Liberties Union?" This expression of outrage could have been genuine, a reaction to an injustice he had not previously known, or calculated to bring those organizations more into the struggle against the segregated military.[4]

Hay's most extensive work in fighting racial discrimination was representation of two of the Trenton Six during their second trial and appeals. In 1948, six African American men were charged with murder of a white shopkeeper based on the basis of forced confessions. The confessions were written by the police, as four of the six men were functionally illiterate. Their arrests and trial were held during an intense media-driven panic over postwar crime. They were convicted by an all-white jury at their first trial; the men were represented on appeal by the Civil Rights Congress of the Communist party and the NAACP. The case became a cause célèbre for the left and liberals. Hays's first involvement in the case was to publicly say that he had donated to the Civil Rights Congress. By expressing his support, he hoped to encourage other "people [made] timid" by the anti-Red hysteria. The appeal that prompted a new trial was the only success of the Civil Right Congress in the case because actions by New Jersey officials caused the Congress's lawyers to withdraw from the case. To assist the NAACP, a new group formed to represent some of the defendants, the Princeton Committee to Free the Trenton Six. That organization hired Hays and local attorney George Pellettieri to represent two of the six. The second trial, in 1951, where lawyers outnumbered clients, turned on questions of the validity of the confessions. Hays was far from the most active of the lawyers, nor among the most effective. His attempt to get key evidence excluded failed, and his attempt to impeach a psychiatric expert witness who denied that men would voluntarily confess to crimes they had not committed was ineffectual. But his question to the expert raising the issue of false confessions by the defendants in the Scottsboro case, although disallowed, showed how Hays understood the New Jersey case as part of a long line of prejudicial policing. In the second trial, the jury split, convicting two (both of Hays's clients), probably on the basis of their confessions—the four found innocent either had seen their confessions thrown out or their lawyers had raised sufficient doubt about them. Pellettieri and Hays wrote a brief seeking a new trial, and that was his last participation in the case; Pellettieri argued and won the appeal in October of 1951. But before the new trial could be scheduled, one of the defendants died in prison and the second pleaded guilty and was paroled six months later.[5]

Hays continued to use lawsuits to educate the larger public about racial discrimination. He did so in Josephine Baker's defamation suit against gossip columnist and radio personality Walter Winchell. After Baker, the famous entertainer, was offered "delayed service" at the Stork Club on October 16, 1951, she charged the club, run by Sherman Billingsley, with discrimination. She implored Winchell to come forward with what he had seen in the club that night. Instead, Winchell, who had a record of supporting civil rights, sided with Billingsley, whose club was a key nexus for his work. Hays was brought into the dispute as Baker's lawyer and appealed to Winchell to support her, praising his record as "a vigorous fighter for the rights of all minorities, including Negroes." But the tactic failed as Winchell, attacked Baker as a Communist. In turn, Hays filed a defamation suit against Winchell, his publisher, and his syndicator in federal court, seeking $400,000 in damages to compensate Baker for harm caused to her reputation and career. Announced from the NAACP headquarters, the amount itself generated headlines and prompted an escalation of attacks and counterattacks in the press. A special investigation by a city body concluded the case for discrimination against Baker by the club was unsubstantiated, and Baker's residence in France and the other circumstances caused delays in scheduling the trial. Indeed, eventually the suit was dismissed in 1955 for failure to meet a filing deadline.[6]

No matter how engaging his work, in his later years Hays turned more of his attention to his family. Hays spent his postwar summers in Long Island, finding the lure of his sailboat and his family irresistible. To beg off a speaking engagement, he admitted, "next week I go with my family to Sands Point on Long Island, and it is hard to get me away from there during the summer." Though he still owned his home in Greenwich Village, over the course of time he spent more time on Long Island, commuting into the city for work. At times, both his daughters were there with him, though after the birth of Lora's daughter, she spent less time there. Jane and her husband, William Butler, became fixtures there in the 1950s. Hays facilitated Jane and Bill's adjustment to married life by supplementing Bill's income as a lawyer as he was just getting established, as well as underwriting a European trip.[7]

Hays never retired from his firm or from public speaking, even as age, losses, and illness slowed him. In 1950, he suffered two major losses in his social circle: McAlister Coleman died and C. Fulton Oursler ended their deep friendship over disagreements about Cold War issues. Hays also began having health problems that year that kept him from the office, including surgery on his face for the removal of presumably a cancer. He took an extended summer vacation in Europe to recover. Three years later he admitted to feeling old and tired, yet he formed a serious relationship with a retired actress, Moon Carroll. He was still effective and in the public eye. For instance, Hays agreed to address the South Shore Human Relations Workshop, a small interracial group in Merrick, Long Island. The well-received talk gained members for the ACLU. Members of his family often drove him to his talks, and Bill and Jane transported him to this one. But he also declined invitations to give talks. In 1952, he refused an out-of-state speaking request by a family member, something that he would not have done in his prime. He excused himself by writing, "I have given it a lot of thought, because I would like to come, but then, as you know, I am well on in years and find trips like this very wearing. I am afraid, therefore, particularly since I have a pretty heavy schedule of work, that I cannot come. I know you will understand and forgive me." Indeed, he was a booked to speak at Cooper Union when he died, and the engagement was repurposed into a memorial service for him.[8]

The world of civil liberties camaraderie continued to sustain him. In the postwar period, Hays helped to welcome former Federal Judge J. Waites Waring into this world. Judge Waring was the federal judge who began breaking down the practices of segregation in South Carolina and, through prompting by his second wife, New York socialite Elizabeth Avery, would become an opponent of segregation. He oversaw a number important cases, including a case that was folded into the *Brown v. Board* case, *Briggs v. Elliott*. In in a dissent in that case, he announced that segregation per se was inequality. In 1952, because of social ostracism and threats, he retired from active service and moved to New York, where he became head of a civil rights organization, the National Committee Against Discrimination in Housing, and vice chairman of the board of the ACLU. His assimilation into this activist world marked how civil rights had become a central part of the civil liberties agenda. Waring and his wife spent some time in the summer of 1952 at Hays's Long Island home. They were there with Hays; his daughter, Jane; and her husband, Bill; as well as another couple. The visit was commemorated by the participants in light verse. Waring's experiences emphasized that the fight against the color line was ongoing, as Hays's remarks at a luncheon praising his opinion in *Briggs* revealed.[9]

In some ways, the fight against segregation was a war Hays fought from a distance. Hays's relationships with African Americans usually extended only to the professional. His connections with activists like A. Phillip Randolph, James Weldon Johnson, Roy Wilkins, and Walter White were driven by their coming together over a case or cause and seldom extended to the personal for long. The African American lawyers with whom he worked, Charles Hamilton Houston, Eunice Carter, Conrad Lynn, and Thurgood Marshall, never became part of his circle of legal intimates; none, for instance, showed up on the list of people to whom he sent free copies of his books. He wrote back and forth with Louis. F. Coles when he was on the Mayor's Commission, but there is no evidence he ever saw him socially or maintained contact with him afterward. His relations with Joshua and Pauline Cockburn seem to have extended no further than that of a lawyer and client. In short, there is no indication that he had close social associations across the color line. Perhaps Hays living in Greenwich Village predisposed him to not socializing much with the activists and lawyers with whom he interacted. He retreated to Long Island, not to the Hudson Valley more easily reached from Harlem. But in Hays's time, and within his orbit, such contacts were possible. For instance, Arthur Spingarn and Thurgood Marshall of the NAACP intertwined their lives. As Jack Greenberg noted, Spingarn spoke of Marshall as a son, and in his will the only bequests outside the immediate family were to Marshall's sons. Marshall spent vacations at the Spingarn home in Amenia, and later he bought that house and sold it back to the Spingarn family. Hays had no such contacts, and his entrance to the race work had been through another white man, Darrow.[10]

Hays's closest associations were with white people. His immediate and extended family formed his core social group, and it reached out to his partners, a few ACLU leaders, a close college friend (McAlister Coleman), and a friend he made of a client (Charles Fulton Oursler). Many were Jewish (especially among his partners and relations by marriage), and all were white. They received invitations to stay at his homes or summer retreats. They were the ones whom he went sailing with or played chess with. They were the ones who sat up late into the night with him in wide-ranging discussions that helped to shape Hays's view of the world. And when Hays re-created one of those conversations as the opening of his book *Democracy Works*, the cast of characters included the host (a free speech absolutist), an activist Socialist, a head of a utility company, a doctor, the host's wife (a long-suffering object of her husband's neglect but also engaged with current affairs), and a questioning young girl. Their conversation was carried on in reaction to hearing a Hitler speech and was portrayed as a "Heartbreak House" gathering, recalling George Bernard Shaw's play of the same name exploring how the British aristocracy failed to perceive the coming crisis of World War I. There was no obvious African American in the group, nor did race enter the conversation. It makes clear that it was not personal contact but ideas that drove Hays's anti-racist work, ideas were shaped by the world of civil liberties activism of 1920s and 1930s, even if Hays did his most prominent race work in the 1940s.[11]

It is important to note that even as the ACLU made race work a key part of its agenda in the 1940s, many did not see the struggle against segregation as a civil liberties issues carried on by cause lawyers. The perceived range of cause lawyers can be seen in a letter Coleman wrote to Hays as they were finishing his final book. "When you come to a description of the work of the ACLU, it would be graceful to mention some of the free work done by the younger lawyers, not only for the Civil Liberties but for other groups." He then listed six names associated with the ACLU or leftist organizations, but no African Americans or African American organizations. It might be that Coleman only had free speech in mind, as this comment amplifying what he was after revealed: "All these younger men are carrying on in the spirit of Darrow and yourself, and as dean of the free speakers, you might mention them." Even Coleman's knowledge that Hays's role in the Sweet case and his involvement in Scottsboro (both of which Coleman wrote up in earlier books with Hays) were connected to Darrow did not prompt Coleman into a discussion of race work. Hays work on the Mayor's Commission and his work in the Cockburn case were treated episodically in the book. In all, it seems to point to categorial thinking that sorted race and civil liberties issues into separate classes. It was never a complete separation, but it was persistent. And it was a hierarchical one, with civil liberties being ranked first. This ranking of course was in line with Hays's conception of what was most important for liberals.[12]

Hays was a liberal. Indeed, he was one of the people who shaped a strain of liberalism within the ACLU and in the greater society. Personal freedom lay at the heart of Hays's liberalism. It was reflected not just in his causes but in little things. Hays was a heavy tobacco user, both pipe tobacco and cigarettes. The portrait he chose for his semi-autobiography shows him lighting his pipe. Many of his speech text pages are marked with tobacco burns. The anti-tobacco activist H. G. Apgar once attempted to persuade him to stop giving tobacco such a good image. Hays explained to Apgar that "I use tobacco because I enjoy it." When Apgar pointed out how the tobacco companies bought silence, using as an example the Hays client Bernarr MacFadden, who, despite being an advocate of healthy living, took tobacco ads in his weekly newsmagazine, Hays answered, stressing his belief in a Darrow-like philosophy, "I am not sure that our views would agree on tobacco; in fact, in general I am pretty well of the opinion that people should be damned in their own way. I do not think you fellows sufficiently regard the importance of doing things merely because you like to do them. However, maybe you are right; and I do appreciate your letter." Hays agreed with Apgar's point that people should make efforts to become healthier, but "for myself I am not quite ready to do this." He never came to grips with Apgar's argument of the corrupting power of industry on public opinion makers. There were blinders to Hays's vision shaped by his commitment to freedom as he perceived it.[13]

Indeed, his views on liberty, especially economic freedom, confused people during his life and after. People at the time of his death asserted wrong things about his views. For instance, Clifford Forrester, ACLU staff counsel, portrayed him in a letter to the *New York Times* as the last of the nineteenth-century liberals who opposed big government. Newspaper man Don Munro declared that "Arthur was to the unknowing thought of as a dangerous radical. Actually, he was an arch conservative and represented half the big firms on Wall Street." To hold those views of Hays, one had to have overlooked his many statements in favor of an extensive government role in social welfare. For instance, in *City Lawyer*, he declared: "We must and can guarantee all citizens a living, even if we give away the necessities of life just as today we provide government, police and fire protection, parks, libraries, museums, golf courses, schools, roads and bridges. There is no difference in principle between distributing food and collecting garbage." Still others thought him a Socialist critic of capitalism. A letter to a reader who wrote him questioning his stance on socialism yields some understanding of Hays's position: "I think I stated: 'I don't like the capitalist system, but it is the only system we have.' It seems to me the important thing to do is to treat specific problems as they arise, instead of trying to remold the world in accordance with some philosophy." He continued, "I have not much faith in any kind of a system. . . . My feeling is that those who put their faith in systems have a religion, and I personally haven't much faith." This "case by case" basis, going after specific problems as they arose, certainly exemplified how Hays approached civil liberties matters and his race work. Still, he was a little less than honest with himself, as he did have a system.[14]

In the final analysis, Arthur Garfield Hays came to his work against the color line through his faith in civil liberties. He captured his view of freedom when he wrote for Edward Morrow's "This I Believe" in 1952. Hays stated: "This I believe—that progress comes from struggle, conflict, and competition of ideas; that freedom is an end in itself, almost as important to the individual as the food he eats or the air he breathes." The Bill of Rights was the "best expression of freedom," and the nation's well-being depended "on our observance" of its "principles." Hays did not want just "platitudinous" observation, though, leading them to supporting "freedom of speech <u>but</u>. . . ." He advocated for untrammeled freedom of speech, provided it did not incite "violent violation of law" even from "unpopular, vicious or discredited" speakers. This absolute right would result in "noxious ideas" losing out to "truth." Still, the struggle was carried out in the legal realm, and "the course of justice is not always straight and swift." He saw progress and had faith that "our time-tested democratic institutions" made "this progress possible." Thus, things that weakened those institutions and pressed on ideas including "Congressional investigation into men's opinions . . . loyalty oaths, guilt by association" needed to be resisted. "I believe that no man should lose his reputation, his liberty or his property except by judgment of court after fair trial according to Anglo-Saxon procedure." It was not just a focus on a due process that he exalted; "Freedom has practical as well as ideological values." Through persuasion and voting, "we have a method of bringing about changes in our society no matter how radical, without force and violence." Freedom made for a "progressive and prosperous" country. He declared he was "unswervingly determined to help keep America free" and said he derived "the deepest satisfaction from doing everything I can to preserve and enlarge" liberty. That of course easily encompassed liberty, regardless of race, to live where one wanted, to be called to the nation's service equally, to be treated without discrimination by the police, and to belong to a professional organization.[15]

A single view of Hays failed to emerge from the two ceremonies held to memorialize him after his death. At the services held on December 16, 1954, presided over by Roger Baldwin, Hays's own presentation of himself predominated. First, his own words formed much of the tribute, as Baldwin quoted extensively from his writings. He repeated Hays's end to the prologue of *City Lawyer*, where Hays, riffing off John Brown's famous statement that he was "worth more for hanging than for any other purpose," wrote that he "had "been worth more for the defense of the right of others to express their ideas." Baldwin noted Hays's lack of faith in "systems," his hatred of seeing "people pushed around," and how that fed his "human urges" to act. Baldwin rightly noted he did so much because "he lived his life with self-confident optimism." Second, the rest of the service reflected how Hays saw himself: It consisted of readings from John Milton's *Areopagitica*, a classic statement of liberty of the press and thought, and Robert Louis Stevenson's romantic poem about how death provided rest from the struggles of life, "Requiem." At the ACLU-organized event at Cooper Union held on March 16, 1955, five speakers spoke for ten minutes each on the different aspects of Hays's work: censorship, labor, race relations, due process, and political expression. The program was later broadcast on the radio station WNYC and the college radio network. Sadly, their comments have been lost. An organizer of the event wrote, "The speakers wove in Arthur's concept of civil liberties with the current scene and the need for vigilance. A number of questions were asked by the audience about civil liberties cases. . . . Arrangements were made for the audience to fill out forms so that information about the ACLU could be sent to them, and this produced about 55 replies" of the estimated 650 attendees. The focus on current cases and building up the civil liberties support were in line with Hays's predilections. In all, the two events did not make it clear how Hays's ideas and actions fit together. Oddly, it was an outsider who did this. Former Governor Herbert Lehman wrote to the director of the ACLU upon Hays's death. His brief letter captured the connections, including how his work against the color line fit into his civil liberties agenda, better than any of his associates had. He described Hays as "a tower of strength in safeguarding the civil liberties of all, regardless of race, color, creed, national origin or political point of view." And, for all his limitations, so he was.[16]

Notes

Introduction

1. Wilkins to Malin, March 4, 1955, American Civil Liberties Union Records, Public Policy Papers hereafter (ACLU Papers), Box 614, folder 1 Seeley G. Mudd Library, Princeton University. The other four areas of his activism discussed were censorship, labor, due process of law, and political opinion; Press Release [1955] ACLU Papers, Box 614, folder 1; W. E. B. Du Bois, *The Souls of Black Folk* (Chicago: A. C. McClurg & Co., 1903), 40. The phrase "Long Civil Rights" was coined by Jacquelyn Dowd Hall, and the duration of the period expanded. Some of the most fruitful work has been done in the period when Hays was most active in confronting racism. Jacquelyn Dowd Hall, "The Long Civil Rights Movement and the Political Uses of the Past," *Journal of American History* 91 (March 2005): 1233–63; Glenda Gilmore, *Defying Dixie: The Radical Roots of Civil Rights* (New York: W. W. Norton, 2008); Thomas J. Sugrue, *Sweet Land of Liberty: The Forgotten Struggle for Civil Rights in the North* (New York: Random House, 2008), Risa L. Goluboff, *The Lost Promise of Civil Rights* (Cambridge: Harvard University Press, 2007. The long civil rights movement concept has been criticized; see Thomas C. Holt, *The Movement: The African American Struggle for Civil Rights* (New York: Oxford University Press, 2021). Also, some scholars have found the struggle for rights a confining paradigm that distorts the full history of African Americans and law. Most notably, Dylan C. Penningroth, in *Before the Movement: The Hidden History of Black Civil Rights* (New York: Liveright Publishing Corporation, 2023), shows how African Americans "thought about and used American law" in ordinary circumstances to "tell a history of Black legal lives . . . to pull back a curtain on seldom-seen parts of Black life itself" (xvii–xix). Significantly, Penningroth uncovers a complex history of African Americans and the law, which, while distinct from the freedom struggle, also interacted and informed it. Such an aligning of regular law and movement law occurred in Hays's representation of clients in a restrictive covenant case; see chapter 3.

2. "Hays, Arthur Garfield," *Current Biography: Who's News and Why* (New York: W. M. Wilson Co.), vol. 3, September 1942, 31–32, clipping in Arthur Garfield Hays Papers, Seeley G. Mudd Library, Princeton University (hereafter AGHP), Box 36, folder 1, Passport, AGHP Box 37, folder 15, "thickset" quoted in and "genial" in clipping, Abraham Silverstein, "An Outstanding American Liberal," *Jewish Tribune,* June 1, 1928, 3, 14 in AGHP, Box 34, folder 14; Hays to John T. Frederick, July 13, 1942, AGHP, Box 11, folder 3; Arthur Garfield Hays, *City Lawyer: The Autobiography of a Law Practice* (New York: Simon and Schuster, 1942), 66; 239; Marian Storm, review of *Let Freedom Ring*, in *New York Evening Post*, Saturday, no date, clipping in AGHP, Box 37, folder 2. In a posed photo of the defense experts, court officials, and lawyers from Scopes trial of sixteen persons, Hays is the only one who is holding a pipe; moreover, he was the only one who had taken off his shirt. In a less posed shot where the experts are working, of the thirteen pictured, Hays is the only one not wearing a tie, and again he has a pipe. Marcel Chotkowski LaFollette, *Reframing Scopes: Journalists, Scientists, and the Lost Photographs from the Trial of the Century* (Lawrence: University Press of Kansas, 2008), 81, 82.

3. Arthur Garfield Hays, *Let Freedom Ring* (New York: Boni and Liveright, 1928), 196–97; Walter White, *A Man Called White* (New York: Arno Press and New York Times, 1969, reprint of 1948), 75–76. The popularizer Irving Stone and the historian Kevin Boyle have retold the tale. I have quoted only the participants in my reconstruction of the event. Kevin Boyle, *Arc of Justice: A Saga of Race, Civil Rights, and Murder in the Jazz Age* (New York: Henry Holt, 2004), 229–30; Irving Stone, *Clarence Darrow for the Defense* (New York: Bantam, 1941), 307–8.

4. Hays, *Let Freedom Ring*, 197.

5. Jack Greenberg, *Crusaders in the Courts* (New York: Basic Books, 1994), 45, 530 note 45, 210; Greenberg was talking about the Trenton Six case, which Hays entered late in 1950 and where he performed quite poorly; see conclusion; Hays, *City Lawyer*, 24; Boyle, *Arc of Justice*, 340.

Chapter 1

1. Alfred Garfield Hays, *City Lawyer: The Autobiography of a Law Practice* (New York: Simon and Schuster, 1942), 17–19; "Champion of Unpopular Causes," *American Hebrew*, April 5, 1929, 755, copy in AGHP, Box 34, folder 3; "Hays, Arthur Garfield," *Current Biography: Who's News and Why* (New York: W. M. Wilson Co.), vol. 3, September 1942, 31–32, copy in AGHP, Box 36, folder 1.

2. Hays, *City Lawyer*, 22–25; Hays to Milton Warner, April 19, 1945, AGHP, Box 14, folder 2. Morris Ernst's family had similar views on new Jewish immigrants; see Samantha Barbas, *The Rise and Fall of Morris Ernst, Free Speech Renegade* (Chicago: University of Chicago Press, 2021), 10–11.

3. Hays, *City Lawyer*, 25, 26, 28–29; Hays to Albert J. Rosenthal, July 1, 1940, AGHP, Box 7, folder 9. Typescript, "March 3/32 AGH Biography," AGHP, Box 10, folder 12.

4. Hays, *City Lawyer*, 28, 35, 46, 66; Hays to Coleman, September 22, 1941, AGHP, Box 9, folder 1; Hays to Cyrus C. Miller, July 8, 1942, AGHP, Box 11, folder 3; Hays, "McAlister Coleman," typescript, May 22, 1950, AGHP, Box 34, folder 12.

5. Ann Pinchot, "Champion of Unpopular Causes," *American Hebrew*, April 5, 1929, 755, 767, copy in AGHP, Box 34, folder 3; Hays, *City Lawyer*, 29, 33, 34–48; "N. R. Lindheim Dies in his 48th Year," *New York Times*, February 9, 1928, 25; "Mr. St. John, Troy Man Dies," *Troy Record*, November 6, 1958, 7; Abraham Silverstein, "An Outstanding American Liberal," *Jewish Tribune*, June 1, 1928, 3, 14, copy in AGHP, Box 34, folder 14; Lindheim's wife, Irma Levy, was president of Hadassah in 1928, which was a leading Zionist organization. Shulamit Reinharz, "Irma Levy Lindheim," The Shalvi/Hyman Encyclopedia of Jewish Women at the Jewish Women's Archives, https://jwa.org/encyclopedia/article/lindheim-irma-levy; typescript, "March 3/32 AGH Biog.," AGHP, Box 10, folder 12.

6. Hays, *City Lawyer*, 76, 47, 48, 26; *Current Biography*, 31, copy in AGHP, Box 36, folder 1"; Lora Hays Spindell, 99, film editor and professor," AMNY, https://www.amny.com/news/lora-hays-spindell-99-film-editor-and-professor/ (hereafter Spindell obituary); "Hays-Marks," *New York Times*, October 12, 1908, 8; Hays to Milton Warner, April 19, 1945, AGHP, Box 14, folder 2.

7. "Found British Court Giving US Justice," *New York Times*, October 3, 1915; "British Acts Against Neutral Trade 'Illegal,' " *New York Times*, January 28, 1917, SM6; Paul B. Urion to Hays, August 20, 1954; Hays to Urion, August 24, 1954, AGHP, Box 16, folder 10. Bound typescript, at Coburg dinner (September 1, 1916), "The Very Blue Book of a New York Lawyer," copy in AGHP, Box 37, folder 15; *New York Times*, August 27, 1915, 14; *Current Biography*, 32: copy in AGHP, Box 36, folder 1; Hays, *City Lawyer*, 50–69; typescript, "March 3/32 AGH Biog." AGHP, Box 10, folder 12.

8. AGH, "Seizure of Mails," October 19, 1916, Box 35, folder 1, Hays, *City Lawyer* 76–77, 83; J. Garry Clifford, "Clark, Grenville," in Roger N. Newman, editor, *The Yale Biographical Dictionary of American Law* (New Haven: Yale University Press, 2009), 108–9; Gerald T. Dunne, *Greenville Clark: Public Citizen* (New York: Farrar, Straus, Giroux, 1986), 36–45; Hays to R. W. Woods, Esq., Procurator General's Office, Whitehall London, January 12, 1918, Box 1, folder 6; Arthur Garfield Hays, *Enemy Property in America* (Albany, NY: Matthew Bender, 1925).

9. "Indict Dr. Rumely and S. W. Kaufmann," *New York Times*, August 3, 1918, 5; "Rumely in Prison," *New York Times*, March 20, 1924, 40; "Hays Loses Tax Case Before Appeals Board, "*New York Times*, July 21, 1925, 2; N. R. Lindheim Dies in his 48th Year," *New York Times*, February 9, 1928, 25.

10. Hays, *City Lawyer*, 50–52, 77, 79, 83 89, 94; "Rumely in Prison," *New York Times*, March 20, 1924, 40; "Hays Loses . . . ," *New York Times*, July 21, 1925, 2; Hays Deposition, April 16, 1952, AGHP, Box 16, folder 4.

11. Hays, "American Liberalism," AGHP, Box 34, folder 1, December 24, 1918.

12. Hays, *City Lawyer*, 70, 248–78; brief for Appellants *New York Ex Rel Doyle v. Atwell* in AGHP, Box 22, folder 5; *New York Ex Rel Doyle v. Atwell* 261 US 590 (1923); Blanche M. Hays to Hays, "Thursday Eve" [January 1942], AGHP, Box 11, folder 1; Blanche Hays to Hays, Sunday in June 1942, AGHP, Box 11, folder 2.

13. Brief for Appellants, 24, in AGHP, Box 22, folder 5.

14. "Greenwich Village Deals," *New York Times*, April 22, 1920, 26. Spindell Obituary; Hays to Henry B. Hoffmann, October 7, 1926, AGHP, Box 1, folder 6; Blanche is one of the "witnesses" in the film *Reds* and later was an activist in founding a Jewish conservative movement in Arizona. *Reds* (1981) film's credit to Blanche Hays Fagan; Jeffrey Fuller to Lora Hays Spindell, February 7, 1955, ACLU, Box 614, folder 2; Fuller to Jane and Bill [Butler], December 23, 1954, AGHP, Box 16, folder 11; Silverstein, "An Outstanding American Liberal," in AGHP Box 34, folder 14; Pinchot, "Champion of Unpopular Causes," 755, 767, copy in AGHP, Box 34, folder 3.

15. "Our New Supreme Rex," copy in AGHP, Box 34, folder 6; Pinchot, "Champion of Unpopular Causes," 755, 767, copy in AGHP, Box 34, folder 3. Hays handled corporate governance cases. "Bank of U. S. Heads Sued for $50,000,000," *New York Times*, December 1930, 1; typescript "March 3/32 AGH Biog.," AGHP, Box 10, folder 12.

16. Hays, *City Lawyer*, 154–60; Spindell Obituary; Radio Guide, *New York Times*, July 2, 1932, 7.

17. Samuel Walker, *In Defense of American Liberties: A History of the ACLU* (New York, Oxford, 1990), 47–71, 69; Robert C. Cottrell, *Roger Nash Baldwin and the American Civil Liberties Union* (New York: Columbia University Press, 2000), 117–23, 174; Peggy Lamson, *Roger Baldwin: A Founder of the American Civil Liberties Union, A Portrait* (Boston: Hughton Mifflin Company, 1976), 133–34.

18. Walker, *In Defense*, 54–55; Hays, *Let Freedom Ring*, 102–22, AGH [Article], no date, 16, AGHP, Box 34, folder 1; Report to ACLU, May 27, 1922, AGHP, Box 32, folder 13; in the spring and early summer of 1935, Hays was again active in the coal fields for the ACLU as the miners attempted to strike. In general, see AGHP, Box 32, folders 15–16.

19. Bernard Taper, "A Lover of Cities, II," *The New Yorker*, February 11, 1967, 45–115, 53; it is ironic that Hays opposed the creation of the antidiscrimination agency Abrams later headed.

20. Clipping, "Charles W. Wood, 'Upholding the Right of Americans to Free Speech and Free Opinions: An Interview with Arthur Garfield Hays," *The World*, Editorial Section, Sunday, December 17, 1922, AGHP, Box 35, folder 3.

21. See "Review of Scopes Trial by Lawyer for the Defense," clipping from unknown newspaper [Lehigh PN 1926] AGHP, Box 37, folder 13, Hays, *Let Freedom Ring*, 25–89; Edward J. Larson, *Summer for the Gods: The Scopes Trial and America's Continuing Debate Over Science and Religion* (Cambridge: Harvard University Press, 1997); Ray Ginger, *Six Days or Forever?: Tennessee v. John T. Scopes* (New York: Oxford, 1958); Marcel Chotkowski LaFollette, *Reframing Scopes: Journalists, Scientists, and Lost Photographs from the Trial of the Century* (Lawrence: University Press of Kansas, 2008).

22. Hays, *City Lawyer*, 208, 461–47; Silverstein, "An Outstanding American Liberal," copy in AGHP, Box 34, folder 14, Typescript "March 3/32 AGH Biog.," AGHP, Box 10, folder 12; Hays to David Levi, November 27, 1945, AGHP, Box 14, folder 1.

23. Walker, *In Defense*, 83–83; Paul S. Boyer, *Purity in Print: Book Censorship in America From the Gilded Age to the Computer Age*, 2nd ed. (Madison: University of Wisconsin Press, 2002) 78, 82, 176–79; Hays, *Let Freedom Ring*, 16–188, 184. Pinchot, "Champion of Unpopular Causes," 755, 767, copy in AGHP, Box 34, folder 3.

24. Clipping, *Jamaica Press*, September 29, 1933 AGHP, Box 37, folder 13; Clipping, *New York Times*, June 4, 1941, AGHP, Box 37, folder 13; Silverstein, "An Outstanding American Liberal," in AGHP, Box 34, folder 14; Communication from Dr. Robin D. Campbell, February, 21, 2021, to author on "Miss." On collaboration, see [Coleman to Hays], September 20 [1938?], Radburn, NJ; Coleman to Hays, [ND], AGHP, Box 1, folder 1; Hays, *City Lawyer*, 199.

25. "Hays Finds Soviet Behind High Tariff," *New York Times*, November 8, 1926, 7; "Debate Proletariat Rule," *New York Times*, December 20, 1931, N3; "Hays and Communist Meet in a Debate," *New York Times*, May 14, 1927, 6; "Arthur Garfield Hays on Russia," *New York Times*, February 21, 1927, 4. Clippings [Unknown Paper, 1926], "American 'Mercury' Defender Arrives," "Arthur J Hays of New York Arrives in Berlin," July 2, AGHP, Box 37, folder 13. Silverstein, "An Outstanding American Liberal," copy in AGHP, Box 34, folder 14; Pinchot, "Champion of Unpopular Causes," 755, 767, copy in AGHP, Box 34, folder 3.

26. "Urges Ignoring Laws That Are Undesirable," *New York Times*, February 6, 1928, 24.

27. This is not the place to tell the full story of the *Sweet* trials; that is done well by Kevin Boyle in *Arc of Justice*, which grounds the case in the social, political, and cultural contexts. Boyle, *Arc of Justice*, 1–11, 131–69; the longer and larger history of violence toward African Americans who moved into "white" neighborhoods is detailed in Jeannine Bell, *Hate Thy Neighbor: Move-in Violence and Persistent of Racial Segregation in American Housing* (New York: New York University Press, 2013).

28. Boyle, *Arc of Justice*, 170–228.

29. Boyle, *Arc of Justice*, 170–228.

30. Boyle, Arc of Justice, 254–55, 273.

31. Boyle, *Arc of Justice*, 268, 273.

32. Boyle, *Arc of Justice*, 268, 284–86; Hays, *City Lawyer*, 208–9.

33. Hays, *Let Freedom Ring*, 214–15.

34. Hays, *Let Freedom Ring*, 217; Boyle, *Arc of Justice*, 287, says that Hays's phrase "so the jury can look you over" "was an unfortunate choice of words, with their echoes of the slave market."

35. Boyle, *Arc of Justice*, 288; Hays, *Let Freedom Ring*, 225–26, 229.

36. Boyle, *Arc of Justice*, 314; Hays, *City Lawyer*, 210.

37. "School Blacklist Charge Is Denied," *New York Times*, May 15, 1926, 12; "Test School Right to Bar Speakers, *New York Times*, May 16, 1926, 23; "Denied Aid to Scopes Barred Hays Speech," *New York Times*, May 17, 1926, 12; "School Blacklist to Get Legal Test," *New York Times*, May 18, 1926, 16; "Thomas Criticizes O'Shea," *New York Times*, May 19, 1926, 14; "School Board Bars Free Speech Rally by Liberties Union," *New York Times*, May 22, 1926, 1; "Liberties Union Fight School Ban Today," *New York Times* November 4, 1926, 45; "School Use Appeal Is Heard in Albany," *New York Times,* November 5, 1926, 12, "Free-Speech Plea by Citizens' Union," *New York Times,* November 26, 1926, 13; " 'Free Speech' Stirs Dispute in Court, "*New York Times,* December 15, 1926, 19; Walker, *In Defense*, 59; Barbas, *Rise and Fall of Morris Ernst*, 73–74.

38. AGH, "Statement of Arthur Garfield Hays," May 18, 1926, AGHP, Box 35, folder 3, Untitled, June 2, 1926, AGHP, Box 35, folder 3.

39. AGH, "American Tendencies and the College Student," *The Frater*, July 1926 issue, 3, 4, Box 34, folder 1.

40. "Files Answer in Libel Suit," *New York Times*, March 8, 1925, 4; "Sees Our Liberties Slowly Vanishing," *New York Times*, July 26, 1927, 9.

41. "My Office Is on Wallstreet," February, 1928, AGHP, Box 10, folder 12; Typescript "March 3/32 AGH Biog.," AGHP, Box 10, folder 12.

42. Hays, *Let Freedom Ring*, 195–236.

43. Hays, *Let Freedom Ring*, 288, 229; Boyle, *Arc of Justice*, 294.

44. A charitable interpretation of this characterization would be that because these attorneys had little role in the case as it went forward, Hays did not interact with them. Hays, *Let Freedom Ring,* 196, 228, 233; Boyle, *Arc of Justice*, 254–55.

45. See press clippings in general: AGHP, Box 37, folder; Harry Hansen, "The First Reader," *New York World*, April 25, 1928, clipping, AGHP, Box 37, folder 2; Fargo, ND, *Forum*, May 19, 1928, clipping, AGHP, Box 37, folder 2, Tulsa, Oklahoma, *Tribune* May 20, 1928, clipping, AGHP, Box 37, folder 2; "Short Notice," Brooklyn, NY, *Citizen*, June 12, 1928, AGHP, Box 37, folder 2; Dewey to Hays, May 5, AGHP, Box 1, folder 14, Durant to Hays, April 28, 1928, AGHP, Box 1, folder 14; Holmes to Hays, AGHP, Box 1, April 20, 1928, folder 14; Hays, *City Lawyer*, 231; the final call letters for WEVD were the initials of Eugene V. Debs, the nation's most famous Socialist.

46. "To our friends," May 14, 1928, AGHP, Box 36, folder 19.

47. "Wakefield-Hays," *New York Times*, March 25, 1930, 34; Spindell Obituary; "Lora Hays in Stage Debut," *New York Times,* September 25, 1931, 33. "Reject Theatre for 'Maya,'" *New York Times*, March 2, 1928, 26; Hays, *Let Freedom Ring,* 237–75; "Sues National City on Peru Bonds," *New York Times*, May 20, 1933, 2.

48. Lamson, *Roger Baldwin*, 134, "Radio Notes," *Washington Post*, January 14, 1938, 9.

49. Silverstein, "An Outstanding American Liberal," copy in AGHP, Box 34, folder 14; Undated bio [1935], AGHP, Box 10, folder 12; Pinchot, "Champion of Unpopular Causes," 755, 767, copy in AGHP, Box 34, folder 3; Memorandum, AGHP, Box 10, folder 12; *Current Biography*, 1933, AGHP, Box 36, folder 1.

50. "Views of Roosevelt and Thomas Debated," *New York Times*, October 24, 1932, 10; "Discuss Radicalism at College Session," *New York Times*, December 30, 1926, 3; "Hays Finds Soviets Behind High Tariff," *New York Times*, November 8, 1926, 7; "Debs in Eulogized at Radio Opening," *New York Times*, October 21, 1927, 28; Radio Address, WOR, Resolved the 18th Amendment shall be Submitted to the American People for a Referendum Vote, [1932], AGHP, Box 33, folder 3.

51. Silverstein, "An Outstanding American Liberal," copy in AGHP, Box 34, folder 14; Kevin Tierney *Darrow: A Biography* (New York: Thomas Y. Crowell, 1979), 369; William Biederman to Hays, December 22, 1919, AGHP, Box 2, folder 4; Hays to Jay B. Van Veen, March 19, 1929, AGHP, Box 2, folder 4; Hays to Pi Lambda Phi Fraternity, June 3, 1929, AGHP, Box 2, folder 4; Pi Lambda Phi to Hays, June 4, 1929, AGHP, Box 2, folder 4; Pi Lambda Phi to Hays, June 29, 1919, AGHP, Box 2, folder 4; Hays to Jay B. Van Veen, July 2, 1919, AGHP, Box 2, folder 4; Hays to Alexander, December 2, 1930, AGHP, Box 2, folder 6; Jerome Alexander to Hays, December 3, 1930, AGHP, Box 2, folder 6, Hays to Heywood Broun, March 15, 1933, Box 3, folder 1; Harvey Strum, "Louis Marshall and Anti-Semitism at Syracuse University," *American Jewish Archives Journal* 35 (1983): 1–12; Marianne R. Sanua, "Jewish College Fraternities in the United States, 1895–1968: An Overview," *Journal of American Ethnic History* 19 (2000): 3–42; Marianne R. Sanua, "The Non-Recognition of Jewish College Fraternities: The Cases of Columbia and Brown Universities," *American Jewish Archives Journal* 45 (1993): 125–45; Hays to Kaus, AGHP, January 29, 1933, Box 3, folder 1.

52. Boyle, *Arc of Justice*, 302; NAACP [James Weldon Johnson] to Hays, January 7, 1926, Box 1, folder 8; NAACP [James Weldon Johnson] to Hays, January 27, 1926, Box 1, folder 8; Isadore Martin to Hays, April 8, 1926, Box 1, folder 8; Hays to Martin, April 10, 1926, Box 1, folder 8, Hays to Frank Halsey, April 8, 1926, Box 1, folder 8.

53. L[ouis] F. Coles to Hays, January 5, 1928, AGHP, Box 1, folder 10; Hays to Coles, January 6, 1928, AGHP, Box 1, folder 10; Hays to Wallace Thurman, November 12, 1928, AGHP, Box 1, folder 14; Hays to Darrow, November 15, 1928, Box 1, folder 14; Darrow to Hays, November 17, 1928, Box 1, folder 14.

54. Silverstein, "An Outstanding American Liberal," copy in AGHP, Box 34, folder 14.

55. Hays to John T. Frederick, July 2, 1942, AGHP, Box 11, folder 3, AGH Article, [ND] AGHP, Box 34, folder 1, 24, 17, 18.

56. Arthur Garfield Hays, *Trial by Prejudice* (New York: Covici, 1933), 25–150; 86–89; Tierney, *Darrow*, 369, 385, 386, 389, 403–7; Dan T. Carter, *Scottsboro: A Tragedy of the American South* (Baton Rouge: Louisiana University Press, 1969, 1979), 98–101; James Goodman, *Stories of Scottsboro* (New York: Vintage Books,1994), 37–38. White, *A Man Called White* (New York: Arno Press and *New York Times*, 1969, reprint of 1948), 128–30.

57. Hays, *Prejudice*, 25–152, 22, frontispiece; Hays, *City Lawyer*, 240–41.

58. Hays, *Prejudice*, 91, 107–9, 149.

59. Hays, *Prejudice*, 3, 20–22.

60. Referring to Scottsboro, AGHP, Box 34, folder 17; Hays to Editor, *New York Times*, November 12, AGHP, Box 3, folder 1.

61. Ray H. Lindman to Hays, January 12, 1934, Box 3, folder 3; Hays to D. B. McCalmont, November 9, 1934, Box 3, folder 3; George T. Bye to Hays, February 6, 1935, AGHP, Box 3, folder 5, Victor Weybright to Hays, December 2, 1935, AGHP, Box 3, folder 5; Hays to Weybright, December 6, 1935.

62. Review, *Lynching and the Law*, AGHP, Box 33, folder 11, 3; "The Issues Before Congress and the Courts," AGHP, Box 33, folder 2.

63. To Harper & Brothers, "Home to Harlem" by Claude McKay, March 8, 1928, AGHP, Box 34, folder 8.

64. His keeping up with developments in Nazi Germany was shown by his going to see Dr. Marie Munk, a German judge of Jewish descent who was returning to Berlin. Note on reverse of: Queens County, New York City, December 13, 1933, AGHP, Box 32, folder 13; AGH speech, undated, Box 33, folder 5; Madison Square Garden, 7/34, AGHP, Box 33, folder 5 (delivered March 6, 1934).

65. Madison Square Garden, 7/34, AGHP, Box 33, folder 5; Arthur Garfield Hays, "What the Jews Want from Hitler," *Liberty*, June 2, 1934, 13–18.

66. Clippings of New York City papers, *Post*, *Herald Tribune*, and *Times*, on December 29, 1934, AGHP, Box 37, folder 14; Clippings, Lakewood, NJ, *Daily Times*, October 29, 1932, November 2, 1932, AGHP, Box 37, folder 13; Pinchot, "Champion of Unpopular Causes," 755, 767, copy in AGHP, Box 34, folder 3.

67. In general, see AGHP, Box 32, folder 7; Bruce Bliven to Hays, December 22, 1933, AGHP, Box 32, folder 7; Hays to *Long Island City Star*, December 26, 1933; Doing Justice, AGHP, Box 34, folder 4.

Chapter 2

1. Villard, "Slumbering Fires in Harlem," typescript, 7, in Arthur Garfield Hays Papers, Seeley G. Mudd Library, Princeton University (hereafter AGHP),

Box 26, folder 5. Until the work of Stephen Robertson, most treatments of the disturbance and investigation were brief. Robertson has captured the disturbance in pointillist detail, creating a full picture of the violence, property destruction, and reactions. His intwined narratives from a wide range of sources are invaluable to understand the start, development, and course of the disturbance. His evidence shows the disturbance was more violent and less focused than previous accounts, including that of the Mayor's Commission. Stephen Robertson, *Harlem in Disorder: A Spatial History of How Racial Violence Changed in 1935* (Redwood City, CA: Stanford University Press, 2024), http://doi.org/10.21627/2024hd, Introduction: "How Racial Violence Changed." Mayor La Guardia establishes an investigation. This work presents a challenge in citation, and I've opted to avoid long strings of numbers and letters to reference the individual titles of sections.

Most scholars who have written before Robertson divide into two schools. Some have centered their work on the sociological factors prompting the event resulting in politics in the street. Others studies bring police action to the forefront and see the event as the first of many struggles to rein in policing. Also, previous accounts of the riot and its investigation (save that of Robertson) have overlooked the importance of Hays to the commission's work on the police. Examples of sociological/politics in the street school are Janet L. Abu-Lunghod, *Race, Space, and Riots in Chicago, New York, and Los Angeles* (New York: Oxford University Press, 2007) and Cheryl Lynn Greenberg, *Or Does It Explode?: Black Harlem in the Great Depression* (New York: Oxford University Press, 1991). The more police-centered works include Dominic J. Capeci Jr., *The Harlem Riot of 1943* (Philadelphia: Temple University Press, 1977); Marilyn Johnson, *Street Justice: A History of Police Violence in New York City* (Boston: Beacon Press, 2003); Clarence Taylor, *Fight the Power: African Americans and the Long History of Police Brutality in New York City* (New York: New York University Press, 2019); and Cathy Lisa Schneider, *Police Power and Race Riots: Urban Unrest in Paris and New York* (Philadelphia: University of Pennsylvania Press, 2014), 43–44. Short but balanced treatments include Michael Lipsky and David J. Olson, *Commission Politics: The Processing of Racial Crisis in America* (New Brunswick, NJ: Transaction Books, 1977), 49–54; Stephen L. Carter, *Invisible: The Forgotten Story of the Black Woman Lawyer Who Took Down America's Most Powerful Mobster* (New York: Henry Holt and Company, 2018); David Levering Lewis, *When Harlem Was in Vogue* (New York: Penguin, 1997, 1979), 305–6; and Thomas Kessner, *Fiorello H. La Guardia and the Making of Modern New York* (New York: Penguin, 1989), 368–76. A brief and lopsided account that does not even mention the role of the police is Marilyn S. Greenwald and Yun Li, *Eunice Hunton Carter, A Lifelong Fight for Social Justice* (New York: Fordham University Press, 2021), 72–74. Almost every scholarly account of the riot and its investigation, before Robertson, bases its conclusion from material from the report *The Complete Report of Mayor La Guardia's Commission of the Harlem Riot of March 19, 1935* (New York: Arno Press, 1969), hereafter *Complete Report*.

2. Greenberg, *Or Does It Explode,* 14–18; Capeci, *The Harlem Riot of 1943,* 31; Clarence Taylor, *Fight the Power,* 57; Abu-Lunghod, *Race, Space, and Riots,* 135–38, 140–41; James Weldon Johnson, *Black Manhattan* (New York: Atheneum, 1968, 1930), 158, 281–84.

3. Abu-Lunghod, *Race, Space, and Riots,* 134; Kesssner, *Fiorello H. La Guardia,* 371–73; Greenberg, *Or Does It Explode,* 18–34, 53.

4. Abu-Lunghod, *Race, Space, and Riots,* 17–18, 141; Greenberg, *Or Does It Explode,* 114–26, 132; Robertson, *Harlem in Disorder,* Communist in Harlem, "Don't Buy Where You Can't Work" campaigns in Harlem.

5. La Guardia opened his administration with statements that he would root out corruption in the police force but appointed as his first police commissioner Major General John F. O'Ryan, who militarized the police conduct while cutting the department's political ties. He did little about corruption and was replaced by Valentine. Johnson, *Street Justice,* 3, 5–6, 10, 41–6, 114, 120, 121; Kessner, *Fiorello H. La Guardia,* 356–57, 368; Terry, Golway, *I Never Did Like Politics: How Fiorello La Guardia Became America's Mayor, and Why He Still Matters* (New York: St. Martins, 2024), 162–63.

6. Johnson, *Street Justice,* 154, 165, 166, 169, 170, 172, 173, 176–77; Kessner, *Fiorello La Guardia,* 153.

7. Johnson, *Street Justice,* 182, 183; Richard Norton Smith, *Thomas E. Dewey and His Times* (New York: Touchstone, 1982), 123–24; Greenberg, *Or Does it Explode,* 177, 192–93; Kessner, *Fiorello La Guardia,* 373; also see in general Shane White et al., *Playing the Numbers: Gambling in Harlem between the Wars* (Cambridge, MA: Harvard University Press, 2010).

8. Shannon King, " 'Ready to Shoot and Do Shoot': Black Working-Class Self-Defense and Community Politics in Harlem, New York, During the 1920s," *Journal of Urban History* 37 (2011): 757–74, 766; Shannon King, *Whose Harlem Is This, Anyway?: Community Politics and Grassroots Activism during the New Negro Era* (New York: New York University Press, 2015), 174–76, 177–85.

9. Johnson, *Street Justice,* 154–55, 167, 180–90; Mark Naison, *Communists in Harlem During the Depression* (Urbana: University of Illinois Press, 1983), 116–17; Robertson, *Harlem in Disorder,* Communist in Harlem.

10. Clipping "Tuesday on the Radio," *New York Times,* August 25, 1932, 17; AGHP, Box 2, folder 11; "Plans to Prosecute Police in Reds' Riot," *New York Times,* March 15, 1930, 3; "Hays Says Police Only Aid Red Cause," *New York Times,* March 25, 1930, 23; Johnson, *Street Justice,* 120, 125; Samantha Barbas, *The Rise and Fall of Morris Ernst, Free Speech Renegade* (Chicago: University of Chicago Press, 2021), 128; clipping, "Secrecy Fought at Riot Inquiry," *New York Times,* March 21, 1934, AGHP, Box 37, folder 5; clipping, *New York World Telegram,* November 28, 1934, AGHP, Box 37, folder 5; "Citizenship Committee of New York County Lawyers' Association to Mulrooney," [1930], AGHP, Box 2, folder 6; Hays to Forrest Bailey [at ACLU], January 23, 1931, AGHP Box 2, folder 9; Bailey to Hays, January 24,

1931, AGHP Box 2, folder 9; Chandler Bennitt to Hays, January 16, 1931, AGHP, Box 2, folder 9; Emilie Bullowa to Hays, June 26, 1931, AGHP, Box 2, folder 9.

11. *Complete Report*, 7–12; Robertson, *Harlem in Disorder*, On the Streets, 2:00 PM to 2:30 PM, 2:30 PM to 3:00 PM, 3:00 PM to 3:30 PM, 4:00 PM to 4:30 PM, 4:30 PM to 5:00 PM, 5:00 PM to 5:30 PM; store workers and police knew such incidents could escalate; see Robertson, *Harlem in Disorder*, Crowds in Harlem.

12. *Complete Report*, 7–12; Kessner, *Fiorello La Guardia*, 370; Greenberg, *Or Does it Explode*, 3–4; Robertson, *Harlem in Disorder*, On the Streets, 5:30 to 6:00 PM, 6:00 PM to 6:30 PM, Inciting Crowds, 6:30 PM to 7:00 PM, 7:00 PM to 7:30 PM, Windows Broken, Deaths.

13. Carter, *Invisible*, 92, 94; Kessner, *Fiorello La Guardia*, 370; telegram, Needle and Thread Workers to La Guardia, March 20, 1935; Walter White to La Guardia, March 20, 1935, in https://www.archives.nyc/blog/2019/3/1/the-Mayors-commission-on-conditions-in-harlem-1935. Hays claimed he replied to the mayor's charge of communist instigation, "you were wise to put liberals on your committee. We'll come back with the truth." Hays, *City Lawyer*, 281; Robertson, *Harlem in Disorder*, In the Courts, Dodge's Grand Jury Investigation, Dodge Announced Grand Jury Hearings.

14. Mayor to People of New York City, March 20, 1935, https://www.archives.nyc/blog/2019/3/1/the-Mayors-commission-on-conditions-in-harlem-1935; Robertson, *Harlem in Disorder*, Mayor La Guardia establishes an investigation.

15. https://www.archives.nyc/blog/2019/3/1/the-Mayors-commission-on-conditions-in-harlem-1935 https://socialwelfare.library.vcu.edu/eras/villard/; other African American appointees were Countee Cullen, Hubert T. Delaney, and Charles E. Toney. John C. Grimley rounded out the white appointees. Villard had long been a supporter; Megan Ming Francis, *Civil Rights and the Making of the Modern American State* (New York: Cambridge University Press, 2014), 65–66; Barbas, *The Rise and Fall of Morris Ernst*, 182–83; NAACP to La Guardia, March 26, 1935, AGHP, Box 26, folder 1; see unknown paper clipping, March 27, AGHP, Box 37, folder 6; Carter, *Invisible* 93; Robertson, *Harlem in Disorder*, "La Guardia's "Representative Citizens," Members of the MCCH (13) Reactions to La Guardia's appointments, Investigations, March 22–March 29.

16. Lindsey Lupo, *Flak-Catchers: One Hundred Years of Riot Commission Politics in America* (Lanham, MD: Lexington Books, 2011), 69, 71, 74–75; Carter, *Invisible*, 93, 94; Greenwald and Li, *Carter*, 72–74; on organization, see Memo on Program, [ND], AGHP, Box 25, folder 19; Frazier, "Statement of the Problem" and "Mr. Frazier's Plan of Study" [Carter handwritten note], AGHP, Box 25, folder 19; Hays's support of the liberal sweeping assessment was expressed in Hays to Arthur L. Swift, May 13, 1935, AGHP, Box 26, folder 1; Robertson, *Harlem in Disorder*, Investigations, March 22–March 29.

17. William Trunbull to Hays, March 21, 1935, AGHP, Box 26, folder 1; Lillye M. Coleman to Hays, March 23, 1935, AGHP, Box 26, folder 1; A. Clayton

Powell Sr. to Hays, March 21, 1935, AGHP, Box 26, folder 1; "Mr. Hays, Rev. Powell Called to Know When You Want Mr. Aiken in Reference to the Tommy Aiken Case Today?," Loose notes [April 21, 1935], AGHP, Box 25, folder 19; Robertson, *Harlem in Disorder*, Investigations, March 22 to March 29.

18. L. F. Coles to Hays, March 23, 1935, AGHP, Box 26, folder 1; Coles to Oswald G. Villard, March 23, 1935; AGHP, Box 26, folder 1; Hays to L. F. Coles, March 27, 1935, AGHP, Box 26, folder 1; James H. Tarter Jr. to Hays, June 10, 1936, AGHP, Box 26, folder 2; Hays to Tarter, June 11, 1936, AGHP, Box 26, folder 2; see Coles's reporting for the *Baltimore Afro-American*, mostly on race issues connected with the military, January 25, 1930, 6; February 8, 1930, 5; August 23, 1930, 6.

19. Kessner, *Fiorello La Guardia*, 373; "Cases of Police Brutality, Discrimination and Mistreatment of Negroes in Harlem," AGHP, Box 25, folder 19; Charles Abrams to Hays, April 1, 1935, AGHP, Box 26, folder 1; Leslie Bain to Hays, March 25, 1935, AGHP, Box 26, folder 1; "Show Movies of Riots in New York to Prove Who Was at Fault," *Chicago Defender*, April 20, 1935, 1, quoted in Ellen Christine Scott, "Race and the Struggle for Cinematic Meaning: Film Production, Censorship, and African American Reception, 1940–1960" (PhD diss., University of Michigan, 2007), 259–60.

20. HNG [Glickstein] to Robert Minor, April 1, 1935, AGHP, Box 26, folder 1; Wolfgang Saxon, "Hyman Glickstein, 91, Dies; Lawyer and Political Leader," *New York Times*, February 17, 1998, section B, 11; Carter to Hays, December 23, 1935, AGHP, Box 26, folder 1; Glickstein to Hays, [ND], AGHP, Box 26, folder 1; Robertson, *Harlem in Disorder*, Investigations, March 22–29; James Tarter's investigation of the killing of Lloyd Hobbs.

21. Robertson, *Harlem in Disorder*, the MCCH investigates.

22. Villard to Rev. Gerald Hamilton, April 17, 1935, AGHP, Box 26, folder 1; Gerald Hamilton to Villard, April 15, 1935, AGHP, Box 26, folder 1; Hays to Hamilton, April 18, 1935, AGHP, Box 26, folder 1. See also William J. Burroughs to Hays, May 1, 1935, AGHP, Box 26, folder 1; Burroughs to Hays, May 13, 1935, AGHP, Box 26, folder 1; Hays to Burroughs, May 13, 1935, AGHP, Box 26, folder 1; on sketching out incidents of police brutality and framing women for prostitution as part of an extortion ring, see also unknown paper clipping, [NPD] March 27, [1935], AGHP, Box 37, folder 6; Robertson, *Harlem in Disorder*, Investigations, March 30–April 5.

23. Robertson, *Harlem in Disorder*, the MCCH investigates, Philipp to La Guardia, August 14, 1935, AGHP, Box 26, folder 1; Robertson, *Harlem in Disorder*, Reactions to the subcommittee report; Villard, "Slumbering Fires in Harlem," 7; Hays, *City Lawyer*, 282.

24. Subcommittee on Crime and Police Hearing Transcript, March 30, 1935, 1–7, 19–21, 21–28, AGHP, Box 26, folder 6 (hereafter Hearing, March 30); Naison,

Communists in Harlem, 42–43; "Loose Notes," AGHP, Box 25, folder 19; Hearing, March 30, 22, 25–26 27; "Report of the Subcommittee Which Investigated the Disturbance of March 19th," AGHP, Box 26, folder 4, 4 (hereafter subcommittee report); *Complete Report*, 8–9; Levering, *When Harlem*, 288–90.

25. Hearing, March 30, 14–19, 28–38, 50–51; Subcommittee on Crime and Police Hearing Transcript, April 6, 1935, AGHP, Box 26, folder 6 (hereafter Hearing April 6). This transcript presents problems of citation; as there are no page numbers, I reference this transcript by speaker (e.g., Coles) or by the subject (e.g., Hobbs case) as best would facilitate the location of the material, Aikins, Hobbs, Lyons, Thompson, and Laurie; "'Inside' Story of Riot is told by Harlem Cops," *New York World Telegram*, March 28, 1935, clipping in AGHP, Box 37, folder 6.

26. Hearing, March 30, 28–38, 50–51.

27. "Hays Scores Harlem Cops," *Amsterdam News*, May 26, 1935, clipping in AGHP, Box 37, folder 13; Hearing, March 30, 11–14; Robertson, *Harlem in Disorder*, Public hearing of the MCCH Subcommittee on crime (March 30).

28. Hearing March 30, 11–14; AGHP, Box 26, folder 6; "Jury Riot Quiz Interrupted," *New York American*, March 27, 1935, clipping in AGHP, Box 36, folder 6; "Harlem Riot Guilty to Be Sifted today," *New York Times*, March 25, 1935, clipping in AGHP, Box 36, folder 6, "Harlem Riot Prober Snubs, ILD Lawyer," *Post*, March 27, 1935, clipping in AGHP, Box 36, folder 6; Robertson, *Harlem in Disorder*, Public hearing of the MCCH Subcommittee on Crime (March 30); in court March 25, confirms that the Communists' office was raided for materials.

29. Dodge to Valentine, Hearing of April 6, 1935, quoted in Hearing, April 6; Samuel Marcus to Hays, April 7, 1935, AGHP, Box 26, folder 1; Hays to Marcus, April 8, 1935, AGHP, Box 26, folder 1; "Order Police to Keep Silent," *New York Sun*, April 6, 1935, clipping in AGHP, Box 37, folder 6.

30. Hearing, March 30, 1–7, 19–21, 21–28.

31. Coles to Hays, April 2, 1935, AGHP, Box 26, folder 1; Coles to Hays, April 9, 1935, AGHP, Box 26, folder 1; Hays to Coles, April 10, 1935, AGHP, Box 26, folder 1.

32. Robertson, *Harlem in Disorder*, On the Streets, 2:00 AM to 2:30 AM, Police find Lino Rivera.

33. Hearing, March 30, 14–19; "'Inside' Story of Riot Is Told by Harlem Cops," *New York World Telegram*, March 28, 1935, clipping in AGHP, Box 37, folder 6; Hearing, March 30, 41–47; Naison, *Communists in Harlem*, 146; Hearing, March 30, 44–45, 46–50; Aikin Case, Battle, Hearing of April 6.

34. Hearing, March 30, 14–19; "'Inside' Story of Riot Is Told by Harlem Cops," *New York World Telegram*, March 28, 1935, clipping in AGHP, Box 37, folder 6. Hearing, March 30, 38–41; Robertson, *Harlem in Disorder*, Public hearing of the MCCH's Subcommittee on Crime (March 30).

35. Hearing, March 30, 41–47; Naison, *Communists in Harlem*, 146; Robertson, *Harlem in Disorder*, The MCCH investigates.

36. Hearing, March 30, 47–50.

37. Ray Dodd, Alfred W. Eldridge, Hearing, April 6; Tauber, Nady McCallen (Kress worker), Aikin Case, Battle, Hearing of April 6; Robertson, *Harlem in Disorder*, The public hearings of the MCCH's Subcommittee on Crime (April 6).

38. Eldridge, Rivera, Battle, Minor, Hearing, April 6; Coles to Hays, April 2, 1935, AGHP, Box 26, folder 1; Coles to Hays, April 9, 1935, AGHP, Box 26, folder 1; Hays to Coles, April 10, 1935, AGHP, Box 26, folder 1.

39. [Moran?] Coles, Hurley, Hearing, April 6.

40. Aikin, Hobbs, Lyons, Thompson, and Laurie, Hearing, April 6.

41. Hearing, April 6; Tarter, Hobbs Documents, AGHP, Box 25, folder 19; "Negroes Accuse Police at Hearing," *New York Times*, April 21, 1935, clipping in AGHP, Box 37, folder 6; Romney, Subcommittee on Crime and Police Hearing Transcript, April 20, 1935, AGHP Box 26, folder 6 (hereafter Hearing, April 20); this transcript, like that of April 6, presents problems of citation, as there are no page numbers. I have referenced this transcript by speaker or by the subject (e.g., Hobbs case) as best would facilitate the location of the material. Also, the final third of the document is a transcript of a hearing on the subject of Relief. Transcript of Arrest Record, March 13, 1935, AGHP, Box 25, folder 19; Loose notes, AGHP, Box 25, folder 19; Sketch, 7th Avenue, Survey made of neighboring storekeepers, AGHP, Box 25, folder 19; Robertson, *Harlem in Disorder*, James Tarter's investigation of the killing of Lloyd Hobbs.

42. Hearing, March 30, 44–45, 46–47; Autopsy report case, 1849, Lloyd Hobbs, AGHP, Box 25, folder 19.

43. Lawyer Hobbs, Hearing, April 6; Robertson, *Harlem in Disorder*, The public hearings of the MCCH's subcommittee on crime (April 6).

44. Mary Hobbs, Hearing, April 6; Robertson, *Harlem in Disorder*, The public hearings of the MCCH's subcommittee on crime (April 6).

45. Tarter, Hearing, April 6; Robertson, *Harlem in Disorder*, The public hearings of the MCCH's subcommittee on crime (April 6).

46. Hearing, April 6; Tarter, Hobbs Documents, AGHP, Box 26, folder 19; Robertson, *Harlem in Disorder*, The public hearings of the MCCH's subcommittee on crime (April 6).

47. Russell Hobbs, McCormic, Hearing, April 6; Robertson, *Harlem in Disorder*, The public hearings of the MCCH's subcommittee on crime (April 6).

48. Hays to Dodge, April 11, 1935, AGHP, Box 26, folder 1; Dodge to Hays, April 12, 1935, AGHP, Box 26, folder 1; Robertson, *Harlem in Disorder*, Investigations (April 6–19).

49. Watterman, Hearing April 20; Sketch, 7th Avenue, Survey made of neighboring storekeepers, AGHP, Box 25, folder 19; Robertson, *Harlem in Disorder*, Public hearing of the MCCH's subcommittee on crime (April 20).

50. O'Brien, Hearing, April 20; in his initial report of March 20, 1935, O'Brien said "a quantity of automobile accessories." Tarter, Hobbs; the Report of March 28; Testimony, and also complaint report, March 20, 1935, and complaint report March 28, 1935, AGHP Box 25, folder 19; Robertson, *Harlem in Disorder*, Public hearing of the MCCH's subcommittee on crime (April 20).

51. Malloy, Hearing, April 20; "Hays Scores Harlem Cops," *Amsterdam News*, May 26, 1935, clipping in AGHP, Box 37, folder 13; Robertson, *Harlem in Disorder*, Public hearing of the MCCH's subcommittee on crime (April 20).

52. "Negroes Accuse Police at Hearing," *New York Times*, April 21, 1935, clipping in AGHP, Box 37, folder 6; Romney, Hearing, April 20; Transcript of Arrest Record, March 13, 1935, AGHP, Box 25, folder 19; Loose notes, AGHP, Box 25, folder 19; Sketch, 7th Avenue, Survey made of neighboring storekeepers, AGHP, Box 25, folder 19; Investigators interview with Mr. Thomas Aikins, at top of page, Transcript of Magistrates Court Record, AGHP, Box 25, folder 19; Hays had this copy before him at the hearing as he has marked Brown's name with a "*" and corrected Harlow's name. He has also written Egan and Cahill and made an equivocal mark by Cahill's; Aikins Hospital record, AGHP Box 25, folder 19.

53. Aikins, Transcript, April 20; Robertson, *Harlem in Disorder*, Public hearing of the MCCH's subcommittee on crime (April 20).

54. Brown, Eaghan, Cahill, Transcript, April 20; Robertson, *Harlem in Disorder*, Public hearing of the MCCH's subcommittee on crime (April 20). The case was robbed of its impact by cross-purposes. Commissioner Robinson interjected that he thought that Aikins had a defense against the officers, which prompted his lawyer to try and limit testimony to showing that Aikins lost an eye as a result of the beating. The Communists, to the contrary, asserted that "the best place to try this case is before the public." Aikins, Robinson, Densch, Minor, Transcript, April 20; the Complete Report gave more detail, some of it slanted, about the Aikins case; it seems to be paraphrasing from a document from the time of the incident, perhaps a report in a newspaper. Complete Report, 116–19.

55. Watterson, Hearing, April 20; Robertson, *Harlem in Disorder*, Public hearing of the MCCH's subcommittee on crime (April 20); "Negroes Accuse Police at Hearing," *New York Times,* April 21, 1935, N4. Representative of much of the mainstream press, the *Times* coverage says that Communists were the leaders of the catcalls and jeering; it also says that Hobbs was "a man."

56. "Harlem Riot Quiz Nearly Broken Up by Angry Charges," *New York Post*, May 4, 1935, clipping in AGHP, Box 37, folder 6. Johnson, *Street Justice*, 188; Robertson, *Harlem in Disorder*, Public hearing of the MCCH's subcommittee on crime (May 4).

57. "Harlem Riot Quiz Nearly Broken Up by Angry Charges, *New York Post*, May 4, 1935, clipping in AGHP, Box 37, folder 6; "Police Are Hissed at Harlem Hearing," *New York Times*, May 5, 1935, 35; [ILD] "Cases of Police Brutality, Discrimination and Mistreatment of Negroes in Harlem," AGHP, Box 25, folder 19;

Delinquency Record of Patrolman Abraham Zakutinksy, AGHP, Box 26, folder 7; the Complete Report renders the officer's name as Labutinaki, Complete Report, 119; Robertson, *Harlem in Disorder*, Public hearing of the MCCH's subcommittee on crime (May 4); Coles to Hays, May 15, 1935, AGHP, Box 26, folder 1.

58. [Tarter], Office Investigation of Mr. Robert Patterson, AGHP, Box 26, folder 7; "Hays Scores Harlem Cops," *Amsterdam News*, May 26, 1935, clipping in AGHP, Box 37, folder 13; "Harlem Riot Quiz Nearly Broken Up by Angry Charges, *New York Post*, May 4, 1935, clipping in AGHP, Box 37, folder 6; "Police Are Hissed at Harlem Hearing," *New York Times*, May 5, 1935, 35; [ILD] "Cases of Police Brutality, Discrimination and Mistreatment of Negroes in Harlem," AGHP, Box 25, folder 19; Delinquency Record of Patrolman Abraham Zakutinksy, AGHP, Box 26, folder 7; Robertson, *Harlem in Disorder*, Public hearing of the MCCH's subcommittee on crime (May 18). See also Johnson, *Street Justice*, 185.

59. Yellow slip, City of New York, Office of the Mayor, Official Communication, April 4, 1935, No. EC-61 and attached circular "Who Fights for the Negro People?," AGHP, Box 26, folder 1.

60. See investigation of the brawl spawned by Communist picketing: Carter to Members, April 3, 1935, AGHP, Box 6, folder 1; loose notes, AGHP, Box 25, folder 19; Hearing, March 31, 1935, 22, 25–26, 27; subcommittee report, 4, AGHP, Box 26, folder, 4. Complete Report, 8–9.

61. Romney to Hays, May 2, 1935, AGHP, Box 26, folder 1; "Hays Scores Harlem Cops," *Amsterdam News*, May 26, 1935, clipping in AGHP, Box 37, folder 13; Johnson, *Street Justice*, 188; Statement, People v. Romney, City Magistrates Court, copy in AGHP, Box 25, folder 19; Naison, *Communist in Harlem*, 146.

62. Hays to Powell, April 29, 1935; Hays to Eustace V. Dench, May 7, 1935, Box 26, Folder; Horace I. Gordon to Hays, May 13, 1935; Hays to Carter, May 14, 1935[?], AGHP, Box 26, folder 1; "Victor Suarez Administration," misfiled as part of Transcript, April 20; Petition to Mayor, April 26, 1935, AGHP, Box 26, folder 19, 2.

63. Notes—Mayor's Committee Harlem Investigation, AGHP, Box 26, folder 3; "Hays Scores Harlem Cops," *Amsterdam News*, May 26, 1935 clipping in AGHP, Box 37, folder 13; Hays to Villard, May 23, 1935, AGHP, Box 26, folder 1; Villard to Hays, May 27, 1935, AGHP, Box 26, folder 1 Robertson, *Harlem in Disorder*, The subcommittee on crime's report, Preparing the subcommittee report.

64. Villard to Hays, May 27, 1935, AGHP, Box 26, folder 1; Hays to Villard, May 29, 1935, AGHP, Box 26, folder 1; Villard to Hays, June 1, 1935, AGHP, Box 26, folder 1; From Rockledge Farm, Thomaston, CT; Hays to Villard, June 3, 1935, Box 26, Folder 1, AGHP, Box 26, folder 1; Robertson, *Harlem in Disorder*, Villard's draft of the subcommittee report, The MCCH and the subcommittee report.

65. Report of the Subcommittee, 1.

66. Report of the Subcommittee, 3, 9.

67. Report of the Subcommittee, 2, 3, 4, 5, 9.

68. Report of the Subcommittee, 6, 7.

69. Report of the Subcommittee, 8, 9. The friendly attitude recalled the famous reformer Police Commissioner Arthur Wood's policies.

70. Report of the Subcommittee, 8.

71. Report of the Subcommittee, 9; Hays was thinking of Darrow's service starting the previous year on the Review Board of the National Recovery Administration, see Kevin Tierney, *Darrow: A Biography* (New York: Thomas Crowell, 1979), 427–34; Andrew E. Keresten, *Clarence Darrow: American Iconoclast* (New York: Hill and Wang, 2010), 238–39.

72. Report of the Subcommittee, 9.

73. Report of the Subcommittee, 5, 6; Transcript, March 31, 1935, 44.

74. Only Father McCann refused to sign it, and two others (who were away) did not sign, Randolph and Schieffelin; the report was supposed to be the subject of a meeting between members of the commission and the mayor. Unfortunately, Hays, the author of the document and the person who had presided over all the crime and police hearings, was traveling, and apparently the meeting was canceled. Lipsky and Olson, *Commission Politics,* 51; Lupo, *Flak-Catchers,* 75; Hays to Mayor La Guardia, June 11, 1935, AGHP, Box 26, folder 1; Carter to Hays, July 11, 1935, AGHP, Box 26, folder 1; Secretary to William Jay Schieffelin, July 15, 1935, AGHP, Box 26, folder 1; Hays to Villard, July 16, 1935, AGHP, Box 26, folder 1; Coles to Hays, July 17, 1935, AGHP, Box 26, folder 1; Hays to Coles, July 18, 1935; Hays to La Guardia, July 18, 1935; Robertson, *Harlem in Disorder,* Reactions to the subcommittee report.

75. Baldwin to Hays, August 8, 1935, AGHP, Box 26, folder 1; Hays to Honorable Anna M. Kross, August 12, 1935; Hays to Kross, August 20, 1935; William J. Robinson to Hays, August 22, 1935; see also Samuel Marcus to Hays, August 27, 1935; Benjamin E. Greenspan to Hays, [ND], AGHP, Box 26, folder 1; *Amsterdam News,* August 10, 1935, Clipping in AGHP, Box 37, folder 13; Robertson, *Harlem in Disorder,* Reactions to the subcommittee report.

76. Coles to Hays, August 15, 1935, AGHP, Box 26, folder 1; written on the letter, not in Hays's hand, "Send report."

77. Philipp to La Guardia, August 14, 1935, AGHP, Box 26, folder 1; Robertson, *Harlem in Disorder,* Reactions to the subcommittee report.

78. La Guardia to Philipp, August 19, 1935, AGHP, Box 26, folder 1; Robertson, *Harlem in Disorder,* Reactions to the subcommittee report.

79. Hays to Valentine, September 25, 1935, AGHP, Box 26, folder 1; Robertson, *Harlem in Disorder,* Reactions to the subcommittee report.

80. Valentine to Hays, September 28, 1935, AGHP, Box 26, folder 1; Robertson, *Harlem in Disorder,* Reactions to the subcommittee report.

81. Villard to Carter, January 6, 1936, AGHP, Box 26, folder 2; Villard to Hays, January [?], 1936, AGHP, Box 26, folder 2; Carter to Hays, AGHP, January

27, 1936; Roberts to Hays, February 7, 1936, AGHP, Box 26, folder 2; Carter to Hays, March 2, 1936, AGHP, Box 26, folder 2; Hays to Villard, March 3, 1936; Carter to Hays, March 7, 1936, AGHP, Box 26, folder 2; Hays to Carter, March 9, 1936, AGHP, Box 26, folder 2; Carter to Hays, March 23, 1936; Ernst to Frazier, February 17, 1936 AGHP, Box 26, folder 2; Ernst twice sent Frazier extensive changes to the report, though none of his suggestions touched upon the issues of policing. Ernst to Carter, March 25, 1936, Box 26, folder 2; Lupo, *Flak-Catchers*, 74–75; Hays to McCook, June 28, 1938, Box 26, folder 2; Robertson, *Disorder in Harlem*, The MCCH final report, Writing the final report, Frazier's report, The MCCH and Frazier's report. In 1938 Hays learned that Frazier had not made the changes he sought. Judge Phillip McCook had obtained a copy of the version of the report where Hays had recorded what he wanted cut and compared it to the *Amsterdam News* version. The passages were still in the report. Typical of their tone was "The outbreak of March 19th, though spontaneous and without leadership, is strengthening the belief that the solution of their problems lies in mass action." Hays confessed to McCook, "I cannot believe that I was stupid enough to have ever signed anything without having made sure that these eliminations were made." Realizing the import, Hays wrote McCook that he wrote the mayor about what had been discovered. But of course it was too late to make a difference. McCook to Hays, June 26, 1938, AGHP, Box 26, folder 2; McCook to Hays, June 30, 1938, AGHP, Box 26, folder 2; McCook to Hays, July 21 1938, AGHP, Box 26, folder 2; Hays to McCook, June 22, 1938, AGHP, Box 26, folder 2; Hays to McCook, September 15, 1938, AGHP, Box 26, folder 2.

82. *Complete Report*, 133–35, The Negro in Harlem, A Report of Social and Economic Conditions Responsible for the Outbreak of March 19, 1935, typescript, Mayors Commission on Conditions in Harlem, 1935, AGHP Box 26, folder 4, 118 (hereafter The Negro in Harlem).

83. Lupo, *Flak-Catchers*: 84–85; Hays to Villard, March 3, 1936, AGHP, Box 26, folder 2; Hays to Schieffelin, January 24, 1936, AGHP, Box 26, folder 2; Arthur F. Irvin to Hays, March 11, 1936, AGHP, Box 26, folder 2.

84. The three non-signers were Ernst, McCann, and Grimley; Carter to Hays, March 23, 1936, Ernst to Frazier, February 17, 1936, AGHP, Box 26, folder 2; Ernst to Carter, March 25, 1936, Box 26, folder 2; Lupo, *Flak-Catchers*, 74–75; Hays to McCook, June 28, 1938, Box 26, folder 2; *Complete Report*, 133–35, The Negro in Harlem, AGHP, Box 26, folder 4, 118; Capeci, *The Harlem Riot of 1943*, 5–7, 9; Kessner, *Fiorello La Guardia*, 375–76.

85. Coles to Hays, July 2, 1936, AGHP, Box 26, folder 2; Hays to Coles, July 6, 1936, AGHP, Box 26, folder 2.

86. The fullest account of La Guradia's actions is found in Robertson, *Harlem in Disorder*, The mayor and the MCCH report; see also Lupo, *Flak-Catchers*, 84–85; Lasker to Hays, April 26, 1936, AGHP, Box 26, folder 2; Hays to Lasker, May 1, 1936, Box 26, folder 2; La Guardia to Hays, May 5, 1936, AGHP, Box 26,

folder 2; "Harlem Riot Probers Meet Mayor Today," *Amsterdam News*, June 10, 1936, clipping in AGHP, Box 37, folder 6; Lupo, *Flak-Catchers*, 82, 84, 90; "Harlem Report Assailed," *New York Times*, August 19, 1936, 4. *Complete Report*, 1.

87. The confusing "release" of the report is covered in Robertson, *Disorder in Harlem*, Releasing the MCCH report; Hays to Roberts, September 4, 1936; Telegram, La Guardia to Villard, September 29, 1936, AGHP, Box 26, folder 2; Villard to Hays, September 30, 1936, AGHP, Box 26, folder 2.

88. Capeci, *The Harlem Riot of 1943*, 5–7, 9; Kessner, *Fiorello H. La Guardia*, 376, 526–36.

89. Hays to Judge Frederic J. Kernochan, November 15, 1935, AGHP, Box 26, folder 2; William A. Walling to Hays, November 15, 1935, AGHP, Box 26, folder 2. In reply, he received a letter that held little hope for mercy.

90. Hays, *City Lawyer*, 281–82.

91. In 1948, NAACP created its own review board in New York City to provide legal counsel for victims. An investigating commission on the problems of policing in the city in 1949 under Mayor William O'Dwyer recommended creation of a monitoring agency for the police department. O'Dwyer ignored the suggestion. See Greenberg, *Or Does It Explode*, 194; Taylor, *Fight the Power*, 10, 11, 88, 89. For the continuing history of police and community violence in New York City, see Schneider, *Police Power and Race Riots*, 44–87, 135–79.

92. Kessner, *Fiorello H. La Guardia*, 532; Golway, *I Never Did Like Politics*, 217–18; Hays to *New York Times*, August 4, 1943, AGHP, Box 12, folder 9, and Box 26, folder 2; "May 29th 1935 Report of Subcommittee, 8–9; Capeci, *The Harlem Riot of 1943*, 176.

93. Mary M. Stolberg, *Fighting Organized Crime: Politics, Justice and the Legacy of Thomas E. Dewey* (Boston: Northeastern University Press, 1995); Villard, "Slumbering Fires in Harlem," typescript, AGHP, Box 26, folder 5.

Chapter 3

1. Michael J. Klarman, *From Jim Crow to Civil Rights: The Supreme Court and the Struggle for Racial Equality* (New York: Oxford University Press, 2004), 79–83; Jeffrey Gonda, *Unjust Deeds: The Restrictive Covenant Cases and the Making of the Civil Rights Movement* (Chapel Hill: University of North Carolina Press, 2015); Richard Rothstein, *The Color of Law: A Forgotten History of How Our Government Segregated America* (New York: Liveright Public Corp., 2017), 44–54; Richard R. W. Brooks and Carol M. Rose, *Saving the Neighborhood: Racially Restrictive Covenants, Law and Social Norms* (Cambridge: Harvard University Press, 2013), 17–41; Elizabeth A. Herbin-Triant, *Threatening Property: Race, Class, and Campaigns to Legislate Jim Crow Neighborhoods* (New York: Columbia University Press, 2019), 112–28, 142–92.

2. Clement E. Vose, *Caucasians Only, the Supreme Court, the NAACP, and the Restrictive Covenant Cases* (1959; repr., Berkeley: University of California Press, 1973); 3, Brooks and Rose, *Saving the Neighborhood*, 41–43.

3. Brooks and Rose, *Saving the Neighborhood*, 41–43, 45; Rothstein, *The Color of Law*, 46–47, 49; Klarman, *From Jim Crow to Civil Rights*, 142–43; Herbin-Triant, *Threatening Property*, 223–39; the arc of actions that led to the rise of restrictive racial covenants is covered in Jeannine Bell, *Hate Thy Neighbor: Move-in Violence and Persistent of Racial Segregation in American Housing* (New York: New York University Press, 2013), 13–23.

4. Brooks and Rose, *Saving the Neighborhood*, 56–62; Gonda, *Unjust Deeds*, 45; Michael Jones Currea, "The Origins and Diffusion of Racial Restrictive Covenants," *Political Science Quarterly* 115 (1973): 261–82.

5. Vose, *Caucasians Only*, vii, 1–8; Brooks and Rose, *Saving the Neighborhood*, 56–73; Antero Pietila, *Not in My Neighborhood: How Bigotry Shaped a Great American City* (Chicago: Ivan R. Dee, 2010), 48.

6. Vose, *Caucasians Only*, 3–4; Brooks and Rose, *Saving the Neighborhood*, 56–73, 81.

7. Vose, *Caucasians Only*, 7, 8, 9, 10, 12–13; Brooks and Rose, *Saving the Neighborhood*, 83; Klarman, *From Jim Crow to Civil Rights*, 145.

8. Vose, *Caucasians Only*, 5, 17–19, 50–55; Kevin Boyle, *Arc of Justice: A Sage of Race, Civil Rights, and Murder in the Jazz Age* (New York: Henry Holt, 2004), 203–14, 229; Brooks and Rose, *Saving the Neighborhood*, 51–55.

9. Vose, *Caucasians Only*, 54–55; Brooks and Rose, *Saving the Neighborhood*, 116–29; 131–32; Klarman, *From Jim Crow to Civil Rights*, 144.

10. Paige Glotzer, "Exclusion in Arcadia: How Suburban Developers Circulated Ideas about Discrimination, 1890–1950," *Journal of Urban History* 41 (2015): 479–94; see also Patricia Burgess Stach, "Deed Restrictions and Subdivision Development in Columbus, Ohio, 1900–1970," *Journal of Urban History* 15 (1998): 42–68; Rothstein, *The Color of Law*, 51, 52. 84. The experience of Baltimore exposes the connection between anti-Semitic and white supremist thought and action that animated residential segregation through covenants. See Pietila, *Not in My Neighborhood*, x–xi, xiii, 33–42, 54, 56; Brooks and Rose, *Saving the Neighborhood*, 81.

11. Boyle, *Arc of Justice*, 144–46; Rothstein, *The Color of Law*, 79–80.

12. As these notes make clear, I am in debt to Thomas Quirk and Nicholas Soares, who have delved deeply into the stories of Pauline and Joshua Cockburn. Thomas Quirk, "The Cockburn Legacy and Northern Jim Crow," Secret History of Scarsdale, March 2, 2013, https://thomas-quirk.com/2013/03/02/the-cockburn-legacy/ (hereafter Quirk, Cockburn Legacy); Tom Quirk, "Of Realtors and Racism," blog post, October 24, 2016, https://medium.com/@tomquirk_64141/of-realtors-and-racism-7da773af2d9d (hereafter Quirk, Of Realtors and Racism); Nicholas A. Soares, "Seeing Color in Black and White: New York Defines its Color

Line in *Ridgway v. Cockburn* in 1937" (MA thesis, University at Albany, State University of New York, 2016), 10–12,13–14 (hereafter Soares, "Seeing Color"); for a summary of the story, see Cindy Korek, "Deed Covenants in a Criminal Rights Story: The Edgemont, New York Incident of 1937" (2013) in The Rhetoric of the Civil Rights Movement https://sites.psu.edu/civilrightsrhetoric/deed-covenants-in-a-criminal-rights-story-the-edgemont-new-york-incident-of-1937/.

13. Quirk, of Realtors and Racism; https://shiphistory.org/2020/01/20/the-black-star-line/; Brittany Hancock, "Marcus Garvey's The Black Star Line: Hopes, Dreams, and The *S.S. Yarmouth*," *Journal of Caribbean History* 52 (2008): 68–104, 75, 76, 81, 86, 52; Soares, "Seeing Color in Black and White," 16–20.

14. Quirk, "Of Realtors and Racism"; Quirk, "Cockburn Legacy"; Soares, "Seeing Color," 20–21.

15. Quirk, "Cockburn Legacy"; Quirk, "Of Realtors and Racism"; "Capt. Cockburn Must Move from $20,000 Home," *Pittsburgh Courier*, June 12, 1937, 1; "Cockburn Net Tourney at Lincoln This Week," *Pittsburgh Courier*, June 19, 1937, 17.

16. Quirk, "Cockburn Legacy"; Quirk, "Of Realtors and Racism"; Soares, "Seeing Color in Black and White," 23.

17. Soares, "Seeing Color," 10, citing US Department of Labor and US Bureau of Labor Statistics; *100 Years of U.S. Consumer Spending Data for the Nation, New York City, and Boston*, 20, http://www.bls.gov/opub/uscs/report991.pdf; Quirk, Cockburn Legacy; "Judge Denies Housing Ban," *Amsterdam News*, February 13, 1937, 1.

18. Covenant quoted in "Brief of Pauline Teresa Cockburn in Opposition to Motion for Temporary Injunction, *Ridgway v. Cockburn*," Supreme Court of the State of New York, Westchester, cover, 2–3; copy in Arthur Garfield Hays Papers (hereafter, AGHP), Box 28, folder 5 (hereafter, Brief in Opposition), 1–2; Quirk, "Cockburn Legacy"; *Ridgway v. Cockburn*, 163 Misc. 511 (N.Y. Sup. Ct 1937), 511–12.

19. Quirk, "Cockburn Legacy"; Quirk, "Of Realtors and Racism"; Soares, "Seeing Color," 26; on the relator firm, "James M. Bridges 240 South Tenth avenue, Mount Vernon was one of the brokers in the purchase of the Cockburn's lot and house." The firm is still in business and proclaims itself one of the oldest African American owned real estate firms in the state. https://www.facebook.com/lw.bridges.re.co9/.

20. Soares, "Seeing Color," 27–29.

21. Clipping in AGHP, Box 37, folder 13.

22. NAACP Report of the Secretary [Walter White] (For the February Meeting of the Board), 7; Folder: 001412-006-0126; Date: January 4, 1937–December 31, 1937; Papers of the NAACP, Part 01: Meetings of the Board of Directors, Records of Annual Conferences, Major Speeches, and Special Reports (hereafter NAACP Board Papers); Marshall's role was minimal in this case. He had just moved to

New York to take up these duties; not only was he quite busy, but he did not yet have the autonomy that later emerged after the development of the Education and Legal Defense Fund. He was present at the hearing, but Hays argued the case. Jack Greenberg, *Crusaders in the Courts* (New York: Basic Books, 1994), 30.

23. Soares, "Seeing Color," 14–15, 17–19.

24. Soares, "Seeing Color," 24–26, 28–29; "Brief in Opposition," 4; it is likely that Joshua Cockburn was saying that Zaubler delivered a summons after another failed negotiation, which was the amended summons for a temporary injunction.

25. Soares, "Seeing Color," 10–12, citing Pauline Teresa Cockburn, Affidavit in Opposition to Motion (Supreme Court: Westchester County. Marion A. Ridgway, Plaintiff against Pauline Teresa Cockburn, Defendant), January 25, 1937, 2–3; Joshua Cockburn, Affidavit in Opposition to Motion (Supreme Court: Westchester County. Marion A. Ridgway, Plaintiff against Pauline Teresa Cockburn, Defendant), January 25, 1937, 2.

26. Franz Boas, Affidavit quoted in Brief in Opposition, 20–21; Charles King, *Gods of the Upper Air: How a Circle of Renegade Anthropologists Reinvented Race, Sex, and Gender in the Twentieth Century* (New York: Anchor Books, 2019), 95, image between 210–11, 215, 302, 303–4, 309, 311. Hays's turn toward social science presaged the later use of what Jeffrey Gonda called "scientific antiracism." Gonda, *Unjust Deeds*, 140–42.

27. Mark Anderson, *From Boas to Black Power: Racism, Liberalism, and American Anthropology* (Stanford: Stanford University Press, 2019), 60–89, 88; Boas quoted in King, *Gods of the Upper Air*, 98–100, 103; Carl N. Degler, *In Search of Human Nature: The Decline and Revival of Darwinism in American Social Thought* (New York: Oxford University Press, 1991), 61–83; Franz Boas, *Anthropology and Modern Life* (New York: W.W. Norton & Company, 1932), 39; Soares, "Seeing Color," 30–32.

28. Boas Affidavit quoted in Brief in Opposition, 20–21; King, *Gods of Upper Air*, 215, 216; Anderson, *From Boas to Black Power*, 60; Franz Boas Affidavit (Supreme Court: Westchester County. Marion A. Ridgway, Plaintiff against Pauline Teresa Cockburn, Defendant), 1; Soares, "Seeing Color," 30–31.

29. Brief in Opposition, 2–3; Hutson L. Lovell to *The Crisis*, August 5, 1926, W. E. B. Du Bois Papers (MS 312). Special Collections and University Archives, University of Massachusetts Amherst Libraries, http://credo.library.umass.edu/view/full/mums312-b173-i217; Thomas Yenser, ed., *Who's Who in Colored America* (Brooklyn: Thomas Yenser, 1942), vol. 6, 125; *People ex Rel. Butts v. Morehead*, 173 Misc. 1061, 18 N.Y.S.2d 696 (N.Y. Sup. Ct. 1940).

30. Brief in Opposition, 5–6.

31. Brief in Opposition, 7–10.

32. Brief in Opposition, 10–16.

33. Brief in Opposition, 16–20; see Brooks and Rose, *Saving the Neighborhood*, 56–62.

34. Brief in Opposition, 19; Richard Kluger, *Simple Justice: The History of Brown v. Board of Education and Black America's Struggle for Equality* (New York: Vintage, 1977, 1975), 309–10, 313, 319, 439, 502; Klineberg was an important social scientist connection for the NAACP in the school education cases that culminated in *Brown v. Board*, and notable for his mentorship of Kenneth Clark; Degler, *In Search of Human Nature*, 179–86.

35. Brief in Opposition, 20–21.

36. Brief in Opposition, 21–22.

37. Brief in Opposition, 22–23.

38. Brief in Opposition, 23–25.

39. Brief in Opposition, 28–30; see William E. Nelson, *The Legalist Reformation: Law, Politics, and Ideology in New York, 1920–1980* (Chapel Hill: University of North Carolina Press, 2001), 26.

40. Brief in Opposition, 31–32.

41. NACCP Report of the Secretary [Walter White] (For the February Meeting of the Board), 7; Folder: 001412-006-0126; Date: January 4, 1937–December 31, 1937, NAACP Board Papers; "Ex-British Ship Captain Opposes Ban: Counsel Says Neighbors Can't Judge Man's Race," *Afro-American*, February 6, 1937; local papers cited in Soares, "Seeing Color," 41–42: "Anti-Negro Clause Tested in Court" *Scarsdale Inquirer*, February 5, 1937; "Woman Insists Court Remove Her Neighbor: And Now It's up to Judge to Determine 'What Is Negro?,'" *Daily Item*, February 2, 1937; "Judge Aldrich to Rule on Local Question: 'What Is a Negro?,'" *Dobbs Ferry New York Register*, February 5, 1937.

42. "Judge Denies Housing Ban," *Amsterdam News*, February 13, 1937, 1; "Racial Plea Denied in Residential Suit," *New York Times*, February 10, 1937, 25; "Court Refuses to Remove Man from 20,000 Home," *Pittsburgh Courier*, February 20, 1937, 1.

43. Hays to White, February 19, 1937, PNAACP, "NAACP Administrative File—Segregation—Residential—White Plains, NY, December 7, 1930–June 18, 1937," Part 5, reel 2, frame 219); "'What's Race' Asks Arthur Garfield Hays," *Amsterdam News*, March 6, 1937, 4; NAACP, Report of the Secretary (For the March Meeting of the Board), NAACP Board Papers.

44. "'What's Race' Asks Arthur Garfield Hays," *Amsterdam News*, March 6, 1937, 4; NAACP, Report of the Secretary (For the March Meeting of the Board), NAACP Board Papers.

45. "Garvey Captain Poses Teaser for N. Y. Court," *Pittsburgh Courier*, February 13, 1937, 1, 4.

46. "Private Lives," *Life*, February 15, 1937, 62; this story was the limit of the racial liberalism of the magazine, the same issue contained a spread on a high society party that featured blackface and "native" dress and another where Tennessee used its African American chain gang convicts to reinforce levees during a flood, 11, 18.

47. Elizabeth M. Smith-Pryor, *Property Rights: The Rhinelander Trial, Passing, and the Protection of Whiteness* (Chapel Hill: University of North Carolina Press, 2009), 61–62, 70–72, 336, note 17; see also in general: Earl Lewis and Heidi Ardizzone, *Love on Trial: An American Scandal in Black and White* (New York: W. W. Norton, 2001); "Lee Parsons Davis Dies at 79; Lawyer Was a Retired Justice: Ex-Member of State Supreme Court Was Former District Attorney of Westchester," *New York Times*, November 24, 1961, 31.

48. "House Ouster Seen as Spite," *Amsterdam News*, February 6, 1937, 1; Arthur Garfield Hays, *City Lawyer: The Autobiography of a Law Practice* (New York: Simon and Schuster, 1942), 207; Smith-Pryor, *Property Rites*, 244, quoting Wilkins to Myra Logan, March 16, 1937, PNAACP; "NAACP Administrative File—Segregation—Residential—White Plains, NY December 7 1930–June 15, 1937, part 5, reel 2, frame 232; on Hays's firm Italian and Italian-American clients, see correspondence with and about the Nora and Vacira families, AGHP, Box 26, folders 10 and 11.

49. "Negro Ouster Suit in Westchester," *New York Times*, March 21, 1937, 2; "Court Defers Race Ruling: Two-Day Hearing for Injunction to Oust Family Ends," *Daily Argus*, March 24, 1937, quoted and cited in Soares, "Seeing Color," 47. One local news account said that Hays conceded the common idea that the "presence of his clients in the neighborhood would depreciate rental and sale values," presumably because of the prejudice of the homeowners in the area. Since this point contradicts what had been put in the brief, how the matter was framed for and by the African American press, and what Joshua Cockburn had said in his deposition, it seems unlikely that Hays said it unless it was part of a conditional that he then dismissed.

50. Hays, *City Lawyer*, 207; "Negro Ouster Suit in Westchester," *New York Times*, March 21, 1937, 2; "Race Barrier Suit Closed," *New York Times*, March 24, 1937, 16.

51. Zaubler's accusation was not in his affidavit, Local papers quoted and cited in Soares, "Seeing Color," 46–47; "Court Defers Race Ruling: Two-Day Hearing for Injunction to Oust Family Ends," *Daily Argus*, March 24, 1937; "Spite Charged in Race Fight: Disappointed Builder Blamed for Effort to Oust Greenburgh Couple," *Mount Vernon Daily Argus*, March 23, 1987.

52. *Ridgway v. Cockburn*, 512, 513.

53. *Ridgway v. Cockburn*, 513, 514.

54. *Ridgway v. Cockburn*, 514–15.

55. *Ridgway v. Cockburn*, 516.

56. Negro Ban Upheld in Edgemont Hills," *New York Times*, June 8, 1937, 22; "Edgar T. Rouzeau, "Capt. Cockburn Must Move from $20,000 Home," *Pittsburgh Courier*, June 12, 1937, 1; "The Menace of Restrictive Covenants," *Pittsburgh Courier*, June 19, 1937, 10.

57. Marcus Garvey, "How Foolish," *The Black Man* (August 1937), reproduced in Quirk, Cockburn Legacy; Soares, "Seeing Color," 62–63.

58. "No Longer a Negro," *Pittsburgh Courier*, October 23, 1937, 15; as to her association with the UNIA, see https://www.afrigeneas.com/forum-aarchive/index_2.cgi/md/read/id/27133/sbj/followers-of-marcus-garvey-check-the-names/; the reference is to Jeremiah 13:23.

59. "Chicagoans Will Fright Residential Jim-Crow," *Pittsburgh Courier*, July 31, 1937, 3.

60. "Housing Ban Pact Upheld: Ordered to Leave $20,000 Home," *Baltimore Afro-American*, June 12, 1937, 1; Hays, *City Lawyer*, 208.

61. "World's Fair Recognition Demanded by Harlem Group," *Pittsburg Courier*, April 2, 1938, 7; Soares, "Seeing Color," 63; Quirk, Cockburn Legacy; the anchor as of 2021 was still there.

62. Hays, *City Lawyer*, 206–8.

63. Hays, *City Lawyer*, 206–8.

64. Hays, *City Lawyer*, 206–8.

65. Hays, *City Lawyer*, 208.

66. *Ridgway v. Cockburn*, 512.

67. Anderson, *From Boas to Black Power*, 81; King, *Gods of the Upper Air*, 84; *Takao Ozawa v. United States*, 260 U.S. 178; *United States v. Bhagat Singh Thind*, 261 *U.S.* 204.

68. Vose, *Caucasians Only*, 60–61, 68–69, 84–88, 129–30, 134, 227–46; Brooks and Rose, *Saving the Neighborhood*, 130–31; Gonda, *Unjust Deeds*, 82–83, 230, note 54. Both Gonda and Brooks and Rose mistakenly assert that the undermining of racial definitions was pioneered by later lawyers.

69. Wilkins to Hays, June 12, 1937, AGHP, Box 4, folder 6. Hays to Wilkins, June 14, 1937, AGHP, Box 4, folder 6.

70. Wilkins to Hays, June 12, 1937, AGHP, Box 4, folder 6.

71. ACLU Memo (P.P.S.), Deprivation of Rights of Negroes in National Parks, AGHP, Box 5, folder 2; Letter of Robert Marshall, US Forest Service, February 11, 1938, AGHP, Box 5, folder 2.

72. Hays, *City Lawyer*, 199–202, 221–24, 226, 236; Samuel Walker, *In Defense of American Liberties: A History of the ACLU* (New York: Oxford University Press, 1990), 127–33; Arthur Garfield Hays, *Democracy Works* (New York: Random House, 1939); Irma Lindheim to Hays, June 29, 1942, AGHP, Box 11, folder 2; clipping, *New York Times*, June 4, 1944, AGHP, Box 37, folder 13; Hays to Archey B. Ball, October 21, 1938, AGHP, Box 5, folder 6; Hays to John Strachey, December 9, 1938, AGHP, Box 32, folder 1; Hays to Mrs. Edward A. Norman, November 28, 1939, AGHP, Box 6 folder 8; Clipping, *Vineyard Gazette*, [1938/9?], AGHP, Box 36, folder 8; Hays to Fredric March, March 4, 1941, AGHP, Box 9, folder 4; Hays to Charles Yale Harrison, July 16, 1941, AGHP, Box 9, folder 3; Hays to Alma

Stern, September 4, 1941, AGHP, Box 9, folder 1; Coleman to Hays, September 9, 1941, AGHP, Box 9, folder 1; Hays to Richard L. Simon, September 16, 1941, AGHP, Box 9, folder 1; Hays to Howe, December 26, 1941; Hays to Coleman, October 20, 1941, AGHP, Box 9, folder 1; Hays to Random House, January 16, 1939, AGHP, Box 6, folder 3; Hays to Mrs. Clarence Darrow, January 6, 1939, AGHP, Box 6, folder 3; Hays to Mr. Russell Owen, January 31, 1939, AGHP, Box 6, folder 7; on American League to Abolish Capital Punishment, see in general AGHP, Box 7, folder 9.

Chapter 4

1. Hays to John Haynes Holmes, April 15, 1943, Arthur Garfield Hays Papers, Seeley Mudd Library, Princeton University [hereafter AGHP], Box 12, folder 7.

2. Hays to Holmes, April 15, 1943, AGHP, Box 12, folder 7. The ABA itself on its online timeline of its history mentions that the 1943 Chicago convention passed a resolution against discrimination but dates the admission of African Americans to seven years later, https://www.americanbar.org/about_the_aba/timeline/; Jerold Auerbach delved deeply into the establishment of the color bar but skims the surface of the ending. Clay Smith's exhaustive history of African American lawyers relates the story more fully, but mistakenly says that Rivers was admitted in 1943 when he was not. Neither details how the members (especially Jewish members like Hays) went about ending the color line. Jerald S. Auerbach, *Unequal Justice: Lawyers and Social Change in Modern America* (New York: Oxford University Press, 1976), 65–66, 216, 348, note 47; Clay Smith, *Emancipation: The Making of the Black Lawyer, 1844–1944* (Philadelphia: University of Pennsylvania Press, 1999), 539–45, 587–88, notes 19–32.

3. David Levering Lewis, "Parallels and Divergences: Assimilationist Strategies of Afro-American and Jewish Elites from 1910 to the Early 1930s," *Journal of American History* 71 (1984): 543–64; August Meier and John H. Bracey, "The NAACP as a Reform Movement, 1909–1965: 'To Reach the Conscience of America,'" *Journal of Southern History* 59 (1993): 3–30; "Susan D. Carle, "Race, Class, and Legal Ethics in the Early NAACP (1910–1920)," *Law and History Review* 20 (2002): 97–146.

4. Smith, *Emancipation*, 41, 545; Auerbach, *Unequal Justice*, 63–64; Lawrence M. Friedman, *American Law in the 20th Century* (New Haven: Yale University Press, 2002), 40–41.

5. Friedman, *American Law*, 30–31, 39–40; William H. Harbaugh, *Lawyer's Lawyer: The Life of John W. Davis* (Charlottesville: University of Virginia Press, 1990, 1973), 41–50, 251–55.

6. Friedman, *American Law*, 32–33; Auerbach, *Unequal Justice*, 102–29; Michael E. Parrish, *Felix Frankfurter and His Times: The Reform Years* (New York: Free Press, 1982), 155.

7. Smith, *Emancipation*, 546–47; Friedman, *American Law*, 40–41; for Marshall, see Victoria Saker Woeste, *Henry Ford's War on Jews and the Legal Battle Against Hate Speech* (Stanford: Stanford University Press 2012), 55–64; Harbaugh, *Lawyer's Lawyer*, 287–89; on Jewish firms, see Richard A. Hawkins, "The Marketing of Legal Services in the United States, 1855–1912: A Case Study of Guggenheimer, Untemyer & Marshall of New York City and the Predecessor Partnerships," *American Journal of Legal History* 53 (2013): 239–64; Philipp Strum, *Louis D. Brandeis: Justice for the People* (Cambridge: Harvard University Press, 1984), 12–29; Thomas K. McCraw, *Prophets of Regulation: Charles Francis Adams, Louis D. Brandeis, James M. Landis, Alfred E. Kahn* (Cambridge: Harvard University Press, 1984), 82–87; Samantha Barbas, *The Rise and Fall of Morris Ernst, Free Speech Renegade* (Chicago: University of Chicago Press, 2021), 38–43, 58–60, 79–81.

8. Smith, *Emancipation*, 539–44; Auerbach, *Unequal Justice*, 65–66.

9. Lothrop Stoddard, *The Rising of Tide of Color: The Threat Against White World-Supremacy* (New York: Charles Scribner's Sons, 1920); Madison Grant, *The Passing of the Great Race: Racial Basis of European History* (New York: Charles Scribner's Sons, 1916); William E. Nelson, *The Legalist Reformation: Law, Politics and Ideology in New York, 1920–1980* (Chapel Hill: University of North Carolina Press, 2001), 3.

10. Smith, *Emancipation*, 539–44; Auerbach, *Unequal Justice*, 65–66; James Edmund Boyack, "American Bar Ass'n Drops Ban on Race," *Pittsburgh Courier*, September 4, 1943, 1, 4; see "3 Quit Bar Group on Race Issue," *Chicago Defender*, April 17, 1943, 1.

11. Barbas, *The Rise and Fall of Morris Ernst*, 130, 377, notes 23, 24; Wigmore to Hays, postcard [1929], AGHP, Box 2, folder 4.

12. Michael J. Klarman, *From Jim Crow to Civil Rights: The Supreme Court and the Struggle for Racial Equality* (New York: Oxford University Press, 2004, 48, 117–35, 171–289.

13. Klarman, *From Jim Crow*, 151; Kenneth W. Mack, *Representing the Race: The Creation of the Civil Rights Lawyer* (Cambridge: Harvard University Press, 2012), 77–81, 111–17; Harbaugh, *Lawyer's Lawyer*, 251–55.

14. Klarman, *From Jim Crow*, 48, 117–35, 171–289; Smith, *Emancipation*, 545. Friedman, *American Law*, 32.

15. Genna Rae McNeil, *Groundwork: Charles Hamilton Houston and the Struggle for Civil Rights* (Philadelphia: University of Pennsylvania Press, 1984), 74–75, 86–155; Rawn James, *Root and Branch: Charles Hamilton Houston, Thurgood Marshall, and the Struggle to End Segregation* (New York: Bloomsbury Press, 2010), 30–46, 92–131; Hays to Stern, August 11, 1943, AGHP, Box 12, folder 9; Smith, *Emancipation*, 544, 587, notes 19 and 20.

16. Mack, *Representing the Race*, 38–60; Pauli Murray, *The Autobiography of a Black Activist, Feminist, Lawyer, Priest, and Poet* (Knoxville: University of Tennessee Press, 1989), 270–82; Victor Rabinowitz, *A History of the National Lawyers Guild: 1937–1987* (NP: National Lawyers Guild Foundation, 1987), 7–8,

10, 12; Auerbach, *Unequal Justice*, 198–204; Barbas, *The Rise and Fall of Morris Ernst*, 221–24; Conrad Lynn, *There Is a Fountain: The Autobiography of a Civil Rights Lawyer* (Westport, CT: Lawrence Hill and Company, 1979), 52–58, 73–76.

17. Hays to Stern, August 11, 1943, AGHP, Box 12, folder 9; Smith, *Emancipation*, 544, 587, note 19; Arthur T. Vanderbilt II, "Arthur T. Vanderbilt," in *The Yale Biographical Dictionary of American Law*, ed. Roger K. Newman (New Haven: Yale University Press, 2009), 558–59; "Arthur T. Vanderbilt," New Jersey Supreme Court Virtual Museum, https://www.njcourts.gov/courts/supreme/vm/vanderbilt.html.

18. Hays to Hogan, August 10, 1938, AGHP, Box 5, folder 5. Hays encouraged even more cooperation with the Bill of Rights Committee. Hays to Arant, October 30, 1942, AGHP, Box 10, folder 4; Arant to Hays, October 28, 1942, AGHP, Box 10, folder 4.

19. Clipping, *New York Age*, August 20, 1938, in AGHP, Box 37, folder 5; Smith, *Emancipation*, 544, 587, note 20; significantly, Smith does not see that the press stories in 1938 were instigated by Hays. Rabinowitz, *A History of the National Lawyers Guild*, 10, 12.

20. Hogan to Hays, August 22, 1938, AGHP, Box 5, folder 5.

21. Hogan to Hays, August 22, 1938, AGHP, Box 5, folder 5.

22. Hogan to Hays, August 22, 1938, AGHP, Box 5, folder 5; Gerald T. Dunne, *Greenville Clark: Public Citizen* (New York: Farrar Straus Giroux, 1986), 36–37.

23. Hays to Hogan, October 27, 1938, AGHP, Box 5, folder 5.

24. Phillip McGuire, *He, Too, Spoke for Democracy: Judge Hastie, World War II, and the Black Soldier* (New York: Greenwood Press,1988), xiii; Gilbert Ware, *William Hastie: Grace Under Pressure* (New York: Oxford University Press, 1984), 3–93, 144–45; *Unequal Justice*, 216, 348, note 47.

25. Smith, *Emancipation*, 547–50, especially note 3; Smith presumed the bylaw was still in effect, but that seems unlikely given what Frank Coleman said; see Coleman to Samuel Seabury, April 30, 1943, AGHP, Box 12, folder 7.

26. Irma Lindheim to Hays, June 29, 1942, AGHP, Box 11, folder 2; clipping, *New York Times*, June 4, 1944, AGHP, Box 37, folder 13; Hays to Archey B. Ball, October 21, 1938, AGHP, Box 5, folder 6; Hays to John Strachey, December 9, 1938, AGHP, Box 32, folder 1; Hays to Mrs. Edward A. Norman, November 28, 1939, AGHP, Box 6, folder 8; C. Fulton Ousler, *Behold this Dreamer! An Autobiography* (Boston: Little Brown and Company, 1964), 235–36; *Washington Post*, January 14, 1938, 9; William J. Butler to Hays, April 17, 1953, AGHP, Box 16, folder 6; Clipping, *Vineyard Gazette*, [1938/9?] AGHP, Box 36, folder 8. Hays also traveled to France on business in the spring of 1939. Hays to Herbert W. Smith, March 29, 1939, AGHP, Box 6, folder 3; [Lora] to Dearest Pop and Maaamy [Arthur and Aline Hays], Tuesday [1941], AGPH, Box 9, folder 3; Hays to Fredric March, March 4, 1941, AGHP, Box 9, folder 4; Hays to Charles Yale Harrison, July 16, 1941, AGHP, Box 9, folder 3; Harrison to Hays, August 13, 1941, AGHP,

Box 9, folder 3; Hays to Alma Stern, September 4, 1941, AGHP, Box 9, folder 1; Coleman to Hays, September 9, 1941, AGHP, Box 9, folder 1; Hays to Richard L. Simon, September 16, 1941, Box 9, folder 1; others, e.g., Hays to Channing Pollock, December 12, 1941; Hays to Howe, December 26, 1941; Hays to Coleman, October 20, 1941, AGHP, Box 9, folder 1; some evidence of the estrangement by the 1940s is the fleeting indication that Hays had formed a relationship with someone else; see Coleman to Hays, October 20, 1942, AGHP, Box 11, folder 8.

27. Walker, *In Defense of American Liberties*, 127–33, 153–58; Barbas, *Rise and Fall of Morris Ernst*, 137–44, 253–66.

28. Barbas, *Rise and Fall of Morris Ernst*, 251–53; Rabinowitz, *A History of the National Lawyers Guild*, 12; Auerbach, *Unequal Justice*, 200–4.

29. He kept up very heavy speaking engagements 1939; see in general AGHP, Box 6, folders 7 and 8. List, AGHP, Box 36, folder 8; Hays to Alma Stern, September 4, 1941, AGHP, Box 9, folder 1; Coleman to Hays, September 9, 1941, AGHP, Box 9, folder 1; Hays to Richard L. Simon, September 16, 1941, Box 9, folder 1; others, e.g., Hays to Channing Pollock, December 12, 1941; Hays to Howe, December 26, 1941; Hays to Coleman, October 20, 1941, AGHP, Box 9, folder 1; Hays to Simon, November 25, 1941, AGPH, Box 9, folder 1; Arthur Garfield Hays, *Democracy Works* (New York: Random House, 1939); Arthur Garfield Hays, *City Lawyer: The Autobiography of a Law Practice* (New York: Simon and Schuster, 1942).

30. Vivian Pierce to Hays, March 15, 1938, AGHP, Box 5, folder 5; Hays to Pierce, March 16, 1938, AGHP, Box 5, folder 5; Hays to Pierce, March 25, 1938, AGHP, Box 5, folder 5; Hays to Michael A. Musmano, November 19, 1941, AGHP, Box 9, folder 4.

31. Press Release, Press Service of NAACP, February 27, 1942, AGHP, Box 9, folder 10; Draft Letter, 3/19/42, AGHP, Box 9, folder 10; Forester to Hays, March 20, 1942, AGHP, Box 10, folder 1; Hays to Thomas O. H. Smith, March 25, 1942, AGHP, Box 10, folder 1.

32. Smith, *Emancipation*, 403–4; Stephen L. Carter, *Invisible: The Forgotten Story of the Black Woman Lawyer Who Took Down America's Most Powerful Mobster* (New York: Henry Holt and Company, 2018), 165, 189, 202–3, 212, Geraldine R. Segal, *Blacks in the Law: Philadelphia and the Nation* (Philadelphia: University of Pennsylvania Press, 1983), 173–74. Jack Greenberg, *Crusaders in the Court: How a Dedicated Band of Lawyers Fought for the Civil Rights Revolution* (New York: Basic Books 1994), 210; Harlem Lawyers Fight A.B.A. Jim-Crow Ban," *Chicago Defender*, May 1, 1943, 3; "3 Quit Bar Group on Race Issue," *Chicago Defender*, April 17, 1943, 1.

33. *Guide*, Jonah J. Goldstein Papers, American Jewish Historical Society, Center for Jewish History, New York, NY, http://digifindingaids.cjh.org/?pID=365004; Smith, *Emancipation*, 403–4; for Herlands, see https://www.fjc.gov/node/1382081.

34. "Judge Watson Accepted by Bar Association; F. S. Rivers of Hogan's Staff Is Rejected," *New York Times*, August 28, 1943, 24; Smith, *Emancipation*, 54, 588;

Jewish Telegraph Agency Archives, April 11, 1943, https://www.jta.org/1943/04/11/archive/judge-jonah-goldstein-quits-bar-association-because-it-bars-negro-from-membership.

35. Hays to American Bar Association, April 8, 1943, AGHP, Box 12, folder 8; Hays to Holmes, April 15, 1943, AGHP, Box 12, folder 7; Hays to Stern, August 11, 1943, AGHP, Box 12, folder 9; "Hayes Quits Bar Assc," *Boston Morning Globe*, April 9, 1943, clipping in ACLU Archives, Reel 214, "Negro Clippings," the story bylined in the *New York Herald Tribune*; "3 Quit Bar Group on Race Issue," *Chicago Defender*, April 17, 1943, 1.

36. Hays to Goldstein, April 8, 1943, AGHP, Box 12, folder 7; Goldstein to Hays, April 9, 1943, AGHP, Box 12, folder 7.

37. Quoted in Smith, *Emancipation* at 548.

38. Harry A. Poth to Hays, AGHP, January 29, 1937, Box 4, folder 2; Hays to Biddle, June 3, 1941, AGHP, Box 8, folder 4; Walker, *In Defense of American Liberties*, 113; Hays to Clark, January 19, 1938, Box 5, folder 4. Gerald T. Dunne, *Grenville Clark: Public Citizen* (New York: Farrar Straus Giroux, 1986), 97–109.

39. Hays to Oursler, May 26, 1950, AGHP, Box 15, folder 12; Hays to Mrs. I. Witkin, April 15, 1954, AGHP, Box 16, folder 9; Hays to Berger, May 3, 1954, AGHP, Box 16, folder 9.

40. Holmes to Hays, April 12, 1943, AGHP, Box 12, folder 7; Dunn to Hays, April 9, 1943, AGHP, Box 12, folder 8; White to Hays, April 20, 1943, AGHP, Box 12, folder 8; Wadhams to Hays, April 10, 1943, AGHP, Box 12, folder 9; Welling to Hays, April 10, 1943, AGHP, Box 12, folder 9; Hays to Holmes, April 15, 1943, AGHP, Box 12, folder 7; Abrahams to Hays, April 14, 1943, AGHP, Box 12, folder 6; Finkelstein to Hays, April 26, 1943, AGHP, Box 12, folder 7.

41. Hays to Holmes, April 15, 1943, AGHP, Box 12, folder 7; Bratter to American Bar Association, April 9, 1943, AGHP, Box 12, folder 6; Von Holst to Hays, April 19, 1943, AGHP, Box 12, folder 7; Stanton to Hays, April 14, 1943, AGHP, Box 12, folder 9.

42. "Urges Anti-Nazis to Lead Fight on Prejudice," *Pittsburgh Courier*, June 29, 1942, 14.

43. Katz to Hays, April 9, 1943, AGHP, Box 12, folder 7; Levin to Hays, April 12, 1943, AGHP, Box 12, folder 7; Hays to Katz, April 12, 1943, AGHP, Box 12, folder 7; Hays to Levin, April 13, 1943, AGHP, Box 12, folder 7.

44. House to Morris, April 16, 1943, AGHP, Box 12, folder 7; Severn to Hays, April 10, 1943, AGHP, Box 12, folder 9; Severn to Morris, April 10, 1943, AGHP, Box 12, folder 9; Hays to Severn, April 12, 1943, AGHP, Box 12, folder 9.

45. Hartstein to American Bar Association (April 13, 1943) AGHP, Box 12, folder 7, Smith, *Emancipation,* 547–50; Morris to Hartstein, July 26, 1943, AGHP, Box 12, folder 7; James Edmund Boyack, "Hays Refutes ABA's Denial of Jim Crow," *Pittsburgh Courier*, May 1, 1943, clipping in AGHP, Box 37, folder 13.

46. "Harlem Lawyers Fight A.B.A. Jim-Crow Ban," *Chicago Defender*, May 1, 1943, 3.

47. "Harlem Lawyers Fight A.B.A. Jim-Crow Ban," *Chicago Defender*, May 1, 1943, 3; "N.Y. Lawyers Probe Bar Assn. Ban," *Chicago Defender*, April 24, 1943, 5; "Bar Group Seeks Facts," *New York Times*, April 13, 1943, 27.

48. Isidor Fox to Hays, April 13, 1943, AGHP, Box 12, folder 7; Hays to Isidor Fox, April 15, 1943.

49. How close Jackson and Hays were is unclear. Hays wrote the foreword to Jackson's book, in which he disagreed with some of Jackson's proposals for changing the legal system to improve its efficiency. Percival E. Jackson, *Look at the Law: The Law Is What the Layman Makes It* (New York: E. P. Dutton, 1940); Jackson to Morris, April 9, 1943, AGHP, Box 12, folder 7; Hays to Jackson, April 12, 1943, AGHP, Box 12, folder 7; "Percival Jackson, Lawyer Is Dead," *New York Times*, August 23, 1970, 70.

50. Voorhees to Jackson, April 16, 1943, AGHP, Box 12, folder 7; Hays to Jackson, April 21, 1943, AGHP, Box 12, folder 7; Jackson to Bond, April 27, 1943, AGHP, Box 12, folder 7; Bond to Jackson, April 28, 1943, AGHP, Box 12, folder 7.

51. Beardsley to Hays, April 18, 1943, AGHP, Box 12, folder 6.

52. Hays to Beardsley, April 23, 1943, AGHP, Box 12, folder 6; Beardsley to Hays, May 19, 1943, AGHP, Box 12, folder 6; Boyack, "Hays Refutes ABA's Denial," *Pittsburgh Courier*, May 1, 1943, clipping in AGHP, Box 37, folder 13; see also "Hays Insists ABA Bars Negroes as Members," *New York World Telegram*, April 24, 1943, cited in Smith, *Emancipation*, 587, 588, note 22.

53. Smith, *Emancipation*, 544; Morris to Stern, July 26, 1943, AGHP, Box 12, folder 9.

54. Stern to Hays, August 7, 1943, AGHP, Box 12, folder 9; Stern to Morris, July 26, 1943, AGHP, Box 12, folder 9; Hays to Stern, August 11, 1943, AGHP, Box 12, folder 9.

55. Stern to McLaren, August 18, 1943, AGHP, Box 12, folder 9; Stern to Hays, August 18, 1943, AGHP, Box 12, folder 9.

56. Smith, *Emancipation*, 403–4.

57. "Judge Watson Accepted by Bar Association; F. S. Rivers of Hogan's Staff Is Rejected," *New York Times*, August 28, 1943; Smith, *Emancipation*, 54, 588, notes 29–31; Greenberg, *Crusaders in the Courts*, 210; James Edmund Boyack, "American Bar Ass'n Drops Ban on Race," *Pittsburgh Courier*, September 4, 1943, 1, 4; "Seabury Report Adopted," *New York Times*, October 20, 1943, 41; "Judge Rivers Is Elected to A.B.A." *Pittsburgh Courier*, March 4, 1944, 14.

58. Auerbach, *Unequal Justice*, 216, 348, note 47.

59. "Three Women Lawyers Admitted to NAWL," *Pittsburgh Courier*, September 4, 1943, 1, 4; Smith, *Emancipation*, 546–49, 588 n.31.

60. Nelson, *The Legalist Reformation*, 130; Walker, *In Defense of American Liberties*, 162–67; Ronald Takaki, *Double Victory: A Multicultural History of America in World War II* (Boston: Little, Brown, and Company, 2000), 171–289; Kevin M. Kruse and Stephen Tuck, *Fog of War: The Second World War and the Civil Rights Movement* (New York: Oxford, 2012); Richard Polenberg, *War and*

Society: the United States, 1941–1945 (Philadelphia: J. B. Lippincott, 1972), 99–130.

61. Hays to Stern, August 11, 1943, AGHP, Box 12, folder 9; Mamolen to Hays, October 13, 1943, AGHP, Box 12, folder 8; Hays to Mamolen, October 14, 1943, AGHP, Box 12, folder 8.

62. Gilbert Ware, *William Hastie*, 29; Hays to Baldwin, July 14, 1938, AGHP, Box 5, folder 1.

63. Irving Bush to Hays, June 17, 1944, AGHP, Box 13, folder 5; Barbas, *Rise and Fall of Morris Ernst*, 211.

64. Hays to Herbert A. Rothman, October 24, 1952; Herbert A. Rothman to Hays, October 21, 1952, AGHP, Box 16, folder 5; Rothman to Hays, March 9, 1953, AGHP, Box 16, folder 8; Milner to Hays, June 11, 1941, AGHP, Box 8, folder 4; Clarice F. Brows to Hays, March 26, 1941, AGHP, Box 8, folder 2; Hays to Brows, ACLU, April 15, 1941, AGHP, Box 8, folder 2; Hays to ACLU, Miss Brows, April 24, 1941, AGHP, Box 8, folder 2; Hays to Brows, May 14, 1941, AGHP, Box 8, folder 2.

Chapter 5

1. Conrad Lynn, *There Is a Fountain: The Autobiography of a Civil Rights Lawyer* (Westport, CT: Lawrence Hill and Company, 1979), 94; the fullest treatment of the case, detailing how it fit in with the military's and government's entrenched racism and was part of the struggle to change the practices, is found in Thomas A. Guglielmo, *Divisions: A New History of Racism and Resistance in America's World War II Military* (New York: Oxford University Press, 2021), 47–51, 136–37; it is mentioned but not explored deeply in Philip A. Klinkner with Rogers M. Smith, *Unsteady March: The Rise and Decline of Racial Equality in America* (Chicago: University of Chicago Press, 1999), 163–64; Michael J. Klarman, *From Jim Crow to Civil Rights: The Supreme Court and the Struggle for Racial Equality* (New York: Oxford University Press, 2004; Samuel Walker, *In Defense of American Liberties: A History of the ACLU* (New York: Oxford University Press, 1990), 160–63; George Q. Flynn, "Selective Service and American Blacks During World War II," *Journal of Negro History* 69 (1984): 14–25, 22–23; Ronald Takaki, *Double Victory: A Multicultural History of America in World War II* (Boston: Little, Brown, and Company, 2000), 25–26; F. Michael Higginbotham, "Soldiers for Justice: The Role of the Tuskegee Airmen in the Desegregation of the American Armed Forces," *William & Mary Bill of Rights Journal* 8 (1999–2000): 273–321, 291–96; Phillip McGuire, *He, Too, Spoke for Democracy: Judge Hastie, World War II, and the Black Soldier* (New York: Greenwood Press, 1988), 17; S. P. Breckinridge, "The Winfred Lynn Case Again," *Social Service Review* 18 (1944): 369–71.

2. Richard Polenberg, *War and Society: The United States, 1941–1945* (Philadelphia: J. B. Lippincott, 1972), 243; John B. Kirby, *Black Americans in the Roosevelt Era: Liberalism and Race* (Knoxville: University of Tennessee Press, 1980), 221; Kevin M. Kruse and Stephen Tuck, "Introduction," in *Fog of War: The Second World War and the Civil Rights Movement*, ed. Kevin M. Kruse and Stephen Tuck (New York: Oxford University Press, 2012), 3–14, 7; Steven White, *World War II and American Racial Politics: Public Opinion, the Presidency, and Civil Rights Advocacy* (Cambridge: Cambridge University Press, 2019), 16–17, 29–30, 58–59, 65; Daniel Kryder, *Divided Arsenal: Race and the American State During World War II* (Cambridge: Cambridge University Press, 2010), 7–11; Klinkner with Smith, *Unsteady March*, 179.

3. The case was what Klarman called litigation as "a method of protest." Klarman, *From Jim Crow*, 7.

4. Lynn, *Fountain*, 34–36, 46, 49, 52, 53; Jay B. Itkowitz, "Winfred Lynn, Fought Army Bias in '42," *Long Island Press*, February 23, 1973, https://web.archive. org/web/20130930140945/http://www.itkowitz.com/mam1965text.php?aid=251; *13th Census of the United States, 1910, Population, Rhode Island, Newport*; *14th Census of the United States, 1920, Population, New York, Hamstead*. My thanks to Sheila Curran Bernard for providing information on the Lynn family.

5. Lynn, *Fountain*, 34–36, 46, 49, 52, 53; on Jamaica, see Peter Eisenstadt, *Rochdale Village: Robert Moses, 6,000 Families, and New York City's Great Experiment in Integrated Housing* (Ithaca: Cornell University Press, 2010), 46–51, 47, 157.

6. "The Story of Winfred Lynn," attached to Wilkins to Hastie, October 13, 1943, Papers of the National Association for the Advancement of Colored Persons (hereafter PNAACP), Group II, Part 9, Series B, reel 10; Lynn, *Fountain*, 71, 92, 93; Guglielmo, *Divisions*, 48, reproduces Lynn's draft registration card.

7. Quoted in Dwight Macdonald, "The Novel Case of Winfred Lynn," *The Nation*, January 20, 1943, 268–70, 268; also see "The Story of Winfred Lynn," 1, attached to Wilkins to Hastie, October 13, 1943, PNAACP, Group II, Part 9, Series B, reel 10; Lynn, *Fountain*, 92, 93; "Another Refuses to Answer Draft Call," *Baltimore Afro-American*, November 21, 1942, 3; Melissa A. Geddis, "Segregation *Is* Discrimination: A Case Study of *Lynn v. Downer* and the African American Resistance to Racialized Military Service in the Second World War" (MA thesis, Rutgers University, 2015), 12–13.

8. Lynn, *Fountain*, 35–37, 39, 42, 43–53; "Conrad J. Lynn, a Veteran Civil-Rights Lawyer, Is Dead at 87," *New York Times*, November 18, 1995, New York City edition, 112.

9. Lynn, *Fountain*, 52–53, 86–87, 92–93.

10. Geddis, "Segregation," 14, 40; Flynn, "Selective," 23; Pauli Murray, *The Autobiography of a Black Activist, Feminist, Lawyer, Priest, and* Poet (Knoxville: University of Tennessee Press, 1989), 152; Richard B. Sherman, *The Case of Odell*

Waller and Virginia Justice, 1940–42 (Knoxville: University of Tennessee Press, 1992), 16–17; Lynn, *Fountain*, 61.

11. Guglielmo, *Divisions*, 26–28; Richard Polenberg, *One Nation Divisible: Class, Race, and Ethnicity in the United States Since 1938* (New York: Penguin Books, 1982), 76; McGuire, *He, Too*, 2; John Morton Blum, *V Was for Victory: Politics and American Culture During World War II* (New York: Harcourt Brace Jovanovich, 1976), 184; Polenberg, *War and Society*, 123.

12. Guglielmo, *Divisions*, 24–26; Harvard Sitkoff, *A New Deal for Blacks* (New York: Oxford University Press, 1978), 298–99; Oscar R. Williams, *George S. Schuyler: Portrait of a Black Conservative* (Knoxville: University of Tennessee Press, 2007), 19, 104; Neil A. Wynn, *The Afro-American and the Second World War* (New York: Holmes & Meier Publishers, 1975), 21, 22; McGuire, *He, Too*, 2, 3; Nancy J. Weiss, *Farewell to the Party of Lincoln: Black Politics in the Age of FDR* (Princeton, NJ: Princeton University Press, 1983), 274; Doris Kearns Goodwin, *No Ordinary Time: Franklin and Eleanor Roosevelt: The Home Front in World War II* (New York: Simon & Schuster, 1994), 165; Klinkner with Smith, *Unsteady*, 132–35; Julian E. Zelizer, "Confronting the Roadblock, Congress, Civil Rights and World War II," in Kruse and Tuck, eds., *Fog of War*, 32–50.

13. Gerald T. Dunne, *Greenville Clark: Public Citizen* (New York: Farrar, Straus and Giroux, 1986), 127–31; Goodwin, *No Ordinary*, 139, 140–42, 144–45, 148–49; Wynn, *Afro-American*, 22–23, 26–27; Richard M. Dalfiume, *Desegregation of the U. S. Armed Forces: Fighting on Two Fronts, 1939–1953* (Columbia: University of Missouri Press, 1969), 22–24; Selective Service System [Campbell C. Johnson], *Special Groups*, Special Monograph No. 10 (Washington, DC: Government Printing Office, 1953), I, 41–45; Klinkner with Smith, *Unsteady March*, 150–52; Lee Finkle, *Forum For Protest: The Black Press During World War II* (Cranbury, NJ: Associated University Presses, 1975), 150–51.

14. Fish had a strong record in support of African American rights. His command of African American troops in World War I made him believe in their value to the services, and he had advocated for the federal anti-lynching law in 1940. Neil A. Wynn, *The African American Experience during World War* II (Lanham: Rowman and Littlefield, 2010), 27; Maggi M. Morehouse, *Fighting in the Jim Crow Army: Black Men and Women Remember World War II* (Lanham: Rowman & Littlefield, 2000), 4–5; Peter N. Nelson, A *More Unbending Battle: The Harlem Hellfighters' Struggle for Freedom in WWI and Equality at Home* (New York: Basic Civitas, 2009), 228; Morehouse, *Fighting*, 4–5; McGuire, *He, Too*, 3–4; 50 USCA (1940) Appendix, Section 3041, Act of 1940; 1; Sitkoff, *A New Deal*, 303; Wynn, *Afro-American*, 22; Dalfiume, *Desegregation*, 30–31; Jack D. Foner, *Blacks and the Military in American History: A New Perspective* (New York: Praeger, 1974), 136–37.

15. Hershey quoted in Macdonald, "Novel," 268; McGuire, *He Too*, 10; Wynn, *Afro-American*, 22–23; Klinkner with Smith, *Unsteady March*, 162; Selective

Service, *Special Groups*, I, 103; Hershey and others involved in the draft pushed against the Army's policies with limited success, Guglielmo, *Divisions*, 44–47.

16. Macdonald, "Novel," 69; clipping, Horace R. Cayton, "Army Policy," *Pittsburgh Courier* [date unknown in], 1944, in Arthur Garfield Hays Papers, Mudd Library, Princeton University (hereafter AGHP), Box 37, folder 14; Selective Service, New York City Headquarters, Memo, attached to Office Memorandum, Civilian Aide to the Secretary of War, February 7, 1947, Records of the Office of the Assistant Secretary of War, Civilian Aide to the Secretary, Subject File [General Correspondence (Judge Hastie), 1940–1948)], ProQuest History Vault Folder ID 12613-922-0853, National Archives, College Park, RG 107 (hereafter CASW); Flynn, "Selective Service," 20; Ruth Danenhower Wilson, *Jim Crow Joins Up: A Study of Negroes in the Armed Forces of the United States* (New York: The Press of William J. Clark, 1944), 91.

17. Flynn, "Selective Service," 19; Guglielmo, *Divisions*, 41–42.

18. Harvard Sitkoff, "Racial Militancy and Interracial Violence in the Second World War," *Journal of American History* 58 (December 1971): 661–81, 664; 676, 679; Gilbert Ware, *William Hastie: Grace Under Pressure* (New York: Oxford University Press, 1984), 110–11, 124–29, 168; Blum, *V*, 185–88; on FEPC, see chapter 6.

19. "Lynn Relates Experience with Jim Crow in U.S. Army," *Atlanta Daily World*, November 1, 1945, 1; Carey McWilliams, *Brothers Under the Skin* (Boston: Little Brown and Company, 1943), 33–34; Guglielmo, *Divisions*, 21–26; Sitkoff, "Racial Militancy," 666; Wynn, *The Afro-American*, 25–26; Kryder, *Divided Arsenal*, 180; Foner, *Blacks*, 145; Selective Service, *Special Groups*, I, 50–51; Wynn, *African American*, 29–31.

20. Patrick S. Washburn, *The African American Newspaper: Voice of Freedom* (Evanston, IL: Northwestern University Press, 2006), 143–78; *Courier* quoted at 148; McGuire, *He, Too*, 15–16; Geddis, "Segregation," 50–51; Lee Finkle, "The Conservative Aims of Militant Rhetoric: Black Protest During World War II," *Journal of American History* 60 (1973): 692–713, 705–9; Takaki, *Double Victory*, 22–57.

21. Lynn, *Fountain*, 84–91, 87, 91. I have used Lynn for the facts; his later interpretations of them are not supported from the contemporary records; see Flynn, "Selective Service," 23.

22. Geddis, "Segregation," 14; Robert A. Hill, ed., *The FBI's RACON: Racial Conditions in the United States During World War II* (Boston: Northeastern University Press, 1995), 472, 482; Lynn, *Fountain*, 93. Wiley B. Rice to NAACP President, November 23, 1942; Marshall to Rice, November 27, 1942, quoted in Geddis, "Segregation," 31–32; Wynn, *Afro-American*, 25, 26; *Baltimore Afro-American*, November 20, 1943, quoted in Finkle, "Conservative Aims of Militant Rhetoric," 709; Murray, *The Autobiography*, 20; Candace Stone to Hayes [Hays], November 30, 1942, AGHP, Box 10, folder 4; Konvitz to Dwight Macdonald, April 21, 1944, PNAACP, Part 9, Series A, reel 9; Finkle, "*Forum for Protest*, 151; Selective Service,

Special Groups, I, 51. On NAACP in these years, see Beth Thompkins Bates, "A New Crowd Challenges the Agenda of the Old Guard in the NAACP, 1933–1941," *American Historical Review* 102 (1997): 340–77; Jack Greenberg, *Crusaders in the Courts* (New York: Basic Books, 1994), 19–15; Richard Kluger, *Simple Justice* (New York: Vintage, 1977), 221; Mark V. Tushnet, *Making Civil Rights Law: Thurgood Marshall and the Supreme Court, 1936–1961* (New York: Oxford University Press, 1996), 20–41. Many reasons probably prompted the NAACP's refusal. African Americans' real progress in the military and war industries cast Lynn's refusal to serve unless the draft was integrated as needlessly confrontational. Also, the experience, up to then, was summary dismissal of most challenges raised about the draft by African Americans. And Conrad Lynn's politics probably caused the NAACP leaders to fear the effects of red-baiting on its programs, and his personal life raised questions about social mixing that NAACP wished to avoid.

23. Walker, *In Defense*, 165; Lucile B. Milner, "Report on the Work of the Committee on Race Discrimination in the War Effort," ACLU, January 7, 1943, in AGHP, Box 12, folder 5.

24. Lynn, *Fountain*, 93–94; Stone to Hayes [Hays], November 30, 1942, AGHP, Box 10, folder 4; Flynn, "Selective Service," 17. Born in Palestine, Konvitz became an American citizen in 1926; he earned his law degree from New York University in 1930 and his doctorate in philosophy in 1933 from Cornell University. Tushnet, *Making Civil Rights Law*, 34; he had published an article in the journal of the National Lawyer's Guild in 1940 attacking the quota on African American recruitment as an adoption of the Czarist quotas on Jews. Guglielmo, *Divisions* 39, 404, note 49; finding aid of Milton R. Konvitz papers, Cornell University Library, https://rmc.library.cornell.edu/EAD/htmldocs/KCL04039.html; "JOHNSON, Campbell Carrington" (2015). Manuscript Division Finding Aids, 108, https://dh.howard.edu/finaid_manu/108.

25. Lynn, *Fountain*, 93–94.

26. Lynn, *Fountain*, 94–95, 104; Hays to ACLU, December 4, 1942, AGHP, Box 10, folder 4; Konvitz to Hays, December [1942], AGHP, Box 10, folder 4; *New York Times*, December 5, 1942, 11; "Lynn Relates Experience with Jim Crow in U.S. Army," *Atlanta Daily World*, November 1, 1945, 1; Macdonald, "Novel," 268–70.

27. Macdonald, "Novel," 268–70; Lynn, *Fountain*, 95–96; Copy of petition attached to Office Memorandum, Civilian Aide to the Secretary of War, February 7, 1947, CASW; Memo [from J. Edgar Hoover] to General Hershey dated December 11, 1942, quoted in Flynn, "Selective Service," 23.

28. *politics*, February 1944, 23–26; the brief cited an article by Konvitz, which suggests he might have begun the brief that Lynn finished. Conrad Lynn's account does not mention Konvitz. Lynn, *Fountain*, 92–93.

29. Hays to ACLU, January 7, 1943; Baldwin to Hays, January 12, 1943, PNAACP, Group II, Part 9, Series B, reel 10; *politics*, February 1944, 23–26.

30. Lynn, *Fountain*, 96; Macdonald, "Novel," 269; *United States ex Rel. Lynn. v. Downer*, 140 F.2nd 397, 398; Hays to ACLU, January 7, 1943, Baldwin to Hays, January 12, 1943, PNAACP, Group II, Part 9, Series B, reel 10.

31. Hays to Conrad Lynn, January 13, 1943, PNAACP, Group II, Part 9, Series B, reel 10; Lynn, *Fountain*, 96–100; Ware, *Grace Under Pressure*, 110–11.

32. Lynn, *Fountain*, 96–101, 100; Macdonald, "Novel," 269, Dwight Macdonald, "The Supreme Court's New Moot Suit," *The Nation*, July 1, 1944, 13–14, 13; see also Geddis, "Segregation," 21, 24–27, 28–29.

33. Hays was asked to join in the defense of Dr. Edgar Keemer, an African American doctor who had refused induction to challenge segregation. William Henry Gallagher to Hays, July 26, 1943, AGHP, Box 12. See also Paula J. Yancey to Hays, May 4, 1943, PNAACP, PT9, series A, reel 9, 283, Emily Hickman to Hays, December 21, 1942, AGHP, Box 12, folder 1; typescript copy of HAS [Harmon ?] to May, December 4, 1942, on the sheet headed Morton to Harmon, December 8, 1942, AGHP, Box 12, folder 1.

34. Geddis, "Segregation," 62; Kerr to White, January 21, 1943; Kerr to White, January 21, 1943, PNAACP, Group II, Part 9, Series B, reel 10; in 1934 Kerr ran on the Socialist line for an Assembly seat in New York; *Brooklyn Daily Eagle*, October 29, 1934, 18.

35. Geddis, "Segregation," 23–24; Andrew E. Kersten, *A. Philip Randolph: A Life in the Vanguard* (Lanham: Rowman and Littlefield, 2007), 25; Paula F. Pfeffer, *A. Philip Randolph, Pioneer of the Civil Rights Movement* (Baton Rouge: Louisiana State University Press, 1990), 66–67; Ashley L. Totten to Hays, February 14, 1941, AGHP, Box 9, folder 6.

36. "Nancy Macdonald Dies at 86; Aided Spain's Loyalist Exiles," *New York Times*, December 16, 1996, B, 13; Macdonald, "Novel," 268; *Baltimore Afro-American*, May 6, 1943, 1; FBI's RACON, 482, 483.

37. "Albert Gilbert," *New York Times*, May 10, 1965, 33; Michael Wreszin, *A Rebel in Defense of Tradition: The Life and Politics of Dwight Macdonald* (New York: Basic Books, 1994), 115; Lynn, *Fountain*, 109; Lawrence Erwin to Konvitz, May 28, 1943, PNAACP, Group II, Part 9, Series B, reel 10; Juan Williams, *Thurgood Marshall, American Revolutionary* (New York: Random House, 1998), 125; Tushnet, *Making Civil Rights Law*, 35–36.

38. Kerr to White, January 21, 1943; Ashley L. Totten to Walter White, February 24, 1943; Roy Wilkins to Layle Lane, April 15, 1943; Lane to Wilkins, April 17, 1943; Lane to Wilkins, April 20, 1943, PNAACP, Group II, Part 9, Series B, reel 10; Geddis, "Segregation," 23, 46, 59–63. This pamphlet is not extant, but we know its contents since it was attacked in a Trotskyite paper and the FBI also digested the pamphlet but did not detail the section on Lynn; FBI's RACON, 484–86; "J.R. Johnson [C.L.R. James] "Pamphlet Points at Scandal of "Jim-Crow in Uniform," *Labor Action*, May 24, 1943, 6, https://www.marxists.org/archive/

james-clr/works/1943/05/jimcrow.htm; Wreszin, *A Rebel*, 116; letter of Mary Herbert, New York *Amsterdam News*, October 2, 1943, 13. It is revealing that she used both the old name of the committee and its address at the MOWM; FBI's RACON, 474, 477, 478, 483.

39. [Untitled report], September 23, 1943, Papers of A. Philip Randolph, Subject file: Subject File, Library of Congress, ProQuest History Vault, Folder ID 001608 021 0700 (hereafter Randolph Papers); Pfeffer, *Randolph*, 67; Randolph to Hays, November 23, 1943, AGHP, Box 12, folder 4; Hays to Randolph, December 2, 1943, AGHP, Box 12, folder 4. In a postwar forum, with people from the Committee against Jim Crow in Military Service (including Winfred Lynn), Johnson asserted that the Selective Service wanted the case tried on its merits, opposed the attempts to have the case dropped or ruled moot, and had nothing to do with Lynn's transfer to the Pacific; untitled transcript [Col. Johnson], Folder 2, 9, Committee against Jim Crow in Military Service and Training Records, Schomburg Center for Research in Black Culture, New York Public Library (hereafter CAJC), CAJC.

40. "The Story of Winfred Lynn," PNAACP, Group II, Part 9, Series B, reel 10 [untitled report], September 23, 1943, Randolph Papers.

41. Wilkins to Hastie, October 13, 1943, 357; Kerr to White, January 21, 1943; Totten to White, February 24, 1943; Lane to Wilkins, April 17, 1943; "The Story of Winfred Lynn," Wilkins to Hastie, October 13, 1943, all in PNAACP, Group II, Part 9, Series B, reel 10; "Lynn Relates Experience with Jim Crow in U.S. Army," *Atlanta Daily World*, November 1, 1945, 1.

42. Copy of brief, Randolph Papers; Selective Service, *Special Groups*, I, 50; see also "Corporal Seeks Army Discharge by Habeas Corpus," *Chicago Defender*, December 18, 1943, 7.

43. *New York Times*, February 13, 1944, 42; Press release, National Citizens Committee, [n.d.], Albert K. Levin to President, December 14, 1943 PNAACP, Group II, Part 9, Series B, reel 10.

44. *United States Ex Rel. Lynn. v. Downer* 140 F.2d 397, "Court Backs Split in Draft of Races," *New York Times*, February 4, 1944, 17.

45. *United States Ex Rel. Lynn. v. Downer* 140 F.2d 397.

46. Lynn, *Fountain*, 101; "Real Significance of the Lynn Case," *Norfolk New Journal and Guide*, February 19, 1944, B8; *New York Times*, February 6, 1944, 36; Klarman, *From Jim Crow*, 171–73, 178, 196–212, 217–20, 225–32; "Army Policy," *Pittsburgh Courier* [date unknown in] 1944 in AGHP, Box 37, folder 14; Memo, Roy Wilkins from Mr. Konvitz, Marshall to Hays, January 6, 1945 [4], PNAACP, Group II, Part 9, Series B, reel 10; Tushnet, *Making Civil Rights Law*, 36. For example, in a January 1944 response to a letter asking about the role of Hays, the NAACP, and the ACLU in the case, the national office skirting over that the NAACP had rejected being involved at the start and hid that it did not cooperate with the Lynn Committee until after the Circuit Court decision. Ast.

Secretary to Lorraine B. Johnson, January 19, 1944, PNAACP, Group II, Part 9, Series B, reel 10.

47. Dear Friends Letters, [n.d., 1944] with National Committee letterhead altered, Randolph Papers.

48. Hays to Marshall, May 12, 1944; Konvitz to Hays, May 17, 1944; Marshall to Osmond Frankel, May 11, 1944; NAACP brief, 4, Hays to Marshall, May 12, 1944, PNAACP Group II, Part 9, Series B, reel 10; Hays, *politics*, April 1944, 86; Lynn, *Fountain*, 101. Conrad Lynn did nothing on the appeal to the Supreme Court, though he remained in contact with Hays, who, according to him, undertook "the enormous amount of paperwork involved in seeking a *certiorari* from the Supreme Court." Lynn, however, a few days after the decision—which would make his filing a suit against segregated service more difficult—was assigned to a segregated unit on Long Island. Albert Gilbert was also struck from the National Citizen's Committee stationary; "dear Friends" [n.d.] Randolph Papers.

49. *politics*, February 1944, 23; Lillie M. Jackson to Wilkins, March 28, 1944; Memorandum to Wilkins from Mr. Konvitz, January 3, 1944, Press release, NAACP Files Brief in the Winfred Lynn Case, February 17, 1944, PNAACP Group II, Part 9, Series B, reel 10.

50. "On the Conduct of the Lynn Case," *politics*, April 1944, 85–88; Konvitz to Macdonald, April 21, 2944, PNAACP Group II, Part 9, Series B, reel 10; see also Stephen J. Whitfield, *A Critical American: The Politics of Dwight Macdonald* (Hamden, CT: Archon Books, 1984), 57–58; Gregory D. Sumner, *Dwight Macdonald and the* politics *Circle: The Challenge of Cosmopolitan Democracy* (Ithaca: Cornell University Press, 1996), 100–2; Guglielmo, *Divisions*, 136–37.

51. Macdonald, "Moot Suit," 13; Walker, *Defense*, 165; 322 U.S. 756; 323 U.S. 817; Major General J. A Ulio to Hays, June 23, 1944, Memorandum: Konvitz to Wilkins, June 1, 1944, 422, PNAACP, Group II, Part 9, Series B, reel 10; Hershey quoted in Flynn, "Selective Service," 22. On the other hand, after the war, Johnson made clear he opposed military segregation and thought future draft laws or universal service should have an antidiscrimination clause, which he implied meant no segregation. He also thought that the Court decision did not settle the issue [Untitled transcript (Col. Johnson)] [n.d., 1948?], 1–6, CAJC, Folders 2, 9.

52. Lynn, *Fountain*, 103; Conrad and Winfred Lynn quoted in Guglielmo, *Divisions*, 50; Memorandum, Konvitz to Marshall, June 1, 1944; Memorandum, Konvitz to Wilkins, June 1, 1944, PNAACP, Group II, Part 9, Series B, reel 10; "Expect to File for Rehearing," *Cleveland Call and Post*, June 10, 1944, 18.

53. Macdonald, "Moot Suit," 13; Walker, *Defense*, 165; 322 U.S. 756; 323 U.S. 817; Major General J. A. Ulio to Hays, June 23, 1944, PNAACP, Group II, Part 9, Series B, reel 10; Press release, Lynn Committee to Abolish Segregation in the Armed Forces, July 7, 1944, PNAACP, Group II, Part 9, Series B, reel 10; "NAACP Seeks to Reopen the Winfred Lynn Case, *Philadelphia Tribune*, July 8,

1944, 1; Rehearing Plea in Lynn Case Filed," *Baltimore Afro-American*, August 5, 1944, 16; "Ask Rehearing in Lynn Case," *Pittsburgh Courier*, August 12, 1944, 2.

54. The organization again shifted its office space to another building on 125th Street and named new co-chairmen with Kerr; Lynn, *Fountain*, 103; *politics*, June 1944, 137–40; Brown to Hays, April 18, 1945, AGHP, Box 13, folder 9; "Dear Friend" [July 14, 1944] on Lynn Committee to Abolish Segregation in the Armed Forces letterhead, "4 Questions to the President of the United States . . ." [n.d.] PNAACP Group II, Part 9, Series B, reel 10; *politics*, August 1944, 197–98; Guglielmo, *Divisions*, 125–26; Michael Cullen Green, *Black Yanks in the Pacific: Race in the Making of American Military Empire after World War II* (Ithaca: Cornell University Press, 2010), 17–18.

55. Memo, CP [CF? Clifford Forster] from RNB, November 2, 1944, AGHP, Box 13, folder 2; 322 U.S. 756; 323 US 817.

56. Guglielmo, *Divisions*, 126–28; Macdonald, "Moot Suit," 13; Walker, *Defense*, 165; Major General J. A. Ulio to Hays, June 23, 1944, Kerr to "Dear Friends" [July 14, 1944], enclosing "4 questions . . . ," Press release, Lynn Committee, July 7, 1944, PNAACP Group II, Part 9, Series B, reel 10; "Lynn Relates Experience with Jim Crow in U.S. Army," *Atlanta Daily World*, November 1, 1945, 1; "Harlem to Greet Lynn Case Hero," *Baltimore Afro-American*, October 27, 1945, 19 [untitled transcript (Col. Johnson)], folder 2, CAJC; Lynn, *Fountain*, 104–5; Wilfred H. Kerr, "Negroism: Strange Fruit of Segregation," *politics*, August 1944, 212–17, followed by increasingly bitter exchanges over it in November 1944, 317, December 1944, 344; Pffefer, *Randolph*, 135–136. It might be that Randolph had originally planned for Bayard Rustin to play a key role in the organization, but his being sent to prison in October 1944 for refusing to be inducted thwarted such plans. Selma De Kroft to Randolph, June 7, 1945; Bertha Gruner to Randolph, June 13, 1945, Randolph Papers; in the war theater, Lynn participated in a work action, refusing to dig latrines for white troops; in a letter he commented about the growing refusal among African American troops to tolerate racism and also noted upon his arrival in Fort Dix for demobilization that segregation was still in force, Guglielmo, *Divisions*, 339, 342, 373.

57. Office Memorandum, February 7, 1947, CASW; Lynn, *Fountain*, 93, 1045, 108; Press release, Lynn Committee [received stamp May 23, 1944]; Kerr to "Dear Friends" [received stamp July 14, 1944], enclosing "4 questions . . . ," Press release, Lynn Committee, July 7, 1944, PNAACP, Group II, Part 9, Series B, reel 10; "Lynn Relates His Experience with Jim Crow in U. S. Army," *Atlanta Daily World*, November 1, 1945, 1; "Harlem to Greet Lynn Case Hero," *Baltimore Afro-American*, October 27, 1945, 19 [untitled transcript (Col. Johnson)], Folders 2, 9, CAJC; Lynn, *Fountain*, 104–5; Itkowitz, "Winfred Lynn, Fought Army Bias in '42," *Long Island Press*, February 23, 1973. According to Conrad Lynn, Winfred only worked five months a year and spent his spare time playing and teaching bridge. He died in 1973. Conrad dedicated his autobiography to his late brother.

58. Dalfiume, *Desegregation*, 107; *Black Yanks*, 9, 10–12, 17–18, 22–23: Maria Höhn and Martin Klimke, *A Breath of Freedom: The Civil Rights Struggle, African American GIs, and Germany* (New York: Palgrave Macmillan, 2010), 39–88; A. Philip Randolph, "Nobody Knows" [description of pamphlet], Folder 1 CAJC.

59. Dalfiume, *Desegregation*, 154–55, 164, 169; Kersten, *Randolph*, 78–83; Pfeffer, *Randolph*, 135–46. Potential cases to being drafted into a segregated military did emerge under the new system; see Devreaux Tomlison to Darius Keene, December 7, 1948, PNAACP, Group II, Part 9, Series B, reel 10.

60. Pfeffer, *Randolph*, 136–49; White, *World War II*, 128–55; John L. Newby II, "The Fight for the Right to Fight and the Forgotten Negro Protest Movement: The History of Executive Order 9981 and Its Effect Upon *Brown v. Board of Education* and Beyond," *Texas Journal on Civil Liberties and Civil Rights* 10 (2004–2005): 83–110.

61. Sabra Holbrook to Hays, January 29, 1940, AGHP, Box 8, folder; Luella S. Laudin to Hays, January 2, 1940, AGHP, Box 8, folder 1; for not using script, see Hays to Milam, May 23, 1940; Hays to Henry Holt, June 4, 1940, AGHP, Box 8, folder 1; Hays to Lyman Bryson, June 20, 1940, AGHP, Box 8, folder 1; Hays to M. Lincoln Schuster, February 8, 1943; Max to Hays, February 11, 1943, Survey of 105 Letters AGHP, Box 12, folder 9; Hays to Clark, February 10, 1942, AGHP, Box 10, folder 10.

62. Walker, *In Defense*, 165; McGuire, *He, Too*, 17; Finkle, *Forum for Protest*, 152–54; Geddis, "Segregation," 45–63; on what success they had in placing the story in mainstream media, see Guglielmo, *Divisions*, 406–7, note 74.

63. Finkle, "Conservative Aims," 694–95, citing Frank Luther Mott, *American Journalism: A History of Newspapers in the United States through 250 Years 1690 to 1940* (New York: Macmillan, 1941); Frank A. Warren, *Noble Abstractions: American Liberal Intellectuals and World War II* (Columbus: Ohio State University Press, 1999), 64–65; a story of school segregation protests from the time of the *Lynn* case shows the lack of mainstream media coverage. See Thomas Sugrue, "From Hillburn to Hattiesburg: Activists Protest Locally, Think Globally," in Tuck and Kruse, eds., *Fog of War*, 87–102, 97; and Clarence Taylor, "To Be a Good American: The New York City Teachers Union and Race during the Second World War," in *Civil Rights in New York City: From World War II to the Giuliani Era*, ed. Clarence Taylor (New York: Fordham University Press, 2011), 10–31, 13. The Lynn story did show up in a few mainstream publications: two books by white liberals and one short review of Supreme Court actions in a sociology journal: McWilliams, *Brothers*, 33–34; Wilson, *Jim Crow Joins Up*, 91–103; Breckinridge, "The Winfred Lynn Case Again," 369–71; some of the idea of the gap between African American and white awareness of the case is shown by Manning Marable's treatment of it in his biography of Malcolm X. Marable writes, "Malcom may have heard about the well-publicized case of Winfred W. Lynn." Presumably Marable was speaking of African American publicity, as whites

mostly ignored the case. Manning Marable, *Malcolm X: A Life of Reinvention* (New York: Viking, 2011), 59–60.

64. Lynn's admiration of Hays may have been strengthened when Hays worked for the commutation of the sentence of Puerto Rican nationalist Oscar Collazo, who had been sentenced to death after the attack on President Truman. Lynn had strong links with Puerto Rican nationalists through his wife and defended Ruth Reynolds and Albizu Campos on charges of sedition. Hays knew Reynolds, and in 1953 they had a spirited exchange of letters about various public figures on the island, which underscored Hays's sympathy for the nationalist cause, though he deplored their methods. Lynn, *Fountain*, 93–94, 123–40; Hays to Sara Ehrman, June 10, 1952; Ehrman to Hays, June 11, 1952, AGHP, Box 16, folder 3; Hays to Ehrman, July 1, 1952, AGHP, Box 16, folder 3; Ehrman to Hays, July 14, 1952, AGHP, Box 16, folder 3; Ruth Reynolds to Hays, July 14, 1953, AGHP, Box 18, folder 2, Hays to Reynolds, July 27, 1953, AGHP, Box 18, folder 12.

Chapter 6

1. Hays to Charles Fulton Oursler, February 27, 1945, Arthur Garfield Hays Papers, Seeley G. Mudd Library, Princeton University (hereafter AGHP), Box 14, folder 2.

2. John Morton Blum, *V Was for Victory: Politics and American Culture During World War II* (New York: Harcourt Brace Jovanovich, 1976), 188; Andrew E. Kersten, *A. Philip Randolph: A Life in the Vanguard* (Lanham: Rowman and Littlefield, 2007), 63; Steven White, *World War II and American Racial Politics: Public Opinion, the Presidency, and Civil Rights Advocacy* (New York: Cambridge University Press, 2019), 125; Louis Ruchames, *Race, Jobs, and Politics: The Story of FEPC* (New York: Columbia University Press, 1953), viii.

3. Steel firm quote in Doris Kearns Goodwin, *No Ordinary Time: Franklin and Eleanor Roosevelt: The Home Front in World War II* (New York: Simon & Schuster, 1994), 246; Tod M. Ottman, "'Government That Has Both a Heart and a Head': The Growth of New York State Government During the World War II Era, 1930–1950 (PhD diss., University at Albany, State University of New York, 2001), 139; Myrdal quoted in Ruchames, *Race, Jobs, and Politics*, 11–13, 12.

4. Andrew Kersten, *Race, Jobs and the War: The FEPC in the Midwest, 1941–46* (Champagne: University of Illinois Press, 2007), 13–14; Philip A. Klinkner with Rogers M. Smith, *Unsteady March: The Rise and Decline of Racial Equality in America* (Chicago: University of Chicago Press, 1999), 154–59; Ruchames, *Race, Jobs, and Politics*, 14–21; Kersten, *A. Philip Randolph*, 57–62; Paula F. Pfeffer, *A. Philip Randolph, Pioneer of the Civil Rights Movement* (Baton Rouge: Louisiana State University Press, 1990), 45–97; Cornelius L. Bynum, *A. Philip Randolph and the Struggle for Civil Rights* (Urbana: University of Illinois Press, 2010), 155–84;

Blum, *V Was for Victory*, 185–88, Daniel Kryder, *Divided Arsenal: Race and the American State During World War II* (Cambridge: Cambridge University Press, 2010), 53–65; Risa L. Goluboff, *The Lost Promise of Civil Rights* (Cambridge: Harvard University Press, 2007), 186–237; Dovey Johson Roundtree and Katie McCabe, *Mighty Justice: My Life in Civil Rights* (Chapel Hill: Algonquin Books of Chapel Hill, 2019), 73–90.

5. Kryder, *Divided Arsenal*, 77; Blum, *V Was for Victory*, 196–98; Richard Polenberg, *War and Society: The United States, 1941–1945* (Philadelphia: J. B. Lippincott, 1972), 118; Blum, *V Was for Victory*, 198–99.

6. Kersten, *Race, Jobs and the War*, 2; Blum, *V Was for Victory*, 174, 196; Polenberg, *War and Society*, 117, 121; Klinkner with Smith, *Unsteady March*, 169–70, 178; Kryder, *Divided Arsenal*, 75; Ruchames, *Race, Jobs, and Politics*, 22–56.

7. Alexa B. Henderson, "FEPC and the Southern Railway Case: An Investigation into the Discriminatory Practices of Railroads During World War II," *Journal of Negro History* 61 (1976): 173–87; Pfeffer, *A. Philip Randolph*, 90–94; Blum, *V Was for Victory*, 196; Kryder, *Divided Arsenal*, 81, 178; Lee Finkle, *Forum for Protest: The Black Press During World War II* (Cranbury, NJ: Associate University Presses, 1975), 68–69, 98–99; Kersten, *A. Philip Randolph*, 64.

8. Goluboff, *The Lost Promise of Civil Rights*, 129, 135, 137–38; Polenberg, *War and Society*, 119–22; Kersten, *A. Philip Randolph*, 65; Kryder, *Divided Arsenal*, 98, Klinkner with Smith, *Unsteady March*, 191–92; Blum, *V Was for Victory*, 212–15.

9. Polenberg, *War and Society*, 119, 123; Ruchames, *Race, Jobs, and Politics*, 73–99.

10. Scholars debate how much of this change came from the FEPC or from other actors (the War Labor Board or state agencies like New York's) and market forces. Klinkner with Smith, *Unsteady March*, 191–92; Polenberg, *War and Society*, 116–17; Kersten, *Race, Jobs and the War*, 3, 6; Ruchames, *Race, Jobs, and Politics*, 137–64.

11. Bynum, *A. Philip Randolph and the Struggle for Civil Rights*, 183; Kersten, *A. Philip Randolph*, 65; Pfeffer, *A. Philip Randolph*, 97–98; Samuel Walker, *In Defense of American Liberties: A History of the ACLU* (New York: Oxford University Press, 1990), 162; Michael J. Klarman, *From Jim Crow to Civil Rights: The Supreme Court and the Struggle for Racial Equality* (New York: Oxford University Press, 2004), 190, 192; Anthony Chen, *The Fifth Freedom: Jobs, Politics and Civil Rights in the United States, 1941–1972* (Princeton: Princeton University Press, 2009), 8–9, 19–21, 46.

12. Lehman quoted in Ottman, "Government That Has Both," 127–93, 127. I draw heavily on Ottman to explain New York developments. Chen, *The Fifth Freedom*, 88–114; Norton Smith, *Thomas E. Dewey and His Times* (New York: Touchstone, 1982), 443–48.

13. Ottman, "'Government That Has Both,'" 143–53; Chen, *The Fifth Freedom*, 90–94.

14. Ottman, "'Government That Has Both,'" 175–88; Klinkner with Smith, *Unsteady March*, 199–200; Chen, *The Fifth Freedom*, 100–14, 116; Smith, *Thomas Dewey*, 447.

15. Ottman, "'Government That Has Both,'" 175–88; Klinkner with Smith, *Unsteady March*, 199–200; Chen, *The Fifth Freedom*, 100–14, 116; Smith, *Thomas Dewey*, 447.

16. Ruchames, *Race, Jobs, and Politics*, 165, 166, quoting Maslow; Kevin Schultz, "The FEPC and the Legacy of the Labor-Based Civil Rights Movement of the 1940s," *Labor History* 49 (2008): 71–92; White, *World War II and American Racial Politics*, 125; Walker, *In Defense of American Liberties*, 163; Chen, *The Fifth Freedom*, 45, 115–69; Klarman, *From Jim Crow to Civil Rights*, 190; Stuart Svonkin, *Jews Against Prejudice: American Jews and the Fight for Civil Liberties* (New York: Columbia University Press, 1997), 92, 94.

17. "Ten Commandments for Civil Rights Include," AGHP, Box 9, folder 3; Hays to Gordon Dorrance, July 1, 1940, AGHP, Box 7, folder 9; Hays to Dorrance, July 12, 1940, AGHP, Box 7, folder 9; Hays to Dorrance, June 5, 1941, AGHP, Box 9, folder 3; Hays to Dorrance, November 19, 1941, AGHP, Box 9, folder 3; Arthur Garfield Hays, *City Lawyer: The Autobiography of a Law Practice* (New York: Simon and Shuster, 1942), 234–35; Hays's ideas can be traced to his friend H. L. Mencken's ideas pulled together in his multiple volumes called *Prejudices*, Arthur Garfield Hays, *Let Freedom Ring* (New York: Boni and Liveright, 1928), xx.

18. *Chicago Defender*, April 24, 1943, 14.

19. "Hays Explains Stand," *Chicago Defender*, [n.d.], clipping in AGHP, Box 37, folder 13; Hays, *Let Freedom Ring*, 233.

20. Untitled Speech, starting "It is said," AGHP, Box 33, folder 3; Hays, *Let Freedom Ring*, 200–1; Hays, *City Lawyer*, 234–35; Morris Ernst also confronted anti-Semitism at his retreat on Nantucket. Samantha Barbas, *The Rise and Fall of Morris Ernst, Free Speech Renegade* (Chicago: University of Chicago Press, 2021), 82–83.

21. Hays to Lehman, AGHP, May 12, 1937, Box 4, folder 2; Holmes to Hays, September 17, 1943, enclosing draft letter, AGHP, Box 12, folder 4; Thomas Kessner, *Fiorello H. La Guardia and the Making of Modern New York* (New York: Penguin, 1989), 546–48.

22. Daniel R. Ernst, *Tocqueville's Nightmare: The Administrative State Emerges in America, 1900–1940* (New York: Oxford University Press, 2014), 6, 79–105.

23. Untitled article draft, opening, "We have heretofore brought to your attention . . ." AGHP, Box 35, folder 3, 1–3.

24. Walker, *In Defense of American Liberties*, 102–3.

25. Arthur Garfield Hays, *Democracy Works* (New York: Random House, 1939), viii, 99–104; for his support of government action, see 233–59.

26. Hays to ACLU, January 26, 1939, AGHP, Box 5, folder 6; Hays to Baldwin, January 24 1940, AGHP, Box 7, folder 1.

27. Hays to William L. Ransom, May 1, 1940, AGHP, Box 7, folder 9; *Hearings before Special Committee to Investigate the National Labor Relations Board, House of Representatives* 76 Congress 3rd Session (Washington: Government Printing Office, 1940), vol. 24, Part II, Appendix, 5819; Hays to George Slaff, June 3, 1942, AGHP, Box 10, folder 2; Slaff to Hays, June 14, 1942, AGHP, Box 10, folder 6.

28. Hays to Thurman Arnold, February 15, 1941, AGHP, Box 9, folder 2; Shad Polier to Hays, November 10, 1942, AGHP, Box 12, folder 1; "Memorandum to the Members of the Firm, April 26, 1946, AGHP, box 14, folder 9.

29. Coleman to Hays, "Friday" early January 1942, AGHP, Box 11, folder 1; Hays, *City Lawyer*, 97–124, 115–20; 119. On SEC, see William O. Douglas, *Go East Young Man* (1974; repr., New York: Vintage Books, 1983), 257–96; Thomas K. McCraw, *Prophets of Regulation: Charles Francis Adams, Louis D. Brandeis, James M. Landis, Alfred E. Kahn* (Cambridge: Belknap Press, 1984), 153–203; Jerald S. Auerbach, *Unequal Justice: Lawyers and Social Change in Modern America* (New York: Oxford University Press, 1976), 180–93.

30. Herbert A. Cone to Hays, August 5, 1942, AGHP, Box 11, folder 5; Polier to Hays, November 10, 1942, AGHP, Box 12, folder 1.

31. "To the Editor of the American Magazine," July 29, 1943, AGHP, Box 12, folder 6.

32. Hays to the *Labor Defender*, May 12, 1937, enclosed statement on Herdon case, AGHP, Box 3, folder, 9.

33. Hays to ACLU, August 8, 1945, AGHP, Box 13, folder 9; Hays to Forster, May 3, 1944, AGHP, Box 13, folder 1.

34. Walker, *In Defense of American Liberties*, 115–18; Barbas, *The Rise and Fall of Morris Ernst*, 144–45.

35. Walker, *In Defense of American Liberties*, 115–18.

36. Richard W. Steele, *Free Speech in the Good War* (New York: St. Martin's Press, 1999), 84.

37. "How Shall We Meet Nazi Propaganda," November 4, 1937, AGHP, Box 33, folder 2; within the ACLU, Morris Ernst advocated the same points in defending himself from criticism in defending American Nazi's free speech rights; Barbas, *Rise and Fall of Morris Ernst*, 144–45.

38. "How Shall We Meet Nazi Propaganda," November 4, 1937, AGHP, Box 33, folder 2.

39. Hugo Marx to Hays, November 1, 1942, AGHP, Box 12, folder 1; Hays to Marx, November 2, 1942, Box 12, folder 1.

40. Libels against Race and Religion, AGHP, Box 34, folder 11; the ACLU did not mention that the action against Edmondson was begun by Mayor La Guardia directly as a magistrate and was at first very popular among New York City Jews, see Dov Fisch, "The Libel Trial of Robert Edward Edmondson: 1936–1938," *American Jewish History* 71 (1981): 79–102; Kessner, *Fiorello H. LaGuardia*, 402.

41. AGH, Discussion, "On Free Speech," *Menorah Journal* [n.d., 1939], offprint in AGHP, Box 34, folder 4.

42. Milner to Hays, January 20, 1940, AGHP, Box 7, folder 1; Draft, Memorandum Submitted in Opposition to New York state Assembly Bill _____ Proposed by Mr. Goldstein, February 14, 1940, AGHP, Box 1, folder 7; Minutes of Meeting of Sub-Committee to Consider the Group Libel Bills, February 21, 1940, AGHP, Box 7, folder 1; Britchey to Robert J. Burton, February 13, 1940, AGHP, Box 7, folder 1; Memorandum on Group Libel Laws Submitted by Professor Jerome Michael, April 4, 1940, AGHP, Box 7, folder 2 (Hays apparently had the ACLU's only copy of the proposal); Baldwin to Members of the Board of Directors, March 9, 1944, AGHP, Box 13, folder 4.

43. Baldwin to Members of the Board of Directors, March 9, 1944, AGHP, Box 13, folder 4; "The Control of Attacks on Race and Religion," May 1944, AGHP, Box 13, folder 3; Barbas, *The Rise and Fall of Morris Ernst*, 263–56.

44. Hays to Editor of the *Jewish Frontier*, March 15, 1944, AGHP, Box 13, folder 1; "Letter to the Editor," *Jewish Frontier*, April 1944, clipping in AGHP, Box 37, folder 13.

45. Hays to Minoru Yasui, February 5, 1943, AGHP, Box 12, folder 9; *Yasui v. United States*, 320 U.S. 115 (1943); Peter Irons, *Justice at War* (New York: Oxford University Press, 1983), especially 81–87, 113–14, 135–43, 171–73, 222–27.

46. Hays to Alexander, September 22, 1942, AGHP, Box 10, folder 4.

47. Hays to Friedenberg, June 29, 1942, AGHP, Box 10, folder 2.

48. Stuart Svonkin, *Jews Against Prejudice*, 79–85, 84; Kersten, *Race, Jobs and the War*, 129; Walker, *In Defense of American Liberties*, 163.

49. Hays to Seymour P. Kassewitz, August 31, 1942, AGHP, Box 10, folder 3.

50. Fred G. Clark to Hays, November 9, 1942, AGHP, Box 10, folder 10.

51. Bernard Gittleson to Hays, November 27, 1943, AGHP, Box 12, folder 4.

52. Hays to Gittleson, November 30, 1943, AGHP, Box 12, folder 4; the social/legal distinction in understanding anti-Semitism was strong among Jews, see Britt P. Tevis, " 'Jews Not Admitted': Anti-Semitism, Civil Rights, and Public Accommodation Laws," *Journal of American History* 107 (2021): 847–70.

53. Hays to Ramsey Black, January 9, 1943, AGHP, Box 13, folder 7; Hays to Celler, January 16, 1945, AGHP, Box 13, folder 7.

54. Hays to Goldstein, December 20, 1944, AGHP, Box 13, folder 4; Hays to Goldstein, January 5, 1945, AGHP, Box 13, folder 7; Hays to Senator James E. Murray, August 9, 1944, AGHP, Box 13, folder 2.

55. Arnold Aronson to Hays, August 21, 1944, AGHP, Box 13, folder 2; ACLU to Samuel D. Jackson, Telegram n.d. [July 17, 1944], AGHP, Box 13, folder 2; Samuel Jackson to Hays, July 31, 1944, AGHP, Box 13 folder 2.

56. Hays to Nathan D. Pearlman, December 27, 1943, AGHP, Box 12, folder 4; *Declaring Certain Papers, Pamphlets, Books Pictures and Writings Nonmailable*

Hearing before the Committee on Post Office and Postal Roads, 78 Congress, 2nd Session H. R. 2328, Part II, February 15, March 16, March 17, 1944 (Washington, DC: Government Printing Office, 1944), esp. Pearlman at 119–23.

57. Goluboff, *The Lost Promise of Civil Rights*, 112, 122; Baldwin to Rotnem, March 17, 1944, AGHP, Box 13, folder 1.

58. G. M. Cohen to Hays, April 24, 1944, all AGHP, Box 13, folder 6; Hays to Cohen, May 1, 1944, AGHP, Box 13, folder 6; Cohen to Hays, May 5, 1944, AGHP, Box 13, folder 6; Hays to Cohen, May 25, 1944, AGHP, Box 13, folder 6; Cohen to Hays, May 31, 1944, AGHP, Box 13, folder 6.

59. "What Shall We Do to Be Saved?," reprint from the *Jewish Post*, AGHP, Box 35, folder 5.

60. "What Shall We Do to Be Saved?," reprint from the *Jewish Post*, AGHP, Box 35, folder 5.

61. "What Shall We Do to Be Saved?," reprint from the *Jewish Post*, AGHP, Box 35, folder 5.

62. "What Shall We Do to Be Saved?," reprint from the *Jewish Post*, AGHP, Box 35, folder 5.

63. Coleman to Hays, n.d. [summer 1939], AGHP, Box 6, folder 5; Leonard Dinnerstein, *Antisemitism in America* (New York: Oxford University Press, 1994), 128–49, 133, 136, 139; Richard F. Hamm, "The Limits of the Law: A 1943 Case of Anti-Semitism in the Lower Hudson River Valley," *Hudson River Valley Review* 31 (Spring 2015): 2–15; Clarence Taylor, "To Be a Good American: The New York City Teachers Union and Race during the Second World War," in *Civil Rights in New York City: From World War II to the Giuliani Era*, ed. Clarence Taylor (New York: Fordham University Press, 2011), 10–31, 12–16; Kirsten Fermaglich, "What's Uncle Sam's Last Name?': Jews and Name Changing in New York City during the World War II Era, *Journal of American History* (December 2015): 719–45, 720.

64. Hays to Cohen, June 1, 1944, AGHP, Box 13, folder 6; Hays to Cohen, June 7, 1944, AGHP, Box 13, folder 6; Hays to Cohen, June 9, 1944, AGHP, Box 13, folder 6; Newman Levy to Hays, June 16, 1944, AGHP, Box 13, folder 7; Jim Luitweiler to Hays, June 15, 1944, AGHP, Box 13, folder 7; Oursler to Hays, May 25, 1944, AGHP, Box 13, folder 7; see also Van Doren to Hays, AGHP, June 6, 1944, Box 13, folder 7.

65. Hays to Oursler, February 27, 1945, AGHP, Box 14, folder 2; Merle to Oursler, March 22, 1945, AGHP, Box 14, folder 2; Hays to C. Salkin, September 15, 1944, AGHP, Box 13, folder 2.

66. Burlingham quoted in Chen, *The Fifth Freedom*, 102, 329, note 30.

67. Letters to the Times, *New York Times*, February 13, 1945, 22.

68. Letters to the Times, *New York Times*, February 15, 1945, 18; Letters to the Times, *New York Times*, February 20, 1945, 18; Letters to the Times, *New York Times*, February 21, 1945, 18.

69. ACLU scrapbook; Reel 214, ACLU American Liberties Union Archives (1943), reel 214, 2479; "Negro Clippings," Frame 63 PM, April 15, 1943; clipping 'Hays Opposes Anti-Bias Laws"; Svonkin, *Jews Against Prejudice, 83.*

70. Maslow to Hays, March 31, 1945, AGHP, Box 13, folder 8; Maslow to Hays, April 10, 1945, AGHP, Box 14, folder 2.

71. Maslow to Hays, March 31, 1945, AGHP, Box 13, folder 8; Charles King, *Gods of the Upper Air: How a Circle of Renegade Anthropologists Reinvented Race, Sex, and Gender in the Twentieth Century* (New York: Anchor Books, 2019), 317.

72. Maslow to Hays, March 31, 1945, AGHP, Box 13, folder 8.

73. Hays to Maslow, April 7, 1945, AGHP, Box 13, folder 9; Maslow to Hays, March 31, 1945, AGHP, Box 13, folder 8.

74. Maslow to Hays, April 10, 1945, AGHP, Box 14, folder 2.

75. Maslow to Hays, April 10, 1945, AGHP, Box 14, folder 2.

76. Chen, *Fifth Freedom,* 116–18, quoting Maslow; Klarman, *From Jim Crow to Civil Rights,* 192.

77. Ruchames, *Race, Jobs, and Politics,* 166–77, 179, 169; *New York Herald Tribune* quoted at 169, 182–83; Svonkin, *Jews Against Prejudice,* 93, 242, note 47; Tevis, "Jews Not Admitted," 860.

78. AGH, *Brooklyn Barrister,* April 1951, vol. 2, no. 7, clipping in AGHP, Box 37, folder 13; Address, October 26, 1949, New Chapter American Council for Judaism, AGHPH, Box 33, folder 1; transcript, "What Do We Mean by un-American Activities?," Wake Up America, copy in AGHP, Box 37, folder 13; Hays to Coleman, January 14, 1946, AGHP, Box 14, folder 9; on his activities, see Hays to Walter Lippmann, May 12, 1954, AGHP, Box 16, folder 9; Hays to Edmond H. Heisler, March 13, 1951, AGHP, Box 16, folder 1; Mary E. Dreier to Hays, December 3, 1952, AGHP, Box 16, folder 4; Hays to Stephen Gendzier, October 9, 1951, AGHP, Box 15, folder 12.

Conclusion

1. Evalyn Coppoc, "Americans Of Good Will," *Pittsburgh Courier,* July 14, 1945, clipping in Arthur Garfield Hays Papers, Seeley G. Mudd Library, Princeton University (hereafter AGHP), Box 37, folder 14.

2. Hays to Rotnem, August 27, 1942, AGHP, Box 11, folder 6. Rotnem toyed with writing Hays's biography. Christmas letter of Marion John and Vic Rotnem to [Jane Butler], January 1, 1955, AGHP, Box 16, folder 11.

3. Hays to Singh, April 7, 1944, AGHP, Box 13, folder 6; Monroe Schneider to Hays, September 28, 1946, AGHP, Box 14, folder 17. Hays also worked with an organization of mostly American Jewish doctors with foreign medical degrees who were being denied medical licenses in the United States; Hays to Schneider, October 23, 1946, AGHP, Box 14, folder 17.

4. Press Release, Committee against Jim Crow in Military Service and Training Records (hereafter CAJC), Schomburg Center for Research in Black Culture, New York Public Library, folder 1; Transcript, CAJC, 6, folder 2.

5. Cathy D. Knepper, *Jersey Justice: The Story of the Trenton Six* (New Brunswick, NJ: Rivergate Books, 2011), 119, 164, 169, 189, 193, 198; "Hays 'Thinks Twice' but Sticks to His Guns," *Daily Worker*, March 29, 1950, clipping in AGHP, Box 37, folder 14; "Hays Enters 'Trenton 6' Case as Counsel For 3," *Trenton Evening Times*, January 5, 1951, clipping in AGHP, Box 37, folder 14; "Hays Joins Defense of Jersey Trial of 6," *New York Times*, January 6, 1951, clipping in AGHP, Box 37, folder 14.

6. "Walter Winchell . . . of New York," *Washington Post*, December 17, 1951, 89; "Baker Sues W. Winchell," *Pittsburgh Courier*, December 29, 1951, 1; Greenberg, *Crusaders in the Courts*, 139–40; "Bias Case Unfounded, Group Advises Mayor," *New York Times*, December 22, 1951, 13; "Jo Baker in NY to Fight Winchell," *Chicago Defender*, June 19, 1954, 1; "Winchell Suit Dropped," *New York Times*, July 22, 1955, 19.

7. Hays to Marian Burr, May 22, 1945, AGHP, Box 14, folder 1; Hays to Coleman, June 15, 1945, AGHP, Box 14, folder 1; Hays to Lora Hays Lenauer, AGHP, December 10, 1945, Box 14, folder 2; Hays to Lora, December 14, 1945, Box 14, folder 2; Hays to Betty Hyde Moore, May 14, 1945, AGHP, Box 14, folder, 2; Hays to Joseph O'Keffe, October 29, 1945, AGHP, Box 14, folder 2.

8. "McAlister Coleman," May 22, 1950, AGHP, Box 34, folder 12; Richard F. Hamm, " 'I Want You to Realize How Unfair You Have Been:' The Cold War's Effect on the Friendship of Arthur Garfield Hays and C. Fulton Oursler," *American Communist History* 17 (2018): 318–39; Hays to Roy Jansen, April 16, 1953, AGHP, Box 16, folder 7; Hays to Joseph Leftoff, April 22, 1953, AGHP, Box 16, folder 7; Francine Leffler to Hays, January 7, 1953; Hays to Leffler, February 10, 1953, AGHP, Box 16, folder 7; Betty (Mrs. Albert) Stern to Hays, August 5, 1953, AGHP, Box 16, folder 8; Mrs. Henry Lazere to Hays, January 16, 1954, AGHP Box 16, folder 10. Hays's will left his estate to his daughters and his girlfriend divided equally. His earlier will had divided the estate between his wife, Aline, and his daughters. "A. G. Hays Will Filed," *New York Times*, December 28, 1954, 20; Secretary [Theresa H. Saper] to Mr. Hays, July 5, 1950, AGHP, Box 15, folder 10; Hays to Butler, July 30, 1948, AGHP, Box 15, folder 2.

9. Richard Kluger, *Simple Justice* (New York: Vintage, 1977), 295–305, 356–57, 365–66; William H. Harbaugh, *Lawyer's Lawyer: The Life of John W. Davis* (Charlottesville: University of Virginia Press, 1990, 1973), 484–92; "Poems," July 1952, AGHP, Box 37, folder 15; "Ex-Judge Waring Is Honored Here," *New York Times*, April 17, 1952, 43.

10. Jack Greenberg, *Crusaders in the Courts* (New York: Basic Books, 1994), 20.

11. Arthur Garfield Hays, *Democracy Works* (New York: Random House, 1939), 3–10.

12. Coleman to Hays, November 28, 1941, AGHP, Box 9, folder 1.

13. Hays to H. G. Apgar, May 27, 1941, "Apgar to Hays, May 31,1941, AGHP, Box, 9, folder 2; Hays to Apgar, July 21, 1941, AGHP, Box, 9, folder 2.

14. Clifford Forster, letter to editor, *New York Times*, December 23, 1954, clipping in Box 37, folder 7, dated 12, 15, 54; Don Munro, "Arthur Garfield Hays," *Endicott New York Bulletin*, December 16, 1954, clipping Box 37, folder 7; Hays to Morris Sommers, February 15, 1938, AGHP, Box 5, folder 6; Arthur Garfield Hays, *City Lawyer: The Autobiography of a Law Practice* (New York: Simon and Schuster, 1942), 246.

15. "This I Believe," "AGHP, Box 35, folder 2. I have quoted the draft version of the statement, not what was printed later in newspapers, as the draft was more representative of his thought. "This I Believe," *Washington Post*, February 23, 1952, B5; typical of Hays, half of the speech was aimed at what he thought the most pressing civil liberties threat of the day, the anti-Red hysteria.

16. Roger Baldwin, "Arthur Garfield Hays," ACLU Records, Box 1890, folder 6; Baldwin edited Hays, who had added that he often defended "a great many" ideas to which "I have not agreed." See Hays, *City Lawyer*, xiii; *New York Times*, December 17, 1954, clipping in Box 37, folder 7. Freda Kirchwey made the same point about Hays's self-confidence, saying how attacks "bounced off the armor of self-confidence," Freda Kirchwey, "Arthur Garfield Hays," *The Nation*, December 25, 1954, clipping in AGHP, Box 37, folder 7; Memorandum, to: PMM [Malin] From AR [Reitman], March 17, 1955, ACLU Records, Box 614, folder 1; Roy Wilkins to Malin, March 4, 1955, ACLU, Box 614, folder 1; Press release, Cooper Union, [March 1955], Box 614, folder 1; Herbert Lehman to Malin, December 17, 1954, ACLU Records, Box 614, folder 2.

Select Bibliography

Archival Collections

American Civil Liberties Union Records. Seeley G. Mudd Library, Princeton University.

Arthur Garfield Hays Papers. Seeley G. Mudd Library, Princeton University.

Committee against Jim Crow in Military Service and Training Records. Schomburg Center for Research in Black Culture. New York Public Library.

NAACP, Papers. Part 01: Meetings of the Board of Directors. Records of Annual Conferences, Major Speeches, and Special Reports, Library of Congress Microfilm edition.

Papers of A. Philip Randolph, Subject file: Subject File, Library of Congress, ProQuest History Vault.

W. E. B. Du Bois Papers. Special Collections and University Archives, University of Massachusetts Amherst Libraries.

Newspapers and Magazines

Atlanta Daily World
Baltimore Afro-American
Chicago Defender
Life
New York Times
Norfolk New Journal and Guide
Pittsburgh Courier
politics
The Nation
Washington Post

Books and Articles

Abu-Lunghod, Janet L. *Race, Space, and Riots in Chicago, New York, and Los Angeles.* New York: Oxford University Press, 2007.

Anderson, Mark. *From Boas to Black Power: Racism, Liberalism, and American Anthropology.* Stanford: Stanford University Press, 2019.

Auerbach, Jerald S. *Unequal Justice: Lawyers and Social Change in Modern America.* New York: Oxford University Press, 1976.

Barbas, Samantha. *The Rise and Fall of Morris Ernst, Free Speech Renegade.* Chicago: University of Chicago Press, 2021.

Bates, Beth Thompkins. "A New Crowd Challenges the Agenda of the Old Guard in the NAACP, 1933–1941." *American Historical Review* 102 (1997): 340–77.

Bell, Jeannine. *Hate Thy Neighbor: Move-in Violence and Persistent of Racial Segregation in American Housing.* New York: New York University Press, 2013.

Blum, John Morton. *V Was for Victory: Politics and American Culture During World War II.* New York: Harcourt Brace Jovanovich, 1976.

Boas, Franz. *Anthropology and Modern Life.* New York: W.W. Norton & Company, 1932.

Boyer, Paul S. *Purity in Print: Book Censorship in America From the Gilded Age to the Computer Age.* 2nd ed. Madison: University of Wisconsin Press, 2002.

Boyle, Kevin. *Arc of Justice: A Saga of Race, Civil Rights, and Murder in the Jazz Age.* New York: Henry Holt, 2004.

Britt, P. Tevis. "'Jews Not Admitted': Anti-Semitism, Civil Rights, and Public Accommodation Laws." *Journal of American History* 107 (2021): 847–70.

Brooks, Richard R. W., and Carol M. Rose. *Saving the Neighborhood: Racially Restrictive Covenants.* Cambridge, Harvard University Press, 2013.

Bynum, Cornelius L., and A. *Philip Randolph and the Struggle for Civil Rights.* Urbana: University of Illinois Press, 2010.

Capeci, Dominic J., Jr. *The Harlem Riot of 1943.* Philadelphia: Temple University Press, 1977.

Carle, Susan D. "Race, Class, and Legal Ethics in the Early NAACP (1910–1920." *Law and History Review* 20 (2002): 97–146.

Carter, Dan T. *Scottsboro: A Tragedy of the American South.* Baton Rouge: Louisiana University Press, 1969.

Carter, Stephen L. *Invisible: The Forgotten Story of the Black Woman Lawyer Who Took Down America's Most Powerful Mobster.* New York: Henry Holt, 2018.

Chen, Anthony. *The Fifth Freedom: Jobs, Politics and Civil Rights in the United States, 1941–1972.* Princeton, NJ: Princeton University Press, 2009.

The Complete Report of Mayor La Guardia's Commission of the Harlem Riot of March 19, 1935. New York: Arno Press, 1935.

Cottrell, Robert C. *Roger Nash Baldwin and the American Civil Liberties Union.* New York: Columbia University Press, 2000.

Currea, Michael Jones. "The Origins and Diffusion of Racial Restrictive Covenants." *Political Science Quarterly* 115 (1973): 261–82.

Dalfiume, Richard M. *Desegregation U. S. Armed Forces: Fighting on Two Fronts, 1939–1953*. Columbia: University of Missouri Press, 1969.

Degler, Carl N. *In Search of Human Nature: The Decline and Revival of Darwinism in American Social Thought*. New York: Oxford University Press, 1991.

Du Bois, W. E. B. *The Souls of Black Folk*. Chicago: A. C. McClurg & Co, 1903.

Dunne, Gerald T. *Greenville Clark: Public Citizen*. New York: Farrar, Straus, Giroux, 1986.

Eisenstadt, Peter. *Rochdale Village: Robert Moses, 6,000 Families, and New York City's Great Experiment in Integrated Housing*. Ithaca: Cornell University Press, 2010.

Ernst, Daniel R. *Tocqueville's Nightmare: The Administrative State Emerges in America, 1900–1940*. New York: Oxford University Press, 2014.

Fermaglich, Kirsten. "What's Uncle Sam's Last Name?': Jews and Name Changing in New York City during the World War II Era." *Journal of American History* 102, no. 3 (2015): 719–45.

Finkle, Lee. *Forum For Protest: The Black Press During World War II*. Cranbury, NJ: Associated University Presses, 1975.

Finkle, Lee. "The Conservative Aims of Militant Rhetoric: Black Protest During World War II." *Journal of American History* 60 (1973): 692–713.

Fisch, Dov. "The Libel Trial of Robert Edward Edmondson: 1936–1938." *American Jewish History* 71 (1981): 79–102.

Flynn, George Q. "Selective Service and American Blacks During World War II." *Journal of Negro History* 69 (1984): 14–25.

Foner, Jack D. *Blacks and the Military in American History: A New Perspective*. New York: Praeger, 1974.

Francis, Megan Ming. *Civil Rights and the Making of the Modern American State*. New York: Cambridge University Press, 2014.

Friedman, Lawrence M. *American Law in the 20th Century*. New Haven: Yale University Press, 2002.

Gilmore, Glenda. *Defying Dixie: The Radical Roots of Civil Rights*. New York: W. W. Norton, 2008.

Ginger, Ray. *Six Days or Forever?: Tennessee v. John T. Scopes*. New York: Oxford University Press, 1958.

Glotzer, Paige. "Exclusion in Arcadia: How Suburban Developers Circulated Ideas about Discrimination, 1890–1950." *Journal of Urban History* 41 (2015): 479–94.

Goluboff, Risa L. *The Lost Promise of Civil Rights*. Cambridge: Harvard University Press, 2007.

Gonda, Jeffrey. *Unjust Deeds: The Restrictive Covenant Cases and the Making of the Civil Rights Movement*. Durham: University of North Carolina Press, 2015.

Goodman, James. *Stories of Scottsboro*. New York: Vintage Books, 1994.

Goodwin, Doris Kearns. *No Ordinary Time: Franklin and Eleanor Roosevelt: The Home Front in World War II*. New York: Simon & Schuster, 1994.

Grant, Madison. *The Passing of the Great Race: Racial Basis of European History*. New York: Charles Scribner's Sons, 1916.

Green, Michael Cullen. *Black Yanks in the Pacific: Race in the Making of American Military Empire after World War II*. Ithaca: Cornell University Press, 2010.

Greenberg, Cheryl Lynn. *Or Does It Explode?: Black Harlem in the Great Depression*. New York: Oxford University Press, 1991.

Greenberg, Jack. *Crusaders in the Courts*. New York: Basic Books, 1994.

Greenwald, Marilyn S., Yun Li, and Eunice Hunton Carter. *A Lifelong Fight for Social Justice*. New York: Fordham University Press, 2021.

Guglielmo, Thomas A. *Divisions: A New History of Racism and Resistance in America's World War II Military*. New York: Oxford University Press, 2021.

Hall, Jacquelyn Dowd. "The Long Civil Rights Movement and the Political Uses of the Past." *Journal of American History* 91 (March 2005): 1233–63.

Hamm, Richard F. "'I Want You to Realize How Unfair You Have Been:' The Cold War's Effect on the Friendship of Arthur Garfield Hays and C. Fulton Oursler." *American Communist History* 17 (2018): 318–39.

Hamm, Richard F. "The Limits of the Law: A 1943 Case of Anti-Semitism in the Lower Hudson River Valley." *Hudson River Valley Review* 31 (2015): 2–15.

Harbaugh, William H. *Lawyer's Lawyer: The Life of John W. Davis*. Charlottesville: University of Virginia Press, 1990.

Hawkins, Richard A. "The Marketing of Legal Services in the United States, 1855–1912: A Case Study of Guggenheimer, Untemyer & Marshall of New York City and the Predecessor Partnerships." *American Journal of Legal History* 53 (2013): 239–64.

Hays, Arthur Garfield. *City Lawyer: The Autobiography of a Law Practice*. New York: Simon and Schuster, 1942.

Hays, Arthur Garfield. *Democracy Works*. New York: Random House, 1939.

Hays, Arthur Garfield. *Let Freedom Ring*. New York: Boni and Liveright, 1928.

Hays, Arthur Garfield. *Trial by Prejudice*. New York: Convic Freide, 1933.

Henderson, Alexa B. "FEPC and the Southern Railway Case: An Investigation into the Discriminatory Practices of Railroads During World War II." *Journal of Negro History* 61 (1976): 173–87.

Herbin-Triant, Elizabeth A. *Threatening Property: Race, Class, and Campaigns to Legislate Jim Crow Neighborhoods*. New York: Columbia University Press, 2019.

Higginbotham, F. Michael, and S. P. Breckinridge. "Soldiers for Justice: The Role of the Tuskegee Airmen in the Desegregation of the American Armed Forces." *William & Mary Bill of Rights Journal* 8 (1999): 273–321.

Hill, Robert A., ed. In *The FBI's RACON: Racial Conditions in the United States During World War II*. Boston: Northeastern University Press, 1995.

Höhn, Maria, and Martin Klimke. *A Breath of Freedom: The Civil Rights Struggle, African American GIs, and Germany.* New York: Palgrave Macmillan, 2010.

Holt, Thomas C. *The Movement: The African American Struggle for Civil Rights.* New York: Oxford University Press, 2021.

Jackson, Percival E. *Look at the Law: The Law Is What the Layman Makes It.* New York: E. P. Dutton, 1940.

James, Rawn. *Root and Branch: Charles Hamilton Houston, Thurgood Marshall, and the Struggle to End Segregation.* New York: Bloomsbury Press, 2010.

Johnson, Marilyn, *Street Justice: A History of Police Violence in New York City.* Boston: Beacon Press, 2003.

Kersten, Andrew E. *A. Philip Randolph: A Life in the Vanguard.* Lanham: Rowman and Littlefield, 2007.

Kersten, Andrew. *Race, Jobs and the War: The FEPC in the Midwest, 1941–46.* Champagne: University of Illinois Press, 2007.

Kessner, Thomas. *Fiorello H. La Guardia and the Making of Modern New York.* New York: Penguin, 1989.

King, Charles. *Gods of the Upper Air: How a Circle of Renegade Anthropologists Reinvented Race, Sex, and Gender in the Twentieth Century.* New York: Anchor Books, 2019.

King, Shannon. " 'Ready to Shoot and Do Shoot': Black Working-Class Self-Defense and Community Politics in Harlem, New York, during the 1920s." *Journal of Urban History* 37 (2011): 757–74.

King, Shannon. *Whose Harlem Is This, Anyway?: Community Politics and Grassroots Activism during the New Negro Era.* New York: New York University Press, 2015.

Kirby, John B. *Black Americans in the Roosevelt Era: Liberalism and Race.* Knoxville: University of Tennessee Press, 1980.

Klarman, Michael J. *From Jim Crow to Civil Rights: The Supreme Court and the Struggle for Racial Equality.* New York: Oxford University Press, 2004.

Klinkner, Philip A. with Smith, Roger. *Unsteady March: The Rise and Decline of Racial Equality in America.* Chicago: University of Chicago Press, 1999.

Kluger, Richard, *Simple Justice: The History of* Brown v. Board *of Education and Black America's Struggle for Equality.* New York: Vintage, 1977.

Knepper, Cathy D. *Jersey Justice: The Story of the Trenton Six.* New Brunswick, NJ: Rivergate Books, 2011.

Kruse, Kevin M., and Stephen Tuck, eds. *Fog of War: The Second World War and the Civil Rights Movement.* New York: Oxford University Press, 2012.

Kryder, Daniel. *Divided Arsenal: Race and the American State During World War II.* Cambridge: Cambridge University Press, 2010.

LaFollette, Marcel Chotkowski. *Reframing Scopes: Journalists, Scientists, and the Lost Photographs from the Trial of the Century.* Lawrence: University Press of Kansas, 2008.

Lamson, Peggy. *Roger Baldwin: A Founder of the American Civil Liberties Union, A Portrait*. Boston: Hughton Mifflin, 1976.

Larson, Edward J. *Summer for the Gods: The Scopes Trial and America's Continuing Debate Over Science and Religion*. Cambridge: Harvard University Press, 1997.

Lewis, David Levering. "Parallels and Divergences: Assimilationist Strategies of Afro-American and Jewish Elites from 1910 to the Early 1930s." *Journal of American History* 71 (1984): 543–64.

Lewis, David Levering. *When Harlem Was in Vogue*. New York: Penguin, 1997.

Lewis, Earl, and Heidi Ardizzone. *Love on Trial: An American Scandal in Black and White*. New York: W. W. Norton, 2001.

Lipsky, Michael, and David J. Olson. *Commission Politics: The Processing of Racial Crisis in America*. New Brunswick, NJ: Transaction Books, 1977.

Lupo, Lindsey. *Flak-Catchers: One Hundred Years of Riot Commission Politics in America*. Lanham, MD: Lexington Books, 2011.

Lynn, Conrad. *There Is a Fountain: The Autobiography of a Civil Rights Lawyer*. Westport, CT: Lawrence Hill and Company, 1979.

Mack, Kenneth W. *Representing the Race: The Creation of the Civil Rights Lawyer*. Cambridge: Harvard University Press, 2012.

Marable, Manning. *Malcolm X: A Life of Reinvention*. New York: Viking, 2011.

McCraw, Thomas K. *Prophets of Regulation: Charles Francis Adams, Louis D. Brandeis, James M. Landis, and Alfred E. Kahn*. Cambridge: Harvard University Press, 1984.

McGuire, Phillip. *He Too Spoke for Democracy: Judge Hastie, World War II, and the Black Soldier*. New York: Greenwood Press, 1988.

McNeil, Genna Rae. *Groundwork: Charles Hamilton Houston and the Struggle for Civil Rights*. Philadelphia: University of Pennsylvania Press, 1984.

McWilliams, Carey. *Brothers Under the Skin*. Boston: Little Brown and Company, 1943.

Meier, August, and John H. Bracey. "The NAACP as a Reform Movement." *Journal of Southern History* 59 (1993): 3–30.

Morehouse, Maggi M. *Fighting in the Jim Crow Army: Black Men and Women Remember World War II*. Lanham: Rowman & Littlefield Publishers, 2000.

Murray, Pauli. *The Autobiography of a Black Activist, Feminist, Lawyer, Priest, and Poet*. Knoxville: University of Tennessee Press, 1989.

Naison, Mark. *Communists in Harlem During the Depression*. Urbana: University of Illinois Press, 1983.

Nelson, Peter N. *A More Unbending Battle: The Harlem Hellfighters' Struggle for Freedom in WWI and Equality at Home*. New York: Basic Civitas, 2009.

Nelson, William E. *The Legalist Reformation: Law, Politics, and Ideology in New York, 1920–1980*. Chapel Hill: University of North Carolina Press, 2001.

Newby, John L., II. "The Fight for the Right to Fight and the Forgotten Negro Protest Movement: The History of Executive Order 9981 and Its Effect Upon

Brown v. Board of Education and Beyond." *Texas Journal on Civil Liberties and Civil Rights* 10 (2004): 83–110.

Oursler, C. Fulton. *Behold This Dreamer! An Autobiography.* Boston: Little Brown and Company, 1964.

Parrish, Michael E. *Felix Frankfurter and His Times: The Reform Years.* New York: Free Press, 1982.

Penningroth, Dylan C. *Before the Movement: The Hidden History of Black Civil Rights.* New York: Liveright Publishing, 2023.

Pfeffer, Paula F. *A Philip Randolph: Pioneer of the Civil Rights Movement.* Baton Rouge: Louisiana State University Press, 1990.

Pietila, Antero. *Not in My Neighborhood: How Bigotry Shaped a Great American City.* Chicago: Ivan R. Dee, 2010.

Polenberg, Richard. *One Nation Divisible: Class, Race, and Ethnicity in the United States Since 1938.* New York: Penguin Books, 1982.

Polenberg, Richard. *War and Society: the United States, 1941–1945.* Philadelphia: J. B. Lippincott, 1972.

Rabinowitz, Victor. *A History of the National Lawyers Guild: 1937–1987.* New York: National Lawyers Guild Foundation, 1987.

Robertson, Stephen. *Harlem in Disorder: A Spatial History of How Racial Violence Changed in 1935.* Redwood City, CA: Stanford University Press, 2024.

Rothstein, Richard. *The Color of Law: A Forgotten History of How Our Government Segregated America.* New York: Liveright Public Corp., 2017.

Roundtree, Dovey Johson, and Katie McCabe. *Mighty Justice: My Life in Civil Rights.* Chapel Hill: Algonquin Books of Chapel Hill, 2019.

Ruchames, Louis. *Race, Jobs, and Politics: The Story of FEPC.* New York: Columbia University Press, 1953.

Schultz, Kevin. "The FEPC and the Legacy of the Labor-Based Civil Rights Movement of the 1940s." *Labor History* 49 (2008): 71–92.

Segal, Geraldine R. *Blacks in the Law: Philadelphia and the Nation.* Philadelphia: University of Pennsylvania Press, 1983.

Selective Service System [Johnson, Campbell C.]. "Special Groups." *Special Monograph* I, no. 10 (1953).

Sherman, Richard B. *The Case Odell Waller, and Virginia Justice.* Knoxville: University of Tennessee Press, 1992.

Sitkoff, Harvard. *A New Deal for Blacks.* New York: Oxford University Press, 1978.

Sitkoff, Harvard. "Racial Militancy and Interracial Violence in the Second World War." *Journal of American History* 58 (December 1971): 661–81.

Smith, Clay. *Emancipation: The Making of the Black Lawyer, 1844–1944.* Philadelphia: University of Pennsylvania Press, 1999.

Smith, Richard Norton. *Thomas E. Dewey and His Times.* New York: Touchstone, 1982.

Smith-Pryor, Elizabeth M. *Property Rights: The Rhinelander Trial, Passing, and the Protection of Whiteness.* Chapel Hill: University of North Carolina Press, 2009.

Stach, Patricia Burgess. "Deed Restrictions and Subdivision Development in Columbus, Ohio, 1900–1970." *Journal of Urban History* 15 (1998): 42–68.

Steele, Richard W. *Free Speech in the Good War.* New York: St. Martin's Press, 1999.

Stoddard, Lothrop. *The Rising of Tide of Color: The Threat against White World-Supremacy.* New York: Charles Scribner's Sons, 1920.

Stolberg, Mary M. *Fighting Organized Crime: Politics, Justice and the Legacy of Thomas E. Dewey.* Boston: Northeastern University Press, 1995.

Stone, Irving. *Clarence Darrow for the Defense.* New York: Bantam, 1941.

Strum, Philippa. *Louis D. Brandeis: Justice for the People.* Cambridge: Harvard University Press, 1984.

Sugrue, Thomas J. *Sweet Land of Liberty: The Forgotten Struggle for Civil Rights in the North.* New York: Random House, 2008.

Sumner, Gregory D. *Dwight Macdonald and the Politics Circle: The Challenge of Cosmopolitan Democracy.* Ithaca: Cornell University Press, 1996.

Svonkin, Stuart. *Jews against Prejudice: American Jews and the Fight for Civil Liberties.* New York: Columbia University Press, 1997.

Takaki, Ronald. *Double Victory: A Multicultural History of America in World War II.* Boston: Little, Brown, and Company, 2000.

Taylor, Clarence, ed. *Civil Rights in New York City: From World War II to the Giuliani Era.* New York: Fordham University Press, 2011.

Taylor, Clarence. *Fight the Power: African Americans and the Long History of Police Brutality in New York City.* New York: New York University Press, 2019.

Tierney, Kevin. *Darrow: A Biography.* New York: Thomas Y. Crowell, 1979.

Terry, Golway. *I Never Did Like Politics: How Fiorello La Guardia Became America's Mayor, and Why He Still Matters.* New York: St. Martins, 2024.

Tushnet, Mark V. *Making Civil Rights Law: Thurgood Marshall and the Supreme Court, 1936–1961.* New York: Oxford University Press, 1996.

Vose, Clement E. *Caucasians Only, the Supreme Court, the NAACP, and the Restrictive Covenant Cases.* Berkeley: University of California Press, 1959.

Walker, Samuel. *In Defense of American Liberties: A History of the ACLU.* New York: Oxford University Press, 1990.

Ware, Gilbert. *William Hastie: Grace Under Pressure.* New York: Oxford University Press, 1984.

Warren, Frank A. *Noble Abstractions: American Liberal Intellectuals and World War II.* Columbus: Ohio State University Press, 1999.

Washburn, Patrick S. *The African American Newspaper: Voice of Freedom.* Evanston, IL: Northwestern University Press, 2006.

Weiss, Nancy J. *Farewell to the Party of Lincoln: Black Politics in the Age of FDR.* Princeton, NJ: Princeton University Press, 1983.

White, Shane. *Playing the Numbers: Gambling in Harlem between the Wars.* Cambridge, MA: Harvard University Press, 2010.

White, Steven. *World War II and American Racial Politics: Public Opinion, the Presidency, and Civil Rights Advocacy.* Cambridge: Cambridge University Press, 2019.

White, Walter. *A Man Called White.* New York: Arno Press and *New York Times,* 1969.

Whitfield, Stephen J. *A Critical American: The Politics of Dwight Macdonald.* Hamden, CT: Archon Books, 1984.

Williams, Juan. *Thurgood Marshall: American Revolutionary,* 1998.

Williams, Oscar R. *George S. Schuyler: Portrait of a Black Conservative.* Knoxville: University of Tennessee Press, 2007.

Wilson, Ruth Danenhower. *Jim Crow Joins Up: A Study of Negroes in the Armed Forces of the United States.* New York: The Press of William J. Clark, 1944.

Woeste, Victoria Saker. *Henry Ford's War on Jews and the Legal Battle against Hate Speech.* Stanford: Stanford University Press, 2012.

Wreszin, Michael. *A Rebel in Defense of Tradition: The Life and Politics of Dwight Macdonald.* New York: Basic Books, 1994.

Wynn, Neil A. *The African American Experience during World War II.* Lanham: Rowman and Littlefield, 2010.

Wynn, Neil A. *The Afro-American and the Second World War.* New York: Holmes & Meier Publishers, 1975.

Dissertations and Theses

Geddis, Melissa A. "Segregation Is Discrimination: A Case Study of Lynn v. Downer and the African American Resistance to Racialized Military Service in the Second World War." MA thesis, Rutgers University, 2015.

Ottman, Tod M. " 'Government That Has Both a Heart and a Head': The Growth of New York State Government During the World War II Era, 1930–1950." PhD diss., University at Albany, State University of New York, 2001.

Soares, A. "Seeing Color in Black and White: New York Defines Its Color Line in Ridgway v. Cockburn in 1937." MA thesis, University at Albany, State University of New York, 2016.

Index